The IRA, 1926–1936

To my father and the memory of my mother

The IRA, 1926–1936

BRIAN HANLEY

FOUR COURTS PRESS

Set in 10 on 13 point Janson
by Linda Longmore for
FOUR COURTS PRESS LTD
7 Malpas Street, Dublin 8, Ireland
e-mail: info@four-courts-press.ie
and in North America
FOUR COURTS PRESS
c/o ISBS, 5824 N. E. Hassalo Street, Portland, OR 97213

© Brian Hanley 2002

A catalogue record for this title
is available from the British Library.

ISBN 1-85182-721-8

Printed in England
by MPG Books, Bodmin, Cornwall

Contents

LIST OF ILLUSTRATIONS   6

ACKNOWLEDGEMENTS   7

INTRODUCTION   9

1   Leaders and men   11

2   The day-to-day working of a 'secret army'   28

3   The IRA and nationalist culture   50

4   Enemies and antagonists   71

5   Allies and rivals   93

6   The IRA and Fianna Fáil in opposition, 1926–1932   113

7   The IRA and Fianna Fáil in government, 1932–1936   126

8   The IRA in Northern Ireland   145

9   The IRA outside Ireland   161

10   The IRA and Irish society, 1926–1936   175

APPENDICES   191

NOTES   213

BIBLIOGRAPHY   273

INDEX   283

Illustrations

(appear between pages 128 and 129)

1   Moss Twomey, November 1926.

2   The Dublin IRA at the 1931 Easter Commemoration, O'Connell Street.

3   IRA prisoners released at the conclusion of the Civil War.

4   Crowds greet the released IRA prisoners at Arbour Hill, March 1932.

5   Frank Ryan, *An Phoblacht* editor, speaks to the 30,000-strong rally in College Green to welcome the released prisoners, March 1932.

6   Moss Twomey at Easter Commemoration, Glasnevin, April 1932.

7   Prisoners released from Arbour Hill and Mountjoy, March 1932.

8   Peadar O'Donnell, a leading IRA member until 1934, at the 1930 European Peasants Congress in Berlin.

9   Sighle Humphreys, the driving force behind Cumann na mBan in Dublin from 1926 onwards.

10   Twomey gives the oration at Bodenstown, 1933.

11   The Tralee IRA at Bodenstown, 1934.

12   *An Phoblacht,* Saturday 5 May 1934.

Acknowledgements

This book is substantially based on a PhD thesis completed under the supervision of Professor David Fitzpatrick from 1997 to 2001. I must thank Professor Fitzpatrick for his help and guidance, criticism and encouragement over those years. Michael MacEvilly has been of tremendous assistance, in both sharing his own knowledge of republicanism and introducing me to his vast range of contacts. Fr Maurice Twomey deserves thanks for ensuring his father's collection will continue to enthral future researchers; I hope his desire to see his father's political life *critically* evaluated will be satisfied somewhat by this study. I have gained some sense of the atmosphere of my period of study by speaking or corresponding with a number of people, of varying political persuasion, who lived through it. My thanks to Eamon Corcoran, Jim Savage, Charlie Byrne, Maura Ó Nualláin, Joe Briscoe, Mick Dowling, Patsy McGuinness, Packy and Sheila Early and Uinseann MacEoin. I would like to thank the staff of the various libraries and archives in which I have worked, especially Seamus Helferty and the staff at UCD Archives. I must also mention the late Commandant Peter Young at Military Archives and the ever helpful staff at the Gilbert Library. A large number of historians and fellow researchers have assisted me in various ways. I thank Eunan O'Halpin, Fearghal McGarry, Anthony Coughlan, Seán O'Mahony, Seán Cronin, Emmet O'Connor, Manus O'Riordan, Brian Murphy, Richard English, Joost Augusteijn, Aindrias Ó Cathasaigh, Conor Brady, Matt Tracey, Gerry Cronin, Carlo Pellizzi and Tommy Graham. My colleagues in room 3077 at TCD were a never-failing source of humour, camaraderie and occasional cynicism! Thank you all. I am very grateful to Martin, Ronan and all the staff at Four Courts Press. My family have been of tremendous support. I thank my father, Paddy, my sisters, Úna and Patricia and my brother, Dara for their encouragement during those long years of research. My mother first interested me in history many years ago and I only wish she were alive to see the publication of this work. Finally my heartfelt thanks to Órla Doherty for making the period in which I completed this book such a happy one.

Introduction: The IRA, 1926–36

The history of the Irish Republican Army has been the subject of numerous studies, ranging from general histories of the organization to critiques of its politics. However, relatively little attention has been paid to its membership and their activities in any detail. In the past the main problem identified by historians was the absence of primary source material. Hence one study of the organization concluded that 'it is no real exaggeration to contend that there are little or no readily available written records, primary or secondary, for a study of the IRA'. Another scholar concurred in his study of the Republican press of the 1930s, writing that the IRA left 'no membership roles, no minutes of meetings, and no records of conventions and debates among leaders where important decisions were made'.

However, the IRA *did* keep very detailed records. We know this thanks to the papers of the single most important IRA figure in this period, Maurice (Moss) Twomey, now open to researchers. Twomey, chief of staff of the IRA from 1926 to 1936, kept in his possession a vast quantity of correspondence, orders, and minutes from his period as leader.[3] We also now have access to the papers of other republican activists such as Sighle Humphreys, and of government ministers like Seán MacEntee of Fianna Fáil, and Desmond FitzGerald of Cumann na nGaedheal.

While the 1920s and 1930s have long exercised a fascination for historians, scholarship has tended to concentrate on the IRA's relationship with the far left, leaving its role in Irish society as a whole to general histories. Republicans themselves have largely ignored the period, possibly because of the lack of an armed campaign. None of the IRA members who met violent deaths during that era is listed in the record of republican dead, the *Last Post*, and the same publication refers to the years between 1923 and 1940 as 'a valley period' of 'inaction and playing with politics'.

In reality, the period from 1926 onwards was of vital importance for Irish republicanism. Despite its defeat in the civil war and the subsequent founding of a constitutional rival, Fianna Fáil, the IRA remained a significant factor in political life in Ireland north and south. Its very existence as a substantial armed organization, dedicated to the overthrow of both states, and claiming to be the rightful inheritor of the revolutionary mantle of 1916–21 gave the IRA considerable importance. Outside its ranks there also existed a sizeable republican constituency which could be mobilized in support of its activities. The Cumann na nGaedheal government faced grave difficulties caused by the IRA and its allies between 1926 and 1932. Fianna Fáil were thankful for its support in the general elections of 1932 and 1933 and even offered the IRA the chance of a merger with their party on the eve of the 1932 election. While the situation in Northern Ireland was very different, the IRA also played a significant part in politics there on occasion. This study examines the day-to-day organization of the IRA itself, its shifting priorities and fluctuating ideologies.

1/Leaders and men

How many people were actually involved with the IRA after the civil war? J. Bowyer Bell's estimate for 1927 is 20,000 to 25,000 IRA members; but the most reliable documents indicate that the figures were actually much smaller. A report compiled for the IRA leadership in August 1924 gives an estimate of 14,541 members. These figures were incomplete, the IRA's calculations being based on strength on paper, rather than on active membership.

Table 1. IRA strengths, 1924

Division	Area	Strength
1st Southern	Cork, Kerry	2,904
2nd Southern	Tipperary, Kilkenny, Waterford	1,983
3rd Southern	Tipperary, Leix, Offaly	1,594
1st Western	E. Clare, M. Clare, S. & W. Galway	2,018
2nd Western		347
4th Western	W. Mayo, N. Mayo, W. Connemara,	
	E. Connemara, N.W. Mayo, S. Mayo	1,723
Eastern Division	S. Wexford, N. Wexford, Carlow, Wicklow	962
4th Northern		944
Midland		628
Limerick County	Mid, East & West	504
Tyrone		100
Dublin No. 2		250
Belfast		240
Britain		344
		14,541

The situation immediately after the civil war found the IRA in a disorganized and shambolic state, with little contact between the various Divisions. In one senior IRA officer's view, the only way of maintaining their organization was to 'train for war ... otherwise we can never hope to keep anything but the semblance of an Army together'. There was no reopening of hostilities with either government in Ireland over the next two years and, while the IRA saw considerable changes in leadership personal and political strategy, the organization did not grow in numbers; in fact it shrank drastically. By November 1926 the IRA's membership had declined to only 5,042.

Table 2. IRA strengths, 1926

Armagh	142	Claremorris	227	Galway	20	Offaly	216
Antrim	23	Connemara	22	Kerry 1	380	Sligo	80
Bantry	23	Cork No.1	200	Kerry 2	100	Tipperary	80
Belfast	242	Cork No. 2	60	Kildare	30	Tirconaill	175
Boyne	146	Caherciveen	80	Kilkenny N.	50	Tyrone	30
Carlow	40	Derry	40	Kilkenny S.	185	Waterford	135
Carrick/Sh	80	Down	40	Leix	150	Wexford	70
Clonakilty	20	Dublin	533	Limerick	60	Wicklow	20
Cavan	30	Dub. Battn	50	Mayo N.	520	Scotland	100
Clare	260	Dundalk	97	Midlands	200	England	89
Total							5,042

In the interim, the IRA had been reorganized to take account of its declining strength. Until December 1924, the organization was still operating on a divisional basis. In 1925, the divisions were replaced by brigades or battalions according to their strengths. There were several factors for this decline in the IRA's strength. The new Fianna Fáil party had been formed in May 1926, and included many of the IRA leadership of 1924, but there was still a considerable cross-over in membership between the two organizations which would continue for some years, especially at rank and file level. Of greater importance was the effect of emigration from the Free State and the loss of members who drifted out of the organization through disillusionment. As the IRA army council noted, 'large numbers of volunteers from all along the west coast emigrated, and a considerable number also from other parts of the country. The reason for which most of these men emigrated was because there was no hope of their obtaining a livelihood in Ireland in the near future.'

During 1926 Irish Army Intelligence noted the emergence of a younger and more militant leadership within the Dublin IRA. This grouping including Michael (Mick) Price and Seán Russell were believed to have planned the 'decidedly successful' breakout of 19 IRA prisoners from Mountjoy jail as well as other aggressive activities. The IRA had attempted to forge a united electoral pact between Fianna Fáil, Sinn Féin and themselves prior to the June 1927 election, but this effort failed. When Fianna Fáil did enter Leinster House that autumn, the IRA took a relatively pragmatic view. The presence of Fianna Fáil TDs in the Dáil who consistently denounced government attempts to suppress the IRA was of use to the organization over the next five years.

In this period IRA activities ranged from attempts to disrupt Remembrance Day ceremonies in Dublin, to destruction of 'Imperialist' symbols and a growing emphasis on social agitation, beginning with a campaign against payment of land annuities to Britain. Despite these activities there was to be no rapid increase in IRA strength. Estimates during 1930 point to IRA membership stagnating rather than growing.

Table 3. IRA strengths, 1930

Armagh	169	Belfast	177	Derry	12
Tyrone	136	South Dublin	65	Antrim	17
Dublin Brigade	262	Kerry 1st Batt.	70	Kerry, 2nd Batt.	51
South Tipperary	270	Mid Tipperary	28	Sligo	155
Donegal	138	Limerick City	65	East Limerick	25
N. Galway	36	Connemara	50	Claremorris	40
South Galway	62	Galway City	30	Drogheda	37
East Clare	124	West Clare	119		
Total					1,833

IRA active strength was often even less than shown in these figures. South Tipperary counted only 135 out of 270 as its parade strength, and Donegal 60 out of 138. During 1930 Seán Russell found there was no serious attempts being made to train or drill the IRA in south Tipperary, while the IRA in west Limerick had not paraded since 1923. Similarly in Sligo and south Galway there were few parades and no training being carried out. One inspecting officer wrote that it was 'painful' to see the decline of the IRA in Westmeath. A major problem the IRA leadership located within their ranks was the belief among many of their men that 'there was no serious intention ... to ever resume the fight again'. Allied to this there was a marked tendency for 'old hands' to dismiss the possibility of recruiting young men who were thought to be 'not the right type ... too fond of amusement' and therefore could not be trusted.

A further feature of the IRA's political direction during 1930 was a close association with organizations like the Irish Labour Defence League and the Friends of Soviet Russia. Government sources considered that the IRA was entering into an alliance with communism, even suggesting leaders like Seán Russell had been won over to the Comintern. On the eve of the government's clampdown of October 1931, which to a large degree depended on the belief that the IRA was a growing threat, the Special Branch estimated the organization had a membership of just 4,800. To put these figures into perspective, they were accompanied by garda reports which stressed that they (the garda) were losing control of the countryside, and that unless draconian measures were implemented by the government the state would not survive.

There were indications the IRA *was* increasingly recruiting new members during 1931. The IRA's journal *An t-Óglách* claimed that 'several companies and Battalions have doubled and trebled their strengths in the present year'.

Twomey told Joseph McGarrity of the IRA's American support organization, Clan na Gael, that he could 'scarcely credit himself the extraordinary growth of the Volunteer movement'. The IRA was benefiting both from the radicalization brought about by the effects of the Great Depression, and its own moves to exploit this discontent. As Twomey explained, 'the stoppage of emigration is adding to the feeling of unrest and dissatisfaction: young people want to know how they are to exist unless something is done to fundamentally alter conditions.' He also claimed that the IRA was now having 'little difficulty' in recruiting and that the turnout for an IRA funeral and the breaking of a ban on the Wolfe Tone commemoration at Bodenstown had 'alarmed' the government who now seemed to be 'losing their grip'. The IRA's policy now was to encourage its units to 'come out as openly as morale of the men will allow'. With what the IRA called 'the improvement in feeling', its units were ordered to confine appointments to men under the age of 25. Where possible, local IRA units were to invite 'all the available young lads' in their area to an IRA recruitment meeting.

During 1931, the IRA had also decided to set up a political organization to organize the 'revolutionary feeling' it believed was growing because of the economic crisis. During 1930 the IRA in west Clare had experimented with a civilian support organization which was a success in giving practical support and helping develop contact with local people. As a result the radical Saor Éire was launched in September that year. By the summer of 1931 Twomey was already aware that a government clampdown on the IRA was likely and the organization made plans to deal with it. Indeed he suggested that if the government attempted to use force in order to stay in power that could benefit the IRA. In October the IRA faced an intense attack on its organization, politically through a 'red scare' endorsed by the Catholic Church and organizationally through a Public Safety Act allowing for trial by military tribunal and use of the death penalty. While Twomey claimed that this 'coercion act' had helped recruitment in some areas and that his organization was weathering the storm, in reality the IRA did face severe difficulties.

While the IRA did not emerge from this period unscathed, its contribution to Fianna Fáil's victory in March 1932, and the enthusiasm this victory generated, meant the organization was able to recruit relatively openly throughout that year. Just prior to the election, Frank Aiken had approached Twomey with an offer of a merger between Fianna Fáil and the IRA; but the IRA rejected this offer and Fianna Fáil formed a minority government with the support of the Labour Party.

The IRA's increasing confidence was expressed in orders such as the following given to its Tralee unit that they had 'an opportunity now that we have been looking for years and every advantage should be taken of it in order to improve the training and morale of our organisation'. Younger members of Fianna Fáil were reported to be leaving the party for the IRA in some areas. Other units claimed increased recruitment and a 'great wave of enthusiasm' towards the IRA. Increasingly, public parades and drilling and the further boost of activity in the January 1933 general election saw IRA membership reach its post civil war high point. Seán Russell bemoaned how few trained officers he had now that 'recruits were pouring in'. The IRA's policy for much of 1932 was to avoid confrontation with the new government in the Free State and to mobilize popular support for the 'Economic War' with Britain (resulting from the Fianna Fáil government's withholding of land annuities) in the hope that military conflict with Britain would result. During the year it made overtures to Fianna Fáil about a united campaign of republican and labour forces, but these offers were rejected. While it has often been asserted that the IRA embarked on a campaign of intimidation against its enemies after Fianna Fáil came to power, it is significant that the IRA themselves thought they were behaving with restraint. Indeed, the Department of Justice considered that the IRA had been comparatively 'quiet' during 1932 and the first half of 1933.

During this period, though, the IRA also involved itself in attempts to force the pace of the economic war by launching a campaign against British goods. The IRA was a very public organization during these years. Its members paraded openly at dozens of local commemorations, at political meetings and at the nation-wide Easter and Bodenstown events. Often IRA rallies were accompanied by 'Aeridheacht' featuring local bands and football or hurling competitions. Its leadership was identified as such by newspapers and a press description of Twomey as chief of staff would not have met with denial or a writ for libel.

The actual strength of the organization at this stage is difficult to gauge. Tim Pat Coogan has given a figure of over 30,000 IRA members in the Free State alone, but an examination of the IRA's own unfortunately incomplete estimates do not bear this out. There is certainly widespread evidence of increasing confidence and recruitment, but nothing to suggest a figure that high. An element of caution was also sounded by Twomey himself during this period when he claimed that with 'open recruiting' the IRA could recruit 'thousands' but that they wanted to select recruits and avoid a reoccurrence of the period after the truce of July 1921. However, there was also a sense of annoyance that with such great possibility of growth the Dublin IRA still had 'less than 500' active members by the years end. The IRA also began to grow in Northern Ireland, where membership had been low since the mid 1920s. Increasing activity in the north saw the IRA active in political campaigns, with an appeal to the Orange Order during 1932 and the standing of four IRA members as candidates in the 1933 Stormont elections. IRA members were also involved in paramilitary activities during the 1932 outdoor relief dispute and the 1933 rail strike.

Table 4. IRA strengths, 1932

Dublin	Ulster No.1	Leitrim	Sligo	Tirconaill 1	Tirconaill 2
472	564	330	286	132	90
Connemara	Waterford	N. Clare	Tipperary	Clonmel	N. Cork
57	89	102	121	140	73
Caherciveen	Dingle	Killarney	Tralee	Roscommon	Offaly
189	122	300	138	180	260
Total					3,645

The Ulster No. 1 area included 513 members in Belfast City itself and the surrounding area. The Dublin figure did not include a large number of new recruits who were on probationary membership or the membership in south Dublin. The membership levels reflect both increased activity and a new enthusiasm north and south. By 1933 there had been further increases in the strengths of key units.

Table 5. IRA strengths, 1933

Dublin	Tirconaill 2	Laoghis	Offaly	W. Cork	Leitrim
630	132	178	285	412	465

What is notable about these figures is that they include both the key Dublin Brigade and Belfast areas as well as the rural strongholds of Kerry and Leitrim, yet only Dublin and Kerry numbered over 500. This evidence suggests that 10,000 to 12,000 members would be closer to the real figure for the IRA's strength at its peak from 1932 to 1934. At two successive General Army Conventions Peadar O'Donnell referred to a figure of 12,000 as the organization's total membership. The IRA's only public pronouncement on the subject was when *An Phoblacht* claimed 16,000 IRA members had paraded at Bodenstown in 1933.

This would make the IRA significantly smaller than the Blueshirt movement, which at its height could claim almost 48,000 members. Indeed in west Cork, an area of strong Blueshirt support, the IRA found itself under severe pressure during 1933 and 1934. By 1933 violence between republicans and the Blueshirts had become endemic in the Free State. On the one hand this led to IRA recruitment, as 'extraordinary life' was put into the organization by the rise of the Blueshirts, but increasing violence exposed the inability of the organization to control its membership.

There were several reasons for the beginning of the IRA's decline after 1934. Firstly there was a split at the 1934 general army convention which saw the departure of several leading officers and later a number of the rank and file to form the Republican Congress. Since 1932 the IRA had been wracked by internal disagreement about its adoption of radical social and economic policies. At the 1933 general army convention there had been substantial opposition from the organization's junior officers to association with communism and 'anti-religious' beliefs. As a result, the organization had published a new 'Constitution and Governmental Programme' which it hoped would mollify 'clerical opposition'. This along with a ban on IRA members taking political initiatives without leadership sanction disillusioned many of the socialists within the movement's ranks. Other sections of the organization continued to complain about too much emphasis being put on social policies, leading Twomey to ask in response just what 'would they put before the people?'

There was also increasing garda and government attention focused on the IRA, and growing numbers of its members were finding themselves behind prison bars as a result of their activities. While conflict with the Blueshirts had some support among the broader republican constituency, the IRA's activities during 1934 and 1935 saw it increasingly in conflict with Fianna Fáil supporters. The launch of a Volunteer Reserve of the National Army in 1934 provided an alternative pole of attraction for republican-minded young men. Most importantly the Fianna Fáil government was beginning to satisfy the aspirations of the majority of republicans. The base for militant republicanism began to contract and many of the IRA's rank and file simply drifted away from the organization. How dramatic that shift was is difficult to assess. The few figures we have for 1934 do not point to a collapse of membership.

Table 6. IRA strengths, 1934

Belfast	Caherciveen	W. Clare	N. Clare	E. Limerick
460	233	66	69	132

The gardaí reported that during late 1934 in Clare and Kerry the IRA was continuing to 'flourish'. Furthermore the IRA's Wolfe Tone commemoration that year drew 17,000 to Bodenstown, the largest attendance to that date. The split that produced the Republican Congress led to the departure of many influential officers from the IRA, but the numbers involved were comparatively small. The decline in units such as those in Clare was certainly not due to defections to Congress, as the local IRA had declared themselves against the new departure. Small numbers of men were lost to the IRA in the Dublin area but it was generally officers rather then rank and file members who supported Congress.

Seán Cronin has estimated the IRA's strength in September 1934 as 8,036. This figure seems realistic as it points to a slow decline from a membership of around 10,000 rather than a dramatic collapse from 30,000. During 1935 the

IRA's intervention in the Dublin Tram strike would lead to mass arrests and its leadership having to go on the run for the first time since 1931. Membership had fallen to 7,358 by the end of that year. By this stage Twomey was seemingly resigned to accepting a declining 'Army' telling McGarrity that the IRA would never be a mass force except in 'time of war or of great enthusiasm'. After two particularly shocking murders in early 1936 the government was able to further clamp down on the IRA. The organization was banned on 18 June, the following day Twomey was jailed for three years, and the Bodenstown commemoration was prohibited. Significantly the gardaí noted that for the first time rank and file IRA members were wary of being openly identified with their organization. By November 1936, the IRA had been reduced to 3,844 members, its lowest strength since the civil war.

The next two years saw Seán MacBride, Tom Barry and Mick Fitzpatrick successively become IRA chiefs of staff and bitter division wrack the organization over political and military policy. Eventually Seán Russell in alliance with the American Clan na Gael and elements within the northern IRA gained control of the organization in 1938. Despite being accused of sabotaging the previous leadership's military plans, Russell committed the IRA to a bombing campaign in Britain. It was also at this stage that closer connections were made between the IRA and representatives of Nazi Germany, Tom Barry later claiming that the Nazis agreed to finance the bombing campaign. The campaign was a disaster, and by 1940 the IRA in the 26 counties had less than 2,000 members, many of whom were jailed or inactive.

LEADERS AND MEN

The make-up of the IRA leadership changed very little between 1926 and 1936. The organization's chief of staff, Moss Twomey, was first elected onto the IRA executive at the November 1925 general army convention. During 1926 he acted as chief of staff in the absence of Andy Cooney, and in 1927 he was confirmed in that position. He remained the IRA's leader until his imprisonment in 1936. Twomey was a native of Clondulane, near Fermoy, Co. Cork. The son of a labourer at Hallinan's Flour Mills in the town, Twomey went to work there at the age of 14. He rose to the position of works manager, and by 1917 became active in the Irish Volunteers. By 1918 he was adjutant of the Fermoy battalion and a year later he became an adjutant of the Cork No. 2 brigade. Twomey took part in an ambush of British troops in Fermoy in September 1919, one of the first attacks on British soldiers in Ireland since 1916. During 1920 he helped direct IRA intelligence in his Brigade area. He was a staff commandant of Liam Lynch's 1st Southern Division when he was captured and imprisoned on Spike Island during 1921. He managed to escape from the prison by row boat along with Dick Barrett, Tom Crofts and Bill Quirke. Twomey opposed the Anglo-Irish Treaty, although he was critical of the tactics adopted by the anti-Treaty forces in Dublin during June 1922. He eventually became adjutant general on Liam Lynch's staff and was with Lynch when he was killed on the Knockmealdowns in April 1923. Twomey was imprisoned at the conclusion of the civil war. During 1924 he became involved in reorganizing the IRA, inspecting its southern divisions that summer and its northern units during 1925. From 1926 Twomey was a full-time IRA activist, although he listed his occupation as 'journalist' and did contribute regularly to the IRA's weekly newspaper *An Phoblacht*. Twomey also visited the United States secretly during 1930. In that year he married Kathleen MacLaughlin from Donegal, a UCD graduate who was five years his senior.

Twomey has caused problems for historians of the IRA. His organizational ability is readily acceded to, but assessments of his politics are often based on lazy assumptions. Coogan's description of Twomey as a 'dedicated, right-wing Fenian' is frequently quoted to explain Twomey's supposed opposition to radicalism within the IRA. In fact far from being an 'apolitical militarist', Twomey was central to the IRA's adoption of radical politics by the late 1920s. Twomey's influence was crucial in convincing militarists like Seán Russell and later Tom Barry, that the IRA should promote social policies. Twomey argued that his organization were 'more than soldiers' and that the IRA had lost the civil war because it had not developed a political strategy. Twomey did not develop these ideas overnight but as a response to the decline and stagnation of the IRA by the late 1920s. He was not a socialist, but he was content to allow those who were, like Peadar O'Donnell, help politicize the IRA. Twomey was highly regarded by all of the tendencies within his organization because as well as his military record he was considered 'reasonable and capable of seeing another's viewpoint'; but he did regard 'building up the military movement' as the key task of the IRA. Within that he was prepared to concede that 'there was a great deal' in George Gilmore's argument for more open socialist policies, as well as tolerating Tom Barry's 'reactionary' views. When the expected disillusionment of republicans by Fianna Fáil did not occur and as the IRA became increasingly embroiled in confrontation, the unity that Twomey worked hard to maintain was sundered (Table 7).

Twomey as chief of staff was 'supreme in all military matters' within the IRA. He was responsible for the appointment of all IRA officers and the general training of the organization. After the C/S the most important officer was the adjutant general. The A/G was responsible for disciplinary matters, the keeping of records and communication with local units. During Twomey's period of leadership Jim Killeen, Seán MacBride and Donal O'Donoghue all held this

Table 7. The IRA leadership of 1933

Name	Rank	Age	Birthplace	Occupation
Moss Twomey	General	36	Cork	Chief of Staff
George Gilmore	Staff Comdt	35	Dublin	F/T IRA
Michael Price	Comdt Gen.	37	Dublin	Director of Training
James Killeen*	Staff Comdt	40	Westmeath	F/T IRA
Frank Ryan	Staff Captain	31	Limerick	Editor, *An Phoblacht*
Seán MacBride	Comdt Gen.	29	France	Journalist
Peadar O'Donnell	Staff Captain	40	Donegal	Journalist
Patrick McLogan	Staff Captain	39	Armagh	Publican
John Joe Sheehy	Comdt	34	Kerry	Insurance Agent
Donal O'Donoghue	Staff Comdt	36	Cavan	Adjutant Gen.
Seán Russell	Comdt General	40	Dublin	Qtr Master Gen.
Michael Fitzpatrick	Staff Captain	40	Wexford	Trade Union Official
Seán O'Farrell	Comdt	n/a	Leitrim	Income Tax Inspector

*Prior to the 1933 Convention James Killeen was adjutant general. See Appendix 1.

position. The quartermaster general was responsible for the supply and distribution of IRA arms, equipment and ammunition. From 1927 to 1936 the QMG was Seán Russell. The director of intelligence attempted to oversee the workings of intelligence officers in the IRA's local units. This involved building up information on the state forces, the IRA's political enemies and rival organizations. Other positions such as director of engineering or director of training could also be filled according to the organization's needs. Five of these men made up the army council which was the ruling body of the IRA appointed by a twelve-man Executive. The editor of *An Phoblacht* was usually a member of the IRA leadership, Peadar O'Donnell, Frank Ryan and Seán MacBride all holding that position during this era.

How typical was Twomey of the men who made up the IRA leadership? In 1933 all of the leadership had some experience of military conflict from Seán Russell who joined the Irish Volunteers in 1913 to Frank Ryan, just old enough to have played a minor role in the civil war. Most had been active in the period 1919–23, generally at officer level. The average age of the leadership was 36, the oldest being 40 and the youngest 29. Ten came from outside Dublin but all but three lived there by 1933. Only one, Patrick MacLogan, was from outside the 26 counties. Seven of them worked full-time for the IRA, while six held jobs outside the movement, although in the case of MacBride and O'Donnell their occupation allowed them to operate as essentially full time activists as well. All had experienced imprisonment at various stages. Two notable absentees from this list are George Plunkett, director of engineering for the IRA during the late 1920s, and Tom Barry, who had only rejoined the organization in 1932. Even with these additions the occupational background of these men, although varied, was universally white collar. The IRA's leadership therefore resembled IRA officers of the 1919–21 period in social background.

Was this pattern continued at junior officer and rank-and-file level? The IRA described itself as an organization 'almost solely composed of workers and peasants'. It took for granted that 'as a rule the Volunteer officer is a poor man'. Certainly in Dublin and Belfast its officer corps was overwhelmingly working class. In early 1933 out of 70 officers in the IRA's Dublin brigade, just two were businessmen and only 11 were in white collar occupations. This contrasts with the Dublin IRA of the 1919–21 period in which officers were more likely to be drawn from white collar occupations than was the case in 1933.

Table 8. Occupations of IRA Dublin brigade officers, 1933

Labourers	18
Unemployed	11
Skilled and semi-skilled	20
Clerks	4
Shop assistants	3
Insurance agents	3
Businessmen	2+
School teachers	1

The RUC captured the IRA's Belfast leadership during April 1936. Their occupational background much resembled that of the Dublin Brigade.

Table 8a. Occupations of Belfast officers, 1936

Anthony Lavery, O/C	Labourer
James Steele, Adjutant	Plasterer
Liam Mulholland, Finance	Labourer
Charles McGlade, QM	Printer
Michael Trainor, communications officer	Sheet metal worker

Outside of Dublin and Belfast the picture was more complex. A sample of 17 officers shows a higher proportion of those in white collar occupations (Table 9).

Of course, a list like this hides a diverse range of experiences. Brian Corrigan from Achill became the officer commanding West Mayo in January 1933. He was employed as an agent for the New Ireland Assurance Company by that stage but, until 1931, Corrigan had supported his elderly parents by farming on

Table 9. Local leadership

Name	Area	Occupation
David Matthews	Belfast	House painter
T.J. Ryan	West Clare	Farmer
Terence Ward	Derry City	Journalist
James O'Connor	Waterford City	Carpenter
Michael Ferguson	Longford	Shop assistant
Seán McCool	Donegal	Teacher
Patrick McKeon	North Roscommon	Road ganger
Tadgh Lynch	West Cork	School teacher
Patrick Fleming	Killarney	Hospital attendant
Brian Corrigan	West Mayo	Insurance agent
John McAdams	Derry City	School teacher
Michael O'Kane	Tyrone	Farmer
Seán McGuinness	Offaly	Farmer
Martin Kyne	Galway	School teacher
Michael Gallagher	Tyrone	Farmer
Tomás Maoiléoin	Tipperary	School teacher
J.J. Rice	Tralee	Commercial agent

Owenduff, Achill. During his imprisonment over the winter of that year, his potato crop had failed, hay had been lost and his parents got heavily into debt with local shopkeepers. Similarly Seán McGuinness of Offaly had been a farmer but while spending some years on the run in the United States he had lost his farm. By 1932 he was dependent on his brother for a place to live. In contrast Terry Ward, from Derry's Waterside, had been a journalist with the *Derry Journal*, while also the local IRA commander. Under the pen name 'Rory' he had written on GAA affairs for the newspaper. The number of school teachers who were IRA officers continued a trend identified by historians of Irish nationalism, although there was also marked differences in the experiences of these men. Tadgh Lynch, a head teacher at Mount Pleasant School in Bandon, Co. Cork, only joined the IRA in 1932. However, Seán McCool from Stranorlar, Co. Donegal, had been active in the civil war, was jailed during the Anti-Annuities campaign and spent time undergoing hospital treatment in the USSR.

The military experience of local officers was also varied. David Matthews was considered a 'competent gunman' by the RUC having been involved in sniping in the Kashmir Road area of Belfast during 1922. He had been imprisoned on several occasions. J.J. Rice had been an officer in the Kerry IRA from 1919 to 1923. Tomás Ó Maoileóin had been brigade commandant of the East Limerick IRA under the alias 'Seán Forde'. By the mid-1930s however the number of IRA officers with direct experience of the Anglo-Irish war and the civil war was declining. Men too young to have been involved like Patrick Fleming in Kerry and Con Lehane in Dublin increasingly gained prominence within the organization. One reason why the IRA favoured younger officers is that married men were sometimes unwilling to take risks or responsibility.

Notable too were the number of prominent personalities who had family connections with the republican movement. George and Jack Plunkett were brothers of Joseph Mary Plunkett the executed 1916 leader. Tomás MacCurtain, a young IRA member in the early 1930s, was the son of the murdered mayor of Cork City. Cork IRA officer Seán MacSwiney was a brother of Terence MacSwiney, MacCurtain's successor as mayor of Cork, who had died on hunger strike in October 1920. Dublin's Seamus Mallin was the son of executed Citizen Army officer, Michael Mallin. At a rank-and-file level, the Walsh brothers of Galway, arrested for seizing a copy of the film *Gallipoli* during 1933, were sons of an IRA man killed by the Black and Tans.

In religious terms, the IRA was an overwhelmingly Catholic organization at both leadership and rank and file level; but there were Protestant IRA members, the best known being the Gilmore brothers of Dublin; others included R.G. Bradshaw of Sligo, Victor Fagg of Athlone and Walter Mitchell from Offaly.

Membership of the IRA did not preclude holding elected office in this period. The most prominent IRA member to do so was army council member Patrick McLogan, elected as a Stormont MP for South Armagh in 1933. Several other IRA members were also elected as county councillors in the Free State during this period. The commander of the north Westmeath IRA, Thomas Maguire was chairman of Westmeath county council during 1933. Army council member Seán O'Farrell was elected onto Leitrim county council in June 1934, as were Seán Lynch in Longford and Michael O'Donnell in Kerry. In all nine 'Independent Republicans' as the IRA candidates titled themselves were returned in the 1934 local elections. This was less part of a concerted strategy by the IRA and more a response to local pressures to challenge Fianna Fáil; still, the organization maintained a flexible attitude to electoral intervention throughout this period.

The IRA rank-and-file were drawn mainly from the working class and rural poor. In 1934 nearly 70 per cent of the Belfast IRA were unemployed. The majority of the south Carlow IRA were also out of work in 1932. In Cork during 1930 the IRA members who had worked at Ford's motor plant were now 'idle'. The Drogheda IRA reported that because of unemployment they could not sell Easter lilies during 1931 unless they were allowed keep some of the proceeds. In Tralee during 1932 an IRA company refused to parade for fear that it might jeopardize their chances of being offered jobs as labourers on road schemes. Already several other IRA members had been given jobs labouring on the roads and at Tralee Hospital. That situation was similar in other parts of the west. Parades during summer 1931 were abandoned by the Donegal IRA because so many of its members had to leave for work in Scotland. A year later the north Mayo IRA reported that greater numbers of their members were leaving for work as migratory labourers in Britain than ever before. The failure of the battalion to mobilize for a training camp that summer was explained by the fact that the IRA in Mayo 'have not the richer element of the people ... but all who have to send their boys to England and Scotland during summer and autumn'. Three years later a member of the IRA in Achill forecast a low turnout from the area at Bodenstown because 'the crowd who would support us are away in England'. The gardaí dismissed Drogheda IRA members as being of the 'corner-boy type'. Of seven Drogheda IRA members arrested for leading an anti-Blueshirt riot in 1934, five were labourers and two clerks. An IRA man, James Glynn, killed in a clash with Blueshirts in Ennis, Co. Clare, was a member of the local Ennis Labourers' Union, as was his father and brother.

The IRA also included students, some of whom would become doctors or solicitors. The College company of the IRA in Dublin had members at UCD, TCD and St Patrick's Teacher Training College. At UCD a Republican Club had been formed during the 1920s which had organized protests against the establishment of an officer training corps of the National Army at the university. Its members included Todd Andrews, Frank Ryan, Con Lehane and Cearbhall Ó Dálaigh. The College company was hostile to radical politics within the IRA and its membership were dismissed as 'young prigs' by Peadar O'Donnell. Militant republicanism continued to have an attraction for some of those from middle-class backgrounds during the 1930s.

In general, the IRA does seem to have been composed of 'poor working men'. This in turn contributed to the constant problem of funding the organization. An attempt to raise extra revenue at the 1934 convention met with hostility as units argued their members could not afford to contribute extra money to the IRA. A Leix officer again stressed that his men were 'farmers' sons and casual labourers' who simply could not afford extra contributions. This intensified the reliance of the IRA on funding from supporters in the United States which, because of the Great Depression, was also greatly restricted. A practical consequence of this for an IRA member was that imprisonment could affect their livelihood. An Offaly IRA member who made his living cutting turf in summer and selling it in winter found himself in dire straits having been jailed for a period over the summer.

By 1932 the 'bulk' of the IRA membership was dominated by young men who had 'attained manhood' after the civil war. The appointment of young officers had helped generate enthusiasm and these men were considered the 'heart and soul' of the organization. This occasionally still produced tension as 'old Volunteers' resented the newer recruits. Young men living at home could also face parental censure. An IRA member from Lisburn was thrown out by his parents after they learned of his arrest by the RUC at an IRA training camp. More importantly the youth of the IRA's membership increasingly became a weapon used against the IRA by its political enemies. When a Drogheda IRA man facing charges of possessing ammunition refused to recognize the court, a garda superintendent pointed out that the defendant was only twelve when the Treaty was signed yet he called himself 'a soldier of the IRA'. Objecting to the IRA's Boycott British campaign, Cork Labour TD T.J. Murphy referred to Tadgh Lynch as the 'kind of soldier' produced by peacetime. When Fianna Fáil sought to stress its credentials as the bearers of revolutionary legitimacy it increasingly pointed to its leaders' records of the 1916–23 period and contrasted them with those of the IRA's membership. As Seán MacEntee reminded IRA members who were heckling him, he had faced a death sentence when they were 'not even in the cradle'. In the Free State of that period there were many contenders for the title of true inheritors of the revolutionary flame of 1919–21 and several of them had convincing credentials. However, the claims by Fianna Fáil that by 1934 the IRA was not 'the Army that fought the Black and Tans' did have an important impact on republican support.

In numerical terms the IRA was consistently strongest in Dublin and Belfast, but Mayo, Clare and Tipperary (very strong areas in 1926 and 1930) had declined by 1932. By 1933 Leitrim and west Cork were areas of substantial IRA strength. Kerry also saw impressive growth after 1932. Belfast's IRA membership also grew between 1932 and 1934. These figures would seem to show some connection between confrontational activity and IRA strength as west Cork, Kerry and Leitrim saw considerable violence between the IRA and the Blueshirts. Dublin as the centre of the IRA's organization as well as the largest centre of population might be expected to maintain a steady membership, not all of whom of course would necessarily be Dubliners. The IRA's growth in Belfast would seem to be connected an increase in its activities following the Outdoor Relief strike of 1932, culminating in the Stormont election campaign of November 1933.

Was there a connection between activity by the IRA during the revolutionary period and residual strength? West Cork saw an exceptional level of violence between 1917 and 1923. However, by 1933 the Blueshirts were numerically much stronger in that area than the IRA. Belfast experienced intense, if often confused, conflict in that period, but the majority of its IRA members had taken the pro-Treaty side in the civil war, leaving the anti-Treatyites to rebuild from a demoralized shell. Leitrim saw comparatively little activity in either the 'Tan war' or the civil war, yet by 1933 it had one of the IRA's strongest battalions. This may suggest that people who would not have joined the IRA in 1920 may have been attracted to it by the 1930s.

Was there a connection between IRA strength and more generalized republican support? Certainly the rural areas where at various stages the IRA had sizeable units were also areas of strong support for Fianna Fáil. There was a slight decrease in Fianna Fáil support in Kerry in the 1937 election, which may reflect some republican disillusionment, but it was the Labour party that seems to have gained from this. Republican candidates who challenged Fianna Fáil at bye-elections were comprehensively defeated. Generally, the IRA and its periphery were never large enough to have a serious impact on electoral politics.

In Kerry, over 67 per cent of the vote went to Fianna Fáil in 1933, making it 'the outstanding Republican county' in Ireland according to one local newspaper. There it does seem that there was a direct link between IRA support and the region's history during the revolutionary period. One garda officer believed that because the county had been 'ruthlessly treated in the past', the civil war would remain 'a bitter memory to a big section of the youth' and as a result the IRA would receive support. As if to prove his point, the Killarney IRA demonstration he was reporting on had among its number the relatives of men killed during the civil war. This theory was echoed several years later when Irish Army Intelligence examined why the IRA, which had almost vanished elsewhere, was able to maintain an organization in Kerry. One observer pointed to republican sympathies among the 'poorer people' who lived along the seaboard and to an 'under-current' of illegality which was said to prevail in Tralee. Another officer believed that small groups of people in Kerry would aid the IRA despite knowing little about their 'present day' policies. He believed that a family 'tragedy ... in the Tan or civil war period' was the reason for this residual support. Whatever the reasons for it, the IRA's numerical strength in the Kerry region was something of a mixed blessing for its leadership as its membership there had an unrivalled reputation for indiscipline.

The post-1926 IRA was never a mass movement, indeed following the civil war it declined in strength and was stagnating until 1931. Then reorganization and the effect of the Great Depression made the IRA a focus for opposition to the Free State. It benefited from the wave of popular republicanism following the coming to power of Fianna Fáil in 1932. By 1934 internal political turmoil about how to relate to the Fianna Fáil government began to divide the organization. By 1936 its increasingly desperate tactics had largely marginalized the IRA from broader republicanism.

A study of the IRA of the 1930s helps illustrate the contradictory influences within militant Irish republicanism. Despite its opposition to parliamentarianism, the IRA would actively assist Fianna Fail in two crucial general elections. It rejected majority rule, but wanted to head a popular revolution. It was overwhelmingly Catholic in membership, but often bore the brunt of clerical condemnation. It carried out activities which were widely seen as sectarian yet genuinely believed it could convince northern Protestants of the virtues of republicanism. For a period it enthused about the Soviet Union and was the Comintern's closest ally in Ireland, while a few years later it would deny charges of communist influence. It denounced partition, yet remained very much an organization focused on the overthrow of the southern rather than the northern state. It trained for warfare, yet often tried to prevent its members involving themselves in confrontation with their enemies.

This study contends that the IRA formulated its policies in reaction to pressures from both within and outside of its organization. Its adoption of radical policies during the late 1920s was a genuine attempt to grapple with the discontent brought about by the Great Depression as well as arrest its own decline. The IRA's slow disavowal of these polices was a response to the increasingly conservative atmosphere of the 1930s and the hostile reaction of much of its own rank and file. In both its scale, politics and day-to-day concerns the IRA of 1926 to 1936 was a very different organization from either its civil war predecessor or its 1940s successor.

2/The day-to-day working of a 'secret army'

Between 1926 and 1936, the IRA did not engage in any military campaign; in fact, the average IRA member's activities were closer to those of a member of a political party than a soldier. It was largely IRA members themselves who pasted up wall posters advertising commemorations or Easter lily sales; it was also the IRA who painted slogans denouncing government repression or the treatment of imprisoned republicans on walls and roads across Ireland. During election campaigns IRA members canvassed and did election work on behalf of republican candidates. The organization helped look after the financial needs of families of its jailed members; it occasionally paid for medical care for members who could not afford it themselves, and would even organize visits to members from the country who were hospitalized in Dublin and had no relatives in the city.

Despite these activities, the IRA was neither a political party nor a welfare organization for republicans. Political instruction for its membership was given by senior officers at parades rather than at political meetings. The IRA regarded itself as an army, dedicated to bringing about an independent Irish republic by force of arms. To do this, it would have to be at least as well armed as the forces of both states in Ireland. It had to train its membership in the use and care of arms and explosives; it needed to maintain a disciplined cohesive organization, which could withstand bouts of government repression without fracturing; it also had to ensure that its members did not engage in unofficial activities, or use their access to arms for criminal purposes. For most of this period the IRA was illegal or semi-legal and therefore had to organize much of its activities in secret. It had to ensure its members did not reveal the whereabouts of its meeting places and arms dumps; it had to guard itself from infiltration but also try to develop its own intelligence network. The ways in which the IRA tried to carry out these tasks can help us to assess how much of a serious revolutionary threat the organization posed during this period.

A year after the conclusion of the civil war, the IRA's quartermaster general, Andy Cooney, compiled a list of arms available to the organization. Although Cooney believed the list was not a complete one, it does give some sense of how well equipped the organization was. What is immediately apparent is that the IRA had more members than it had weapons to arm them with (Table 10).

For an estimated 14,000 men, the IRA could muster 3,900 rifles, 124 machine guns and 1,400 handguns. This did mean that as the IRA shrunk in size over the next six years it was to become proportionally better armed. However,

Table 10. IRA arms, July 1924

Service rifles	3,801	*Ammunition*	
Mauser	171	.303 Ammo	140,154
Lewis MG	66	Mauser	610
Thompson MG	46	.45 Auto	16,895
Vickers MG	4	.45	10,386
Maxim MG	6	.38 Auto	1,900
Parabellum MG	2	Parabellum	2,543
Revolvers .45	1,232	'Peter'	1,057
Handguns		Mills Bombs	256
Automatics .45	32	'our make'	465
Revolvers .38	31	Explosives	3,211lbs
Automatics .38	17	Detonators	3,438
Parabellum	67	Fuse	75 yds.
'Peter'	43		
Luger	4		

large numbers of these weapons never left their hiding places and the organization could never claim to be adequately armed.

The results of another arms inspection in 1930 again illustrate how poorly
armed the IRA actually was. Even in the areas that seemed relatively well armed
such as Tipperary, in reality few IRA members had access to the weapons the
unit claimed. In the aftermath of the civil war many arms were abandoned and
knowledge of them completely lost to the IRA as was the case in west Limerick.
In Sligo during 1930 there were weapons in dumps that had not been touched
for almost five years (Table 11).

Control of its weapons was to remain a problem for the IRA. During 1925
substantial amounts of weapons in Tyrone, including 30 rifles in Omagh, were
no longer under IRA control. Following the formation of Fianna Fáil, numbers
of its adherents seem to have taken IRA weapons with them when they left the
organization. As late as 1932 the IRA believed Fianna Fáil supporters had control of at least 50 rifles in north Cork. For security reasons only a few IRA members could be aware of the location of arms dumps. This also meant that if an
individual emigrated (for example, as occurred in Connemara during 1930, or
Kilkenny a year later), the location of the local dump was lost. Fear of being
arrested with weapons meant that in many areas arms were left unattended in
dumps for long periods. The safe-keeping of arms in dumps was dependent on
great care being taken to ensure the dump was dry, had adequate ventilation and
that the weapons themselves were stripped, cleaned, and stored in greased cloth.

Table 11. Arms inspection 1930

Area	Rifles	Handguns	Machine-gun
West Limerick			2
Limerick City	6		
West Clare	34	4	
East Clare	22	4	1
Kerry	110	10	2
Sth. Tipp.	144	44	1
Nth. Tipp.	47	11	
Cork No. 1	247	28	15
Nth. Cork	40		1
Sligo	73	26	5
Galway C.		6	
Connemara	38	4	
Claremorris	4		
N. Galway	1		
Waterford	17	8	
Kilkenny	76	18	2
Totals	859	163	29

If ammunition was allowed to become dirty or if explosives became damp, then it was no longer safe to use them. The IRA leadership were complaining during 1929 of its members 'nervousness' which was leading to weapons becoming useless through neglect.

As well as its own figures, we know that the IRA lost substantial amounts of its weaponry due to capture by the police. Between 1923 and 1931, 985 rifles, 1,270 handguns and 9 machine-guns were seized by the gardaí. While not all of these arms necessarily belonged to the IRA, we can be sure most of them did. Two of the organization's biggest losses came in the Dublin area with the capture of dumps at St Enda's College in 1926 and at Killakee in 1931. IRA units usually wanted more arms or ammunition than they had. During 1930, the IRA in Templemore complained that they had no rifles for training; in south Wexford they asked for a 'few small guns' as they had almost no arms; and the Dundalk unit made 'anxious' inquiries for an ammunition drum for their one Thompson gun.

As well as the shortage of arms and ammunition, the IRA's weaponry was made up of a variety of types and calibres, most of which dated back to the 1916-23 period. The Monaghan IRA had among its arms in 1930 a Martini Henry rifle, which had been the British Army's rifle until 1907, and an 'Ulster

Volunteer' rifle of unspecified type. The Connemara IRA also had a Martini Henry, and several Mauser and Lee Enfield rifles. The Mauser was of German origin, and numbers of these had reached Ireland pre-1914 for both Nationalist and Unionist use. The great majority of the IRA's rifles seem to have been Lee Enfield Service rifles, however. The Lee Enfield had been the standard-issue British Army rifle of the First World War and was used by both the Irish National Army, the British Army and Commonwealth forces well into the 1950s. The various handguns that IRA members had access to were the Webley revolver, the Smith and Wesson revolver, the Colt Automatic and the Parabellum and 'Peter' automatics. The two most common machine-guns were the Lewis and the Thompson. The Lewis was a light machine-gun which had been widely used by Allied forces during the First World War. The Thompson sub-machine gun has become one of the most famous and recognizable weapons of all time, although during the 1920s it was associated more with American gangsters than with military use. The IRA also developed its own explosives, of which 'Irish Cheddar' and 'Paxo' were the best known.

Despite the problems outlined above, it could be argued that the IRA possessed quite enough weapons to carry out a deadly, if limited, armed campaign. Indeed, given the use these weapons were put to during this period (largely, assassinations, occasional destruction of war memorials and shooting up of houses and offices), the organization had more than enough equipment for its task; but it did not envisage engaging in a guerrilla war against either government in Ireland; it saw itself leading an insurrection or coup d'etat and then waging a revolutionary war against Britain. As early as 1925 it was recognized that attempts to overthrow the government in the Free State by 'obstructive or guerrilla tactics' would end disastrously. Instead a republican government would only come to power on the back of a coup d'etat. Defeat in the civil war was blamed on 'hit and run' tactics and an exaggerated sense of regional identity cultivated by the IRA during the 1919-21 period. As the left within the IRA began to gain influence, the language of 'mass revolutionary' action became current. The IRA was to be the 'Army of the revolution' containing the leadership of a mass popular movement. It was this type of thinking that informed IRA decisions in 1932 and 1933 to concentrate their efforts on 'building up the military movement.' Therefore IRA training was theoretically geared toward producing a regular soldier, not a guerrilla.

There were a number of occasions between 1926 and 1936 when the IRA leadership felt a 'military situation' could emerge to their benefit. Prior to the May 1927 general election, the IRA felt that if a republican coalition won a majority, then the Free State Army could be demobilized and replaced by the IRA. Then a conflict might ensue with the British government over the Treaty. During 1931, Twomey speculated that, if the Cumann na nGaedheal government lost the forthcoming general election, they might refuse to give up office. For the IRA that would have been 'the very best thing to happen'. It would expose the Free State as the dictatorship republicans already considered it to be, and create division among the National Army, possibly opening the way for an IRA-led seizure of power. After 1932, the growing tension between the Irish and British governments which produced the Economic War was taken as evidence that an Anglo-Irish military conflict was in the offing. By late 1932, the IRA was speculating that the Army Comrades Association might attempt a coup, which, if met by an IRA counter-attack would possibly unleash revolution; in 1933 Twomey was talking in terms of seizing power in Ireland 'within the next twelve months'; and, the following year, the IRA were still planning to intensify training so its men could 'take the field within a year'.

To carry out such a revolution the IRA, would of course, need to be much better armed, equipped, and trained than it was. Therefore much time and energy was spent attempting to rectify these problems. One obvious way it could arm itself was to steal weapons. Large numbers of people owned shotguns for example, and nearly 3,000 of these weapons were recovered from IRA dumps by the gardaí between 1923 and 1931; but shotguns were not a match for rifles or machine guns, and ownership of weapons like these was much more restricted. In Belfast, where after the turbulent events of the early 1920s there seemed to have been many arms in private hands, the IRA engaged in a number of arms raids. There were dangers in attempting to steal from civilians, as the Mayo IRA discovered when a raid for arms resulted in the shooting of one of their members in 1932. While elements within the IRA pushed for a mass seizure of arms from civilians during 1933, the organization's Convention voted against this. It was argued that stealing shotguns would unnecessarily alienate farmers and that the IRA should recognize the right of private individuals to bear arms. The tactic was not abandoned, however, as the theft of explosives from the magazine at Ballymullen barracks, Tralee, later that year showed. As late as 1936 Cork IRA members were arrested for stealing arms from a dump controlled by Fianna Fáil TD Martin Corry.

The organization could and did order former members to give up weapons in their possession, but it is hard to judge how successful this was. In Co. Tipperary during July 1932 a number of ex-IRA men formed a 'Land Settlement Committee' that became embroiled in a dispute with a local farmer. Using weapons that they had kept since their IRA days, these men fired on the farmer's house and killed one of his livestock. IRA members in Clare had a reputation inside the organization for the use of arms in private disputes. During October 1932 two ex-IRA members in the north of the county effectively 'terrorized' their former comrades with a series of threats and violence which included an attack on local IRA leader Martin Whyte. The dispute was caused by the refusal of the men to hand over their weapons to the IRA. IRA members from west Clare were brought in to threaten the former members with retaliation if they persisted.

The main method of gaining modern equipment was to purchase it abroad and smuggle it to Ireland. During the 1920s the IRA still had contacts in Europe from the revolutionary period. During 1925, an officer reported on the widespread opportunities for arms buying in Germany and Belgium. There were already 50,000 rounds of ammunition in Hamburg awaiting transport to Ireland and rifles, handguns and even light artillery were available for dealers there at reasonable prices. There was also a smuggling line controlled by the IRA between Antwerp and Southampton. One difficulty, however, was that the German dealers were untrustworthy, and it was suspected that if given the 'slightest opportunity' for swindling the IRA they 'would probably avail of it'. Another firm had already apparently defrauded Robert Briscoe and Charles McGuinness on a earlier arms-buying mission. Because the League of Nations had forbidden the export of arms from Germany to Ireland their transport would have to be consigned to 'some South American republic'; this meant more problems with custom officials and consuls. In contrast the Belgian suppliers were prepared to ship from Antwerp to the 3-mile limit off the Irish coast and offered machine guns and rifles at cheaper rates than the Germans; they were also willing to manufacture ammunition. Previously there had been some weapons ordered but not collected by the IRA, so the Belgians were demanding assurances about any future deal. The main difficulty for the IRA, however, was that it did not have the funds to pay for any large quantity of arms.

Other options open to the IRA in this period were link-ups with Egyptian and Indian revolutionaries in Britain and the prospect of shipping small quantities of arms through London. The subsequent arrest of Jim Killeen in London during 1925 with a consignment of revolvers seems to have ended this route. The IRA in Britain also opened up a connection with the Soviet Union, and were prepared to trade information in return for military favours; however, the IRA stressed they wanted to be given 'absolute equality' with the representatives of the Russian government rather than be considered agents of theirs. By the late 1920s, the IRA was looking towards the United States as the main source of military technology. In 1932 Seán Russell visited the US, and Twomey expressed the hope that as well as political work that Russell would do 'something which we will all be pleased with-in his own particular line!' By 1933 the Clan na Gael was holding nearly 490 Thompson guns and 100,000 rounds of ammunition for the IRA, but getting this material to Ireland was posing a major problem. There were routes used by the IRA for smuggling through Galway, Cobh and London. The organization also employed the services of sympathetic fishermen off the west coast of Ireland and Irish staff on board cruise liners;

it also had contacts at the B and I depot at North Wall who could 'get a packet through without being examined by Customs'; during 1932 the IRA also utilized returning emigrants from the US to smuggle in weapons, although it claimed not all these were making their way to its organization. Most of these were only capable of bringing in relatively small amounts of arms. In late 1932 the IRA were stressing that if the ACA did mount a coup, the IRA did not have the ammunition to fight for more than a day; yet the Clan were suggesting selling half the Thompson guns in order to procure money for more ammunition, a suggestion the IRA reacted to angrily. Many of the Thompsons did eventually reach Ireland during the 1930s and several theories exist as to how this occured. Certainly 40 Thompsons were delivered to the IRA in March 1937. The Special Branch believed that Seán Russell organized the smuggling of 400 Thompson guns through Cork in late 1936. Irish military intelligence however, thought that several hundred machine guns were brought through Cobh when the Kerry football team returned from a tour of the US in 1938. There is however no evidence of smuggling during the early 1930s on the scale suggested in some contemporary reports. Twomey believed that the gardaí, (especially Eoin O'Duffy) and the British press, were exaggerating tales of gun running to undermine the Fianna Fáil government. The IRA's smuggling operations were small-scale and never likely to bring the organization the amount of arms it desired.

The IRA regarded the US as important for its military plans in a number of other ways. It believed the US was the most militarily developed nation at the time and that the IRA's allies in America should make use of this. IRA men who emigrated were urged to join the US Army, Air Force or Reserve Forces in order to receive military training. Manuals and publications issued by the US armed forces were supposed to be scrutinized for information that would be useful to the IRA. Information needed to be gathered about the latest methods of warfare, including developments in wireless and chemical technology. Of particular interest to the IRA were developments in armoured, mechanized, and aerial warfare and especially counter-tactics to the use of these. The organization wished to discover the best methods of securing a coastline against attack, 'assuming little artillery and heavy guns are at the disposal of the defenders'. It was unhappy that the Clan seemed to be ignoring these developments and that IRA members were not taking an interest in improving their military skills. One exception was the training of five IRA men as pilots at Curtis Air School in Chicago. Russell visited the air school and was very happy with the progress of the IRA fliers during 1932. While the training was proving costly, Russell stressed that if the IRA 'ever go into active service we will need such men'. The IRA's interest in air and coastal defence point to its belief that after a successful revolution it would be engaged in defending Ireland against an external enemy. Despite the potential republican air force, though, it was to be largely disappointed in its hope that its US supporters would prove to be a source of military knowledge.

While procuring arms was one problem, the training of IRA members in their use presented other difficulties. In 1930 Russell complained about the limited number of training officers the IRA possessed. A small number of officers, among them Donegal's Seán McCool, were sent to different areas for weeks at a time to help train the local IRA. When the IRA began recruiting heavily, this problem became even more apparent. During 1933 the IRA began to send instructors from Dublin, who were conversant in drilling and arms training to the countryside at weekends; they included Bob Bradshaw, a young Belfast man on the run following the killing of an RUC officer in Belfast. Another major difficulty was that the IRA could only carry out weapons training in secret. While lectures on arms and some instruction could be given indoors, most weapons training had to take place outside. Secure and secluded locations had to found by the IRA, and scouts posted to warn of approaching strangers. The Dublin IRA, for example, carried out training at the Pine Forest, near Glencullen in the Dublin mountains, and explosive training at quarries in Crumlin and Rathfarnham. Even then there was no guarantee of avoiding attention from the police as mass arrests at Carnlough outside Belfast in 1932 and Giles Quay outside Dundalk in 1935 showed. Less dramatically, bad weather could force the cancellation of training classes, as it did in Kerry during 1930. The risk involved in being caught could cause fainthearted IRA officers to 'forget' to bring rifles to a training camp, as occurred in Leix. Inattentive scouts who allowed local people to gather and become 'interested onlookers' at a training camp in Westmeath forced its abandonment. For theoretical knowledge of arms, the IRA largely relied on British Army manuals, many of them collected by Russell.

Even if training went ahead, then the results were often very mixed. There was only a limited time period available to IRA members and the amount of time devoted to actually firing weapons was a fraction of this. Participants in a Dundalk officer's training camp (OTC) were given only a half an hour to practise shooting after a seven hour training session. Even then most only got to fire one shot from a rifle. This was not unusual. A major OTC was planned for west Cork during May 1933. Participants were guaranteed just one shot with the rifle. Similarly in Caherciveen during 1934 the standard rifle training involved firing just two shots a month. At the Dundalk camp each man was also given an opportunity to fire a burst from a Thompson gun, but neither this nor a single shot from a rifle would be enough to gain proficiency. Aside from target practice, mastering the Lee Enfield rifle would require hours spent learning to judge distance, and take account of wind and cover. Not surprisingly, it was difficult to train men in these skills in a limited period of time. While rural IRA men often had a better sense of the use of cover and skills of observation than those from urban backgrounds this was not always the case. One instructor found it surprising that 'country-bred' officers found it impossible to locate men placed in 'rather ordinary cover'. IRA officers reports point to great variations in the level of military expertise among their rank and file. One officer judged the Midland battalion as 'hopeless' with military knowledge and arms training 'non existent' in its ranks. In west Clare however a visiting officer was pleased with the proficiency displayed by members in musketry. The presence in that case of a 'capable instructor' or a man with military experience made a major difference. Most major training sessions had to take place on weekends when IRA members did not have work commitments – as in Dublin during 1930, when members left the city for training on Saturday night and Sunday mornings. For rural units, however, this could interfere with farm work as in Leix, where numbers of men decided to remain 'working at the corn' while the weather was fine rather than attend a camp. Even when a training session was successfully run, Russell noticed how men unused to military training tired after about five hours and were unable for 'further exertion'. All the evidence points towards the IRA having great difficulties in training its membership in the use of arms.

The majority of the IRA's training was not in the use of weapons however. Most IRA parades and training camps involved hours of drilling. While this was partly so the IRA would look impressive in its public appearances at parades and commemorations there was a more important reason. As Jim Killeen explained, it was 'only on the parade ground that a sense of discipline and obedience can be instilled'. Drilling is how recruits to regular armies learn quick reactions to verbal commands. The IRA leadership knew many of its members felt parades were 'irksome' and that repetition jarred on them; though they stressed that 'constant training and parading and repetition' was absolutely vital. The IRA believed a man who would not parade regularly would not be prepared to fight when necessary. The weekly parade was the centre of the IRA man's activity. It was there that he received political instruction and the leadership imparted their analysis to the membership. It was at parades, too, that recruits were sworn into the IRA in the presence of their peers. Non-attendance at parades was a cause for dismissal from the IRA, and many members were expelled for that reason. Whether or not an individual was prepared to give up his spare time to drill and be ordered about by another civilian was obviously a mark of their commitment to the IRA; but given the nature of the IRA's membership there was rarely full attendance at its parades. Members with valid reasons for non-attendance would be excused, but this could be taken too far, as in Dundalk in December 1930 when 'owing to the Christmas rush' parades were sparsely attended. If parade strength was an indication of a healthy state of organization, then the figures confirm that large numbers of IRA units were in a poor state during 1930. Most IRA parades were taken up with forming fours, squad and section drill, and practice at extended order drill and section formations rather than weapons training. Weapons were carried only when parades were held in secluded areas. The IRA also realized that lectures on weapons and the promise of training with them were necessary to maintain members' interest in parading. It was noted that men would not 'cheerfully parade for squad drill' but would turn up when firing practice was promised.

During 1932 the IRA decided to take advantage of the changed political circumstances to embark on intensified training. The army council intended to organise week-long training camps in various locations in the Free State. However only one went ahead, at Donamon Castle in Co. Roscommon, where IRA officers from the north west gathered in August 1932. From the course of activities held there we gain a sense of how the IRA would have liked to organise its training. From 6 a.m. every day IRA members were drilled, given lectures on arms and equipment and engaged in field exercises. In the evening they had an hour and half of football before 'lights out' at 9 p.m. The weeks activities were overseen by the IRA's director of training, Mick Price. While those who attended were said to have benefited greatly from the experience, the political reaction to the event meant the IRA were wary of organizing similar events elsewhere. The leadership also complained that the reaction to its plans for training camps had been very unenthusiastic within the IRA itself. While some were conversant with arms and their use, the majority of the membership had not enough opportunities to become proficient.

Armies by their very nature are not democratic institutions. They demand obedience to a chain of command and have the power to inflict punishments on members who disobey orders. The IRA recruited on the basis that it was a revolutionary organization, and it encouraged a certain level of political discussion among its members. Delegates to its conventions were elected, but this also meant that political disagreements could lead to splits within its ranks. It claimed to depend on a 'spirit' that members' duties were 'voluntary and for Ireland'. Since the organization was likely to attract those who were rebellious, it faced a problem with how to maintain discipline. Its members had to accept orders which had no formal basis in Irish society. On paper, the organization laid down rigorous strictures which prevented its members recognising courts of law and answering police questions. Did the IRA's adherence to a formal military structure mask a more anarchic reality?

The best known of the IRA's rules and regulations was General Order No. 24 which forbade members from recognizing courts in either the Free State or Northern Ireland. It also prohibited the signing of statements, of undertakings of good behaviour and essentially any co-operation with the authorities. Permission to employ legal defence was only given in 'very special' cases. Members were also forbidden from having 'voluntary communication' with the police. The reality was that these rules were broken on numerous occasions. In 1929 three Dundalk IRA men were dismissed for recognizing the courts and employing legal defence. A young IRA member in Dublin recognized the court and admitted involvement in an assault on a guard during 1930. Indeed, Garda Commissioner Eoin O'Duffy was boasting of having at least 30 undertakings signed by IRA men in the Dublin area that year. At a parade in north Kerry during 1930, the IRA's inspecting officer was outraged to discover that his visit was common knowledge among the local community. This meant that large numbers of people turned up to watch the parade, as did a number of gardaí and detectives. The local IRA commander then arrived, quite clearly drunk, and agreed to accompany the gardaí to a nearby pub! In 1931 a battalion adjutant was court-martialled in Leitrim for losing IRA weapons, recognizing the court and giving an undertaking to the gardaí. During 1932 a section leader in the IRA in Dungannon was dismissed for recognising the court after being arrested for possession of *An Phoblacht*. During the same month a Dundalk man pleaded guilty to possessing ammunition and agreed to co-operate with gardaí. IRA men questioned about slogan painting in Co. Roscommon willingly gave both their own names and that of their commanding officer to the gardaí. In a highly embarrassing case for the IRA, its Belfast O/C and a former election candidate both signed undertakings to discontinue political activity in early 1934. At that year's Convention, Moss Twomey described how 'frightful humiliation' had been caused to the organization by the numbers of men giving information when questioned. Later that year Donal O'Donoghue complained that the 'usual breading down ... under interrogation' of IRA prisoners was occurring in Kerry.

Over a ten-year period these could be judged relatively isolated incidents. Indeed, they were due to a variety of different factors. In a number of cases family pressure influenced men to recognize courts. The mother of the young IRA member on trial for assaulting a garda accused Seán MacBride of 'sheltering behind foolish young men' like her son and convinced him to participate in the trial. The Dundalk man caught with ammunition initially refused to recognize the court, until his mother's 'tears and entreaties' induced him to do so. The Dungannon IRA member was the son of a hotel owner and the IRA believed his social background convinced him he was untouchable. The shock of facing a prison sentence taught him otherwise. The three Dundalk men were likewise 'young and inexperienced' and panicked when confronted with possible imprisonment. The IRA was having difficulty getting what it described as 'undisciplined ruffians' in its Kerry units to obey any of its directives by 1934. The case of the parade fiasco in north Kerry illustrates another difficulty for the IRA. It was obvious to the inspecting officer that the local commander should be dismissed. It was also made clear to him that this would lead to the resignation of other officers in the area. To preserve its organization the IRA was forced to tolerate this amazing display of indiscipline.

When the IRA was faced with a major government crackdown however, sections of its organization did show an alarming tendency to break ranks. In October 1931 the Cumann na nGaedheal government introduced the Constitution (Amendment 17) Act to halt what it saw as the alarming rise in subversive activity. The Act introduced a tribunal made up of army officers to try those charged with anti-state activities. This military tribunal had the power to impose the death penalty and there was no right to appeal its sentence. The IRA was banned along with ten other organizations, and the left and republican press censored. The organization responded with orders for its members to maintain 'discipline and cohesion' and not to be provoked into violence.

Some of the first proceedings before the tribunal saw two Achill men, Brian Corrigan and John Mulgrew breach IRA orders by pleading 'not guilty'. Two Leitrim men agreed to give undertakings to sever their connection with the IRA and to assist the gardaí in any way they could. It transpired that another 13 Leitrim men had given similar assurances. A Kerry IRA officer agreed to leave the organization and a Waterford youngster also severed his connection with the IRA. Three IRA company O/Cs in Listowel signed undertakings as did at least two men in Dublin. An IRA company commander in Strokestown, Co. Roscommon, also signed a garda undertaking. In Castlecomer, Co. Kilkenny, two IRA members signed undertakings, one agreeing to help the gardaí find arms dumps in the area. In a highly embarrassing case seven Galway IRA men including a Fianna Fáil councillor, Martin Fahy, admitted to several inept but destructive activities, revealed details of secret meetings and publicly denounced the organization.

It must be said, however, that many of the IRA men tried before the Tribunal conducted themselves in the manner the organization expected. Once jailed, most embarked on a protest at not being treated as prisoners of war and faced the winter of 1931–32 in solitary confinement. Twomey actually claimed that the clampdown was increasing recruitment to the IRA, arguing that 'times like these make an appeal to the best type of young men'. Certainly after the initial panic the IRA does seem to have weathered the storm reasonably well. In both Dublin and Cork the spirit of the organization was said to be good and 'encouraging' meetings were being held. The clampdown did put pressure on the IRA, though, and, had it not been for its political unpopularity, might have severely damaged the organization.

There could be a certain flexibility in the IRA's approach to General Order No. 24. Men who disobeyed it could be readmitted but it largely depended 'on the type of men and the circumstances' which induced their indiscipline. Corrigan was allowed back into the IRA partly because he served his sentence but also because he was popular in Achill. The welcome Corrigan received in Achill on his release showed that the IRA's image had not suffered because he pleaded 'not guilty'. The IRA took into account that in cases where there was a possibility of the death sentence prisoners could employ a legal defence. Despite the fact that a Leitrim officer believed that 'you could not blame' many of the men who signed undertakings there because they believed they were about to be executed, these men were not re-admitted to the IRA.

At times the IRA's internal rulings could seem extremely petty. A Belfast man was refused membership because some years before he had been expelled from the IRA for being part of a band that had played 'God Save the King' at the conclusion of a concert! A double standard seems to have been employed at times. Another Belfast man, a veteran of the War of Independence and the civil war had applied to Queen's University for a teaching diploma. The school where he was to train was run by the Northern Ireland Ministry of Education and teachers had to swear an oath of allegiance. The man in question had never had a job, due to imprisonment and IRA activity, and he begged for a chance to gain that 'individual independence that we all crave for'. His request to be exempted from General Order No. 24 in this case was refused. On the other hand, Seán MacBride's IRA career does not seem to have suffered after he undertook not to engage in 'objectionable activity' if released from prison to complete audits for the Roebuck Jam Company in 1929.

Despite the real problems the IRA faced in living up to what were often unrealistic expectations of refusal to deal with the process of law there is no doubt that in many cases their members did adhere to General Order No. 24. The real sacrifices that prisoners who experienced solitary confinement and withdrawal of privileges made in order to be considered republican soldiers undoubtedly helped IRA morale. But discipline was not simply about obeying directions on dealing with the courts. There was also the question of obeying the IRA's political instructions and avoiding involvement in activities that would reflect badly on the IRA. Here the organization was again publicly embarrassed on several occasions.

Tension which had existed between older more conservative officers and younger militants was defused with the departure of most of the older officers to Fianna Fáil. Until 1932, the IRA was not overly troubled with internal political problems. While political differences certainly existed there was little public reflection of these. This changed with the IRA's decision not to obstruct Fianna Fáil in government and the organization's gradual disavowal of socialism. A minor dispute emerged after Dundalk IRA officers claimed that the local Fianna Fáil cumainn had been informed of the IRA's decision to support the party in the 1933 general election before they had. A number of Dublin IRA members had formed a secret 'Republican Workers' Group' which was holding its own meetings in early 1933. The IRA leadership moved to ensure control over its members participation in non-IRA activities by passing several related motions at its March 1933 convention. The most important of these demanded that members seek permission before writing or speaking publicly on political matters. As a result, some RWG members left the IRA and the issue festered to re-emerge at the 1934 convention.

Shortly after the 1933 convention, however, these issues were exposed publicly by events in Dublin. Premises owned or associated with communists in Dublin came under attack from large crowds. Over several nights mobs besieged the Communist headquarters, Connolly House, and eventually succeeded in storming it. An IRA member, Charles Gilmore, took part in the defence of the building, firing shots at the crowd and wounding a man. Gilmore was arrested and when questioned claimed he had the authority of the IRA to carry arms. The IRA adjutant general publicly disputed this in the daily newspapers. Gilmore's brother Harry, an IRA commander in south Dublin, refuted the IRA leadership's claim in both the *Irish Press* and *An Phoblacht*. He argued that his brother had every right to defend Connolly House and to carry IRA weapons. The potential consequences of this should not be underestimated. An IRA member had taken weapons from a dump and used them to shoot a civilian without official permission. The leadership's explanation had been publicly contradicted in the national press by a junior officer; it was a serious case of indiscipline but the leadership took no action against the Gilmores. One part of the explanation for this is that politics aside, the Gilmores were popular within the IRA. A feeling that 'Gilmore should not be let down' was current among sections of the Dublin Brigade. In fact, while a dramatic case, the incident was symptomatic of numerous local affairs where IRA members became embroiled in unauthorized actions which the leadership was largely powerless to prevent.

It was obvious that an organization like the IRA could be seriously effected by problems of indiscipline. While it considered itself an army in fact the link between the leadership and local units was often tenuous, depending on a visit from a touring officer. The fact that the members had some access to firearms meant the IRA could be drawn into all sorts of local disputes. If members did indeed involve themselves in unauthorized activities then how could the IRA punish them? How could it prevent others committing similar acts?

IRA members involved in a trade dispute attempted to blow up a bakery in Donnycarney in 1926. Following the sacking of an IRA man in Belfast his comrades shot up his former employer's house, and boasted that he now lived in 'constant dread'. In Kilrush, armed and masked IRA men raided a farmer's house to force him to stop dealing with a local strike bound merchant. In Roscommon, because of a perceived injustice to a local widow, IRA members threatened the executor of her husband's will. Not all these activities were connected to labour or land issues. IRA members in Clare asked for permission to threaten a hairdresser, whose 'slush' was blocking a neighbour's drains! All these activities were capable of causing embarrassment to the IRA, especially if the participants were apprehended as they were in the bakery explosion case. An IRA member in Kildare who stole flour from a local merchant was arrested and arms and ammunition captured in his home, giving the IRA a 'terrible' image locally. A Dublin IRA man was dismissed publicly from the organization after he took part in a robbery during 1930. A raid on the home of an ex-Free State officer in Sligo resulted in the wounding of an IRA member, whose comrades fled leaving him to be arrested.

The IRA's dilemma was how to prevent members engaging in these acts but still maintain the loyalty of members who joined so they could take part in armed action. A great deal of IRA intervention in strikes and land disputes was sanctioned by the leadership, if sometimes only reluctantly. In some cases as in Kilrush, the members involved were demoted. Here the IRA also publicly denied involvement in the dispute. It also denied the authorship of dozens of threatening letters sent its name throughout Ireland in this period. In some cases, as in that of a doctor in Clonmel, and a Kildare Cumann na nGaedheal TD, the IRA's denials were probably genuine. In others however it is impossible to tell, as local IRA members obviously carried out activities without informing the Dublin leadership. Some of these exposed the levels of indiscipline, illpreparedness and local prejudice which informed many IRA activities. In the Sligo case the IRA were reacting to ACA provocation. However, they attempted a raid on an ex-soldier, who was known to be armed, with only one gun and two rounds of ammunition between them. When the first shots were fired they abandoned the raid. The IRA intended punishing their 'cowardice' by dismissal from its ranks. In the end they were merely demoted and 'severely lectured'.

The story of the Galway IRA unit which recanted before the Military Tribunal was an even more pitiful one. This unit had previously blown up an unoccupied garda post in Kilreacle and intimidated a teacher who was accused of taking a job from a local woman. There was a strong suspicion that the attack they were charged with, a raid on the state solicitor's office in Ennis, was less about the Anti-Annuities campaign and more about the family debts of one of the IRA men involved. However, it was decided after, it was alleged, direction from Peadar O'Donnell, to 'wreck' the office and destroy all the Land Commission's ledgers and accounts. The affair was carried out with less than military precision. It was intended to borrow a car but, due to the owner's suspicions, permission was refused. The car was then stolen, despite its owner knowing most of the thieves. After arriving in Ennis, one member of the group attempted to gain entrance to the office by stealth. While he knocked at the solicitor's door, his comrades became restless and made so much noise that the solicitor became suspicious. The IRA men panicked and sprayed the house with Thompson and revolver fire, nearly shooting their own comrade in the process. They then abandoned the raid and fled. On the way back to Galway there was a row about whether or not to shoot up the garda station in Crusheen. They intended to refill the car with petrol and leave it near to its owner's home to mollify him, but it was left miles from its owners, with the tank almost empty. Following the men's performance at the military tribunal they were denounced by the IRA as 'arrant cowards' and dismissed with ignominy. It is hard to see how dismissal from the IRA carried weight with the majority of those who broke its rules. Like much of the IRA's rules and regulations it only meant something if a person was a dedicated member. If they were already disenchanted or simply did not care, dismissal was hardly a frightening prospect.

The alternative, of course, was for the IRA to impose its will on its members by fear. In Kildare during 1932, an IRA member was stripped and caned by his superior officer for an unnamed misdemeanour. Even the officer in this case admitted this treatment was likely to prove counter-productive. In the case of anonymous letter writers the IRA recommended chaining the culprits to chapel gates as punishment. In general, however, the IRA was hidebound by its own nature, as an unofficial body which no man was 'forced to join' but which demanded the discipline of a regular army.

It became obvious during 1933 and 1934 that the IRA leadership's rulings on preventing clashes with the Blueshirts were being wilfully ignored. The army council demanded stringent new powers to punish indiscipline at the 1934 convention. The reaction from the majority of delegates was hostile. John Joe Sheehy objected to the 'young lads' who were joining the IRA being described as 'ruffians'. He warned against giving 'Dublin' too much power. Tadgh Lynch argued that the IRA could not have the 'iron discipline' of regular armies. Another officer felt the army council's suggestions were 'ridiculous' and were reminiscent of the military tribunal. George Gilmore weighed in to argue that the IRA's problems could not be solved by wielding the 'big fist'. The problem facing the leadership was that the areas where their members were increasingly undisciplined like Kerry, Drogheda or Leitrim, were also areas where the IRA was strong. To dismiss large numbers of men or to take action against their officers would have split their organization. While some brutal and humiliating punishments were inflicted on individual IRA men who upset the organization, to a large extent unauthorized activities by its members were tolerated.

The setting up of the Republican Congress following the 1934 convention illustrated the unreal nature of the IRA's disciplinary procedure. Peadar O'Donnell and Mick Price were court-martialled and dismissed with ignominy, but as they had already left and were in the process of forming a new organization this had absolutely no practical effect. It was gleefully pointed out to the

IRA that any of their members could secede with virtual impunity and that their court-martial procedure was 'futile'. It is relevant that later in 1934, IRA members who joined the Volunteer Reserve were subjected to violent attacks. The embarrassment caused by the IRA's inability to stop the Congress defections may have influenced this shift in tactics.

Aside from political indiscipline did the IRA's armed capacity lend itself to involvement in crimes for personal gain? Some members of the IRA stole from their own organization. One Galway man, resident in Detroit for a period, had been asked to bring £70 to the IRA by the Clan na Gael; but he spent the money and found himself court-martialled by the IRA. While 'drastic action' of an unspecified nature was threatened against him the IRA eventually settled for repayment of the £70. Patrick Hickey, the IRA commander in west Clare for a period, was dismissed from the organization for stealing from his unit's funds. His dismissal was publicized in *An Phoblacht* and he agreed to pay back the misappropriated money. In these two cases at least the IRA did not severely punish the offenders. In January 1927 a man was shot dead by gardaí during an attempted bank raid in Ballinamore, Co. Leitrim. W.T. Cosgrave claimed that the man was a member of an IRA gang. The IRA denied this and claimed that the organization had not carried out bank robberies since the civil war. There is evidence to support the IRA's claim in this case, as they had been attempting to ascertain the identity of the gang involved in a number of robberies in the area and were contemplating using violence against those involved. During 1932 a visitor from the US was robbed by men claiming to be from the IRA in Elphin, Co. Roscommon. The local IRA commander claimed to have 'some important clues' as to who was responsible but denied it had anything to do with his unit. Eoin O'Duffy suggested that Fianna Fáil supporters in Co. Clare had made use of their previous career in the IRA to amass takings from robberies which never went into IRA coffers.

A number of former members did carry out a robbery in Tipperary during 1929, which because of the later career of one of them, George Plant, has been described as an IRA operation. However, Plant, whom gardaí considered a 'courageous' if 'dangerous' man because of his record from the 1919-23 period, does not seem to have been acting on behalf of the IRA. He had left Ireland with his brother, James, after the civil war and gardaí believed he had returned in order to put the knowledge he had of the area to use in robbing several banks. Plant was believed to have been motivated by both personal gain and also a desire to clear debts on his elderly mother's farm. In April 1929 the Plants, along with another former IRA man, robbed the Bank of Ireland in Tipperary town. Gardaí were aware the Plants had returned from the US and surprised the heavily armed gang three days after the robbery. The men were jailed for seven years and the IRA gave no indication that they were members of its organization.

There is little evidence to suggest the IRA involved itself in widespread criminal activity to finance itself in this period.

There were various means which the IRA adopted in order to safeguard their organization's secrets. This was one area of their members activity that the IRA took extremely seriously. The only offence that the IRA killed its own members for in this period was for giving information to the police. At its most basic the IRA leadership had to find secure means of communicating regularly with its units. Routine, relatively non-sensitive material was sent by post. The IRA operated a system of covering addresses, usually in women's names to which a letter could be addressed. Twomey for example, could be contacted via a Mrs Emmet in Sandymount or a Mrs Kelly in Marino. For more important communications a 'hand-line' system was employed. IRA members whose work involved travel or sympathetic non members who worked as drivers or travellers were used to bring messages from one area to another. This often meant that dispatches had to pass through several hands, and it would take over a week for a message from Armagh to reach Dublin, as the message was sent to Keady then to Castleblaney and finally to Dublin.

These methods were obviously not completely secure. An IRA report form sent to a covering address in Dundalk was returned to the post office as it was undelivered. The post office attempted to forward it to 'Adjutant General, Oglaigh na h-Eireann' in Dublin but not surprisingly this led to its interception by the gardaí. The gardaí were aware that female sympathisers allowed their addresses to be used for communications and obtained postal warrants to search their mail. An uncollected parcel sent from Dublin to Armagh by bus aroused the suspicion of the bus inspector who opened it and contacted the RUC, leading to the arrest of a local IRA man.

A necessity for the IRA was the provision of safe accommodation for its members and secure premises for the holding of meetings and storing of documents. This largely depended on the goodwill of its supporters. An undated list of 45 Dublin 'safe houses' illustrates this. Only five of the householders wanted monetary reward for aiding the IRA although the IRA considered several of the others were 'poor' and entitled to some remuneration. Thirty-two of the houses were listed in women's names. Some of these aided the IRA for reasons of family history. One of the women was a relative of Seán MacDermott, another the mother of an IRA man killed in the civil war. A few could also offer rooms for meetings like the owner of a sweetshop in Thomas Street, or the use of space for an office over a shop near Hardwicke Street. Nine of the houses were compromised having been raided on occasion. Some had been used by the IRA during the 1919-21 period (one as a bomb factory), and so were also possibly known to the gardaí.

The IRA's rejection of the label of being a secret society and its efforts to present a military image hindered the organization in several ways. It demanded local units store communications and orders from headquarters arguing that safe hiding places could always be found. Units were also instructed to build up a supply of military manuals and maps. Inevitably, these meant that when IRA arms dumps were discovered or members homes raided, the authorities often captured IRA documentation as well. The IRA's contacts with the Soviet Union came to light as a result of the Killakee arms find. The practice of the IRA in drilling and parading openly where possible also gave the police an opportunity to observe its activists, its local leaders and estimate local support.

The IRA also attempted to assess the strengths and weaknesses of its enemies, and to counter their efforts to undermine it. During late 1932 all its units in the Free State were instructed to ascertain the names and records of the 'principal people' involved in the local ACA. The Belfast IRA compiled a list of those who it believed had been involved with the Ulster Protestant Association during 1922. The value of such information could often be limited depending on the judgment of the men concerned. For example the Belfast IRA were convinced that the British Fascisti would become a major force in northern politics. Similarly, the Leitrim IRA were informed that Dr T.F. O'Higgins had been to Germany to buy arms for the ACA and that plans were afoot to land them by plane!

The IRA also made continual attempts to build up intelligence on the army and police north and south. The Kildare IRA were expected to supply regular reports on the Curragh camp. In Armagh the local IRA was supposed to gather information on the British garrison there. For news of garda movements the *Garda Review*, a 'very useful publication', was scrutinized. A more systematic effort to gather information on the Irish Army was attempted during 1930. The IRA had a number of incomplete maps of various army bases and hoped to update their knowledge. They also required details of army strengths, equipment and of sleeping quarters and billets within the barracks. They had some success with gaining information on the Islandbridge barracks in Dublin and on the barracks in Athlone, Limerick and Templemore. They had also been supplied with estimates of the number of officers and men in the Curragh camp and their armament. The response of the Dublin Brigade to the intelligence gathering effort had been poor and information on McKee, Collins, Arbour Hill and Portobello barracks was still lacking. It was hoped that an 'inside touch' the IRA had in Portobello barracks would be of some help. The IRA was keen to cultivate contacts with sympathetic soldiers or policemen. During 1925 the IRA hoped to be able to make use of the friendly attitude of some of the British garrison based in Omagh. A former Connaught Rangers' mutineer who had joined the National Army had supplied information on Renmore barracks in Galway to the IRA during 1924. It was claimed that a garda had informed the IRA of checks taking place within the force on officers family's political links. A 'detective friend' warned the IRA that the CID would be watching the 1927 Sinn Féin ard fhéis for any appearance by Twomey. He also informed them that the gardaí had captured a dispatch for Russell at a shop used by the IRA and were now watching the premises.

Much of the IRA's intelligence was based on attempting to prevent infiltration by civilian agents and betrayal by informers. A list of 20 alleged 'touts' was produced by Dublin IRA intelligence in late 1927. A number were Detectives and were therefore in the strictest sense not informers. One interesting suspect ran a troupe called the 'Black Jesters' who performed in cinemas in the Dublin area. He apparently used this to help collect information. The difficulty for the IRA was that fear of infiltration tended to generate a paranoia about informers. During 1932, a Waterford IRA member who was 'very loose in his talk and generally indiscreet' was suspected of being an informer. The IRA in Armagh received notice that the RUC knew about a visit by Twomey to the area in May 1932. This was taken very seriously and the IRA leadership believed the 'safety of the organization in the six counties' depended on the informer being discovered. During 1933 the IRA in Dublin became aware that former members of the organization were now gathering information on it for the Fianna Fáil government. Twomey warned officers to be wary of discussing IRA business with former comrades who were now 'Fianna Fáil CID'.

The IRA would operate its own counter-intelligence system with greater or lesser degrees of efficiency. IRA misinformation led to a garda superintendent being dismissed on suspicion of passing information to them during 1928. It made contact with the foreman of a jury in the case involving two of its Belfast members and gained a promise from him to split the jury. Despite these efforts, both men were jailed. In Dublin its usual tactic in such cases was a little less sophisticated, amounting to threatening the jurors themselves which was occasionally effective. In another case in Belfast a young IRA member was ordered to pose as an innocent bystander, caught up in a mass arrest in order to convince a judge that the accused had not been engaging in disruption. In that case the IRA ruse was successful.

The IRA were correct to be wary because there were several informers in its ranks over this period. An IRA inquiry into the capture of the arms dump at St Enda's made such alarming reading that the IRA's commander in Dublin feared that, if it became public knowledge, the organization would not have a 'single Volunteer left' in the city. The IRA discovered that the officer in charge of the dump had revealed its whereabouts and that of others to a number of his friends. They included a number of inactive or ex-IRA members, some of whom being unemployed decided to put the knowledge to use. An old pre-Truce dump was 'given away' to the gardaí in exchange for monetary reward. Some of the men then suggested removing arms from St Enda's to commit a robbery but before this was done another member of the gang sold its location to the gardaí.

Many informers may simply have supplied low level information of no great importance, like a young 'boy' involved in Fianna Eireann in Limerick during 1929. In the same period the gardaí claimed to have a 'prominent and trusted' IRA member in Clonmel working for them. As we have seen an organization in which the poorer sections of the urban and rural population were over repre-sented financial incentives could make supplying information seem attractive. In Dublin, the IRA were informed that an ex-member who had been unem-ployed for a long period was offered £4.10s. to begin work for the gardaí. Two Cork IRA officers were offered the more considerable sum of a 'couple of hun-dred' pounds to give away the location of dumps in their area during 1930. In the case of a young Clare man, Patrick Murray, the loss of his job as a tailor, and the offer of 'monetary enticement' from a detective who had been on friendly terms with him, induced him to become an informer. Unfortunately for him the local IRA commander, T.J. Ryan who had trusted Murray 'implicitly' was alert-ed to the possibility of an informer in his ranks and Murray disappeared from his home in May 1929 and was never seen again.

As the IRA made clear, the penalty for 'treachery' to the organization was death. The IRA discovered during late 1927 that the man offering money to ex-members in return for information was Seán Harling, a republican and former Dail courier. He was confronted with this accusation in October 1927 but denied it. An attempt to murder him in February 1928 resulted in the death of an IRA man, Timothy Coughlan. Ironically, Coughlan had been associated with the gang who had given information about St Enda's to the gardaí. Harling left Ireland for a period but returned a few years later. Despite apparent IRA plans to avenge Coughlin, he was not harmed. In 1931, the organization did succeed in killing Patrick Carroll, an officer of the Dublin Brigade's third battalion. He had been an informer for three years and had supplied the gardaí with much 'valuable information'. Carroll had also interested himself in the IRA's links with left-wing groups and was a member of several of these as well. That an agent was so well placed within the IRA created some unease within the orga-nization. Not all those found guilty of informing were murdered by the IRA. A member who admitted to being an informer was chained outside a church in Collinstown with a sign bearing the slogan 'spies and informers beware' hung round his neck during 1929. While the IRA's Dublin commander had hoped that the 'most extreme' punishment would be meted out to the informants in the St. Enda's case, they were simply 'debarred' from ever again being involved with the IRA! Initially, exile was the punishment meted out to another alleged informer, Dan Turley from Belfast. Turley had been director of elections for Sinn Féin in Belfast during 1918, and had served numerous terms of imprison-ment in Derry, Belfast and Larne and on the *Argenta* prison ship. During 1932 he was the subject of an affectionate tribute in *An Phoblacht* while he was serving another term of imprisonment in Belfast. Turley had attended the meeting with Twomey in Armagh during May that year and this may be what drew suspicion upon him. After being accused of informing in August 1933 he left Ireland and lived for a period in Southampton. In 1936 he returned home and was shot dead by the IRA. In 1945 an RUC raid on the Turley home uncovered letters Turley had sent to his family from Southampton. In these Turley described how he had been taken for questioning by the IRA to a house across the border where he alleged he was beaten and tortured with pliers and a poker.

In the most notorious IRA killing of this period, that of Minister for Justice Kevin O'Higgins, the organization seemed to have kept its secrets well. IRA members assassinated O'Higgins but the men involved were never arrested or imprisoned. The seriousness with which the gardaí took an accusation from Seán T. O'Kelly that the men who had killed O'Higgins were still working for the state, points to the lack of real knowledge they had about the affair. During 1930 the gardaí found that the IRA also affected to regard the O'Higgins murder 'as a mystery'. Evidence would actually point toward the IRA too being largely ignorant of its members involvement. During late 1927 the IRA believed the government was trying to blame the killing on Michael Price. They also received information that former IRA director of training, General Emmet Dalton, had carried out the assassination. The three men involved seem to have acted spontaneously and it is likely that they never informed their superiors about their action, hence ensuring that it did remain a secret. One of the men was Timothy Coughlin, killed less than a year later by Seán Harling. Another was Bill Gannon, who remained active in the IRA until 1933 and was a founding member of the Communist Party of Ireland. The final assassin was Archie Doyle, who by 1930 had been dismissed from the IRA for robbery. The gardaí believed that Doyle had left the IRA some time before that. After a spell in prison Doyle became active within the IRA again and was suspected of involvement in a number of robberies during the 1940s.

The IRA possessed enough arms to be a serious irritant to both Irish states and to carry out a terrorist campaign, but they did not possess the necessary equipment to carry out the insurrection they themselves envisaged. The majority of their membership were never sufficiently trained to master the skills of modern warfare. The organization was prone to involvement in unauthorized activities and intervention in local disputes. The IRA was forced to tolerate these problems in order to maintain its organization. To enforce discipline within the IRA the leadership veered from leniency to brutality, never solving the problem with either tactic. A major part of the IRA's attraction was its paramilitary nature but its real importance lay in its role as a force for opposition to the Irish states rather than in its prospects of actually overthrowing them.

3/The IRA and nationalist culture

Part of the importance of the IRA was its ability to mobilize numbers beyond its immediate membership in displays of support for its politics. One way of doing this was through commemorations such as the annual 'pilgrimage' to Bodenstown. Another was with its newspaper, *An Phoblacht*. The IRA also attempted to relate to the struggles of people it considered part of the republican constituency by supporting strikes and campaigns against evictions. The IRA's belief in promoting indigenous Irish industries inspired the 'Boycott British' movement of 1932–3, which while leading to arrests and violence, failed to arouse enthusiasm either inside or outside of the IRA. Culturally, the IRA operated within an Irish nationalist milieu, encouraging support for Gaelic games and the Irish language. But most IRA members did not speak Irish and the organization had a very mixed relationship with the GAA. The Catholic Church often denounced the IRA, but most IRA members remained practising Catholics and clerical hostility to the organization exacerbated internal tensions.

The annual Wolfe Tone commemoration at Bodenstown was the IRA's most important public event. Its successful defiance of a government ban in June 1931 had signalled its increasing confidence. The IRA's failure to break a similar ban in 1936 illustrated its decline. The IRA's organization for this event between 1932 and 1936 was very public. *An Phoblacht* published the mobilization orders for the day, giving details as to which IRA units would lead the procession and assigning places to supporting organizations. The organization of the event required the IRA to book buses and trains from across Ireland and railway and bus companies facilitated this. For example, Great Northern Railways (GNR) published posters advertising special trains to Bodenstown from Belfast and Derry. In June 1931 the IRA was able to mobilize for Bodenstown despite the government's cancelling of rail traffic because the Irish Omnibus Company (IOC) agreed to allow passengers with train tickets to travel with them. This was despite the IRA having attacked IOC staff and property during the bus strike of 1930. In 1933, the organization would carry out similar attacks on GNR trains and buses. Still, it made economic sense for these companies to facilitate the IRA as Bodenstown generated considerable business. Gardaí estimated 20 trains and 30 buses had brought people to the 1934 commemoration. In 1935, advance rail bookings from Dublin totalled 2,000 places with 1,224 travelling in the end. A total of 2,765 tickets were booked from across the south and west. As well as train passengers at least 17 buses were travelling from Armagh, Tyrone and

Derry. The organizers of the 'pilgrimage' also faced the usual mundane difficulties of putting on a large-scale public event, renting fields from local farmers and dealing with complaints about damage to their property.

The entire spectrum of the IRA and its affiliates, Cumann na mBan,
Cumann na gCailíní, the American Clan na Gael and the Women's Prisoners
Defence League paraded at Bodenstown. Aside from these, at various stages
Fianna Fáil, Sinn Féin, 'Old IRA', Irish Citizen Army, trade union branches and
the Communist Party all attended the commemoration. There is evidence that
the event only began to attract large numbers, even from the IRA itself, after
1932. That year, 70 IRA members from Sligo, 40 from Roscommon and 50 from
Leitrim were expected to travel to Bodenstown. This figures were substantially
smaller than the number of IRA members in each area. Other areas reported
difficulties in moblising for the event as well. The Dublin IRA presence was also
small that year due apparently to its more devout members attending a retreat
sermon instead. Attendances at Bodenstown also reflected the schisms within
the republican movement. After 1931 Fianna Fáil no longer attended the event,
organizing its own commemoration from 1933 onwards. Sinn Féin boycotted the
event on several occasions. In 1933 the Communist Party had literature seized
from their members by the IRA. The 1934 commemoration gained notoriety for
the clashes between the IRA and the Republican Congress, which were replicated on a smaller scale a year later. However, confrontations at Bodenstown
were the exception rather than the rule. In 1934 the gardaí noted how IRA stewards engaged in 'friendly co-operation' helping gardaí manage the large numbers attending the event. The gardaí claimed that republicans 'behaved with
admirable restraint' when taunted by drunken Fine Gael supporters on their
way back to Sallins. The IRA itself specified that no alcohol be served on trains
it booked for Bodenstown.

While waiting in the assembly field at Sallins, IRA supporters could listen to
the various marching bands and sample tea and packed lunch in tents courtesy
of the Nas na Riogh Hotel in Naas. Some of the bands featured were affiliated
to the IRA like the Cork Volunteers Pipers' Band and the O'Rahilly Brass and
Reed Band from Dublin. The Workers' Union of Ireland (WUI) band supported the event for ideological reasons, while others were local bands who were
offered discounted travel to play at the event. Some, such as Dublin's Fintan
Lalor Pipe Band played at both the IRA and the Fianna Fáil Bodenstown commemorations. Traditionally a celidhe was held in Dublin's Mansion House following the event.

Using attendances at Bodenstown to assess levels of IRA support is prob-
lematic. In 1934, the pro-Fianna Fáil *Irish Press* admitted that the IRA's event
was the 'biggest tribute' yet paid to Tone's memory with about 17,000 attending.
A week later Fianna Fáil's commemoration drew a crowd of between 8,000 and

10,000. Yet this does not adequately reflect the balance of forces within republicanism at the time. Following the ban on the event in 1936 just 1,000 attended a protest rally in Dublin. A year later the commemoration was allowed to proceed but only 1,140 were present, at what according to the gardaí was a 'half hearted' affair. This would suggest that while Bodenstown was a largely peaceful display of republican support it could draw large crowds, but when risk was attached to attending support would dwindle. While 1931 was an exception, which was related to increasing IRA confidence, the largest turn-outs at Bodenstown were from 1933 to 1935 when the occasion was largely risk free.The numbers attending the event during the war years point to the steady decline of militant republicanism.

It is clear that the IRA was capable of mobilizing large numbers of people outside its own ranks for specific occasions, especially commemorations, although sometimes these numbers could mask the relatively small size of the IRA itself. The 30,000 strong crowd who gathered in Dublin's College Green to welcome released IRA prisoners in March 1932 contained just 620 members of the organization's Dublin Brigade. For major public occasions the IRA also attempted to persuade its old or inactive members to parade, which again would give an exaggerated impression of the number of active members in a particular area.

The IRA also sought to mobilize its constituency through the newspaper *An Phoblacht*. From April 1926 when the IRA took control of the paper it was the movement's main method of publicising its views. As Jim Killeen put it, *An Phoblacht* was 'the only means' the IRA had of giving 'open expression' to its policies. From Peadar O'Donnell onwards, all its editors were IRA members though not all of their assistants were. It was published on a weekly basis, although because of government suppression there were several periods during which it did not appear or was replaced by a similar publication. From May 1929 it was officially published by the Republican Press Ltd. The paper was sold by IRA members themselves, outside church gates for example, by 'newsboys' at Dublin's Nelson's Pillar and in shops such as Eason's. Despite its brushes with the law, it secured advertising even from semi-state bodies such as the Electricity Supply Board.

Despite its importance the IRA often had difficulty circulating the paper among its own members. During 1930 officers reported that 'only a few' of the IRA's Midland Battalion read *An Phoblacht*. In west Mayo many IRA members never saw the paper and there appeared to be a distinct 'lack of interest' in it. Two years later Jim Killeen had to remind Tralee officers that it was the duty of all IRA members to sell and support *An Phoblacht*. Furthermore he warned that unless 'more interest' was taken in sales of the paper the IRA might be forced to close it down. In Northern Ireland *An Phoblacht* could not be sold openly and had to be distributed in secret. Recurring problems seemed to have plagued the IRA as a result of this. In 1929 the paper was arriving in Belfast a fortnight or more out of date and could not be sold. By 1933 the Belfast IRA were still finding that their supply would lie for weeks 'somewhere between Dublin and Belfast'.

This evidence contrasts sharply with garda perceptions of the extent of the paper's influence during 1931. *An Phoblacht* was said to have more influence in Tipperary 'than all other papers combined' and to be 'poisoning' the youth of Kerry. These reports were certainly exaggerating the papers influence. It is possible that *An Phoblacht* could be widely read in one area of the country and unknown in another, but the paper never had anything approaching a mass circulation. In January 1930 Frank Ryan was claiming *An Phoblacht* had a sale of 8,000. Two years later during a period of intense republican enthusiasm following the election of Fianna Fáil, *An Phoblacht*'s print run was 10,000 a week. During May 1932 it sold 27,727 copies. While the paper would be read by wider numbers than those who bought it this still reflects a relatively limited circulation. Furthermore, the paper was a financial drain on the IRA. In September 1932 it was amounting to 50 per cent of the organization's total expenses. Between March and November that year it cost nearly £1,500 to run *An Phoblacht*. There were suggestions of reducing the paper's size and even of closing it down. The paper survived, but figures for numbers being printed two years later do not show evidence of a major increase in sales. In January 1934 just over 11,000 copies of the paper were being printed. From that period onwards *An Phoblacht* was the subject of repeated seizures and proofs of the paper had to be supplied to gardaí before going to press. As a result, many issues appeared with editorials or front-page articles missing. In June 1935 the paper ceased publication for almost a year, the IRA blaming government repression and the failure of debtors to settle accounts. Just prior to its suppression the print run had declined to 7,500 copies. It was revived for a four-month period in March 1936, with just 6,500 being produced weekly before being suppressed again in July that year. Even at that stage the IRA leadership complained that few units made an effort to support it.

The relatively limited sales of *An Phoblacht* mean some caution must be shown when examining the IRA's ideology in this period. While the paper was certainly a guide to the diverse strands of leadership thinking, questions must be asked as to how much of their ideology percolated to the rank and file.

The IRA began to identify with the poorer sections of the Irish population from the mid 1920s. This in itself was evidence of a shift in IRA thinking and the influence of a new, younger leadership. By the 1930s IRA members were admitting that during the 1919-21 period the organization had 'protected employers' and had developed no social programmme to appeal to the working class. This reappraisal meant that when *An Phoblacht* was taken over by the IRA, it was stressed that from then on there would be a 'very friendly' attitude taken in the paper to labour and small farmers. In 1925 Military Intelligence was noting how some IRA Dublin members were supporting Jim Larkin and attacking strike breakers. Indeed, the IRA claimed to have had high hopes that Larkin would ally himself with the republican movement when he returned from the US during the civil war. However this 'wonderful opportunity' was squandered when Larkin came home in a 'maudlin and sentimental' mood and refused to back the anti-Treaty forces. By 1927, the IRA suggested that Larkin was a 'spent force' whose personal ambition and temperament rendered him incapable of giving real revolutionary leadership. Instead it was suggested rather optimistically that following IRA members seizing control of the Irish Transport and General Workers' Union unity with Larkin's WUI would be restored.

Because of its position during the civil war the Labour Party and especially its leader Thomas Johnson were damned as representing 'anaemic liberalism' rather than genuine Labourism. Indeed, the IRA claimed that it reflected the attitudes of Irish workers more authentically than the Labour Party did. Local IRA officers could express the belief that the 'so-called labour gang' should be 'wiped out' but then suggest that independent 'militant labour' might offer the best hope of re-vitalising their own organization. There were in fact occasions when members of the Labour Party associated with the IRA. In Leitrim, the Mohill branch of the party marched in support of the IRA's Seán O'Farrell in 1934. In Ennis, there were also personal connections between the Ennis United Labourers' Association, the IRA and the local Labour Party. Twomey was also fulsome in his praise for Labour's 'splendid' support of the first Fianna Fáil government. More often than not, however, the Irish Labour Party was ignored rather than attacked by the IRA.

Peadar O'Donnell expressed hostility to the presence of British-based unions in Ireland, believing that they had held back the Labour movement from the national struggle. In practice, the IRA adopted a more flexible attitude backing the British-based National Union of Railwaymen (NUR) in strikes during 1930 and 1933, but continued to hold that 'Irish labour organised in Ireland' would be the best situation. During 1929, IRA officers met with Communists to discuss the setting up of a 'Workers' Defence Corps' to take an active part in strikes. The IRA was to form the nucleus of this organization. While the communists wished to confine membership to trade unionists, the IRA successfully convinced them to allow those whose 'social position does not admit membership of Trade Unions' to join. Later that year the IRA were involved in the launch of the Irish Labour Defence League. Dublin IRA officers donated money to strike funds and striking workers took part in IRA commemorations. In Newport, Co. Mayo, during 1932, IRA members who worked on coal boats became embroiled in a strike over wage cuts. In Kerry during late 1933 the ITGWU in Tralee threatened a general strike in support of IRA members arrested following clashes with Blueshirts.

Most IRA intervention during labour disputes was of a violent nature. At its 1933 convention delegates voted in support of a motion authorizing military action in support of strikers, despite opposition from delegates from Armagh and Down. The organization had already been carrying out violent actions during strikes for several years prior to this. The first major IRA intervention in a national dispute was during the IOC strike of 1930. During the strike a bus was held up in Granard, Co. Longford, its driver and conductor beaten up and the bus itself abandoned in a bog. Shots were fired at buses in New Ross, Galway and Clare, and bus windows smashed in Cork and Limerick. Strike breakers were also attacked in Sligo town. The IRA were certainly the driving force behind most of these incidents. The extent that such violence helped cohere the IRA internally should not be underestimated. In Galway the IRA claimed that its organization had improved since the 'attack on buses commenced'. Similar tactics were to be used during the Northern rail strike three years later. Employees of O'Mara's bacon shops in Dublin struck for three months during late 1934 and early 1935. The dispute involved an inter-union argument between the Shop Employees Society and the Commercial Employees Union (CEU) of which the IRA's Mick Fitzpatrick was an official. The Shop Employees were accused of being a 'company union' by the strikers. In late December, four of O'Mara's shops were raided by armed men. Gardaí were held up outside the premises while the raiders broke windows and smashed equipment inside.

Similar tactics were envisaged by the IRA when it intervened in the Dublin tram and bus strike during March 1935. After several weeks, the government moved to ease the lack of public transport by placing Army lorries on the streets. The IRA saw this as an unacceptable strike-breaking move. *An Phoblacht* denounced the government's move as an 'extreme fascist step' and called for a general strike in protest. The IRA issued a statement putting their organization at the disposal of the strike committee. There was initial hesitancy on behalf of the strikers, but eventually a meeting was organized between the strike committee and the IRA. The presence of at least one striking IRA member on the committee helped ease relations. While the official union leaderships of the ITGWU and the Amalgamated Transport Union professed no knowledge of the IRA's intentions, gardaí believed that there were plans to set fire to army lorries. The government responded to the IRA's intervention by arresting 44 republicans and the IRA leadership were forced to go on the run for the first time under Fianna Fáil.

One exception to the IRA's normal practice in industrial disputes was its role during the Dublin newspaper strike of the autumn of 1934. With the three

Dublin daily newspapers strike-bound, and no English or provincial papers on sale in the city, the IRA received permission to publish *An Phoblacht* from the strike committee. Donal O'Donoghue boasted that at last *An Phoblacht* was 'Ireland's only national paper!' For the duration of the strike *An Phoblacht* published three special editions a week as well as its regular paper. It was also the case that while Mick Fitzpatrick was very visible during a campaign by the CEU for shorter working hours, the gardaí believed that the IRA were not being used to augment the union's efforts.

Generally, however, the IRA response to industrial disputes was to intervene militarily on the strikers' side. To what extent this aided the strikers' cause is open to question, but some trade unionists seem to have been prepared to co-operate with it. This meant that the IRA tended to operate outside the mainstream of trade unionism. A similar rationale was applied in more localized disputes. When a number of striking members of the Irish Road and Rail Federation were sacked at Fenit railway station in Kerry the IRA responded by burning down the railway station house. In this case there was also a personal grievance, as IRA member and Kerry county councillor Michael O'Donnell had been one of those sacked. In Clare, during 1932 several violent incidents occurred during a strike, the origins of which the local IRA leader described as so 'complicated and interwoven' that it was impossible for him to write a report on them. Local IRA members were jailed after taking part in an armed raid on the home of a farmer in an attempt to intimidate him into withdrawing support from a local employer.

There were also differences of emphasis in the IRA's attitude to the labour movement. Peadar O'Donnell believed initially that the Irish 'peasantry' were the 'great force' that would overthrow Imperialism in Ireland. Indeed, he expressed some resentment of urban workers whom he claimed had excluded small farmers from trade unions in the 1919–21 period. O'Donnell had a very ambitious and optimistic view of how to win the rural masses to the republican cause and it was to be centred on a campaign against land annuities. Certainly the make up of the IRA in the countryside did mean many members would have instinctive sympathy for people engaged in land agitation. As a detective was alleged to observe in Carlow, it was only 'the small farmers and the labourers' who made up republican support anyway.

Despite the decline in the numbers of agricultural labourers and the lack of any great 'land question' there remained discontent among the rural population. Land owned by or with shooting or fishing rights in the hands of English owners was still a potent mobilizing issue among sections of the rural populace. The Leitrim IRA were able to mobilize local support to forcibly reinstate a tenant of Lord Kingston's in a gatelodge after the man, who had lived in the lodge for 11 years, was evicted. The fact that he was unemployed, with seven children and forced to live in an 'old shed' helped ensure almost all the local people along with the Keadeu Band turned out in a demonstration to support him. The IRA were then able to inform the landlord's steward that they did not recognize 'planters' rights to Irish property. After a controversial Land Commission decision to grant ownership of a quarry near Tralee to a local farmer, the IRA took over the quarry and removed stone the locals wanted to use in the building of a local school. When blatant injustice was perceived as when a 78-year-old woman with an unemployed son and four young grandchildren was threatened with eviction in Sligo, the local IRA clamoured to be allowed take action.

Again many local IRA units responded to attempts to collect annuities or perceived local injustices not with mass agitation but by violence or threats of violence. Galway IRA men fired into the home of the state solicitor for Clare in a botched attempt to destroy land commission warrants, although as we have seen personal factors were also involved in this case. In Waterville, Co. Kerry during 1929 an under-sheriff and his garda escort came under attack from rifle fire as they attempted to seize cattle belonging to a debtor. Gardaí believed the local IRA, whose leader was also secretary of the anti-Annuities campaign, were responsible. In that case as with several others local IRA members wanted to assist people they felt had made sacrifices for republicans in the past. When a man from a remote farm in the Nephin mountains faced eviction, the Mayo IRA felt obliged to assist him as he had given refuge to men on the run during the civil war. Seán McGuinness of the Offaly IRA told his superiors he would not 'stand idly by' while a man who had 'beggared' himself providing assistance to the IRA in 1919-23 was evicted.

The IRA leadership's attitude to these activities was generally lukewarm however. While expressing sympathy with individual cases there was a fear of the organization getting involved in 'bickering'. Officially, the IRA argued that where there was local injustice the 'people in the neighbourhood can be got to protest' and that was a better remedy than the IRA taking action on its own. In the case of the elderly Sligo woman, Twomey agreed that it was obviously an 'outrageous case' but felt that organizing a public meeting and mobilizing local opinion in her support would be more effective than using violence.

There was also certainly a fear of what left-wing officers like McGuinness could drag the organization into. He was severely admonished for writing an article which fondly recalled the shooting of a policeman during the land war and for organizing an anti-eviction protest meeting without informing IRA headquarters. The fact that Peadar O'Donnell had co-operated with McGuinness in doing this intensified growing divisions over tactics among the IRA leadership.

The IRA declined to lead a potential movement for land reform despite being in a position to do so in the autumn of 1932. Meetings were organized by former IRA members in Tipperary and Limerick to demand that republicans benefit from any redistribution of land by the Land Commission. There was local IRA enthusiasm for the project but they were warned by the leadership that the meetings were probably an attempt by Fianna Fáil to establish 'Old IRA' clubs and undermine their organization. While the proposed campaign might be useful in help get unemployed IRA members work or land, the IRA was not to put itself at the head of any movement. Members attending the land reform meetings were instructed to raise issues which had been stressed in *An Phoblacht*, such as repeal of the 1923 Land Act and the seizing of grazing land for tillage. Out of 42 delegates meeting in Thurles, 17 were IRA members including a representative of the leadership. The list of demands drawn up by the meeting reflected IRA thinking, with calls for 'ranches' to be divided among 'landless men', all farmers be required to till at least 50 per cent of their arable land, long term credit to allow the purchase of houses and equipment and a commitment to develop industries in the towns. Despite the election of two IRA members to a committee of seven the organization's leadership were too suspicious of the initiative to push it any further.

The most notorious example of IRA intervention in a land dispute during this era concerned the Sanderson estate in Edgeworthstown, Co. Longford. While attention has focused on the killing of Richard More O'Ferrall, the nature of the dispute itself helps illuminate some aspects of rural politics at the time. The landlord of the estate, Maria Sanderson, was mentally ill and confined to an asylum, so her land was administered by the chief justice. Sanderson's brother-in-law, a Captain Montague, acted as land agent. Every householder in Edgesworthstown was a Sanderson tenant. Discontent with the rent being charged led to the formation of a tenants' association in May 1934. The association first approached local Fine Gael TD Seán MacEoin and his Fianna Fáil counterpart James Victory, with regard to them presenting their demand for a 50 per cent reduction in rent to Captain Montague. When this demand was rejected, Montague's attempt to collect rent was blocked by pickets. Some months later, a local agent, Gerald More O'Ferrall was appointed whom the tenents initially felt would be 'more disposed' to help them. When tenants continued to withold payment of rent, evictions were threatened. In early November, the tenants association passed a resolution calling on the IRA to assist their fight against 'Landlordism'. At a rally held in the town local speakers expressed the hope that they were no longer 'isolated' and an IRA member stressed that landlords 'deserved no pity'. Another IRA member, Hugh Devine, became secretary of the association. Two months later during a raid on the O'Ferrall home in Lissard, the agent's son Richard was fatally wounded.

What is notable about the shooting is despite a major garda investigation and the eventual trial of seven men, the land agitation did not come to a halt. Indeed, during April the IRA tried to forcibly reinstate evicted tenants on the estate only to be prevented by gardaí. Another rally against evictions drew support from Labour as well as republican representatives. The agitation was only halted after the tenants' association accepted terms negotiated by James Victory in June 1935. The jury in the case of the IRA members involved eventually delivered a verdict of 'not guilty' in December 1935. The defendents were met by a torchlight procession in Mullingar, a parade in Longford and 300 people welcomed them back to Edgesworthstown. Where violent activity by the IRA was counter-productive in some cases, in this instance local tension and a general dislike of what was seen as a relic of Ascendancy meant that even a killing had little effect on their support.

In the case of a major IRA initiative to up the stakes in the Economic War, however, the organization badly misjudged feeling both inside and outside their organization. The 'Boycott British' campaign was a logical extension of the IRA's occasional attempts to implement opposition to British produce in Ireland. In 1927, British newspapers had been burnt in Dublin's streets, and in 1931 an attempt had been made to burn a lorry containing Cadbury's chocolates at Dublin port. In the context of the change in government during 1932 and the growing economic tension with Britain, the IRA felt a grassroots campaign against British imports could mobilize mass opinion behind the Economic War. In the autumn of 1932, the IRA leadership sanctioned the launch of a broad-based campaign with the proviso that the IRA maintain ultimate control of it. The first National Executive of the campaign contained four IRA members, two from Cumann na mBan, one from the Fianna Eireann, Maud Gonne, a communist and a representative of the Indian-Irish Independence League.

A decision was taken to form local committees throughout the country and to operate on an 'activist' basis, with canvassing, bill pasting, and road painting to be standard activities. The National Executive of the campaign decided to concentrate on certain specified articles to be boycotted, with an intensive mobilization against these items for about a fortnight. Then having been successful, the campaign would move on to the next items. The first items chosen were 'British ales and sweets' and as Bass was the 'only widely consumed' British ale in the Free State this was chosen as the first target. Hotels and pubs were to be visited, warned against stocking Bass and then given ten days to desist or face having their stocks destroyed. In case of opposition Irish ales such as O'Connells or Cairnes, and chocolates such as 'Urneys' were to be suggested as alternatives.

The campaign immediately ran into difficulties. By November 1932 support for it within the IRA had been, according to the army council 'very disappointing'. Committees existed in twenty-three areas across the Free State but with varying levels of activity. Only five were very dynamic with Waterford the most energetic area. The IRA leadership decided that the only way to intensify interest would be by the 'siezure and destruction' of British goods. Premises of Bass distributers were attacked in Dublin and Cork and casks of ale smashed. Again the response was poor. By late December it was still the case that the campaign had not 'much of a grip' on people's imagination.

There were several reasons for this. Outside the ranks of the IRA many republicans, especially Fianna Fáil supporters, believed that the government's tariffs already provided a 'sufficient boycott'. The hostility of the *Irish Press* to the boycott campaign was also thought to be influencing the IRA's rank and file. There were also claims that the newspapers were ignoring the campaign. Rather than increasing support, the IRA's moves to destroy stocks of Bass had frightened off Fianna Fáil supporters. More importantly, little genuine interest had been shown by IRA members themselves, especially in Dublin. Even in Waterford the IRA had not played an active role in the local campaign. One explanation for this put forward by Donal O'Donoghue was that Bass was not widely consumed in Ireland, and especially not in Dublin. Another problem O'Donoghue identified was that boycotting British goods and promoting Irish produce could be seen as 'boosting up Irish capitalism' which meant that left-leaning IRA members were uncomfortable with the campaign. As a guard against this, Twomey suggested that boycott speakers stress that they were against profiteering by Irish manufacturers and that Irish business should be forced to pay decent wages. The contrived nature of the targeting of Bass itself, on the basis that its owner, Colonel Gretton MP, was a 'bitter public enemy' of the Irish people, made it difficult enough to convince IRA members, let alone the public, that this was a serious campaign. The campaign was also solely a 26-county affair. One northern IRA officer, on receiving notice of the initiative, wished the leadership would 'please point out how this concerns us in six counties'. At the 1933 convention, Seán MacBride suggested that the campaign be kept going in order to keep the IRA in 'training' only to be contradicted by a delegate who argued it was actually obstructing training activities. It was decided to maintain the campaign but only to use violence if the necessary public support had been built up beforehand.

In actual fact the campaign had almost collapsed when the IRA decided to revive it by widespread violence in late 1933. During September stocks of Bass were destroyed by the IRA in Dublin, Tralee, Lucan, Naas, Drogheda and Waterford. A number of publicans were assaulted and £161 of damage caused to Dublin pubs. The IRA's activities led to the jailing of 13 of their members and, hence, to another round of campaigning but had no discernible interest in increasing support for a boycott. De Valera's view that the raids were a 'damn foolhardy business' was probably shared by most of the republican constituency, whose passive support was needed for an effective campaign. By this stage there was little effort to boycott anything except Bass and the desperation of the

IRA in hoping violence would revive the campaign was in fact an admission of its failure. At the 1934 convention the campaign was quietly abandoned.

The IRA's constitution committed to it to making the Irish language the 'everyday language' of the Irish people. Publicly the organization stressed the need to 'replace the English language ... in the pulpit, platform and press'. All the organization's political initiatives from the left-wing Saor Éire to the non-socialist Cumann Poblachta na h-Eireann stressed the importance of the revivial of the language. In reality, like the majority of its constituency, the IRA was an English-speaking organization. Irish language enthusiasts like Frank Ryan were the exception among the leadership. The IRA were not unique in this regard among republicans. At the 1925 Cumann na mBan convention it was decided to reserve one third of the organization's executive for Irish speakers, but a year later this could not be done from the available candidates. All the IRA's internal documents were written and all its discussions carried out in English. At the 1933 convention a motion was passed suggesting the organization's commands be given in Irish. This was agreed to, but only where 'practicable'. In reality, the IRA's verbal commands were almost always in English. The IRA's Dingle battalion, in which a majority were Irish speakers, had expressed a wish to become a completely Irish-speaking unit. While the IRA leadership had no problem with this they did warn that a 'great many technical difficulties' would have to be overcome first. They suggested that the National Army's Gaelic manuals would be of use! A plan by a Connemara officer to form an Irish speaking organization involving his unit as well as the IRA in Dingle and Donegal, was coolly received in Dublin. Young IRA members' inability to speak Irish was ridiculed on occasion by their adversaries. One judge asked of a Dundalk defendant if it was a rule of the IRA 'not to speak Gaelic'. A Clare IRA man was similarly taunted by another district justice. *An Phoblacht* usually carried just one Irish language article a week, and this reflects the fact that like much of nationalist Ireland, the IRA accepted in fact, if not in theory, that English was the language of the majority of Irish people.

The IRA's attitude to other areas of popular culture reflected both the bias of nationalist critics towards 'foreign' influences and the organization's ambivalent but more open attitude to modern trends. *An Phoblacht* contained articles both critical of, and praising, writers like Seán O'Casey and Seán O'Faolain. Republicans, including Hannah Sheehy Skeffington, disrupted performances of *The Plough and the Stars* in 1925, yet by 1933 it was being praised by *An Phoblacht* for its 'grim realism'. The widespread hostility to jazz music in the Free State received an echo with the report of a Gaelic League anti-Jazz rally in Leitrim while in contrast American singer Paul Robeson was hailed as the 'vocalist of an oppressed race'. This coverage also reflects the fact that the IRA did not take these issues very seriously and generally left discussion of them to individual taste.

A good deal more serious was the IRA's enthusiasm for Gaelic games. *An Phoblacht's* coverage of Gaelic sport has been characterized as the paper at its 'narrowest, most exclusivist and racialist'. Indeed, Irish people who professed to enjoy both native and foreign games were condemned as 'mongrels' and 'traitors' by the paper's GAA correspondent. This is a little unusual in that the IRA was strong in a number of areas where there was popular support for soccer, but there is no hint that any IRA member followed this game. Interestingly, the Republican Congress newspaper favoured similar coverage of GAA sports and again did not feature 'foreign' games. Most IRA members who played or followed Gaelic sports did so because they were popular across nationalist Ireland rather than for political reasons. It was also the case that the organization's relationship with the Gaelic Athletic Association was often an uneasy one and reflected the GAA's ability to include within its ranks mutually hostile sections of Irish nationalist society.

In the immediate post-civil war period the IRA had high hopes of gaining political control of the GAA. In 1924 Kerry had refused to play the All-Ireland football final and Limerick and Galway the hurling final as protests against the continued imprisonment of republicans. The IRA were centrally involved in promoting this boycott within the GAA in the respective counties. As a result, the IRA ordered its members to begin to organize within the GAA in the hope of gaining influence in it. This, however, was not to happen, and the IRA remained just one of the many political organizations represented within the GAA. Elements within the IRA remained suspicious of the widespread presence of National Army soldiers and gardaí within the association. There were even suggestions that the GAA sought 'deliberately' to divert young men from involvement in the IRA.[157]

A request by the Clan na Gael as to the affiliations of the visiting Mayo football team in 1932 gives an indication of the broad nature of the association. Of 21 players listed, just one was an IRA member, another was described as 'republican labour', four were Cumann na nGaedheal supporters, five Fianna Fáil, three were gardaí, one was described as an 'imperialist' and four were 'neutral'. The Kilkenny hurlers visiting the US that year again only contained 'a few' IRA sympathizers. The Clan na Gael did have some influence within the GAA in the US with a number of their supporters elected onto its executive in 1927. Teams from Ireland which included players who were prominent Cumann na nGaedheal supporters such as Con Brosnan of Kerry were guaranteed a 'hostile reception' in America. Brosnan, an IRA member from 1919-22 and later a National Army officer, was Kerry organizer for the Army Comrades Association during 1932. He was also a six times All Ireland winner with Kerry and an important figure in the GAA there. The IRA leadership believed that its Kerry organization had missed the opportunity to undermine Brosnan's influence within the GAA during the 1920s. They lamented that it was also impossible to get republicans to complain about Cumann na nGaedheal supporters on the GAA's Connaught council.

One historian of the GAA has argued that the conflicts between the IRA, the Blueshirts and the de Valera government 'hardly' affected the association. In general this was the case, so while individual IRA men may have gained some prominence as players, the GAA was not badly affected by their organization's activities. Depending on locality the GAA county boards could be considered reasonably friendly to the IRA such as in Sligo or Donegal or hostile as in Leitrim or Roscommon. The North Tipperary county board gave permission for the IRA to organize a hurling tournament despite clerical opposition during late 1932. The local IRA were amused to report that several Cumann na nGaedheal supporters and a garda played in the competition!

In Kerry, the one county where the IRA did have real influence among GAA officialdom, the association *was* badly affected by the conflicts of the period. The most senior IRA figure in the county, John Joe Sheehy, had captained the 1930 All Ireland winning side and was an official of Tralee's John Mitchel's club. Another leading IRA member, J.J. Rice, was a member of the Kerry county board and individual officers such as Patrick Fleming and Eugene Powell were also active in the GAA. During 1934 and 1935 in Kerry the local sporting calendar was also severely disrupted as players and entire clubs such as John Mitchel's and Austin Stack's stood down in protest against the jailing of IRA members by the government. Kerry Fianna Fáil TDs were also put under pressure by the Munster council of the GAA to give concessions to the IRA to allow games to resume. The IRA did not have universal support among the local GAA for its protests and in fact was blamed for reducing the status of Kerry Gaelic games to 'below zero'. Soccer and rugby were said to be gaining ground among youngsters in Kerry because the GAA was leaving the field open to them. While the IRA complained of ill treatment of its prisoners, a member of the GAA Munster council reminded them that it was unjust for them to 'hammer young boys on the street' too. The IRA's opponents within the Kerry association even called their Gaelic credentials into question. One member of the Tralee Gaelic League claimed that most of the IRA's membership attended 'foreign' dances and games anyway.

An indication of the unpopularity of the boycott was that in May 1935 the IRA prisoners in the Curragh themselves called on the GAA in Kerry to resume play. However this still did not resolve the problem as the IRA in Kerry was itself divided on the matter. During 1934 J.J. Sheehy had argued for a conciliatory line, warning against disrupting the GAA's jubilee year but had been publicly contradicted by J.J. Rice who pressed for more confrontational tactics. When disquiet mounted over the paralysis of the association, Sheehy lamented that the whole affair was a 'mess' brought about when the IRA 'bit off more than it could chew'. IRA officer Eugene Powell not only declared that the boycott should continue despite the wishes of the prisoners themselves, but that the IRA could 'eat all we have chewed off and more with it if necessary'. When the sport in Kerry returned to something approaching normality in 1936, the *Kerry Champion* reflected that while the association nationally had carried on as normal, the government had remained in office and the IRA prisoners had stayed in jail, the only thing to have suffered from the boycott was the GAA in Kerry itself. While the IRA had the influence within the GAA in Kerry to bring it to a halt for political purposes, it alienated much of that support by its tactics and ultimately failed to attain its demands.

The IRA membership was largely composed of Catholics yet was regularly denounced by the Catholic hierarchy. During the civil war the bishops' pastoral of October 1922 had condemned the anti-Treaty campaign as 'murder before God'. In October 1931, the bishops had issued a pastoral attacking the IRA for wanting through Saor Éire to 'impose upon the Catholic soil of Ireland the same materialistic regime ... as now dominates Russia'. In 1934 and 1935, the Lenten pastorals again denounced the organization. Individual bishops such as O'Doherty of Galway, Kinnane of Waterford and O'Brien of Kerry regularly reminded their flock that no Catholic could 'lawfully belong to the IRA'. There is evidence that some clerical condemnation was directly due to state influence. Prior to William McNeely, the bishop of Raphoe, administering confirmation in Dungloe during 1929 the local garda superintendent had spoken to the area's priests about the Anti-Annuities campaign. As a result, the bishop delivered a long condemnation of the campaign which the gardaí believed had a 'good' effect locally. However as Patrick Murray has shown, even during the civil war there remained an element within the Catholic Church who were sympathetic to anti-Treaty republicanism. Most of this support was to gravitate towards Fianna Fáil however, and aside from a tiny minority of clerics the Church remained hostile to the IRA throughout this period.

Gauging the effect that clerical hostility had on the IRA is difficult. On the one hand the organization maintained itself right throughout the period from the civil war onwards which would suggest most of its members were largely unaffected by the Church's hostility. This was certainly the view argued by the IRA itself. One senior officer conceded that the clergy's hostility had played a 'fairly important' role in the IRA's civil war defeat. Though, since then, he claimed the Church had lost a 'great deal' of its influence. During the 'Red Scare' of late 1931, Twomey found it 'very gratifying' that so few of his men seemed to have been affected by the bishops' pastoral. He argued that the Irish people despite being 'overwhelmingly Catholic' took for granted the hostility of the Church to republicanism and were not influenced by it. He also took issue with a plan by Count Plunkett of Sinn Féin to present an appeal to the hierarchy. Twomey felt that this would only increase the bishops' political influence. Two years later, Twomey again claimed that '70 per cent' of his organization were unaffected by clerical condemnation. The reality was that the IRA was damaged by the hostility of the clergy and particularly by the Church's association of the movement with communism. A number of those who publicly broke with the organization during the 'Coercion' period claimed it was because they had been convinced the IRA was 'against religion'. The organization declined to re-organize Saor Éire because the criticism of it by the 'clergy and press' on the grounds that it was anti-religious had made it difficult to recruit men to the IRA. The new programme that the IRA was drawing up during 1933 was designed to try to nullify these criticisms especially those from the church. At its convention that year many IRA members expressed their disquiet at the association between their organization and 'anti-religious' doctrines. Tom Barry argued that the Church's decree that no Catholic could be a communist was hurting recruitment to the IRA. A Dublin IRA member argued that as the Catholic Church was infallible and it said communism was wrong, he accepted that view. The attacks on the IRA in Catholic papers such as the *Universe* and the *Standard* was said to be causing further damage to its support. Undoubtedly, this influenced Twomey's speech at Bodenstown in 1933 when he disassociated the organization from communism.

The hostility of the clergy had been causing numerous problems for the IRA during 1932. During the 'Coercion' period from 1931-1932 the IRA believed that the clergy in Mayo worked with the gardaí to try to get its members to leave the organization. 'Scarcely veiled' attacks were made from the pulpit on local IRA leader Brian Corrigan. During the same period priests in Offaly put pressure on IRA members to leave the organization. An IRA officer inspecting units in east Clare found that a local priest had denounced the organization and warned his parishioners not to allow strangers in the area. The local IRA were 'very windy' about challenging the priest and hence the officer was left without a place to stay. At a Mass in Anacarty, Co. Tipperary, the parish priest used his sermon about the success of the Eucharistic Congress to remind parishioners that the clerical ban on Saor Éire still held and that it was a mortal sin to join it or the IRA. In Cooraclare, Co. Clare, a priest had told his congregation that the IRA was a communist organization and that they should be forced from the area. In Croghan, near Boyle, Co. Roscommon, the parish priest told parishioners that the local IRA leader, Patrick McKeon, was a member of an 'anti-God organization' and a follower of Leitrim socialist James Gralton.

At organizational level this type of attack certainly had an effect with members leaving the IRA in Waterford and Offaly because of similar accusations. Its effect on individuals at a personal level should not be underestimated either.

The accusations against McKeon were made at a station mass, in the presence of his elderly father and many of his neighbours. The parish priest hinted that the deportation proceedings against Gralton in Leitrim should also be extended to McKeon. In north Clare, an IRA member who taught Irish had one of his classes broken up by people allegedly inspired by clerical accusations about him. A republican teacher sacked from a Christian Brothers school in Kilrush blamed the loss of his job on a 'campaign of slander' by the local clergy who accused him of being a supporter of the Friends of Soviet Russia.

The situation was made even more tense by a revival of popular anti-Communist feeling in Dublin, which was accompanied by violent attacks on communists and those perceived to be their allies. Twomey was in no doubt that the campaign was clerically inspired as 'nine tenths' of the sermons at Lenten lectures were on the subject of communism. He also received a report from Nora Connolly O'Brien which gave detailed examples of sermons given at churches in inner city Dublin which included instructions for listeners to attack communists in order to prevent them 'burning your churches'. This atmosphere, which gardaí believed was partly motivated by news of the Gralton affair, eventually culminated in the storming of the Communist Party's headquarters, Connolly House. Despite Twomey's low opinion of the anti-Communists and his feeling that a few IRA men would have scattered the mob, the IRA officially ignored the rioting at Connolly House. Instead they argued that the attack was brought about by the communists' own activities and it was not the IRA's responsibilty to defend them. The fact that a small number of IRA members attempted to defend the building, and used the IRA's stated aim of defending 'religious and civil liberty' as their reason for doing so, provoked more dissension on the subject within the IRA.

When the IRA defended itself from clerical accusations, it tended to try to avoid any confrontation with the Church itself. Even the most left-wing members of the IRA usually stressed their Catholic credentials when replying to charges made against them. Seán McGuinness of Offaly argued that as a 'sound Catholic' his membership of the IRA and Saor Éire proved that a person's faith was not impaired by these bodies. This did not spare McGuinness from denunciation in the *Catholic Herald* or from losing members in Offaly due to clerical influence. When an IRA member was sacked from his job as caretaker of a Catholic Young Men's Society, he defended himself by assuring the society's chairman that the IRA had never 'transgressed the laws of God or the Holy Catholic Church'.

In the Roscommon case Twomey suggested that a public apology be demanded from the parish priest. Local people were asked to provide statements supporting McKeon, and the woman in whose house the station had been held agreed to give one. She argued that while she had the 'highest respect' for the priest, the 'information he got about Paddy McKeon is all wrong'. The priest, however demanded that McKeon write a statement denouncing communism which he would then read out at Mass. Even with some local support the last resort was a court case, 'either civil or ecclesiastical' and Twomey considered McKeon's chances of winning in either were slim. In most cases, the IRA gave similar advice to its members facing these accusations. Local people should be canvassed for support and then the priests approached for an apology or retraction. If these statements were made outside of a church, at a political meeting for example, then the press could be utilized. There was a marked desire to avoid what could be construed as a 'challenge to the priests, as priests'.

Occasionally republicans took a more openly defiant stand. When a priest told his congregation in Bushfield, Co. Mayo, that the IRA were 'blackguards', 15 local IRA men walked out of the church. At an open air meeting in Achill, 200 young people were asked to give a show of hands against communism. One of the organizers, a local priest, expressed annoyance at the 'lukewarm' atmosphere of the meeting. Things deteriorated further when he was challenged by Brian Corrigan to explain why the republican cleric Fr Fahy was being called an 'anti-Christ'. Corrigan, by this stage a member of the Republican Congress, then mounted the platform and asked for three cheers for the Worker's Republic. The gardaí considered the crowd's reaction to his call to have been 'very responsive'. The IRA nationally defied the Church on occasion, most notably after the sacking of Frank Edwards in Waterford because of his participation in Republican Congress activities. While the bishop of Waterford had issued a pastoral letter forbidding 'under pain of sin' any one attending an IRA meeting in support of Edwards, hundreds of IRA members still participated in the protest.

There did, however, exist within the church a number of clergymen who were prepared to support the IRA. Most notable was Fr John Fahy, the 'patriot priest of Clonfert' who was active in Co. Galway with Peadar O'Donnell in land campaigns during the late 1920s. There were other less well known individuals who also aided the IRA. Gardaí in Co. Galway noted that the parish priest of Shanaglish, an 'enthusiastic republican', had allowed the selling of Easter lilies *inside* his church during 1931. He had also introduced the IRA speaker at the local commemoration. In Tipperary, following the murder of John Ryan by the IRA, gardaí noted whether priests were reading out a letter condemning the murder from the local archbishop. Many condemned the killing, others read the letter and made no comment, while one did not read the letter but asked for prayers for both Ryan and his killers. During 1932 a priest in Kill, Co. Kildare actually advised the young men of his parish to join the IRA and overthrow the 'only aggressor we have – England'. A priest in Waterford addressed a republican meeting that same month and as a result there was a 'splendid feeling' in the area towards the IRA. The existence of a pro-republican clergy could obviously make a major difference to the local perception of the IRA. After the denunciation of the IRA in Cooraclare, an IRA member wrote to the leadership asking if they could produce evidence that the organization was not linked to communism 'Russian or otherwise'. This was important because another local priest, who was a regular reader of *An Phoblacht*, wanted information in order to defend the IRA. Twomey replied that the IRA was 'emphatically' not a communist organization, but that all revolutionary bodies were slandered in this way when they became a threat. This satisfied the local men and the republican priest assured parishioners that there was 'no communism in Cooraclare'. Furthermore, the priest who had made the original accusation was apparently 'laughed at' by parishioners following this.

It must be stressed, however, that the number of clerics who would defend the IRA by 1933 was very small. While Fianna Fáil attained greater respectability, the IRA remained outside the mainstream of Catholic life. When IRA members resigned because of alleged 'communist' influence in Offaly, the Gardai believed that an important influence on them was a local Fianna Fáil-supporting priest. His record meant that he had 'great influence' with the IRA in his parish. The important point is that had he been a Cumann na nGaedheal supporter he would not have had the same influence. A hint of changing circumstances was given in a report written by a Mayo IRA officer during the general election of 1933. He noted how clergymen previously hostile to Fianna Fáil were now supporting de Valera's party. Whereas clerical condemnation of the IRA before 1932 certainly had some effect, the fact that Fianna Fáil remained just outside the political mainstream insulated the IRA to a degree. In 1929, for example, Fianna Fáil members of Galway county council boycotted the town's Catholic Emancipation centenary celebrations in protest against the jailing of Fr John Fahy. By 1933, the vast majority of Fianna Fáil activists had no quarrel with the Church and both the intensely anti-communist atmosphere and the IRA's own increasingly violent activities left it open to clerical attack.

While the IRA publicly stated that as an Irish revolutionary body it expected nothing less than condemnation from the same Church that had denounced the Fenians, the internal repercussions of such condemnation were important. The popular mood of anti-communism was reflected among the IRA's officer corps and rank and file and forced the leadership to articulate their views in ways it was hoped would not draw criticism from the Church. There had always been a tendency to present radical social views as in line with Catholic or at least Christian teaching and this was the case increasingly after 1933. By 1935 the IRA was arguing that its economic and social policy would give 'practical application to the teachings of Christianity'. They were not unique in this as even the left-wing Citizen Army could accuse de Valera of having decided to serve 'Mammon instead of Christ' by implementing capitalist policies. It is important to stress that the worries about IRA policies being contrary to the Church's teaching was not confined to any one region, and much of the most intense hostility to 'communism' came from within the Dublin Brigade. The 1933 IRA convention unanimously accepted the addition of a clause to the 'Constitution of the Irish Republic' which stressed that the 'propagation of irreligious doctrines, or the suppression of religion' were not the aims of the IRA. The period from 1929 onwards saw a major revival in popular Catholicism, with the Emancipation celebrations and the Eucharistic Congress of 1932. Many Belfast IRA members attended the congress and it is probable that many others did also along with the large numbers of ordinary Irish Catholics. Indeed, the IRA ordered its units to take the opportunity of the return of emigrants for the congress to explain its policy to the 'exiles' and attempt to recruit them. Although not all the IRA leadership were Catholic and certainly not all devout, they did operate largely within this milieu. This was reflected in the practice of the IRA in saluting Catholic churches while on parade and saying the rosary at commemorations.

Given the atmosphere in Ireland during the 1930s, could the IRA have reasonably expected to mount a successful attack on clerical influence, even accepting that it desired to? With the exception of the Edwards case, where popular opinion among local Fianna Fáil and trade union branches in Waterford seems to have been strongly against his dismissal, most of those who confronted the Church during the 1930s were very isolated. Again the IRA leadership could not expect to carry its rank and file along with it even if it did decide to do this. In the Gralton case, the Dublin IRA leadership did initially support the campaign against his deportation only to find the Leitrim IRA wishing to stay neutral. Even those among that unit who wanted to defend Gralton stressed their opposition to 'anti-God doctrines'. The IRA could do little except resort to terrorism when the bishop of Galway forced Mártín Ó Cadhain to resign from his teaching post because of his IRA membership.

The IRA did express more open hostility to lay Catholic organizations. The Ancient Order of Hibernians was seen as 'exactly of the same nature' as the Orange Order. The Irish National Foresters on the other hand were non-political, and IRA members were allowed join them if they wished. Twomey saw the emergence of the Knights of Columbanus as a 'worst form of Hibernianism than the AOH'. He believed that Catholic propagandists had exaggerated the influence of the Freemasons in order to create support for groups like the Knights. The Masons were only a 'bogey' while the Knights were dangerous because they seemed to have some influence within Fianna Fáil. He also considered the campaign against Gralton to have been inspired by the Knights. Twomey was correct in his belief that the Knights had made inroads into Fianna Fáil. In fact, several leading figures in the party were members. The question of the Knights was kept in republican minds by the long running controversy over the non appointment of a Sligo republican to the town clerkship. Robert Bradshaw had been editor of the *Connachtman*, the only local newspaper to have taken an anti-Treaty position during the civil war. He had been active in the IRA during that period and was still a supporter in 1932. He was also a Protestant. He seemed to have strong support from Sligo corporation when he was appointed temporarily to the position in 1933, but the Minister for Local Government overruled this decision and replaced him. *An Phoblacht* denounced this as anti-Protestant sectarianism, inspired by a sinister secret society. Bradshaw took his case to the high court where it was alleged that the Knights had instigated a whispering campaign against him, telling people that he was an atheist. Bradshaw lost his case and *An Phoblacht* bemoaned the influence of new 'Irish Klux Klan'. Certainly the minister for Local Government, Seán T. O'Kelly, was a Knight of St Columbanus, as several personalities involved in campaigning for Bradshaw's replacement seem to have been. In a sequel to the case, during 1937 Bradshaw regained the position of town clerk when the previous occupant of the job was dismissed.

The IRA's protestations over the Bradshaw case would carry a little more weight had they not gone along with the tide of objection to the appointment of Letitia Dunbar Harrison as a librarian in Co. Mayo during 1930. The IRA accepted that as a non Irish-speaker she was unsuited to the job but, realizing that most objectors were more concerned about her religion then her mastery of the language had also tried to condemn sectarianism. In this they took no different a position then many within Fianna Fáil.

However, while the IRA certainly made concessions to sectarianism it never tried to lead a movement based on it. The various Catholic Action groups drew their support from other sources. *An Phoblacht* was still the only newspaper where it was likely to find an attack on religious orders exploitation of children through the industrial school system. The IRA argued that the 1929 Emancipation celebrations presented a picture of Catholic suffering and Protestant tyranny only in order to turn young Catholics into 'zealots' devoted to hating 'fellow Christians'. The reports of the vast Christian Front rallies during 1936 contain no mention of republican participation. But it is notable too how little IRA concessions towards Catholic teaching muted clerical hostility. De Valera's populist republicanism satisfied those clerics who had been unhappy with the Treaty settlement and the IRA's radicalism, no matter how non-threatening to Catholic power in reality, was still too dangerous for the Church to tolerate.

4/Enemies and antagonists

In the decade after 1926, the IRA was never engaged in an armed campaign. Yet it did involve itself in violent activity on a regular basis, often directed against particular targets. Some of these targets remained constant, others changed over time. Why did the IRA embark on particular campaigns and was its rationale always political? To what extent was it motivated by sectarian, local or personal factors?

During the mid-1920s the IRA began to target what it considered symbols of British imperialism in the Free State. Over the next decade it organized demonstrations against the celebration of Poppy Day in Dublin, attempted to prevent the public display of Union flags and attacked British Legion halls and even Boy Scout huts. This campaign formed a major part of the IRA's activity until 1932, sometimes involving thousands of people, leading to arrests, violence and even deaths. The most obvious focus for the IRA's hostility to 'imperialist' symbolism were the Remembrance Day ceremonies held every November. Poppy Day was observed by thousands of people, particularly in Dublin during the 1920s. Over 500,000 poppies were sold in the Dublin area in 1924. From 1925 onwards it was also the occasion of republican counter demonstrations. These invariably took the form of public rallies featuring speakers from right across the republican spectrum. Twomey, MacBride and Ryan of the IRA, de Valera for Fianna Fáil, feminist Hannah Sheehy Skeffington, communist Seán Murray, and trade unionist Helena Moloney all appeared on anti-Poppy Day platforms. These rallies were usually held in College Green on the eve of Remembrance Day, attracting crowds of between 5,000 in 1930 and 15,000 in 1932. From the beginning there was substantial disorder associated with these protests. Republicans attacked premises displaying 'imperialist' symbols, snatched poppies from sellers and fought running battles with gardaí. On Remembrance Day itself, republicans would gather in the city centre and attempt to seize Union flags from supporters of the British Legion. In 1930, detectives had to fire shots to disperse a crowd attacking two men wearing poppies in O'Connell Street and in 1932 a car displaying a poppy was overturned in Stephen's Green and its occupants assaulted.

From 1927 the protests were organized under the auspices of the Anti-Imperialist League, which had been formed by the IRA to co-ordinate these activities. The IRA's publicly stated reasoning behind its campaign was that it would not tolerate 'the flying of the Union Jack and the singing of the English National Anthem in an unfree Ireland'. In Ireland, the poppy was the 'emblem of Ascendancy' and the British Legion's Remembrance Day ceremonies 'nothing more or less than homage of loyalty to England's King'. Therefore a great deal of effort was put into disrupting these events as part of the struggle for the 'complete overthrow of imperialism in Ireland'.

The protests involved the mobilization of the entire Dublin IRA. A major attraction for the IRA must have been the opportunity to mobilize their forces in a confrontational manner, thus giving off a show of strength while being relatively insulated from arrest by the numbers of supporters on the street. In an organization, that in theory, prepared for war, but with few opportunities for activity, Poppy Day offered opportunities which could not be overlooked. There was a visible enemy, who could be demonized as representing the 'Black and Tans' only recently departed from Ireland's shores, being protected by the Free State's police. The younger generation of IRA officers, such as Frank Ryan, clearly relished the street fighting that occurred before, during and after Poppy Day.

There was also a class dimension to the disturbances. The gardaí noted that the republican rallies attracted some of the 'roughest elements of the population' in Dublin. While large numbers of ex-servicemen came from working class backgrounds, republican propaganda targeted the Unionist businesses in Grafton Street and College Green as the displayers of 'imperialist bunting'. The most exclusive areas of the city were therefore open to attack from mainly poor crowds. Frank Ryan speculated that the British Legion marchers would be largely composed of 'bank clerks and students of Trinity College'. This, of course, was not true, and a section of working class Dublin continued to identify with its contribution during the First World War well into the next decade; but the image of well heeled pro-British demonstrators was a powerful mobilizing tool – as of course was the sectarian aspect of the imagery used by the IRA's propaganda, for 'bank clerks and students of Trinity College' in 1932 largely meant Protestants.

So were the protests an opportunity for the IRA to encourage sectarian violence? Whatever the motivation was of many who took part in their protests, the IRA denied that religious bigotry or prejudice against ex-servicemen played any role in its activities. In fact, the IRA claimed to support the right of veterans to remember the dead and indeed to sympathize with the plight of ex-sevicemen. Furthermore, the IRA accused the British Legion and Unionists of exploiting the suffering of veterans for their own ends. Motions expressing sympathy with the relatives of Irish war dead were passed at anti imperialist rallies. Frank Ryan accused the British Legion of ignoring the poverty of ex-servicemen and using them as pawns every 11 November. According to the IRA, the 'Irishman who once wore khaki' was as welcome in their ranks as any other. Veterans should 'remember your dead' but also remember that their reward for that sacrifice was 'hunger, starvation (and) unemployment'. The IRA suggested anti-militarism as a reason to disavow Poppy Day, arguing that 'illusions' that the Great War was a 'noble' affair had to be 'torn down'. George Gilmore even claimed that the IRA met with General Hickie of the British Legion to discuss how to avoid clashes on Remembrance Day.

What was significant for the IRA was that their activities around Poppy Day did have an appeal beyond their ranks. There was considerable resentment among many Dubliners towards some aspects of the Remembrance ceremonies. Military intelligence directly connected IRA revival in Dublin with the organization's first involvement in protests against Poppy Day. Because hostility to the event was not confined to them the IRA realized that they could appeal to 'a large section of the public which would nominally be described as friendly to the government'. What annoyed many was the practice of Trinity students halting traffic in College Green ostensibly to observe a two-minute silence but then regaling passersby by singing 'God save the King.' At various stages, senior gardaí complained that Poppy Day was becoming an excuse 'for a regular military field-day' and an occasion for the display of 'anti-Irish and pro-British sentiments'. They argued that the display of Union flags by shops and businesses was provocative and that much of the practices carried out by the British Legion would be illegal if indulged in by the 'irregulars'. They also noted how the IRA were being given opportunities for activity by the commemorations. There was undoubtedly a section of those taking part in Remembrance Day ceremonies who used the occasion to demonstrate Unionist sentiment.

A minor though potent factor in the disturbances was the presence of black-shirted members of the British Fascists at the Poppy Day parades. In 1926 Gilmore was arrested after a violent clash between IRA men and Fascists. Their attendance was also the source of complaint from the gardaí. While the IRA in Dublin did have instructions that allowed 'hitting up' the 'Blackshirt crowd' if possible, they never made opposition to this group a focus for their Poppy Day protests. Eventually, an agreement was reached between the British Legion and the authorities which regulated the ceremonies and Fianna Fáil in power showed quite a flexible attitude to the event. After 1932, their importance to the IRA also declined. By the mid-1930s, Ryan, now a member of the Republican Congress, was organising alternative Poppy Day commemorations featuring ex-servicemen.

These protests were always largely a Dublin affair. Aside from the stealing of poppies from a supplier in Co. Cork in 1928 most of the IRA's aggressive 'anti-imperialist' activities were concentrated in Dublin. Partially this was because the main British Legion ceremonies took place there, making it the 'headquarters for such rank Imperialist display'. Also, outside Dublin the ceremonies do not seem to have raised local republican ire, with a Drogheda officer explaining that those attending the local commemoration were 'in no way aggressive'. Gardaí noted how peacefully commemorations passed off in Cork, Sligo, Tralee and Kilkenny during 1928.

However, while the Poppy Day protests involved the IRA in public activity, the organization also carried out acts of terrorism against 'imperialist' symbols especially during the late 1920s. Beginning in 1925, when the Masterpiece cinema in Dublin was blown up for showing 'imperialist' films, British Legion premises, scout halls and monuments to English monarchs were all targeted. IRA units were also instructed to make off with any Union flags that were prominently displayed in their areas. Motion pictures like 'Mons' in 1927, were targeted on the basis that they glorified the British armed forces rather than truly reflected the 'the horrors of the European war'. The Baden Powell Boy and Sea Scouts were seen as 'British Reservists' and as potential strike breakers. During September 1928, attempts were made to burn scout huts and camps were raided in Wicklow and Dublin. The British Legion hall in Inchicore was set on fire and then bombed on two occasions. The Legion's hall in Killester was also destroyed in an arson attack. On 11 November 1928, attempts were made to destroy the statues of George II in Stephen's Green, King William in College Green and the King Edward fountain in Herbert Park. Again many of these activities were approved of outside the ranks of the IRA.

A more dramatic form of anti-imperialist activity was uncovered by the gardaí during 1930. They discovered an IRA plot to kidnap Earl Jellicoe, the former first sea lord, during a visit to Dublin. As far as is known, the IRA's plan was not to harm Jellicoe but to publicly humiliate him. They had planned to place Jellicoe in a box on top of a donkey cart and leave him chained in O'Connell Street surrounded by signs bearing slogans such as 'Earl Jellyfish'. The entire Dublin IRA had assembled at Amiens Street station on the morning of Jellicoe's visit but the gardaí ensured that there was no opportunity for them to get near their target.

In most cases these activities represented a low-cost strategy to the IRA which provided excitement, and armed activity for its members, with little chance of the opposition hitting back. Nevertheless, they make IRA assertions of non-sectarian motives ring a little hollow. In theory the IRA was as opposed to the Catholic Boy Scouts, a 'sectarian body' as it was to the Baden Powell version. Despite this rhetoric which occasionally went as far as the call to 'smash' the Catholic Scouts, they were never physically attacked, because this would surely have been highly unpopular in the Free State. The anti-imperialist activities also led to the murder of Albert Armstrong, who was shot dead following his giving evidence at the trial of IRA men who had removed a Union flag from his offices.

The IRA's campaign was also largely restricted to the Free State. Their organization in Belfast had produced an impressive list of bodies hostile to it in 1926.

These included the British Fascists, the Orange Order, the Ancient Order of Hibernians and the Knights of Columbanus. Though, possibly because of its own weakness, or simply because it was impossible to do so, the IRA in Northern Ireland did not generally carry out these type of activities.

Evidence does exist to suggest that the IRA in Belfast did consider carrying out an attack which would have been unparalleled in this period. In early 1930, a Belfast IRA report noted how an inquiry had been held to discover the reasons for the failure of a plan to 'bomb the crowd at the City Hall' on 11 November 1929. That day had seen the unveiling of the Belfast Cenotaph and if the IRA was planning to use explosives then there would have been widespread casualties. Because of a misunderstanding of signals between IRA members the plan did not go ahead, but it suggests that hatred of 'imperialist' symbols could have had grave consequences. However, again there was no repetition of this in Belfast or elsewhere, which either suggests that the plan was unauthorized or that it was not intended to produce fatalities.

The 'anti-imperialist' campaign has to be seen in the context of a relatively weak IRA recovering from defeat and in the process of reorganization. Targeting Unionists and ex-servicemen offered opportunities for activities which were exciting and relatively popular. Blowing up monuments gave an impression of military prowess and achieved public notoriety. These activities reflected the new dominance of militants within the Dublin IRA who began to revive their organization through violent activity.

This analysis also helps explain one of the IRA's shortest lived campaigns, that against moneylenders during the summer of 1926. From July to August that year the IRA raided the offices and homes of moneylenders in Dublin and Limerick, taking away account books and notes of transactions. It announced that it was going to 'end to this practice' which exploited the misery and poverty of the 'poorest citizens'. During the raids, several IRA members were captured by police and leading IRA members Mick Price and Donal O'Donoghue found themselves in court charged with their involvement in the campaign. After a raid in Limerick in early September, the IRA ceased their activity on the issue. Negotiations between the IRA and representatives of the moneylenders produced an agreement in early 1927.

What is of interest, however, is that many of those raided by the IRA were Jewish and there has been suggestion that anti-Semitism played a role in the IRA's motivation. From the beginning, the IRA denied this was the case arguing that their attack was on moneylending 'not on Jewry'. The IRA wished it to be known that they opposed moneylending for 'reasons of principle only' and not religious prejudice. They were supported in their claims by the most prominent Jewish politician in Ireland, Robert Briscoe of Fianna Fáil. He argued that he did not see the raids as anti-Semitic, and wished it to be known that he and 'many other members of the Jewish community' abhorred moneylending and expressed his admiration for the IRA's attempts to end 'this rotten trade'.

Like the campaigns against 'imperialist' displays, the IRA had chosen an unpopular target which was even more unlikely to retaliate. There were about 180 moneylenders the Free State during the late 1920s, of whom 147 operated in Dublin. Statements given to a Dáil committee during 1930 point towards there being a large number of Jews involved in the trade in Dublin. There was often great hardship associated with owing debts to moneylenders so there was a possible return in popularity for the IRA in carrying out the raids. Interestingly however, oral testimony points to the relative popularity of Jewish moneylenders among working class Dubliners of the period, with non-Jewish moneylenders often regarded as far worse.

Some of the IRA's propaganda about the evils of 'usury' did parallel contemporary anti-Semitic themes. However, evidence does not support this as a motivation for the raids. Aside from Briscoe, the artist Harry Kernoff would seem to have been the only other Jew publicly associated with the IRA in this period. *An Phoblacht* did, however, condemn an attempt to stir up anti-Semitism during municipal elections in Dublin during 1933.

The agreement eventually supported by the IRA involved an undertaking that moneylenders would not use the courts to collect arrears, that where repayment was agreed it would be made through a committee so that the moneylender did not personally call to collect it and that Robert Briscoe and Peadar O'Donnell be appointed as conduits for negotiations between lenders and debtors. Despite some opposition from IRA officers who argued that a satisfactory conclusion to the raids had not been arrived at, the agreement was publicized in February 1927. The IRA continued to monitor moneylenders for a period after this but never engaged on raids on them again, despite occasional calls for it to do so.

Questions of sectarian motivation arise again however, with the IRA's mobilization against Orange marches during 1931. The Royal Black Preceptory were prevented from holding a walk in Cootehill, Co. Cavan, by a major IRA demonstration. Several hundred men armed with hurleys, sticks and iron bars occupied the route of the walk, while local roads were blocked and telegraph wires cut. A force of gardaí backed by soldiers and an armoured car was required to keep the two sides apart although was little actual physical violence. However, the event sparked disturbances in Portadown, Armagh and Lisburn, where attempts were made to prevent Hibernian parades and a convent was attacked. The IRA claimed the credit for preventing 'an imperialist meeting' asserting that it had responded to demands from local people. A statement had been issued prior to the walk by the IRA's 'Working Farmer's Committee' which attempted to convince 'wage earners of planter stock' that their motives for opposing the walk were not sectarian. This was reiterated in all the IRA's statements on the affair, with the organization claiming it would try to prevent victimisation of Protestants.

The IRA's decision to mobilize against the parade was influenced by increasing tension in the border area following some of the first Orange parades in the region for several years. During July in Newtowngore, Co. Leitrim, the first Orange march for 34 years was disrupted by local nationalists, including both Fianna Fáil and government supporters. At an Orange rally in Bailieboro, Co. Cavan, one speaker had made disparaging references to Catholicism as a 'moneymaking' religion which caused widespread consternation. Therefore, there was potentially local support for an aggressive action by the IRA and furthermore the opportunity for semi-military manoeuvres. Certainly the IRA was pleased at how its Leitrim and Cavan units sealed off Cootehill, took over its town hall and secured the surrounding area until Army and garda reinforcements arrived. Following the affair, one Orange leader remarked that if Protestants were to be treated that way in the south than 'let the other side take what they get from the men in the six counties'.

The amount of time the IRA spent denouncing sectarianism would suggest that in the aftermath of the Cootehill incident their leadership realized that they were the ones that had stirred up the 'sinister forces' they were now condemning. Threatening notices addressed to Protestants in Leitrim were denounced by local IRA leader Seán O'Farrell as the work of 'contemptible blackguards'. The IRA praised their Armagh unit for taking 'exemplary action' against sectarianism by punishing a group of men who had issued threats to local Protestants in the name of the IRA. There is no doubt that the leadership did not want to be seen as sectarian and had realized that 'much education' would be necessary in order to make sure republicans could distinguish 'sectarian animosities' from 'nationality'. They also noted how 'easily' sectarianism was aroused by these events. Indeed, this may have influenced the IRA's decision not to attempt this type of activity again. When the Donegal IRA reported local hostility to an Orange march during July 1932 they were denied permission for a counter protest, and ordered to avoid sectarian clashes.

Later that year, Twomey was asked to allow the IRA become involved in a case where a Donegal republican supporter claimed his cousin had lost her job due to discrimination in favour of Protestants. There had been a demand for IRA members from Leitrim to take action against the manager of Ballybofey station for his alleged bias but Twomey refused to allow IRA intervention.

However, it is doubtful if the suppression of an Orange march in the Free State would be seen by northern loyalists as anything other than an attack on Protestants.

The identification of largely Protestant institutions with 'imperialism' continued to lead the IRA into actions which could only be construed as sectarian. When the 'Boycott British' campaign was launched with a poster campaign in July 1932, TCD, the Masonic Hall and the Kildare Street Club were all covered with posters. The paranoia that some republicans displayed about the Freemasons was reflected in an IRA raid on their hall in Cork during 1935. Shots were fired and furniture destroyed by the raiders but no explanation ever offered as to why the hall was targeted. Again, in theory the IRA was just as opposed to the Knights of Columbanus and the AOH as it was to largely Protestant secret societies but these organizations were never physically targeted.

The IRA regarded itself as the legitimate army of the Irish Republic, sworn to bring about that Republic by 'force of arms'. Therefore the state forces north and south should have been among its foremost targets. In reality the IRA never attempted a sustained campaign against any of these bodies. Indeed, when the IRA did attempt to confront the forces of the Free State directly, with raids on garda barracks during November 1926, it was quickly forced to realize that it had bitten off more than it could chew.

There is an important factor to be taken into account when dealing with IRA attitudes to the gardaí in particular but also to state forces in general. The IRA had emerged from a period when the entire structure of legal authority was effectively demonized in Ireland. Its leadership and middle ranking officers had experience of RIC and British Army atrocities during the War of Independence and also those of the CID in the civil war. To the IRA, every garda action was designed to enforce Free State rule and was therefore illegitimate. While difficult to understand for an outsider this meant that within the republican movement any claims of garda brutality or harassment were believed without question, just as a supporter of the gardaí would automatically dismiss all such allegations as spurious propaganda. So, while the IRA would claim the right to shoot gardaí if necessary, they would complain vociferously if questioned by the gardaí about such an action.

While hostility to the Special Branch, the successors of the hated CID of the civil war era, could be taken as given, the IRA had taken some time to clarify its view of the new civic guards. An army council member writing during 1924 speculated that if the gardaí were 'discreetly handled' they could be of use to the IRA. This was because, according to the IRA's information, the majority of the force was resisting government efforts to make it 'similar to the RIC' by doing political work. Therefore, except in areas where the gardaí were 'hounding' republicans, the organization should have a flexible attitude towards them.

But it was inevitable that conflict would emerge between the IRA and the gardaí as the uniformed garda was more often than not the most apparent local symbol of Free State authority. It was uniformed gardaí who were likely to come across IRA members illegally drilling, or who were called upon to maintain order at political meetings. From an early stage an attitude of hostility to the 'peelers' who were charged with 'upholding His Britannic Majesty's rule' prevailed within the IRA.

In 1929, the IRA reminded its members that the police were not its main enemy. In fact, it claimed that if it wished to, it could overcome them easily. The gardaí were simply the 'lowest and meanest types' employed by the government for its 'lowest and vilest tasks'. The 'unfortunate renegades and perverted types' who were members of the police force should meet with contempt and amusement, but not with fear by IRA members. The language employed by the IRA for its own members was moderated in public. Despite fierce attacks on 'O'Duffy and his underlings' *An Phoblacht* would also claim that the 'vast majority' of gardaí wanted to administer civil law and not interfere with the IRA.

In reality, the IRA had to be careful in how it dealt with the gardaí. Despite bluster about the gardaí playing the same role as the old RIC, violent IRA activity against uniformed officers was not popular. It also tended to lead to increased repression against the IRA, which the organization wished to avoid as it rebuilt its strength during the late 1920s. The IRA learnt this lesson very quickly following its raids on garda barracks during November 1926. Groups of up to 30 IRA members armed with rifles and handguns seized 11 barracks in Cork, Waterford and Tipperary, stealing or destroying official documents before they left. During the raids, one garda was killed and another fatally wounded. In their aftermath a Public Safety Bill was introduced and over 110 republicans arrested.

The IRA claimed that the raids were a response to increased 'spying' on the organization and the raids were intended to make it understood that 'barracks are no safe strongholds'. The IRA further claimed that gardaí would not have been hurt if they had not resisted. In their aftermath the IRA attempted to present the raids as a success claiming that after them the gardaí 'ceased their hunt for Volunteers and arms'. This interpretation is fanciful as in fact the government was able to use the raids to clamp down on the IRA. More importantly, the raids led to internal dissension. A number of republicans publicly distanced themselves from the IRA's actions and a number of IRA officers in Dublin threatened to resign over the affair. The Dublin officers argued that the 'isolated raids' were instrumental in creating an atmosphere in which the government could institute a 'state of war' against the IRA. They also openly stated that they did not find the IRA's explanation for the raids to be satisfactory.

The IRA rode out the storm but it must have realized that clashes with uniformed gardaí were largely counter productive. However, in one sense the IRA did profit from the affair. It later transpired that prisoners in Waterford were subjected to repeated beatings from the gardaí. The gardaí were forced to discipline a number of officers, and the IRA were able to exploit this publicity. There was no repetition of a generalized attack on the gardaí over the proceeding years. Such violence that did occur between the IRA and the gardaí was of a much more localized nature.

The most notorious incidents occurred in west Clare during 1929, capturing nation-wide attention with Fianna Fáil allegations of widespread garda brutality in the county, followed by the murder of a detective in June. Their roots lay in a long-running and very personalized struggle between the local IRA commander T.J. Ryan and garda detectives. Garda Commissioner Eoin O'Duffy regarded west Clare as an area notorious for agrarian and political crime, attacks on the person and 'swilling poteen'. By 1929 it was an area with a strong IRA unit and one in which O'Duffy believed the majority of the populace were hostile to the gardaí. His men had been given instructions to 'effectively ... harass' the IRA and there is no doubt that they were doing this as the IRA and Fianna Fáil's complaints signalled. IRA reports from late 1926 show republicans being the subject of intense harassment involving house raids and searches but mention no violence being used. However, the IRA considered that the CID was employing 'terrorism' in their investigations in west Clare.

O'Duffy had feared an 'outrage' was being planned by the IRA and he was proven correct with the killing of a garda in June. A forged letter, purporting to reveal the location of a box containing ammunition, drew detectives to a trap mine at Tullycrine. O'Duffy had no doubt that T.J. Ryan was behind the murder, although he believed a different officer had been the target. Ryan was believed to have established a very efficient intelligence network in the area and had managed to evade garda observation to that point. However a number of local gardaí had been having some success in 'checking' IRA activity in the area and the murder was a response to this. While the crime committed was extremely serious, the IRA's actions were largely governed by local factors. It did not signal a new phase of violence against the gardaí.

Indeed over the next year the IRA's only major activity directed specifically against the force was the chaining of a garda to railings in Dublin, in revenge for his arrest of one their members. IRA members during this period were instructed not to use violence to resist arrest and use passive means to draw the attention of the public to their plight.

During 1931, however, there was a serious escalation in IRA activity generally. As the organization grew it became bolder and conflict escalated with the gardaí. Again, however, much of the confrontation was localized. In an attempt to check the IRA, the government banned its Bodenstown commemoration in June, but the IRA successfully defied the ban. However, the gardaí in Kerry were largely able to prevent the IRA from that county attending the event. In response the Kerry IRA tore up railway tracks and cut telegraph wires in an attempt to disrupt garda sports in Tralee a month later. In Donegal there was a shoot out between detectives and the IRA after they came upon men trying to tear up tracks in an effort to prevent gardaí travelling to a sports day in Letterkenny.

The most serious occurrence was the murder of a garda superintendent by the IRA in Tipperary. This was almost certainly the result of local tension following prosecutions for illegal drilling, as superintendent Curtin had managed to get IRA members to testify against their officers but, the government believed it signalled the beginning of an offensive against the gardaí. Garda reports from that year reflect a feeling of both helplessness in the face of, and a desire to hit back at, the IRA. The destruction of an unoccupied garda barracks in Co. Galway did little to ease their fears. The gardaí believed that the IRA was preparing to respond to mass arrests by assassination of gardaí nation-wide.

It was the case that the IRA was encouraging its local units to come out in to the open as much as possible, and some used this as an opportunity to test local garda resolve. In Offaly for example, gardaí claimed that Seán McGuinness had told them where he could be found drilling the local IRA unit and dared them to do something about it. He allegedly reminded them of what had happened to the superintendent in Tipperary for 'not minding his own business'. However the gardaí accepted his challenge and arrested him on Easter Sunday.

Despite garda fears, the IRA reacted to the Public Safety Bill of October 1931 not by assassinating policemen but by urging restraint among its members. Another garda was not to die at the organization's hands until 1940. During the clampdown of late 1931–2, the IRA received reports of 'beatings and assaults' on its members in Leitrim and north Clare. In Tipperary the local IRA commander had shots fired at him by gardaí. A Leitrim IRA member, James Vaugh, died after being released from garda custody during December 1931. An inquest ruled that he had died from the effects of influenza, measles and congestion of the lungs. The IRA accused the gardaí of causing his death through ill-treatment. Again what is important is that whatever actually occured while Vaugh was in garda custody, republicans would always believe he was murdered.

Following Fianna Fáil's coming to power, there followed a period of confusion for both the IRA and the gardaí. Contrary to previous interpretations the IRA leadership did not assume that the organization had been given carte-blanche to behave as it liked. The IRA's orders were to avoid confrontation but very rapidly IRA members became embroiled in street clashes which inevitably caused conflict with the gardaí.

There is some evidence that elements within the IRA believed that the gardaí would behave differently towards them under the new government. After an armed garda search of IRA men in Leitrim, the local IRA officer sought clarification about whether the gardaí still had the power to carry out such searches. More seriously, in a sequel to the west Clare events of three years previously, T.J. Ryan and George Gilmore were attacked by detectives in Kilrush and were badly injured. Ryan was clearly caught off guard by this as he had been telling associates that the 'CID' would not dare touch him now that Fianna Fáil were in power. Two gardaí were dismissed as a result of the affair, leading Twomey to speculate that the detective branch was about to be dissolved. Yet again, the IRA did not respond with violence, instead actually issuing orders to continue to avoid conflict.

Nevertheless, street violence did occur increasingly during the autumn of 1932. On several occasions, republican crowds were baton charged by the gardaí and Twomey believed known activists were deliberately singled out for a 'bad battering'. At an anti-imperialist protest in Dublin, two Kilrush based detectives were recognized by republicans and surrounded by a crowd who attacked them shouting 'You're not in Kilrush now!' This occurred on the occasion of Peadar O'Donnell's statement that a 'policeman who put his head between Mr Cosgrave's head and the hand of angry Irishmen might as well keep his head at home'. Given the rhetoric of IRA leaders like O'Donnell and the gardaí's task of maintaining public order, some level of conflict between the IRA and uniformed gardaí as well as detectives was always likely.

More serious attacks on the gardaí during 1933 were related to local conflicts and unlikely to have been centrally directed. In February, a garda sergeant in Tralee was shot and wounded because of his leading role in a baton charge the previous month and after rioting later that year the local garda barracks was fired on. During July, a superintendent's house and car in Drogheda were riddled by gun fire late at night. Again, he had been active in the prosecution of local IRA members. A garda was injured by a bomb thrown by the IRA at a bus passing through Dundalk during the Northern Ireland rail strike.

By March 1935, gardaí were again being deliberately targeted by the IRA with shootings in Tralee and Dublin. The gardaí believed that the motive behind the Dublin shootings was revenge for baton charges against IRA demonstrators on St Patrick's Day. The Tralee shooting was the result of threats made against the local detective branch by IRA officers in the town.

The IRA's main adversaries in terms of day-to-day activity were the gardaí. Despite being quite capable of killing individual policemen the IRA never mounted a generalized offensive against them. While the IRA's murders of four gardaí were terrible in themselves the organization was capable of far worse violence, yet for a variety of reasons it chose not to engage in it. The IRA's attitude to the state forces, north and south, was generally one of caution in this period.

Prison warders accused of ill-treating IRA prisoners were named on republican posters, but were only actively targeted on a couple of occasions. The head warder at Mountjoy was shot and wounded by the IRA in early 1928. Two years later, one of his colleagues was handcuffed to railings with a placard claiming he mistreated prisoners tied around his neck.

While the National Army should have been at least in theory the IRA's main enemy, it was very rarely physically attacked. Generally these attacks occurred when the army was guarding individuals or attempting to quell riots. An army sergeant was wounded during a gun attack on the Ceann Comhairle's residence during late 1930. Troops were used to quell disturbances in Tralee and Kilkenny during October 1933 and to seal off Bodenstown in 1931 and 1936. In a solitary case a former IRA member who had joined the Irish Army was kidnapped and tied to railings in Limerick city during 1934. The IRA claimed that it recognized young men joined the Free State army for economic reasons and not through 'hostility to Irish freedom'. Therefore they also occasionally directed propaganda at rank and file soldiers, calling on 'brother Irishmen' to refuse to play the part of 'Black and Tans'.

In Northern Ireland the RUC were attacked only in the context of strikes or public disturbances. Their first fatality at the hands of the IRA occurred during the 1933 rail strike. The British Army in the north was never targeted. There was only one rather pathetic attempt to attack British forces in the south, with a few shots discharged at a Royal Navy destroyer in Cobh harbour during 1936. The only other attack by the IRA which may be very vaguely described as connected to the British military was the murder of the retired Vice-Admiral Boyle Somerville in Co. Cork. The stated reason, that the seventy-three-year-old was a 'British agent' for giving references to local young men who wished to join the Royal Navy hardly marked a high point in the IRA's campaign against 'imperialism'.

During 1934 the IRA clashed with Dublin street gangs. The so-called 'animal gangs' of Dublin have entered Irish left-wing folklore, being held responsible for almost every attack on socialists during the 1930s and alleged to have been allies of the Blueshirts. While Dublin did see serious street violence against the left during this period, its perpetrators were more diverse than is often allowed.

The 'animal gangs' themselves were territorially based groups involved in a variety of criminal activities as well as violence against rivals. Their reputation appears to have been a mixed one, occasionally seen as local heroes or alternately as thugs. In 1934 the IRA accused them of strike breaking on behalf of the Dublin newspaper employers and of attacking its members. *An Phoblacht* had been the only newspaper that the Print Unions' Strike Committee allowed to publish during a two month strike in the autumn of 1934. The IRA claimed that armed members had visited the Ardee Hall in Talbot Street, one of the 'Animal

Gang's' meeting places and warned them to desist from interfering with the IRA. The Hall was a meeting place for the gangs many of whom worked as 'newsboys' selling papers in Dublin city centre. The incident which gave rise to the threat was a clash between IRA members and 'newsboys' which led to two IRA men being hospitalized. 'Newsboys' had broken windows in *An Phoblacht*'s office and the IRA had mobilized 50 men to guard it. Further clashes erupted with sticks and bottles being used by both sides. After the injuries to their members the IRA then upped the stakes by threatening gang members with guns.

The 'newsboys' had a mixed relationship with the IRA. During the clampdown of late 1931 they had apparently 'stood by' the IRA and distributed *Republican File*. In 1932, *An Phoblacht* praised them for attacking strike-breakers during the *Irish Press* dispute. However, gardaí believed that the violence had erupted when the 'newsboys' had refused to pay extra for the special strike editions of *An Phoblacht*. After they broke windows in republican premises the IRA had been forced to respond, and with many 'newsboys' being gang members, they then responded to the IRA's challenge themselves. The gardaí's report did not mention any possible connection to strike breaking. However, some 'newsboys' raided the Republican Congress offices during the strike, injuring Mick Price and stealing bundles of newspapers so a connection to the strike cannot be ruled out. In any case it was the last recorded clash between the IRA and Dublin gangs in that era.

Perhaps the best known conflicts that the IRA of this period were involved in were those with the Blueshirts. The Blueshirts emerged from the Army Comrades Association in early 1933, and conflict between them and the IRA reached its height between 1933 and 1934. The violence of that period has been well-chronicled, as has the implications of that violence for both the IRA and their opponents. Generally, it has been argued that the period allowed Fianna Fáil to establish its credentials as the guardian of law and order, saw the majority of the Blueshirts' support opt for democratic parliamentary methods and contributed to the further marginalization of the IRA. The IRA never developed a consistent strategy for dealing with the Blueshirts and controversy over conflict with them contributed to the organization splitting in 1934.

The IRA first began to pay attention to the 'Higgins Gang' as it called the ACA, in the autumn of 1932. Units were instructed to gather intelligence on the ACA and to infiltrate it if possible. The IRA wanted to know the 'names and records' of its principal activists in every local area. Reports from around the Free State suggested that the ACA was not recruiting widely but was largely composed of ex-Free State army 'pensioners' with some access to arms. Incidentally the gardaí also noted how in some cases the ACA were 'as well armed as the irregulars'.

The emergence of the ACA gave the IRA a boost, giving units a focus and leading to increased recruitment. No doubt the appearance of a potential rival gave rise to the belief that conflict was at hand. Twomey stressed however that the IRA did not want street 'brawls' as it was a 'short distance' from 'individual scrapping matches to guns'. He also speculated that unless the national army gave backing to the ACA they would 'fizzle out'. The IRA continued to empha-size this even as violence did break out over the winter of 1932, most notably in Killmallock, Co. Limerick. While it argued that anger against the 'white army' was inevitable it was up to the Fianna Fáil government to stamp out their 'trea-son' by withdrawing state pensions from the ACA's membership. Republican violence against the ACA while understandable, would only give them a focus for their activities. A potential for clashes arose when Dublin publicans asked the ACA to protect their premises from attack by the IRA during the 'Boycott British' campaign but in the event conflict was avoided. While belligerent speeches by Peadar O'Donnell and Frank Ryan at an anti - imperialist rally in Dublin during November 1932 have been seen as beginning the 'no free speech for traitors' campaign and certainly increased the temperature politically, the army council did not discuss their policy towards meetings of Cumann na nGaedheal until later that month. It is likely that the IRA leadership responded to grassroots pressure rather than initiated the campaign themselves.

Following the January 1933 general election victory of Fianna Fáil, the IRA concluded that 'as a serious force' the ACA was finished. The IRA leadership's key note statement to be read to all units prior to the 1933 general army con-vention did not mention the ACA at all. There was a brief but significant dis-cussion on the ACA at the convention in March. It was concluded that they were a 'spent force' and any violent action against them by the IRA would only 'jus-tify their reorganization' and therefore the IRA should exercise restraint. However, in cases where the ACA became particularly aggressive towards the IRA, local officers could use their discretion in dealing with them. The IRA's assessment was mistaken, as the summer of 1933 saw the blueshirted National Guard flourish under the leadership of Eoin O'Duffy and become a mass move-ment. In August, the government moved dramatically against the organization, banning a proposed mass march in Dublin. *An Phoblacht* ridiculed the Blueshirts' 'phantom hundred thousand' and again speculated that the organization was on the brink of collapse. However, O'Duffy's 'fascists' as the IRA now increasingly referred to them, instead embarked on a winter of intense activity which saw the most serious street violence since Fianna Fáil had come to power. In October, troops were called in to back up gardaí in both Tralee and Kilkenny as hours of street fighting followed attempted Blueshirt rallies. In Tralee, O'Duffy was assaulted, his car burnt out and the fighting only subsided after the Army had used tear gas.

The IRA's official response to these and smaller scale clashes throughout the winter was to blame government inaction for allowing 'imperialist fascism' to thrive and to warn of more violence unless action was taken to prevent treason. It was also stressed that there were 'definite Army Orders' instructing IRA members to avoid conflict with the Blueshirts. Twomey claimed that most of this violence was 'spontaneous' local reaction to Blueshirt provocations and that most of those involved in it were actually Fianna Fáil members and supporters. The IRA had made it clear to their members that they wanted no 'local feuds'. Following arrests in connection with the Tralee riots the IRA was quick to claim that only six of its members were in jail for offences related to anti-Blueshirt activities. Instead, it suggested that it was the *Irish Press* whipping up 'hysteria' about the Blueshirts that was contributing to the disorder.

The IRA's condemnation of clashes with Blueshirts became ever more shriller during 1934, even as three people died as a result of violence associated with the conflict. The IRA now stressed that 'militancy must be directed' into an attack on the 'privileged interests' behind the Blueshirts. 'Local and isolated clashes' were not the way forward. In response to further clashes in May, the IRA again condemned 'meaningless violence' which only served to divert from the task of 'smashing of the capitalist system'. Twomey warned IRA members not to 'interfere with individual wearers of Blueshirts … but to get out after the financiers of the organization'. In Ballybunion, Co. Kerry, he described attacks on Blueshirts as 'nothing better than … faction fighting' which was carried out by people who considered fighting with 'imperialists' more important than a real challenge to 'imperialism'.

During this period the Blueshirts were also engaged in a campaign against the payment of annuities which involved them in widespread sabotage and clashes with the gardaí, leading to the death of one young man in August 1934. This was arguably more important to them than fighting the IRA, something which they did with much less regularity during late 1934. By 1935 the violence between republicans and Blueshirts had declined perceptibly.

Despite their leadership's very vocal denunciations of it, the IRA were heavily involved in anti-Blueshirt violence. Much of the tempo of the conflict was governed by local conditions, and betrayed how little central control the IRA could exercise over its local units. From an early stage IRA units had expressed a desire to confront the ACA. An IRA officer in Kildare wanted to organize attacks on ACA members parading in Celbridge and Naas in September 1932, but was denied permission from his superiors until official instructions were received from Dublin. In Castlegregory, Co. Kerry, the local IRA felt that if the ACA tried to hold a meeting it should 'hunt them out of the place'. Some sections of the IRA expressed a fear that if Cumann na nGaedheal were given free platforms they could 'stampede the people' against the government.

An important factor in the escalation of conflict was that the ACA seem to have been making their presence felt to the IRA in several districts. In Caherciveen, three IRA members were held up by a detective who threatened them with his revolver and told them that there was now an 'army that would quieten them'. According to the IRA, this detective had been seen in the company of the local ACA. In Sligo, an IRA member was abducted, questioned and beaten up by masked and armed men during late September 1932. The IRA locally were convinced that this was the work of the ACA. In Belcara, Co. Mayo, an ex-Free State officer had drawn a gun on IRA members heckling a speech by former Cumann na nGaedheal minister FitzGerald Kenny. The IRA retaliation for this incident resulted in the shooting of one of its members. Fianna Fáil sources were also informing the IRA of threats they had received which they believed came from the ACA.

In some cases a contributing factor to the animosity was the fact that the participants had clashed in different guises before. The two detectives dismissed over the Kilrush attack on Gilmore and Ryan subsequently took a 'prominent part' in Blueshirt activities. In Offaly an ex-army officer who the IRA had campaigned against during a land dispute became vice-chairman of the local ACA and a member of its national executive a year later. The IRA were also receiving reports that ACA members had fired shots during fighting in Mallow and Cork in early November.

Therefore while the IRA leadership dithered as to what policy to adopt towards Cumann na nGaedheal meetings, local IRA members took the opportunity that these meetings provided to let the ACA know that they would not tolerate them in their areas. The IRA leadership could disavow knowledge on the basis that many other non-affiliated republicans would also be involved in disturbances at these meetings. This too helps explain the often localized nature of the conflict. While the set piece battles during the 1933 election campaign and during the winter of 1933–4 drew much attention, unreported local clashes probably produced more intense bitterness. This situation was still not general in early 1933 however, although the election campaign produced several confrontations. In Kiltimagh Co. Mayo, the IRA claimed that it had disarmed ACA members who had beaten up two local youngsters.

At the IRA's 1933 convention the only area that demanded action on the issue of the ACA was west Cork. There the ACA was said to be 'strong in numbers and rather aggressive'. Tom Barry claimed the ACA was 'wreaking havoc' among the local IRA. He asserted that young IRA members were being intimidated by the ACA and asked for permission to 'execute' their local leadership. Twomey argued that whatever was the case in west Cork, the ACA nationally were 'not a menace' to the IRA. Shooting their leaders would simply bring them sympathy and help revive their organization. However, Barry was given permission to take measures short of this to defend his men. The fact that the IRA were outnumbered by the ACA in many parts of Ireland may have contributed to the intensity of their violence against them. It is not surprising that the first fatality of Blueshirt-IRA violence took place in west Cork. In retaliation for an assault on an IRA member in Bandon during October 1933, two Blueshirts were abducted and beaten up with one of them being shot in both legs. He recovered but the other man died of his wounds in December.

There has been much speculation as to what the IRA had planned for the proposed Blueshirt march on Dublin. Rumours of snipers being placed on rooftops to machine gun marchers, or of armed units taking over train stations have become accepted as fact. Whether the IRA would risk this is open to question. Having spent so much time trying to convince its members that confrontation was counter-productive, why would it have authorized the use of arms, with the potential for mass carnage? In fact, the IRA's preparations may have been a little less grandiose but more in keeping with the temper of the times. It was claimed that groups of men had gathered at Cabra, Kingsbridge Station, and the Royal and Grand Canals, equipped with sticks and stockpiles of stones on the day.

Clashes between the two organizations took several forms. One was mass rioting as seen in Tralee, Kilkenny and Drogheda during late 1933 and early 1934. Here the IRA were not the only participants, but their involvement was very important. In Drogheda, for example, a large crowd had gathered outside a Blueshirt dance. While there was much heckling it was not until the IRA arrived that an attempt was made to storm the dance hall. There followed a night of stone throwing and baton charges. Of the 21 republicans arrested, seven were IRA members. On occasions like this the IRA's organization provided leadership for larger groups of people. The type of incident that typified the conflict in the localities is well illustrated by one which occurred at Ballyclough, Co. Cork, in August 1934. A small group of Blueshirts taunted a passing IRA man, who summoned help from his comrades and a fight took place involving no more than 12 men. Neither side would talk to gardaí about the affair, and no court cases resulted from it. To these IRA men their leadership's orders to ignore 'provocations' and instead concentrate their efforts on attacking 'imperialist strongholds' must have seemed rather abstract. When the organization was challenged locally, the instinct was to respond, whether in order to gain revenge or not to lose face.

Much of the violence was of a tit-for-tat nature. It was also violence which was not one-sided. There has been a recent tendency to see the activities of the Blueshirts as purely defensive. Yet that the IRA was responsible for two deaths and the Blueshirts for only one is more due to accident than design. During early 1934, for example, Blueshirts shot two IRA men, one of whom died, and were involved in another eighteen incidents involving firearms.

It was also the case that anti-Blueshirt feeling had a popular basis in some parts of the Free State. A Cork Fianna Fáil Cumann called on the government to provide garda protection for them because of the 'menacing attitude' of local Blueshirts. After riots in Waterford during May 1934, the gardaí explained that the trouble resulted when Blueshirts armed with batons attacked Labour and Fianna Fáil supporters who had taken part in a trade union march. In Leitrim and Kerry, labour and trade union branches took part in anti-Blueshirt rallies. During February and March 1934 schools in Tipperary, Limerick, Cork and Waterford were disrupted by walkouts in protest at the wearing of Blueshirts by pupils. While there was republican involvement in some cases in others the action seems to have been spontaneous. Rural class tensions undoubtedly also played a part in violence between the Blueshirts and their enemies.

The IRA's involvement in violent anti-Blueshirt activities did have a damaging effect on the organization. Firstly, the obvious participation of its members in actions which it publicly disavowed showed how little control it had over its own ranks. Secondly, it was allowing itself to be further and further associated with disorder and chaos, points made by de Valera when he visited Kerry in December 1933. Twomey claimed that the government was using the violence, even that which involved its own supporters, to attack the IRA. Yet the IRA leadership could do little about this. Their own ranks were split on the issue. By 1934 the left, represented by O'Donnell, Ryan and Gilmore were arguing that the fight against Irish fascism was the most important task for the IRA. Following their departure to the Republican Congress, they claimed that the IRA leadership had failed to give a lead to the struggle against the Blueshirts. Non-left-wing leaders such as Seán O'Farrell and John Joe Sheehy were however, also centrally involved in clashes with the Blueshirts in their localities. At its 1934 convention these differences were expressed openly. Michael Kelly complained that it had been an 'honour' to put the Blueshirts off the streets, but the army council had then forbidden the IRA rank and file from doing this. Tadgh Lynch of west Cork claimed that the Blueshirts were still 'sapping' the morale of the IRA in his area and that action had to be taken against them. In contrast Seán McCool argued that it was 'foolishness' to attack the Blueshirts as instead the IRA should be attacking what they stood for. John Joe Sheehy put the case for aggressive action when he stated that unless the Blueshirts were 'squelched' they would 'spring up like daisies' and crush the IRA.

In the case of the Blueshirts the majority of the IRA, of all political hues, were in agreement on the need for confrontation. Whether this was because the Blueshirts were led by the man who made 'Kerry a graveyard in 1922' or because they represented 'dictatorship as exemplified in Germany (and) Italy' it meant that the IRA were never likely to avoid conflict with them. While evidence exists of some co-operation between imprisoned members of the two organizations the self sustaining nature of the conflict between them meant there was little room for rapprochement. O'Duffy's occasional praise of the IRA was never going to inspire an already unlikely alliance. A degree of toleration for violence against the Blueshirts had to be allowed by the IRA leadership, especially when it could be presented as defensive. When it was highly embarrassing, as with the fatal injuring of an elderly woman in Dundalk, it was disowned.

It was when Fianna Fáil launched an ostensibly republican reserve of the Irish Army that the IRA found itself in widespread conflict with a 'republican' force. The IRA was aware of Fianna Fáil's plans to launch a Volunteer Reserve force from an early stage. Frank Aiken had made it clear the government were going ahead with plans to do so during discussions with the IRA in July 1932. Twomey expressed the fear that the force would exert a great pull on young republicans, because of the likely 'glamour and intense propaganda' that would be behind it. Tom Barry felt that such a force would 'sweep the unattached youth into its ranks'. The IRA realized that when the force was launched 'a high percentage of the youth' who normally might join the IRA would be attracted to it. The IRA decided to do 'everything possible' to discourage the launch of the reserve. However, this essentially meant rhetorical opposition to the idea of such a force rather than anything concrete. A suggestion that the IRA should threaten 'the extreme penalty' (death) to discourage members from joining the reserve was voted down at the 1933 convention.

The Volunteer Reserve was finally launched in 1934. By then the IRA had still not developed any strategy to deal with the Volunteers aside from accusing them of being a 'Free State militia'. Clear divisions on the matter emerged at the 1934 convention where sections of the IRA wanted violent action taken against members of the force. Seán O'Farrell stated that the IRA 'should attack their meetings and bomb and burn their halls'. A Tralee officer claimed that the 'militia' would meet the same reception in Kerry as the Blueshirts did. An officer from Tipperary felt that he would be unable to prevent his men attacking the Volunteers, and that he had only narrowly prevented them burning a Volunteer organizer's car. Senior figures such as Seán MacBride and Tom Barry counselled caution. Attacking the Volunteers would only give the government an excuse to 'crush the IRA'. Barry warned that it would be unwise if the 'militia' were made the 'victims of aggression'. However all realized that the Volunteer Reserve was a threat to the IRA's position as the republican military force. The fact that the men leading it were 'of good records' meant that it was the 'greatest menace' to the IRA. This point was also admitted in the IRA's publicity attacking the new force. 'Young Irishmen' were warned not to be 'misled' by 'plausible' arguments of the promoters of the Volunteers.

While the convention had agreed that opposition to the new force should be confined to 'posters and propaganda', by the autumn IRA members would be carrying out violent attacks on its members. This response can be partially explained by cases of 'treachery' where IRA members went over to the new force. This occurred particularly in Kerry where IRA members in Dingle, Castlegregory, Ardfert and Listowel left to join the new force. A section of the north Carlow IRA also joined the Volunteers as did members in Longford. While this was not a mass phenomenon, the IRA was obviously put under pressure to show that it could not be tolerated where it did occur. The vast majority of violence against the Volunteers would take place in Kerry, where the IRA waged a vindictive campaign against the force during the winter of 1934-35. Outside Kerry, such incidents were more unusual although a Volunteer was shot and wounded in Clare and another had his home raided in Roscommon. In the longer run, this led to the jailing of substantial numbers of IRA men and their isolation from wider republican support.

The following examples were typical of the IRA's campaign in Kerry: In Tralee the IRA raided the home of a Volunteer and stole his uniform. After an IRA man was jailed because of the incident, the Volunteer was beaten up by armed and masked men. A dance hall used by Volunteers in Lixnaw was riddled with rifle and Thompson gun fire. The Ballymullen barracks in Tralee was bombed. Volunteers on recreation in Tralee were subjected to a mass physical attack involving almost all of the local IRA.

Former IRA members who joined the Volunteers were singled out for particularly harsh treatment. A man was tied to the railings of Toomevara church, Co. Tipperary, and had a sign reading 'Deserted from IRA to join Free State imperial militia' pinned to his coat. An ex-captain in the Tralee IRA who joined the Volunteers was badly beaten up by armed men.

By February 1935, 28 IRA members were in jail for attacks on Volunteers. Unlike the IRA's conflict with the Blueshirts, there was no popular basis for their violence against members of the Volunteers. Nor is there any evidence that Volunteers responded to these attacks with violence of their own. The IRA activities against the Volunteers, in the absence of any political strategy, appeared to be those of a bully who had been disobeyed. The extent to which the IRA leadership controlled their Kerry organization's behaviour is of course open to debate. The leadership had made it clear that they did not want attacks on Volunteers, and communications to Kerry units about discipline would seem to bear this out. However, the fact that the IRA did not disown any of its Kerry members for attacks on Volunteers would point to tacit acceptance of their activities at least. The strong influence of civil war bitterness in Kerry, recognized in contemporary garda reports, is possibly another factor in the violence being concentrated in that county. Possibly because the IRA came under more pressure from the government during 1935, the attacks on Volunteers came to an end.

The IRA's range of antagonists was informed by ideology but governed by practical considerations. From 1926 onwards, targets were chosen which were relatively unpopular and which were unlikely to respond aggressively. Where this was not the case, as with the gardaí, serious conflict was generally avoided. The IRA's two most serious campaigns of the post-1932 period, against the Blueshirts and the Volunteer Force, exposed the extent of regional and factional differences within the organization and in the case of the Volunteers contributed to its marginalization. The character and tempo of IRA violence were often governed by the reaction of local activists rather than centrally directed.

5/Allies and rivals

Outside of the IRA a number of other organizations formed the wider extra-parliamentary republican movement. The Sinn Féin party considered itself the authentic political voice of republicanism. Explicitly allied to the IRA was Cumann na mBan, the republican women's organization. From 1934 the IRA faced competition from a rival political organization, the Republican Congress, which was itself briefly allied to a military grouping, the Irish Citizen Army (ICA). There also existed a number of organizations claiming the title of the 'Old IRA'. This chapter assesses the IRA's relationship with these organizations.

In 1925 the IRA had withdrawn itself from the authority of the Second Dáil. From then on the IRA operated as a force independent of any political body, though the organization still contained officers who were members of either Sinn Féin or Fianna Fáil. The IRA attempted to organize a united republican effort for the June 1927 general election but its efforts foundered mainly due to Fianna Fáil's resistance. Sinn Féin then put forward 15 candidates including three IRA officers who then faced court martial for disobeying General Order 28, which forbid the organization's members standing for election. One candidate, Tom Maguire, withdrew, but the others, Dr John Madden and Seán O'Farrell, stood with Madden managing to hold his seat. Sinn Féin's electoral effort was completely overshadowed by that of Fianna Fáil. In the event, the party won just five seats and 41,400 votes, with Austin Stack and Oscar Traynor being its most prominent members elected. Leading figures such as Mary MacSwiney and Count Plunkett, lost their seats. Following the assassination of Kevin O'Higgins, an Electoral Amendment Act disqualified any candidate who refused to take the Oath of Allegiance if elected. Therefore, Sinn Féin did not contest the September election.

Thereafter, Sinn Féin drifted further and further from the IRA. Leading Sinn Féiners became increasingly critical of IRA policies and many IRA members dismissive of Sinn Féin, a trend that was already apparent at the time of the September elections. Then *An Phoblacht* criticized the party's abstentionist policy and stated that it believed 'not much can come out of Sinn Féin'. Sinn Féin's 1927 ard fheis saw another example of this tension. A number of delegates claimed that they had been secretly canvassed by Peadar O'Donnell and Donal O'Donoghue on behalf of the IRA to ensure the election of IRA supporters onto the Sinn Féin Standing Committee. A heated discussion followed with much 'dirty linen' being aired. Delegates then complained that the IRA had allowed the Police to capture too many arms from them in the past two years. This discussion apparently upset the IRA members, including Moss Twomey and Seán

MacBride, who were present, but had taken no part in the discussions. The detective who reported on the ard fheis described it as 'more or less farcical' and unlikely to increase Sinn Féin's standing in political circles.

The persistent campaigning of Mary MacSwiney, in particular, kept Sinn Féin's name in the pages of *An Phoblacht*, but she and her fellow Sinn Féin leaders, J.J. O'Kelly (Sceilg) and Brian O'Higgins, had little direct influence with the IRA. Indeed, MacSwiney would later claim that her attempts to raise the 'fundamental points at issue' failed because there was 'no free discussion in *An Phoblacht.*' Instead the organization began to rely on the monthly *Irish Freedom*, owned by Sinn Féin member Gobnait Ni Brúadair, to publicize its views.

Sinn Féin took no organized part in the campaigns against the Land Annuities or the IRA's anti-imperialist protests. The IRA continued to send observers to Sinn Féin Ard Fheisanna but the discussions there were dominated by statements of loyalty to the Second Dáil's shadow government and denunciations of those who had betrayed it. Sinn Féin's non-attendance at Anti-Imperialist events was explained by the fact that Fianna Fáil supporters were allowed attend. Republicans who wanted to play a more active role drifted away from the party. Women Workers Union leader Helena Molony argued that to stay loyal to SF's rules meant that 'one could not go through ordinary life' because 'one could not fight for the republic if one did not mix with people'. Maire Comerford, a member of the party's executive, was expelled from Sinn Féin because she voted in a Free State election. Not surprisingly, numbers attending the annual SF Ard Fheis declined from 100 in 1929 to 60 in 1931.

Sinn Féin even declined to attend the IRA's Bodenstown commemoration in June 1931 because of the participation of Fianna Fáil and other 'Free State' organizations. The Dublin Brigade of the IRA had earlier refused to have Brian O'Higgins as a speaker for their Easter Commemoration because they wanted a speech identifying the IRA with social revolution and they knew O'Higgins was 'personally opposed' to that idea.

Sinn Féin was not banned under the Public Safety Act of October 1931. Its Ard Fheis that month heard ritual denunciation of the 'Coercion Act' but this was tempered by the fact that the impression given by several Sinn Féin speakers was that the IRA had drawn trouble unto itself by flirting with 'communistic doctrines'. The gardaí also speculated that Sinn Féin resented being 'excluded from the list of proclaimed organizations'. Perhaps this was as they perceptively noted because Saor Éire was 'intended to replace Sinn Féin although the latter body will not admit the fact'.

Sinn Féin played no role in the elections of March 1932 having already signalled that republicans should take 'the hard road of abstention'. Twomey had spelt out his frustration with that policy to Count Plunkett earlier that year, arguing that if they wanted an end to coercion then 'what can those to whom they appeal do except vote them out? that is what it amounts to as far as ordinary citizens are concerned'.

Later that year, an IRA officer in Mayo complained that Tom Maguire of Sinn Féin refused to call on men to join the IRA when speaking at commemorations. When questioned as to why he replied that the IRA were 'not the same as they used to be' and that he himself disagreed with them. The exasperated officer informed HQ that Maguire's attitude showed the 'mentality of our Sinn Féiners in the west'.

Again, Sinn Féin stood aloof from the general election in 1933 and Twomey was aware that some in SF were of the opinion that the IRA had 'gone Fianna Fáil'. There were complaints from SF that IRA recruitment posters called on people to join the IRA and Cumann na mBan but not their party. O'Higgins claimed that the IRA 'ignored us (SF) completely' in arrangements for Easter Commemorations and that the IRA's explanation about this matter had only 'added insult to injury'. There was a further blow to Sinn Féin's influence when the Cumann na mBan decided to belatedly follow the IRA's example and withdraw recognition from the Second Dail. The Cumann na mBan executive justified its decision on the grounds that to 'ask young girls and women to render allegiance to a government which does not and cannot function is simply taxing their powers of credulity beyond reason'. This in turn provoked the departure of Sinn Féin supporters from Cumann na mBan leaving Sinn Féin even more isolated from militant republicanism. Sinn Féin also refused to support the IRA's election effort in Northern Ireland in late 1933 because the IRA were not in MacSwiney's view 'prepared to stand as Dail Eireann candidates and give allegiance to the government of the Republic'.

Following the split in the IRA during March 1934 a meeting was organized between the IRA, Sinn Féin and representatives of 'The Government of the Republic' to discuss possible co-operation but so little was agreed that one Sinn Féin delegate wrote afterwards that it was time they formed their own military force as the IRA were only interested in setting up its own dictatorship. Sinn Féin again attempted during 1935 to convince the IRA to recognize that 'the field of civil activity' belonged to it but once again the discussions failed to produce any concrete result. Again the IRA decided to launch a new political party in 1936, rather than revert to allowing Sinn Féin to play this role. Sinn Féin denounced the IRA's 1935 electoral intervention in the north and made it clear they would not support candidates who had not been 'selected upon purely republican principles'. Even MacSwiney found that statement 'superfluous and provocative', since she claimed that the party had no organization in the north by that stage. Further evidence of how little importance was placed on the organization by the authorities came in 1936 when after making a major effort to prevent the IRA's Bodenstown commemoration going ahead, the gardaí allowed Sinn Féin to hold theirs unhindered.

There is evidence that elements within Sinn Féin occasionally took a more pragmatic view than their leadership. Gardaí believed that the local Sinn Féin organization in Leitrim worked for Fianna Fáil in the July 1929 bye-election there. Despite the acrimonious relationship between the two bodies there were still Sinn Féin members active within the IRA. Both army council member J.J. Sheehy and Belfast commander Davy Matthews were members of the party in 1933. The politics of Sinn Féin certainly had an influence among the northern IRA. There was criticism of the decision to launch Saor Éire among the IRA in Monaghan, who favoured promoting Sinn Féin instead. At the 1933 general army convention there were motions, from Belfast, Armagh and Down, all calling on the IRA to restore relations with Sinn Féin as its 'political arm'. This did not prevent Matthews working as an IRA election organizer during the November Stormont election campaign, which his party was boycotting.

In ideological terms aside from its unshakeable belief in the legitimacy of the Second Dail, the most notable aspect of Sinn Féin's politics was its association of Catholicism with Irish republicanism. In 1929, the SF Standing Committee had addressed a remonstrance to Pope Pius XI in which they declared themselves 'faithful children of the one Holy Catholic Church'. Sinn Féin considered that 'Christian Social Justice' based on the encyclicals of Pope Leo XIII were the best alternative to 'pagan capitalism' and 'eastern materialism'. The IRA's adoption of radical social policies was condemned by O'Higgins as an attempt to link up 'stark, gross materialism' with Irish republicanism, which was 'clean, spiritual and unselfish'. MacSwiney interpreted the 1931 Public Safety Bill as an attempt by Cosgrave's 'Freemason Junta' to bring about a state of affairs where it would be impossible to hold the Eucharistic Congress. In J.J. O'Kelly's case he added a large dose of anti-Semitism to this ideological hotchpotch, believing that Britain was ruled by 'unscrupulous Jews'. Ironically the one dissident from this clericalist ethos was a priest, Fr Michael O'Flanagan. With his long record of activity he was a respected figure with all factions within the republican movement and he became the party's president in 1933. He had caused a sensation at the 1931 ard fhéis when he denounced the pope as an 'enemy of Ireland'. O'Higgins disassociated himself from this statement and refused to share a platform with O'Flanagan until he withdrew it. However, O'Flanagan declined to back down, and on most of the major issues of the day he consistently criticized clerical interference in politics. When O'Flanagan was given the task of editing county histories for use in schools by the Department of Education, this provoked another schism within Sinn Féin. J.J. O'Kelly argued that the project was of a valuable enough national character to excuse acceptance of government money. O'Higgins and MacSwiney disagreed and MacSwiney subsequently quit the party in protest. O'Flanagan was dismissed from the organization himself for the crime of taking part in a state radio re-enactment of the First Dáil in January 1936.

These developments were largely ignored by the IRA leadership. But Sinn Féin ideas did find important echoes inside the organization itself. There was substantial rank and file hostility to the IRA's radical political policies and while this did not necessarily denote sympathy with Sinn Féin, militarists often allied with proponents of 'Christian Social' policies in order to minimilize the influence of the left. After the departure of the socialists in 1934, support for the IRA began to contract, and governmental pressure on the organization increased. *An Phoblacht* was frequently suppressed and eventually banned. Sinn Féin's *Irish Freedom* and later O'Higgin's *Wolfe Tone Weekly* were generally left unmolested and as the only republican publications freely available were able to frame republicanism in their image, (O'Higgins *Wolfe Tone Annual* was very influential in later years). In the longer run, the purist Sinn Féin view came to dominate the public perception of republicanism, despite what many militants thought of its exponents. Ultimately, in 1938 the IRA leadership asked the seven remaining members of the Second Dáil to give it powers of government, although this was driven more by the desire to give the Russell leadership political clothing than by respect for their authority.

Unlike Sinn Féin, Cumann na mBan was quite explicitly linked to the IRA in this period. The organization was pledged to organize and train the women of Ireland to take part in the 'military, political and economic movements towards the enthronement of the Irish Republic'. A major element in this was to assist the IRA in whatever way possible. Despite the perception of Cumann na mBan as an auxiliary of the IRA its leadership were not afraid to undertake activity on their own initiative, or to argue against IRA policies. Indeed on several occasions they clashed with the leadership of the larger organization. At the first Cumann na mBan convention since the conclusion of the civil war, the organization claimed just 648 members organized in 54 branches.

Table 12. Regional distribution of Cumann na mBan branches 1925

Munster	11	Leinster	27	Britain	4
Ulster	4	Connaught	6		

The organization's president, the Countess Markievicz, withdrew at this convention, and joined Fianna Fáil when it was founded the following year. The organization experienced decline during 1926, and its convention that year was its smallest since 1914. Emigration had hit it badly in Kerry, Cork and Connemara, and the split with Fianna Fáil had seen 30 members leave in Dublin. There were now just 70 members in that city and 31 branches nationwide. The organization elected a new president, Eithne Coyle, with Mary MacSwiney as vice-president. Coyle would remain president of the organization until 1940, while Sighle Humphreys, as director of publicity, would be the main driving force behind it in Dublin for the next decade. Cumann na mBan would remain largely southern based with only a handful of branches in Northern Ireland, although Belfast member Mary Donnelly was prominent at *An Phoblacht*. In the years following 1926, the Cumann na mBan only really existed as an active organization in Dublin, where in early 1928 it claimed just 50 members. In 1929 Humphreys suggested that if there were not major changes in the organization's activities it would collapse within 12 months. Cumann na mBan did step up its activities but these were still the work of a handful of activists, with the gardaí estimating about 50 women active in the Dublin area during 1931. Unlike Sinn Féin, the organization was banned in October 1931, and Humphreys jailed along with two colleagues by the military tribunal.

The organization's next convention was held in very different political circumstances in June 1933. The more relaxed atmosphere following the coming to power of Fianna Fáil meant that Cumann na mBan was able to organize openly and parade in uniform. There were now 32 branches of the organization, and five of the newly formed republican girl scouts, Cumann na gCailíní. The departure of Mary MacSwiney and a small group of supporters, who subsequently formed Mná na Poblachta, had little effect on the organization's strength. In fact, the winter of 1933 and spring of 1934 saw a major attempt at expansion by the Cumann na mBan as it appointed a full-time recruitment organizer, May Lavery. Lavery toured country towns in the west and south meeting IRA officers and being introduced to interested local women. Her activities were not especially clandestine as she often wore Cumann na mBan uniform as she cycled from town to town, but her progress was dutifully recorded by the gardaí. The expansion of Cumann na mBan to 74 branches, including many in small towns, was attributed by Coyle to Lavery's work. The gCailíní also grew to 27 branches. At Bodenstown in 1934 an estimated 1,500 women and girls marched in uniform. Despite many innovative activities organized by the Cumann na mBan leadership for its rank and file, the general political situation could not fail to affect the organization. While 1932 to 1934 was a period of 'comparative peace', the next two years saw republicans under increased pressure. By its 1936 convention Cumann na mBan was again in decline, with only 27 branches registered. Coyle blamed the introduction of pensions by the Fianna Fáil government which led to 'demoralisation ... in the face of such odds and many members grew disheartened'. She also believed that many who joined in the 1933–4 period did not understand the organization's politics and were attracted by the image of an organization 'for hey-days and holidays, for showing off a uniform'. How many women those 27 branches represented is difficult to assess, but 597 entered the organization's examination in June 1936 and we can presume that it was the most active members who would be interested in this. Of those who added a prefix to their surname, 195 were single and 25 married women. Garda reports point to its being mostly young women who Lavery addressed on her travels, and in Templemore at least all those who joined were of 'the domestic servant type'. While the organization was not banned along with the IRA in 1936, its activities contracted sharply.

The most successful activity initiated by the Cumann na mBan was the sale of Easter lilies to mark the memory of Irish republican dead. This was suggested in March 1926 by Sighle Humphreys and Fiona Plunkett, and the lily was chosen because 'we consider this would be the most suitable for Easter, and it has also the republican colours'. Within a few years the Easter lily had become the main republican emblem. As well as honouring republican dead the Cumann na mBan also believed that the spread of the Lily could eventually 'rival in magnitude the British Imperialist Poppy Day'. Sale of the lily took several years to fully attain popularity, and some IRA units were slow to take up the practice. During 1930, a Cork IRA officer claimed that as it was only 'the gentler sex' who could sell lilies his area would be able to do little at Easter. In contrast, at the same time northern IRA units were ordering 8,000 lilies and west Limerick 5,000. Since open sale of lilies was not possible in the north and difficult in the south, these are impressive figures. After Fianna Fáil came to power in 1932, the sale of lilies became easier in the Free State. By 1934 the Cumann na mBan were satisfied that the 'object for which the Easter Lily was initiated' had been realized as sales of half a million lilies had made them 'the emblem of commemoration for Ireland's dead'. Monies from the sales of lilies were divided equally between Cumann na mBan and the IRA, as outside Dublin it was the IRA who sold most of them.

It was not for the sale of lilies however, that Cumann na mBan was described by W.T. Cosgrave as 'women who give moral, financial and active support to the (IRA), whose activities include propaganda in favour of violence ... the terrorisation of jurors and citizens and interference with the administration of justice'. From 1926 the organization had decided that efforts should be made to create hostility to 'all visible connections with England, viz.: Governor Generals, Free State Ministers, Free State Army Officials (and) Police'.

Cumann na mBan therefore took an enthusiastic part in the anti-Poppy Day demonstrations in Dublin, and in campaigns against British products. Sometimes these campaigns took on a rather surreal quality, like the attempts to prevent British sweets being sold in Ireland, where shopkeepers were urged to ask customers who wished to purchase an English-made chocolate 'if for the sake of a sweet they are willing to starve 3,200 of their fellow country men'. After 1927 Cumann na mBan were involved in attempts to intimidate jurors in trials involving the IRA. Leaflets signed 'Ghosts' were posted or hand-delivered to homes of jurors, creating an atmosphere of fear especially when the IRA escalated the campaign to shooting jurors. Some 'Ghosts' ranged from appeals to jurors to 'show your appreciation' of the principles of 'one of Ireland's noblest patriot soldiers' by demanding the defendant be set free. Others took a more threatening tone by listing the names and addresses of jurors who had 'helped the infamous "Judge" Sullivan to send the Irish Patriot Con Healy to penal servitude' and announcing that 'these men are traitors ... Death would be their fate in any free country of the world.'

The 'Ghosts' campaign was a Cumann na mBan initiative. Initially, the IRA reacted with hostility to the circulation of letters to jurors and demanded Cumann na mBan cease this practice. The IRA's adjutant general informed the Cumann na mBan leadership that in the cases of IRA prisoners, 'it is we who are responsible for deciding the action to be taken regarding their cases'. What was more, Cumann na mBan's 'futile threats' were considered 'detrimental' to the interests of the prisoners, and the IRA resented their action. In future, he stressed, Cumann na mBan were not to involve themselves in matters in which IRA members were involved. Cumann na mBan replied that they as an organization had not issued the circular, but they agreed with its contents. More importantly, they stated that they were an independent body who were not 'dependent on the goodwill, or approval of any other organization' in actions they undertook in defence of republicanism. Sighle Humpheys subsequently contacted Moss Twomey, admitting that she and some others had drawn up the circular, but she also criticized the A/G's 'impertinent' letter and asked to be informed in future when IRA members would be seeking legal assistance to prove 'what good little boys' they were. Twomey rather dismissively replied that he would not comment on Humphrey's letter as it seemed to have been written from 'irritation.'

The IRA obviously changed its position during 1928, as the 'Ghosts' became a regular feature of republican trials. The campaign caused real problems for the government, leading them to introduce a Juries Protection Act in 1929. At one stage the gardaí were convinced Frank Ryan was the author of 'Ghosts' but a raid on the home of Humphreys in August 1929 produced evidence that she was responsible for at least some of the leaflets. More importantly, a document was discovered in which Humphreys argued that rather than Cumann na mBan cease to exist, it should devote its energies to the disruption of the business of 'enemy administration' particularly in the legal sphere. 'Ghosts' continued to circulate right up to winter 1931. After the release of prisoners by the new government in 1932, the practice ceased for a period. However, as increasing numbers of IRA members found themselves before the courts in 1933, Cumann na mBan made an attempt to return to the propaganda of the 'Ghosts' era. In December 1933 the gardaí discovered that jurors in a Dublin trial had received copies of an appeal from Cumann na mBan through the post. The defendants had been acquitted before gardaí were aware of the circular. A garda noted that it was the 'first case of this nature' in several years. Humphreys had been spotted in the court on the day of the trial. However, with the reintroduction of trial by military tribunal these tactics became of limited usefulness. Agitation on prisoners would continue to be a major part of Cumann na mBan's work. Local branches were instructed to paint 'every dead wall' in their locality with slogans attacking Fianna Fáil. Ceilidh, concerts and plays were organized to raise funds to support the prisoner's dependants.

A great deal of the Cumann na mBan's appeal after 1932 was not in these activities but in its public appearance. Unlike the IRA, Cumann na mBan paraded in full uniform at Easter commemorations and at Bodenstown. Their uniform consisted of 'grey green skirt, grey green military pattern tunic coat, brown beret, brown shoes and stockings'. Officers wore a Sam Browne belt and all ranks wore gloves on parade. Appearance in uniform was the pride and joy of the organization and, like the IRA, a great deal of emphasis was put on drilling and perfecting a military appearance. A strict set of guidelines was laid down as to members behaviour while in uniform with no smoking or talking allowed and the wearing of furs, flowers, and carrying of handbags forbidden. Members without uniforms were instructed to wear white blouse, green tie and dark clothes. The Cumann na mBan badge was worn on the beret. Other regular activities included the organization of entertainment after republican events particularly the major ceilidhte organized in Dublin's Mansion House after Bodenstown Sunday. Also present in uniform at republican gatherings from 1932 onwards were members of the Cumann na gCailíní. This organization was open to girls between 8 and 16 years of age and were obviously less political and confrontational than the Cumann na mBan. The Cailíní were encouraged to learn 'Irish, Irish singing and Irish dancing and the teaching of Irish history through ballads'.

There were attempts by Cumann na mBan members to militarize their organization. At the 1926 convention it was suggested that members be trained 'in the use of firearms and other weapons of war'. One delegate backed this proposal by arguing that 'in other countries women used firearms particularly in Russia and it would be a very good thing to be able to use them even if the occasion never arose'. She felt that being relagated to carrying arms for the IRA was degrading. There were objections to this from other delegates, who did not wish to use guns. Eventually, a compromise was reached whereby members who wanted to could train with firearms. The monthly report to Cumann na mBan branches asked if members wished to be trained in the 'care and use of arms'. How often this offer was taken up is difficult to assess. There are no reports of republican women using firearms in this period.

The Cumann na mBan also placed a great deal of importance in the politi-

cal education of its members especially from 1933 onwards. A educational programme involving lectures and readings of the works of Connolly, Fintan Lalor
and Pearse was drawn up. Eventually, an examination was devised to test members' knowledge of republicanism and prepare them for questions or criticism.
Humphreys complained that many older members had adopted an attitude of
'indifference if not discourtesy' to the exam but stressed the enthusiasm of the
younger women made up for this. Cumann na mBan members were instructed
to read Connolly's *Labour in Irish history* and *The re-conquest of Ireland*, and to be
able to explain how a 'Worker's Republic would differ from a Capitalist
Republic'. Nothing similar existed for education within the IRA. In part, this
was because the IRA was seen primarily as a military force, but also points to the
leadership of Cumann na mBan's adherence to left-wing republicanism.
Cumann na mBan held a flag day in support of the striking outdoor relief workers in Belfast during October 1932. Members were encouraged to join trade
unions and there were plans to organize boycotts of employers who paid low
wages. Local groups were instructed to compile information about the conditions for women working in factories and shops. The dangers that the rise of fascism in Europe posed for women were particularly emphasized by Eithne Coyle
at the 1934 convention. In 1933, the organization committed itself to the 'social
policy of James Connolly'. One member hoped that this meant that 'The days
of drilling and first aid in the ranks of Cumann na mBan are over and done
with;' though, it should be noted that only 37 women attended the 1933 convention, and that the Cumann na mBan leadership was a great deal more politically sophisticated than their rank and file. This was alluded to by Mary
MacSwiney in her letter of resignation, when she noted how she, a member
since 1914, had been outvoted by 'youngsters of two months standing' who she
claimed knew 'nothing' about the issues before the convention. The organization too placed a much greater emphasis on the Irish language than did the IRA.
Every member was 'bound' to learn Irish and branches were questioned monthly on how many members were taking Irish classes and how many had earned
the Fainne. During September 1933, representatives of the Cumann na mBan
met members of the IRA leadership to formulate a common social policy. This
process was halted by the divisions within the IRA which led to the split at their
1934 convention.

The split in the IRA produced the most serious dispute between the two
organizations. The call by ex-IRA members for a Republican Congress was
endorsed by Coyle and Humphreys During late April the Cumann na mBan
executive met firstly representatives of the IRA army council and then with the
resigned officers. The IRA's report of their discussion further alienated Sighle
Humphreys who felt that her opinions were misrepresented by MacBride
among others. The IRA attempted to prevent defections to Congress by inform-

ing a number of Cumann na mBan branches that participation in Congress was prohibited. The Cumann na mBan leadership argued that they were 'an independent organization with a constitution of its own' and there was nothing to prevent their members from working for the Congress if they wished to. Members were reminded that they were only answerable to the Cumann na mBan Executive. Coyle and Humphreys continued to be associated with the Republican Congress until July 1934 when they resigned from its organizing bureau.

In their letter of resignation they argued that instead of building a movement to end capitalism in Ireland the Congress was dominated by people who wished to wreck the IRA. They claimed that Frank Ryan had stated that his aim was to destroy *An Phoblacht* within six months. George Gilmore allegedly wanted to atone for the 'folly and his dishonesty' of his IRA membership by damaging the organization. Coyle and Humphreys felt that the IRA was still the vehicle that would 'eventually overthrow capitalism'. They also argued that Congress was abandoning Connolly's ideals for a 'foreign pagan and materialist philosophy'. This was a strange argument from two of the most prominent left-wing figures within the republican movement. There must have been intense personal pressure on Coyle and Humphreys after they linked up with Congress: they were after all close personal friends with leaders on both sides. However, their only significant political argument with Congress was a perceptive one. They asked if one of Congress main criticisms of the IRA was that it concentrated too much energy on military affairs, why had Congress spend so much time attempting to form its own armed force with elements from the Irish Citizens Army? Did this not prove the 'inability' of Congress to 'hold men together' by other than military means? Furthermore, if the IRA were untrustworthy, what then were the ICA who had not identified with republicanism for 14 years and had allegedly taken part in Free State commemorations?

Following their departure, Coyle and Humphreys were subject to a stinging attack by Peadar O'Donnell. He insinuated that Cumann na mBan existed to 'ginger up' the IRA and push it towards 'headless' activities. Cumann na mBan continued to be relatively open to discussion on these subjects however, and at their 1934 convention, it was admitted that there was still a 'diversity of opinion' on the Congress within its ranks. However opinion among the rank and file would seem to have been heavily pro-IRA and this no doubt also affected Coyle and Humphrey's decision. Cora Hughes, the former commander of UCD Cumann na mBan, and Bobbie Walsh of its Waterford branch remained with Congress.

The Cumann na mBan went through two distinct phases in this period. From 1926 to 1932 it was a small tightly knit relatively clandestine group which pursued various means of disrupting the administration of the Free State and issued propaganda vilifying it. After 1932, it expanded in strength and became in many ways the colourful face of republicanism with its uniformed members visible at demonstrations, collecting money on flag days or selling Easter lilies. Its leadership were highly politicized and eager to maintain an independence from the IRA. Nevertheless, its fortunes were largely dependent on those of the IRA which remained the dominant republican organization.

The role of women in the broader republican movement was not confined to Cumann na mBan. There were several other women prominent in republican circles in that period. Helena Molony was a regular contributor to *An Phoblacht* and a speaker at IRA events. The writer Rosamond Jacob contributed to both *An Phoblacht* and the *Republican Congress* newspaper. Hannah Sheehy Skeffington, whom Twomey considered a 'fine writer', was deputy editor of *An Phoblacht* until March 1933, and a regular speaker at rallies and demonstrations. She was arrested at a banned meeting and spent two months in Armagh jail in early 1933. Former Sinn Féin Executive member Maire Comerford was also active on the republican fringe during this period. Maud Gonne MacBride was involved in almost every republican initiative of that era (she was a member of five of the organizations banned in 1931) but she concentrated on mobilizing support for IRA prisoners. During the civil war Maud Gonne and Charlotte Despard had formed the Women's Prisoners Defence League which held weekly meetings to highlight the cases of IRA prisoners. The group was tiny with perhaps 20 members at most. After being banned during the coercion period, it changed its name to the People's Rights' Association and continued holding protest meetings. The League briefly disbanded in April 1932, but later that year they were revived. During 1934 weekly meetings were held in Cathal Brugha Street. The Sunday morning crowds, usually numbering between 200 to 500, heard furious denunciations of the government, but the gardaí reported no trouble arising from them. Maud Gonne spoke every Sunday and was usually accompanied by Helena Molony and 'John Brennan' (Sidney Gifford). Rarely were issues other than prisoners' welfare mentioned and as the IRA only occasionally had a presence at the meetings they were allowed proceed by the gardaí. The WPDL published a magazine, *Prison Bars*, for a period in the late 1930s, following the ban on *An Phoblacht*. One writer has argued that the relatively high profile given to reports on women's issues by *An Phoblacht* reflected the 'major role' women contributors played at the paper.

The split at the IRA's March 1934 General Army convention was its first major cleavage since the formation of Fianna Fáil and cost the IRA a number of leading officers. The most senior figure to align himself with the call for a Congress was Michael Price, the IRA's director of training. The IRA leadership complained bitterly after Price's departure that he had given no indication that he was dissatisfied with the organization's political development. Indeed, it was the case that Price had publicly argued against the leftward shift in the IRA during 1930. Ironically, in the light of later events it was Price who ordered the confiscation of communist literature at Bodenstown in 1933. Despite his walking out of the convention, Price still received 46 votes for the IRA executive, the seventh highest vote, and enough to elect him had he decided to remain. Peadar O'Donnell was probably the best known left-wing figure in the IRA. He was less prominent in 1934 than he had been during the late 1920s and early 1930s, and claimed that following the 1933 GAC his articles for *An Phoblacht* been censored by the army council. At the 1934 convention he argued the left within the IRA had been 'handcuffed' by restrictions on the right of IRA members to air political views without army council permission. He was still an army council member as well as being nationally known. George Gilmore had been unhappy with IRA policy for some time and had tried to resign from the army council in September 1932. He was already of the opinion during 1933 that there was 'little hope' for the IRA unless it embraced more openly socialist policies, but like Price he had a record of militancy which meant he was admired by all sections of the IRA. Unlike O'Donnell, he was suspicous and critical of, the Irish communists. Gilmore was again elected to the IRA executive at the March 1934 GAC and had to return and inform the convention that he was actually leaving the IRA! Frank Ryan had been increasingly dissatisfied with the IRA, resigning from editorship of *An Phoblacht* in 1933 and refusing to stand for the IRA executive at the GAC that year. He had been engaged in a bitter row with the IRA over *An Phoblacht* and his alleged presence at a communist meeting in early 1933. However, he was one of the IRA's best known street agitators and was immensely popular with its rank and file. All of the four disputed the IRA's claim that they had engaged in a conspiracy to disrupt the 'Army'. O'Donnell claimed that he did not know Price was going to present his resolution to the GAC; though Price had met Gilmore a week before the convention and he may have used this opportunity to discuss his plan.

The departure of the four officers and their call for a meeting of republicans to discuss the idea of a Republican Congress had obvious implications for the IRA. After a meeting in Athlone in early April an organizing committee was set up to co-ordinate the Congress. As well as the two most important figures in Cumann na mBan the committee also included 10 other IRA officers. These included the commanders of battalions in Offaly, North and South Westmeath, Galway, Mayo and junior officers from Leitrim, Galway and Mayo. Also siding with Congress were Brian Kelly the O/C of Dublin South, Harry Gilmore, that Battalion's former O/C, and Charles Gilmore, its quartermaster. Ascertaining how many of the IRA's rank and file sided with these officers is extremely difficult and figures given in other accounts are an overestimation.

Of particular concern to the IRA, however, was that the Congress contained members who had information about IRA weapons. Indeed, the Congress itself attempted to organize its own 'army.' Ex IRA members were instructed to hold onto their weapons (and funds) as 'arms would be neccessary' for the new organization. O'Donnell claimed that the body required would be a 'defence force' for use during strikes rather than a new IRA. During the summer of 1934 negotiations began between the Congress leadership and the tiny Irish Citizens Army about the fusion of Congress' 'armed groups' with the ICA. The ICA had been kept alive in Dublin by a small group of veterans led by Seamus MacGowan, Dick McCormick and Frank Purcell. Apparently in response to the warnings of Labour Party leader William Norton about the threat of fascism, the ICA had decided to re-organize. They approached Congress to suggest co-operation and Gilmore, Price, O'Donnell and Nora Connolly O'Brien were co-opted onto the ICA army council. Another reason why the ICA may have been needed was that Congress were subject to accusations that they would in time become just another political party and the appearance of an armed wing might appeal to IRA members who were wary of politics. Indeed, Ryan suggested as much when he argued that 'now ... that the existence of the Irish Citizen Army is more generally known, Volunteers are not so much afraid that they will cease to be fighters if they participate in Congress'.

The IRA took steps to prevent the formation of a rival armed body when they kidnapped the former quartermaster of their Dundalk unit and questioned him about the whereabouts of weapons he controlled in October 1934. Whether or not the Congress armed groups engaged in much activity is hard to verify. They were probably responsible for armed raids on De Selby quarry during a strike in June 1934. One veteran claimed that, after a period, Congress realized militarism was counter-productive and handed their guns back to the IRA. There seems to have been elements within Congress who did favour using arms, with one Achill Congress supporter telling a meeting that 'they had the guns and ... would use them too'. However, O'Donnell had suggested at an early stage that if the IRA demanded the return of arms, Congress members were not to resist them. Congress members could also find themselves in embroiled in local feuds like those which plagued the IRA. Three Kerry members were arrested for beating up the chairman of the ITGWU in Tralee after he refused to allow the union's band to welcome Nora Connolly O'Brien to the town.

The IRA also took early steps to neutralize the organizational threat of Congress. Within a week of the Congress appeal, the IRA's Galway O/C Charles Reynolds and Adjutant Séamus de Búrca had re-sworn allegiance to the IRA and pledged to resist 'any attempts by you others, (Congress) to seduce volunteers from their allegiance'. Price and O'Donnell were court-martialled (in absentia) and dismissed with ignominy from the IRA. J.J. Hoey remained in the IRA despite his signing the Congress appeal, as did Walter Mitchell of Offaly, who had attended the Athlone meeting. Officers such as Seán McCool and Donal O'Donoghue, who were regarded as being the left of the organization remained within its ranks. One IRA officer later claimed that in the struggle with Congress, the IRA's 'company units lost heavily'. The Department of Justice suggested too, that the IRA lost a substantial number of members to Congress. However, the IRA's Bodenstown commemoration three months after the split drew an estimated 17,000 participants, the largest to that date, which does not point to the IRA having lost many members. An estimate of number of IRA members in Northern Ireland who were attracted to Congress puts their numbers at less than 70. Nevertheless, even when units remained loyal to the IRA such as in Kenmare, Co. Kerry, where officers had destroyed letters from Congress, the split 'had a very bad effect on Volunteers'. Congress would seem to have done moderately well in the first few months of its existence but it was never in a position to challenge the IRA. At the June 1934 local elections it did succeed in getting two candidates elected to county councils in Westmeath and Dundalk.

Any republican schism would lead to some degree of bitterness, and this was the case particularly between Seán MacBride and George Gilmore, although both sides seem to have respected Twomey and Ryan. Donal O'Donoghue was jailed along with Price during April 1935, and claimed to have done 'his best' to help out his former comrade, though he noted that many in the IRA regarded Price as someone who had done 'his best to smash the army'.

There was also some violent confrontation between the two groups most notably at successive Bodenstown commemorations in 1934 and 1935. The 1934 clashes are an established part of left wing republican folklore. The Congress contingent, including a number of Protestant socialists from Belfast, were attacked on the orders of the IRA leadership and their banners destroyed. The IRA claimed to have made it clear that no unauthorized banners would be allowed into the cemetery, an instruction that was obeyed by the Communist Party, who were not involved in the fracas. Accounts differ as to whether the Congress retreated and held an alternative rally or battled through to Tone's grave. The size of the Congress contingent and the numbers of northern Protestants accompanying them are imprecise. The gardaí estimated that the Congress contingent numbered about 600, while one participant claimed Congress had 2,000 supporters present. A contemporary estimate of the east Belfast marchers was just 36. A number of things are notable about the affair. Congress persistently claimed that the IRA members ordered to seize their banners showed no enthusiasm for the task. This would seem to indicate that Congress wanted to retain some contact with the IRA rank and file. It could also mean of course that they wished to deny that IRA members might be hostile to them. It was never alleged that religious sectarianism played a role in the attack.

Finally, Gilmore was allegedly pleased that the fight occurred because of the publicity it gained Congress, and presumably the embarrassment it would cause the IRA. Strangely, Eithne Coyle, still at this stage associated with Congress presented medals to Cumann na mBan members from the official platform and Cora Hughes, also of Congress, was one of the recipients.

These clashes were repeated on a much smaller scale in 1935. Again, there was a struggle over banners, which seems to have been more violent than in the previous year and again Congress claimed that many IRA men would not join the attack. The Congress contingent numbered only 42, the organization having split itself in September of 1934. There is some evidence of increased bitterness in that Gilmore felt that if the IRA leaders had shown themselves during the fight it would have been his 'pleasure to hurt them'. Congress contacted the IRA about participation in the 1936 Bodenstown commemoration with a view to avoiding clashes. They again stressed that they felt previous attacks had been a 'half-hearted affair', but had been 'humiliating' for the republican movement generally. Their request was superfluous, as the commemoration was banned and only a token ceremony took place. Aside from a complaint by Sighle Humphreys about a minor incident in Castlecomer and claims of a kidnapping in Belfast, the Congress-IRA relationship was largely a peaceful if uneasy one.

There were several violent attacks on Congress members during 1936, beginning with assaults on left wing contingents at the Easter Commemoration in Dublin, and culminating with the sacking of the Congress premises after an abortive rally in College Green. There has been speculation that the IRA participated in these assaults. This is unlikely, though, as Gilmore claimed that 'known Blueshirts' were among those instigating attacks on the left at the Easter procession. *An Phoblacht* also strongly condemned the incidents. Incidentally, these attacks almost led to the establishment of another armed force. A meeting of Congress and Communist Party activists, many of whom had IRA backgrounds, set up a 'defence corps' to be led by Gilmore; but, despite opposition from some at the meeting it was decided that it would be unarmed.

There was occasional co-operation between the IRA and Congress. The Department of Justice speculated on widespread fraternization during attacks on Blueshirts and support for industrial disputes, such as the 1934 bacon shops strike. Much of this united activity was probably of the opportunistic type rather than directed by the respective leaderships. However, *An Phoblacht* did occasionally report Congress activities and also listed Congress (and ICA) members in jail as 'anti imperialist prisoners'. That decision was taken at IRA leadership level with the proviso that non-IRA members' credentials were vouched for by the IRA in their locality. In late 1934 Congress and IRA speakers shared the same public platform for the first time since the split, at an unemployed workers' protest in Dublin. The IRA also held a rally, at which Twomey spoke, to support Congress member Frank Edwards who had been sacked from his teaching post at a Waterford Christian Brothers school because of his political views. This lack of hostility may be partially explained by the fact that after the Congress itself split in September 1934 there was little threat of it becoming an alternative to the IRA. Instead, Congress began to co-operate more closely with the Communist Party, and remained a small if active fringe group.

The Irish Citizens' Army having been given a new lease of life by the advent of Congress then played a role in Congress' own rupture. The ICA delegates at the Rathmines conference supported Price's and Roddy Connolly's call for Congress to become an openly socialist political party, agitating for a 'Worker's Republic.' O'Donnell and Gilmore, supported by the communists present, argued that Congress instead attempt to build a united front of republican forces. When this view narrowly prevailed, Price and his supporters left the Congress. They then concentrated their efforts on organizing the ICA. The core group of veterans who had maintained the ICA allied themselves with Price. However, by this stage the ICA had suffered a split of its own. The organization had initially been maintained, according to its veteran leadership, for the 'day when the militant members of the Irish Working Class would realize their need' for a body like the ICA. The organization of the Republican Congress had been seen as that day. After the Congress split, the ICA dismissed Peader O'Donnell and Gilmore from its leadership. It accused them of attempting to disrupt the ICA by 'unscrupulous, dishonest and disloyal' tactics. O'Donnell in particular was singled out as someone who was 'notorious for his disruptive and destructive activities in all organizations to which he belonged'.

Roddy Connolly was also accused of support for the 'ex-IRA' faction, and,. to confuse matters further, he refused to be dismissed and instead continued to claim to have the support of the ICA! He had been involved as early as 1929 in efforts to form an armed 'Workers Defence Corps' as he believed that the IRA 'should not have the monopoly on armed force in Ireland'. In an appeal to his supporters, he claimed that Price was supported only by units which 'sprung to light' by the 'touch of Mick's magic wand'. By January 1935 there were two ICAs, one led by Michael Price and Nora Connolly O'Brien and the other by her brother Roddy. This situation was the subject of some derision in the pages of the *Republican Congress* and the Communist *Irish Worker's Voice*. Roddy Connolly's ICA continued to have a loose association with the Republican Congress. Its importance was dismissed by Price who claimed it only had about 60 members and that its claim to be the real ICA should simply be ignored by his followers.

The ICA's structure was similar in many respects to that of the IRA. Units were drilled and trained in the use of small arms, the Lee Enfield rifle and in handling explosives. In Dublin, the ICA drilled in the Connolly Mallin Hall in Parnell Street, or in Commons Street on the docks. Unlike the IRA, however, the ICA allowed women to become members, and Nora Connolly O'Brien served on its army council as director of finance. It also encouraged its members to recognize the courts if brought before them so as not to give an easy victory to the 'enemy'. The adjutant of the Kilkenny ICA was a member of the National Army Reserve and was encouraged by his superiors to report for training to the Curragh, use the experience to broaden his military knowledge and also to distribute ICA material to any potential sympathizers. Members were also allowed to claim military service pensions from the Free State. Its membership were also encouraged to remain on friendly terms with their local IRA units and co-operate with them if possible. There seems to have been a degree of co-operation in Belfast. In Kilkenny, members were urged to assist IRA disruption of a visit by Eoin O'Duffy in November 1934. Unlike the Congress, the ICA forbade members of the Communist Party from joining because it considered that they were 'rigidly controlled and directed' by the British CP and Russia. The Price faction had almost 300 members in early 1935, with the two largest units in Dublin and Belfast.

Table 13. ICA membership, January 1935

Dublin 105	Cork 40	Kildare 7	Limerick 25	Kilkenny 7
Belfast 59	Westmeath 25	Carlow 6	Ballymore Eustace 10	Glasgow 25

There was no thaw in the relationship between the ICA and Congress. In May 1935 Price claimed that Congress had ceased to exist except for its paper 'which nobody reads'. By June that year he was urging his followers north and south to join their respective Labour parties. The intention was to bring about a merger of the Irish and Northern Irish Labour parties, and force them to take an active role in strikes and unemployment agitation. By November, Price still chief of staff of the ICA, was calling on his followers to push for Labour to declare its commitment to a workers' Republic. Indeed Price would later become a member of the Labour Party administrative council and, joined ironically by both Nora and Roddy Connolly, managed to convince the 1936 Labour conference to adopt the 'Workers' Republic' as an objective. Price later became secretary of the Dublin Labour constituencies' council and the ICA seems to have disappeared with his immersion into Labour politics. It never seriously posed a threat to the IRA's 'monopoly on armed force'.

Throughout this period there existed in the Free State a number of organizations claiming the title of 'Old IRA'. As early as 1926 the IRA was keeping an eye on the 'Old IRA Mans Association' which it saw as a front for those involved in the National Army mutiny of 1924. Indeed in 1924, the IRA had been

approached by elements among the army mutineers but was wary of involvement with them. In 1927, the IRA was warning its members against participation in these associations. While claiming to be interested in the welfare of veterans the IRA considered that these organizations were in fact attempting to
exploit 'good Volunteers' for political motives. Members were advised to keep
away from them. In 1928, a number of veterans of the revolutionary period
formed Clann na nGaedheal, the 'pre-Truce IRA.' Its aim was to foster unity
between men who had fought on both sides of the civil war as well as those who
had remained neutral. Among the founders were Liam Tobin who had fought
on the pro-Treaty side and Leo Henderson, an anti-Treatyite. Also involved
was Dr Patrick McCartan, formerly of Clann Eireann. At this stage it clearly
represented many of those who had been pro-Treaty but felt betrayed by the
perceived abandonment of republicanism by the Free State. Tobin had been a
central figure in the 'IRA organization' within the National Army involved in
the army mutiny of March 1924. The IRA was naturally suspicious of these
developments. The O/C of Cork was warned in the autumn of 1930 to be wary
of the activities of 'Tobin and co'. Allegedly, a number of Cork republicans
including Tom Barry and Florrie O'Donoghue were involved in some alliance
with the 'Old IRA' and were claiming to have access to arms. O'Donoghue and
his allies were 'more dangerous than the enemy' according to Jim Killeen.

At Easter 1931 the Clann held its own commemorations where it stated that
it was in favour of 'complete independence under a Republican form of
Government' but criticized the adoption of 'foreign doctrines' by the IRA. It
also claimed to have more '1916 men' in its ranks then any other organization
in Dublin, and pointed out that membership was only open to men who had
served in the IRA prior to the truce of 1921. Twomey replied on behalf of the
IRA charging that the Clann had forgotten the lessons of the 1918–21 period,
when the independence movement lost because it lacked a clear political and
economic strategy. He also made it clear that any republican organization that
was serious about making progress would have to gain support from those too
young to have been involved in the pre-Truce era.

The Clann was not the only veterans organization in existence during the
1930s. Twomey told Mary MacSwiney in 1933 that the government wanted to
use the 'Old IRA' associations to undermine the IRA and then form the nucleus for a 'National Guard'. The involvement of former Sinn Féin TD and IRA
officer Dr J.A. Madden in a meeting with several Fianna Fáil TDs under the
auspices of a 'Mayo Old IRA' greatly worried Twomey. He argued that these
'freakish combinations of Republicans-Free Staters' had hurt the IRA in the
past. The IRA leadership continued to worry about the machinations of the
'Crofts-Donoghue-Deasy clique'. The IRA's paranoia reached fever pitch during late 1932 when movements for land redistribution in Tipperary and

Limerick were adjudged to be efforts on behalf of Fianna Fáil to create 'Old IRA' bodies. The Clann on the other hand was eager to promote some form of joint activity with the IRA. Their position was that all nationalist organizations should unite at one event and end rivalry over 'sectional' commemorations. As a result of this they began to attend IRA commemorations such as Bodenstown. In some areas, co-operation was closer as in Leitrim where the IRA and the 'pre-Truce' body held joint election rallies. The Clann also held their own events such as a rally in Roscommon in December 1933 where over 140 men heard Frank Thornton and Simon Donnelly appeal for unity among veterans and for support for any government making strides towards the Republic. But on other occasions such as in Crossbarry, Co. Cork, at Easter 1934, the 'Old IRA' association led by Tom Crofts, Liam Deasy and Florrie O'Donoghue refused to join in an IRA procession because of IRA hostility to the Volunteer Reserve.

In other parts of the country, separate IRA (Old Comrades) associations were established whose main activity was agitating for compensation for veterans of the war of independence and for grants of land by the Land Commission. Those taking part in one such Tipperary meeting in early 1934 were known to the gardaí as 'men of good character' who were Fianna Fáil supporters and not connected to the IRA. The Dublin Clann remained in existence for several years, remaining non-political in theory but generally verbally critical of government moves to suppress the IRA. Occasional statements were issued deploring the showing of 'imperial propaganda' in cinemas and supporting anti-British demonstrations. The Clann also objected to de Valera's 1937 Constitution as a retreat from the republic.

While the IRA was initially suspicious of the organization of this group of men with substantial military records, by the mid-1930s the Clann was something of an ally, verbally at least, and certainly no longer a potential threat.

6/The IRA and Fianna Fáil in opposition, 1926–1932

The formation of Fianna Fáil in May 1926 did not see an immediate severing of ties with the IRA by its members. At officer level, many held joint membership of the two organizations until mid 1927. Among the rank and file there existed cases of dual membership until 1932. Both enemies and supporters of republicanism often presumed that both organizations shared broadly the same outlook. Nevertheless, there remained important differences between them which would eventually surface more intensely after Fianna Fáil came to power.

Following its November 1925 general army convention, the IRA elected a 'composite executive' composed of members both supportive of and opposed to de Valera's proposed new departure. The most senior IRA figure to support de Valera was Frank Aiken who, despite being replaced as chief of staff by Andy Cooney, was re-elected to the IRA's executive. Aiken suggested that IRA members who supported his stand should not be debarred from holding positions within the organization. The IRA agreed to this in order to prevent the split in Sinn Féin from adversely affecting the IRA. This fluid situation existed even after the formation of Fianna Fáil. For a period an advisory council combining the IRA, Sinn Féin and Fianna Fáil members met with a view to co-ordinating republican activities, but as relations worsened between Sinn Féin and Fianna Fáil, the council was disbanded.

There are indications that sections of the IRA were unhappy with the what they saw as a passive leadership during 1925. At that year's Convention a motion from the Dublin Brigade argued that the 'spirit and discipline' of the IRA was being destroyed by inactivity. The Tipperary Brigade also expressed suspicion of the 'constitutional' methods of the IRA leadership. At that stage the IRA Executive was still dominated by men who would support de Valera after 1926. These tensions came to a head after the deaths of two gardaí during IRA raids on garda barracks in November that year. As a result, a state of emergency was declared and large numbers of IRA members arrested. Among those detained were a number of Fianna Fáil supporters including Mayo TD Michael Kilroy, Cork county councillor Michael Corry and IRA executive member Michael Murphy. De Valera called for an emergency meeting of IRA officers from all parties, as he believed a 'national crisis' was at hand, but it soon became apparent that numbers of the arrested men were unhappy with their predicament. Several, including Michael Murphy, Thomas Crofts and Frank Buckley publicly disassociated themselves from the IRA's actions. Murphy and his fellow executive member Patrick Murray were suspended from the IRA for their attitude to the raids. Although a public breach was avoided, it was clear that a new IRA leadership were edging out the more cautious supporters of Fianna Fáil.

The wholesale departure of Fianna Fáil supporting officers from the IRA did not take place until May 1927 just prior to the general election. In October 1926 the army council had issued General Order No. 28 which forbade IRA members standing as parliamentary candidates. However, 23 officers allowed themselves to be selected, the vast majority as candidates for Fianna Fáil. Among them were Aiken, Tom Derrig, Mark Killilea and Neil Blaney. Despite the threat of court martial only one, Tom Maguire of Sinn Féin, agreed to stand down. This was highly embarrassing for the IRA because the existence of G.O. 28 was public knowledge and the IRA feared its being disobeyed would 'gravely prejudice discipline' within its own ranks as well as damage its public image.

The pressures which led IRA officers to take the decision to sever ties with their organization are illuminated by explanations given by two of them. Their testimonies also show a continuing attachment to the use of physical force. Patrick Houlihan of Caherfeakle, Co. Clare, had been imprisoned for two years during the civil war, leaving him a 'physical wreck'. He had tried to organize the IRA in his area, but found it impossible as 'the few who have not boarded the immigrant ship are down and out'. Local republicans had 'built their hopes on de Valera' and as he saw no way of 'overthrowing the present government in a hurry' except through Fianna Fáil, he had agreed to stand as one of their candidates. He did stress that if circumstances changed then he would rejoin the IRA. These sentiments were echoed by Patrick Smith of Cavan, who, while believing that the place for all republicans was now in Fianna Fáil, stressed that 'if our present attempt (politically) should be doomed to failure, I hope my action will not prevent me in future taking a line of action in which I have not lost faith'. Both Houlihan and Smith were elected.

Fianna Fáil had 44 candidates elected but refused to enter the Dáil; a decision to do so was forced on them by the government's response to the assassination of Kevin O'Higgins in early July. As well as the Electoral Amendment Act, a stringent Public Safety Act was also introduced. Twenty republicans were arrested for questioning about the assassination and IRA officers were encouraged to go on the run to avoid arrest. One of those arrested, Frank Kerlin, decided to resign his membership of the IRA executive for 'family, business and ... serious financial' reasons. Within a month he stood and was elected as a Fianna Fáil TD.

After Fianna Fáil took their seats in Leinster House there ceased to be a crossover in membership at leadership level with the IRA. But among the rank and file the situation remained more fluid. Defections of officers to Fianna Fáil badly affected IRA organization in Limerick and Mayo during 1930, leaving it without capable organizers. In Doon, Co. Limerick, almost all the local IRA were also members of Fianna Fáil. A similar situation existed in Drumkeen, Co. Donegal, and Ballymacelligot and Scratnaglen, in Kerry. During early 1930 the IRA's south Wexford commander was suspended for his continuing connections to Fianna Fáil. While membership of Fianna Fáil was forbidden by IRA general orders the organization seems to have been forced to tolerate this situation in certain areas. Some of the IRA's 'considerable quantity' of arms in west Limerick were also held by Fianna Fáil members. Martin Fahy, a Galway Fianna Fáil councillor, was also an officer in his local IRA unit. As late as 1932 the local IRA commander in east Clare was secretary of his local Fianna Fáil cumann. However, the available evidence suggests that such cases were uncommon. The IRA regarded Fianna Fáil influence among its units as undesirable, and a factor which induced 'listlessness' and inactivity.

Of more significance was the IRA's political reaction to the electoral potential of Fianna Fáil. In the spring of 1927, speculation was rife that a majority of republican TDs could be returned in that summer's election. Public appeals for republican unity were being made by figures like Dr Patrick McCartan of Clann Éireann and approaches were made to the IRA leadership to help bring this about. The IRA leadership believed that the opportunity presented itself for the defeat of the Cumann na nGaedheal government and an overthrow of the Treaty settlement, provided they secured an electoral pact between Fianna Fáil and Sinn Féin. This would help maintain unity within the IRA's ranks, which contained supporters of both parties, as well as those who favoured neither; it could also possibly produce a situation where the IRA could seize power bloodlessly. While this seems a highly unrealistic prediction, the IRA leadership used this argument to convince its sceptical officers about the value of the effort at unity.

There was substantial resistance to the leadership's initiative from within the IRA. At a meeting to discuss the proposal several officers declared that 'they had no faith in politicians', and that 'Fianna Fáil had already let them down'. Jack Plunkett spoke for this grouping when argued that he was against 'anything that savoured of going near Leinster House' and his brother George felt the proposals would lead to the IRA becoming 'overflooded with compromise talk'. To allay these fears, the IRA leadership argued that the return of a republican majority would open up military possibilities. Twomey used the example of the December 1918 election, saying that the majority of the Dáil elected then were not in favour of war, but war had resulted from their election. Furthermore, the proposal would help maintain IRA unity as supporters of both political parties were willing to 'co-operate in the army'. He also sounded a note of warning that, if the Cumann na nGaedheal government were re-elected, it would be very difficult to maintain the IRA 'for another six years' under what he presumed would be a very repressive regime. The alternative would be to attempt an 'armed revolution' but Twomey suggested that the IRA was not in a position to bring that about successfully. While his officers believed an armed revolt against the Free State was preferable to its overthrow by electoral means, they surely realized that the IRA had been severally weakened since the civil war, and was in no position to carry out a coup. A republican majority on the other hand could change the situation drastically, opening possibilities of being handed control of the state machine. Seán Russell, while assuring the meeting he had 'no liking for political parties' felt that a situation could arise from the election that the IRA could take advantage of. The proposals to bring about unity were passed by a majority of 31 to 9.

The IRA then set about attempting to convince both republican parties of the desirability of a united effort. Its strategy for doing so, though, betrayed a fundamental misunderstanding of Fianna Fáil's *raison d'être*. The IRA believed unity could be achieved with a few concessions on either side as the differences between the organizations were merely tactical. Fianna Fáil had, however, begun the process of freeing themselves from ideological straitjackets and were not keen on returning to them. The IRA drew a memorandum of proposals for co-operation and circulated it among to Sinn Féin and Fianna Fáil. Its main suggestions were that a 'national board' consisting of representatives from the IRA, Sinn Féin and Fianna Fáil be established which would choose a panel of candidates for the election. A manifesto from the National Board would centre on four points:

(a) The repudiation of the Treaty
(b) The repudiation of Partition
(c) The repudiation of all financial and other arrangements or obligations entered into with the Government of Great Britain.
(d) The abolition of a Standing Army and the Organization of the Defence Forces on a territorial basis.

The last point was of particular significance to the IRA because they also proposed that if a republican majority was secured all the National Army's weaponry be put under the IRA's control. All candidates would pledge not to take any oath to the Free State or British government.

Sinn Féin's reaction to these proposals was reasonably positive with their only worry being that Fianna Fáil would enter Leinster House even if they were in a minority once the oath of allegiance were removed. If Fianna Fáil could assure them this would not happen then there was a possibility of a united effort. Fianna Fáil were predictably less positive. They pointed out that it was their policy of agreeing to take their seats if the oath was removed that had made them a political force and to revert to the old absentionist policy would undermine their progress. They also argued that Fianna Fáil would do better electorally without being allied to Sinn Féin. While 'some' of the Fianna Fáil representatives apparently were favourable to the IRA's proposals for dealing with the situation if a majority of republicans were elected, they insisted that they should have 'absolute freedom' to act as they thought fit if a minority were returned. The IRA felt 'no progress' had been made at the meeting.

Nevertheless, the IRA again approached the executive of Fianna Fáil with the proposals in late April. The reply by Gerald Boland and Seán Lemass was swift and disappointing, dismissing the proposals as 'not acceptable as a basis for discussion'. Furthermore, the IRA were informed that their proposals had not been 'discussed in any detail'. Another IRA appeal to de Valera himself was met with the reply that he was in 'complete agreement' with the views expressed by his executive.

The IRA's efforts were motivated first of all by a desire to avoid a split in its ranks. Most of its leadership understood the need for some political action but it remained first and foremost a military organization and the unity effort had to be sold to its members on that basis. While Fianna Fáil contained many who had sympathy for the IRA, its leadership were not about to sacrifice their newly found independence for an alliance of dubious value.

Just prior to the general election the IRA publicly announced that its efforts to secure unity had failed. It criticised both Fianna Fáil and Sinn Féin for being unable to come to an agreement with each other but called on its supporters to 'Vote Solidly Republican'. This also meant that its members could work for Fianna Fáil and Sinn Féin at the election, as neither party was prepared to enter Leinster House. The situation drastically changed following the O'Higgin's assassination. On 11 August Fianna Fáil TDs took their seats in the Dáil. *An Phoblacht* announced itself 'profoundly disturbed' at Fianna Fáil's decision. But it stressed that while some bitterness among republicans was inevitable they should realize that 'thousands of people ... are in the same mood and in the same position as the Fianna Fáil TDs would have done the same thing ... yet one feels that ... if Separatist Ireland tomorrow took to the street barricades, the Gerry Bolands would be among the first to answer the call'. Fianna Fáil were not denounced as traitors, but patronized as a 'tired wing' of republicanism that 'surrendered' in order to prevent wholesale repression of republicans. However there were no talks on united electoral efforts prior to the September general election.

More significantly, Twomey outlined his view of the events later that month. He was 'not very angered' by Fianna Fáil's entering the Dáil, as he had 'for years' felt absentionism was a 'futile and wrong' policy. He did, however, feel that Fianna Fáil had now 'abandoned orthodox republicanism' and was no longer a revolutionary organization. Nevertheless, it was 'certainly not hostile' to the IRA and it would be wrong for the IRA to antagonize a potentially friendly political party.

This relatively pragmatic view was to inform the IRA's attitude to Fianna Fáil over the next five years. While membership of Fianna Fáil was later forbidden by General Order No. 28, it was, as has been said, reluctantly tolerated. There is also evidence of electoral co-operation. At the June 1929 Sligo-Leitrim bye-election, 'practically all' the IRA members in the region 'gave active assistance' to Fianna Fáil. Similarly, IRA officers recognized that in the parts of Kerry local members would 'undoubtedly' support and work for Fianna Fáil during elections.

The next five years saw the IRA undertaking more and more aggressive activities as it slowly rebuilt its organization. In terms of social policy it moved steadily leftwards, supporting strikes and land agitation. All these actions brought it into violent conflict with the state. In this period, Fianna Fáil vocally supported many of the IRA's activities and championed the cause of IRA prisoners. Some of its members were also attracted by the IRA's radicalism though there was a limit to Fianna Fáil's endorsement of both IRA actions and radical agitation.

As early as November 1926 Fianna Fáil had reacted to arrests of IRA members following the raids on garda barracks by demanding the release of republicans detained on 'trumped up charges'. Once inside the Dáil Fianna Fáil TDs kept up a steady stream of attacks on the Garda Special Branch or 'CID'. De Valera claimed that there were 'more gun bullies in the service of the Minister for Justice than in any other organization in the country'. Robert Briscoe accused the Special Branch of encouraging young men in the west of Ireland to rob banks so as to smear republicans. Tom Derrig explained IRA attacks on the gardaí as actions by individuals 'goaded into desperation by incessant raids and attacks by the CID'. Fianna Fáil's newspaper *The Nation* regularly reported 'outrages' by the 'licensed thugs' of the gardaí. There seems little doubt that most Fianna Fáil TDs agreed with Todd Andrews assessment of the Special Branch as a 'pretty low form of humanity'.

Fianna Fáil loudly championed the grievances of imprisoned IRA members. *The Nation* carried weekly 'Prisoner's Notes' by Maud Gonne and printed lists of IRA detainees. TDs regularly asked Dáil questions about the ill-treatment of IRA men and harassment of republican supporters. Leading members of the party openly stated where their sympathies lay. Gerry Boland, questioning the arrest of Peader O'Donnell ('a friend of mine'), claimed that the case proved that the government was trying to ensure that the 'civil war would not die out'. On another occasion he warned that the government would not be allowed make criminals of 'men like (George) Gilmore, Seán Russell and Mick Price'.

Briscoe was particularly active in support for republican prisoners. He infuriated gardaí by arriving 'hot foot' to stations following the arrest of IRA suspects and demanding their release. The gardaí sought means of having him removed as he was causing them considerable problems. This they managed to eventually do, to Briscoe's annoyance. The propaganda value to the IRA of this support for their prisoners was considerable; but also important was its use in keeping up the morale of those in jail. In late 1927, after a debilitating protest in Maryboro' jail (Portlaoise), the IRA sought to encourage an officer by telling him that Fianna Fáil had raised questions in 'parliament', spoke on republican platforms and were meeting the Minister for Justice to discuss his case.

Two major cases where Fianna Fáil became entangled in confrontation between the IRA and the state were those of Timothy Coughlan and T.J. Ryan. Coughlan was shot dead by a garda informant, Seán Harling, in early 1928. The circumstances of his death raised several questions and Fianna Fáil were foremost in demanding an enquiry. Large numbers of Fianna Fáil TDs attended Coughlan's funeral and one of the party's Dublin Cumann was renamed in his honour. Seán Lemass warned that as long as 'men like Harling' held positions in the gardai there was the potential for violence against them. Seán MacEntee promised that when Fianna Fáil came to power 'the murder of Timothy Coughlan will not go unpunished'.

T.J. Ryan, the IRA's leading officer in west Clare, became the focus of national attention in 1929 after allegations that a sustained Special Branch vendetta, including violent attacks, was being waged against him. Fianna Fáil dominated Clare county council and Kilrush urban district council passed motions demanding a halt to garda harassment of Ryan. *The Nation* told its readers that the CID were 'on the rampage' in Clare. Finally de Valera, visiting the Ryan family home, which he found surrounded by detectives, attested to the fact that Ryan bore the marks of severe beatings. This drew the celebrated reply from the Minister for Justice that Ryan had been kicked by one of his own cows!

Government attempts to get to grips with violent IRA activities met consistent resistance from Fianna Fáil within Dáil Eireann. De Valera accused the Minister for Justice of sounding 'like Foster or Balfour ... or Sir Hamar Greenwood' when he attempted to introduce the Juries Protection Bill in 1929. Seán T. O' Kelly told the House on the same occasion that the IRA would continue to exist until Ireland was free. MacEntee warned that when Fianna Fáil came to power the 'CID' would be punished for their 'illegal acts'. Garda commissioner Eoin O'Duffy claimed that this type of rhetoric from Fianna Fáil had placed a 'halo of righteousness' around the IRA. He felt that since Fianna Fáil had entered the Dáil, the situation had become much worse for his men, as they feared condemnation from these parliamentary 'inciters and sympathizers' of the IRA.

While this verbal support encouraged the IRA it also undoubtedly enabled Fianna Fáil to maintain the support of young republicans. West Clare, for example, was an area where Eoin O'Duffy claimed most people were 'actively or passively hostile' to the gardaí. Following an armed attack on debt collecters in Co. Kerry, gardaí reported that they were recieving 'no help or information' from the local population. Throughout the Free State there existed areas where the government and the police were resented. Therefore, Fianna Fáil was reassuring its own activists and a section of its electorate by this stand.

An important area of IRA activity by the late 1920s was opposition to 'imperialist' symbols and ceremonies. Fianna Fáil generally expressed support for these IRA actions. *The Nation* publicized the anti-imperialist protests and questioned whether 'British Reservists' like the Boy Scouts should be allowed organize in Ireland. The success of anti-Poppy Day protests in 1929 was hailed by *The Nation* as evidence that the 'Garrisons day was passing'. De Valera spoke at the IRA's anti-Poppy Day rallies in 1927 and again in 1930. That year Fianna Fáil in Dublin had promised a full turnout of its members to ensure the IRA's demonstration was a success.

A deadlier consequence of the IRA's campaign followed the jailing of a number of their members for attacking premises displaying Union flags. A juror in this case, Albert Armstrong, was murdered in early 1929. One of the jailed IRA members had been an election agent for Robert Briscoe, who was questioned about the murder. While the gardaí did not believe Briscoe was involved in the killing, his attitude is indicative of those Fianna Fáil members who remained close to the IRA. Briscoe claimed that he personally did not approve of the use of arms, but he did not consider Armstrong's death murder, as his killers had surely only meant to frighten their victim. While the Armistice Day protests often involved street disturbances Fianna Fáil had little to lose by supporting them as not only republicans but also large numbers of Dubliners, including even some gardaí, disliked the ceremonies.

Politically, more interesting was the relationship between Fianna Fáil and the IRA's intervention in social agitation. The Special Branch certainly thought that a section of Fianna Fáil were immersed in radical politics. During 1930 it identified the existence of a Fianna Fáil 'left wing' thought to include Frank Aiken, Frank Kearney, Eamonn Cooney, 'Briscoe the Jew', and Senator Seamus Robinson. Oscar Traynor, the 'personification of subterranean crime', was also alleged to be in sympathy with this grouping.

There certainly was an effort by the IRA to involve Fianna Fáil in its most important radical venture of the late 1920s, the Land Annuities campaign. In August 1927 Peader O'Donnell had outlined a plan whereby resistance among small farmers and rural labourers to the payment of annuities to Britain could be channelled into a mass campaign of non payment. The government would be forced to seize livestock in lieu of the withheld money, and the IRA would carry out a campaign to prevent any sale of the livestock within Ireland. Attempts to export the livestock would meet with strike action by dockers, and as the confrontation escalated appeals would be made to the rank and file of the 'largely peasant' National Army to refuse to carry out their orders. Thus a revolutionary situation would be brought about.

What gave this ambitious plan some reality was the fact that large numbers of rural dwellers were in desperate straits by 1927. In March of that year four members of a family in Adrigoole, Co. Cork, had died from influenza and starvation, having been denied state assistance because they owed land annuities. While elements within the IRA were suspicious of O'Donnell's plans, he gained official army council backing for them in January 1928. He had already begun using his journalistic talent to promote the idea through *An Phoblacht*. From the beginning attempts were made to persuade Fianna Fáil to back the non-payment campaign. Some early successes were recorded. In February 1928 Paddy Ruttledge, Dr Jim Ryan and Gerald Boland spoke at an anti-annuities rally at Dublin's Rotunda. Shortly afterwards TDs Frank Fahy and Hugo Flinn shared a platform with O'Donnell in Loughrea, Co. Galway. Clare county council endorsed the campaign, and its chairman Frank Barret helped it organize a rally in June 1928 at which de Valera shared the stage with O'Donnell.

Fianna Fáil was not endorsing O'Donnell or the IRA in its support for the campaign. The policy adopted by Fianna Fáil was for the retention of the annuities money in Ireland not their abolition. O'Donnell's own rhetoric became muted as he tried to entice Fianna Fáil speakers on to anti-annuities platforms. At rallies in Dungloe in early 1929 and Kinsale that summer, where O'Donnell shared platforms with Councillor Eamon Corbett and TDs Tommy Mullins and Martin Corry, he stressed that there was no need for people to resort to 'other than constitutional methods'. O'Donnell also conceded that he had no objection to the Fianna Fáil policy of collecting the annuities but retaining the money in Ireland.

There is also evidence that in some districts the campaign of non-payment had ground to a halt by the beginning of the 1930s. During early 1929 there were popular expressions of support for the campaign in Donegal with crowds stoning gardaí escorting summons servers in Dungloe. However, by May that year strong condemnation of the campaign by the bishop of Raphoe was said by the gardaí to have almost brought it to an end in that disdict. During 1930 an IRA officer found that in Donegal, the birthplace of the campaign, from Letterkenny to Gweedore 'not a single individual' was holding to non-payment of their annuities. In Dungloe, there were a few still withholding payment but 'nothing approaching organized resistance'. Many locals were cynical about the agitation, claiming that some who 'would be foremost' in calling for non-payment would be the first 'to go to the Land Commission and settle on the quiet'. Many people who had made sacrifices at the beginning of the agitation felt that the rest of the country had let them down. Even more worryingly large numbers of people expressed 'utter indifference' to the whole question, which led the officer to conclude there was no future for the campaign. Eoin O'Duffy also claimed that his officers had effectively defeated the campaign in Donegal during 1931. It is possible that O'Donnell's persuasive retelling of the agitation has given it a prominence it does not deserve.

The limits of Fianna Fáil's commitment to social agitation have been widely discussed. But there is no doubt that many of the party's rank and file were open to elements of the radicalism encouraged by the IRA. In its most negative form it meant simply obstructing the normal process of government, driving Eoin O'Duffy to describe the Clare Fianna Fáil councillors as 'irresponsible blackguards who have nothing in the world ... except malicious tongues and facility for playacting and posing'. The fact that rank and file Fianna Fáil members faced occasional garda harassment themselves meant that they also instinctively sided with the IRA when it confronted the state forces.

There were also small number of party members who were prepared to work more closely on left-wing IRA initiatives. Several Fianna Fáil councillors were involved with the Irish Working Farmers Committee, an affiliate of the Kristertern, the Comintern's 'peasant' section. These included Seán Hayes of Clare, and Eamon Corbett and Martin Fahy of Galway. The IWFC was a tiny organization with only 43 attending its conference in Galway during March 1930, but the Special Branch believed Fahy and Corbett were the 'soul of the movement' in the county. All three councillors applied for passports to attend the Kristertern congress in Berlin, but in the end only Peadar O'Donnell represented the Irish section there. The depth of these men's commitment to radicalism is of course open to question. Fahy, who had once told republicans to 'pay no heed whatsoever' to criticism from the bishop of Killaloe, reversed his anticlerical stance when faced with serious charges before the military tribunal in late 1931. There he announced that he had severed his connections with the IRA, since the bishops' pastoral had convinced him that the organization he had thought was 'patriotic and Christian' was actually neither. Hayes, however, chaired the launch of the Saor Éire organization in September that year and remained associated with IRA initiatives well into the 1930s.

The IRA and Fianna Fáil had very different objectives even if this was not readily apparent to their supporters during the late 1920s. Despite their denunciations of the CID and defence of IRA prisoners, Fianna Fáil were careful to disassociate themselves from unpopular IRA activities. The IRA murder of a garda in Clare was denounced by *The Nation* as an 'act of utter cowardice'. Gerald Boland commented after the killing of a young man in Tipperary later that year that the IRA had 'unknowingly gone from the moral plane right down to criminal status'. Of course these condemnations always occurred in the context of denunciation of the government's response to IRA activity but it was becoming clear that Fianna Fáil did not believe that physical force remained a viable option. As *The Nation* commented after the Tipperary murder, 'the conditions which justify the taking of human life were not present' in the Free State. Fianna Fáil also increasingly differentiated between the 'CID' and the 'ordinary Police' who they generally felt were not politically biased.

There were similar processes at work in Fianna Fáil's attitude to the IRA's radical experiments. When the weight of the hierarchy and government launched its attack on Saor Éire in the winter of 1931, Fianna Fáil skilfully avoided the taint of communism while denouncing Cumann na nGaedheal's hypocrisy. Boland explained his 1925 IRA mission to Russia as simply following a 'line that was followed by Irish nationalists from the days of Elizabeth' in seeking aid from England's enemies. Seán Lemass taunted the government that while 78,000 Dubliners lived in rooms unfit for habitation, it was creating a communist bogey rather than implementing a housing programme. De Valera denounced the new Public Safety Act while declaring his commitment to Catholicism and the rights of private property. The one major exception to this was Tommy Mullins of Cork who proudly told the Dáil that he belonged to four of the organizations banned under the new Act. He also suggested that Saor Éire was simply following the policy of James Connolly and that he saw nothing wrong in the efforts of 'Revolutionary Workers' Groups' to improve conditions in factories and coal mines. Furthermore he agreed with their aim of overthrowing 'British imperialism and its ally, Irish capitalism' to begin with.

But Mullins was far from representative of Fianna Fáil thinking on this and other matters. While the IRA still saw military force as the only method of establishing the Republic, and inaugurating a new society, Fianna Fáil had slowly but definitely chosen a different path and objective. This was signalled as early as 1929 when *The Nation* replied to criticism in *An Phoblacht* by pointing out that it was 'not possible to free a people without their support'. It claimed 75 per cent of the Irish people did not endorse physical force methods and to ignore that was foolish. De Valera stressed that IRA arms dumped at the end of the civil war were never intended for use in another civil or indeed class war. Fianna Fáil managed a very delicate but successful manoeuvre in remaining close to militant republicanism but gathering moderate electoral support. It was not that the IRA leadership were blind to this but that much of the time they were so concerned with problems of training and maintaining their 'army' that they paid little attention to Fianna Fáil's pursuit of the middle ground.

The background to the Public Safety Act had been a period of increased IRA mobilization and activity during 1931. The organization had also carried out three killings by the autumn. Less dramatically but more importantly the IRA was growing again after a period of stagnation. It was now their policy to march and drill as openly as was possible. Even with the government preventing special trains running to Bodenstown in June that year, at short notice the IRA hired buses and cars and thousands defied the ban. Significantly, de Valera and leading members of Fianna Fáil marched with the IRA to Tone's grave. It was after this event that the IRA feeling the government was 'undoubtedly losing their grip' decided to launch Saor Éire. Twomey also felt that if the government lost at the polls, there was a chance that they would refuse to step down, creating a crisis the IRA of which could take advantage. That challenge was met by the Public Safety Act and the 'Red Scare' which, while not destroying the IRA, did cause it severe problems, organizationally and ideologically.

As the general election of 1932 approached, the IRA leadership suspended its orders forbidding members to work for political parties in elections and urged its members to 'vote against the candidates of the Cumann na nGaedheal party'. Twomey had signalled the likelihood of this when he informed Joseph McGarrity that he was doubtful if the IRA's attitude to elections could be maintained in the present circumstances. He felt that Fianna Fáil by, in the IRA's view, accepting the 'Free State position' had made things easier for the organization. Where in the past support for Fianna Fáil would have been 'misinterpreted by our own people', now it would be seen as simply tactical. However, the decision was not simply brought about by the opportunity of defeating the government at the polls but also by pressure from the IRA's own ranks. The effects of the clampdown on the organization meant that their 'Volunteers could not be restrained from voting' even if the leadership had tried to prevent them doing so. The army council realized too the potential effect on the IRA's morale if large numbers of members 'insisted on taking part in the election'. There had been no discussion with Fianna Fáil about this decision and it was taken solely to help bring down Cumann na nGaedheal.

Certainly grassroots pressure played a role with Twomey claiming that 90 per cent of his organization, in particular its younger members, was anxious to take part in the ousting of the government; but he also believed that a 'Fianna Fáil phase' of the Irish revolution was inevitable. The IRA were not strong enough to overthrow the Cosgrave government and Fianna Fáil's arguments that peaceful change was possible held sway among the mass of republicans. This would only change when Fianna Fáil was tested in power, when Twomey believed they would 'inevitably lose much of the support they have now'.

So in the spring of 1932 the IRA threw its weight behind Fianna Fáil's election effort. In practice, it meant the IRA undertook election work in their various areas, with Dublin's 3rd battalion canvassing Donnybrook, Rathgar and Ranelagh during early February, while their 1st Battalion 'worked 100%' at canvassing. Most of the Dublin brigade's work was geared towards the Fianna Fáil election effort. While the gardaí feared that the IRA was planning to disable vechicles used by the government party on the eve of the election this did not come to pass. Indeed, canvassing, putting up posters and attending election meetings probably accounted for the majority of the IRA's election effort rather than the more dramatic claims of some writers. Certainly having at least 5,000 extra election workers across the state must have been a considerable boost to the Fianna Fáil election effort.

Fianna Fáil secured 72 seats at the polls, enough to form a minority government with Labour party support. On 9 March, de Valera became head of the new administration. One of the first acts of his government was to release IRA prisoners held in Arbour Hill and Mountjoy. Two days later, the IRA's Dublin Brigade marched in military formation to a rally in College Green, where 30,000 people greeted the released men. Crowds cheered Peadar O'Donnell's assertion that the Cumann na nGaedheal leaders must never again be allowed a public platform but instead be 'put out of public life'. Seán MacBride stressed that the change in government did not mean a change in the policy of the IRA which would remain active until the republic was achieved. To many it must indeed have seemed that the road to the 'republic' would now be a shorter one. Frank Ryan's belief that the IRA would now have a 'soft and easy time ... maybe too soft and easy' was the one note of caution in the otherwise triumphant atmosphere for republicans. The following week these scenes were replicated in smaller scale across the country as ex-prisoners returned home. On 18 March the government suspended the Public Safety Act. The IRA's Easter commemorations were notable for the presence of Fianna Fáil TDs and for the first time the sale of lilies went unhindered by the gardaí. To supporters of Cumann na nGaedheal it must have seemed that the 'Second Apocalypse' had indeed arrived, with Fianna Fáil and the IRA working hand in hand. In reality, the contradictory nature of the personal, social and political relationships between the two organizations were to undergo their most serious tests.

7/The IRA and Fianna Fáil in government, 1932–1936

The IRA's policies remained remarkably consistent towards Fianna Fáil in the aftermath of their election victory in 1932. The 'breathing space' created by the victory of the party was to be used by the IRA to recruit and train. At the same time, critical support was given to the new government and clashes with state forces avoided, in the hope that Fianna Fáil would take steps towards the declaration of a republic. Discussions with Fianna Fáil stressed the need to mobilize support through a united front of republican and labour bodies and galvanize popular opinion. Over the next four years, the IRA leadership clung to the belief that Fianna Fáil would inevitably disillusion its republican supporters, but, rather than Fianna Fáil rupturing, disagreement as to how to deal with the government eventually split the IRA.

Just after polling day in 1932 Twomey received a dramatic proposal from Frank Aiken. Aiken argued that the two men's organizations should 'be fused at once'. Such a fusion would 'double' their strengths and provide a huge boost to republican morale. Furthermore, if as expected the British government and other 'reactionary forces' brought intense pressure to bear on the new administration unity with the IRA would greatly increase its strength. Such a re-alignment was possible, Aiken argued, because 'at bottom' the IRA and Fianna Fáil shared the same outlook with 'less friction between them today than often exists within one organization'. Social justice for the 'labourers and working farmers' would also be achieved rapidly if the IRA could align itself with Fianna Fáil. But this had to be agreed to while neither organization was in a position of power over the other. Aiken believed that the 'cease fire Proposals' of 1923 were now applicable to the current situation and that the IRA could put its arms at the disposal of a government that would work towards achieving the republic. Aiken's proposal suggested that Twomey's 'splendid record' would be rounded off by his support for these suggestions.

While there was no suggestion of material reward for the IRA leadership if they chose this course it must have been probable that Twomey and other senior figures would have secured positions within the army or government. It seems clear however that Aiken's interest was in ensuring that the IRA was brought under the authority of the new government and effectively neutralized. With its arms and men under the control of Fianna Fáil it could be used to siphon off republican enthusiasm among the young and at the same time be unable to launch its own initiatives which had the potential to destabilize the government.

Twomey was sufficiently wary to avoid replying to Aiken before putting the proposals to the army council. They unanimously rejected them and the IRA informed Aiken that there was little point in further discussing the matter.

Fearing that a public statement by Fianna Fáil of its proposals would confuse its rank and file the army council placed the Aiken correspondence before its local leaderships and again the Fianna Fáil proposals were rejected. At its convention that spring the IRA outlined its determination to remain an independent body and to retain control of its arms and equipment. While there were many different political viewpoints represented among the IRA leadership, one point which united all factions was the desire to remain an independent force.

The IRA also decided not 'to hamper' Fianna Fáil in any 'advance it may make towards National Independence'. Noting that the government claimed to seek the establishment of a republic then the IRA also asked it not to hinder their activities towards the same goal. The organization also decided that while Fianna Fáil faced attack over its position on the oath of allegiance the IRA would not act aggressively towards them.

Formal discussions between the two organizations occurred again in July 1932. On a visit to Cork, de Valera had met Tom Barry and told him of Fianna Fáil's plans to launch a volunteer force for 'National Defence'. Barry, who was not an IRA member at this stage, told de Valera that he was impressed by the progress of Fianna Fáil, especially the challenge to Britain posed by the withholding of land annuities. He felt that he could speak to the IRA and possibly convince them of the value of being a part of the new force. Barry spoke to Twomey about the matter on several occasions and Twomey stressed that the IRA saw the situation as one which demanded political rather than military action. Barry, however, was convinced that if the IRA agreed to join the new force they could 'practically control it' and prepare the ground for a military confrontation with Britain.

Barry arranged a meeting between de Valera, Aiken and the IRA leadership to discuss these matters. In the event Aiken represented Fianna Fáil, while Twomey, MacBride and George Gilmore were present for the IRA. They argued that the key was the organization of popular agitation against Britain in the 26 counties and the formation of a united front to co-ordinate this. Aiken 'said very little' except to stress that a volunteer force would definitely be launched. Aiken felt that since the oath was no longer relevant, the Land Annuities being withheld and the governor general 'put in his place' there was no barrier to IRA participation in such a force. With regard to any popular agitation, Aiken made clear that the government would have to have full control of its organization. Fianna Fáil had created the current political situation and could not allow any other groups to take advantage of it. The meeting ended without any agreement.

The IRA impressed upon Barry that for him to call for recruits to the new volunteers would cause them severe problems. He in turn argued that he felt Fianna Fáil were 'travelling as fast' as they could towards the establishment of a republic. The army council then forwarded a proposal to the Fianna Fáil Executive suggesting the formation of a conference of 'national organizations and labour bodies' which could organize a campaign in support of the government's position in the Economic War. Fianna Fáil replied that the proposals were unacceptable and that they were organizing a series of public meetings which the IRA should attend if it wished to support the government.

Again Fianna Fáil had held out a tentative prospect of some IRA involvement in the national forces, but only on their terms. As Twomey noted the IRA had tried to reach an understanding with the government but Fianna Fáil had held out the choice of merging with it or becoming part of its militia.

After these discussions there was little leadership contact between Fianna Fáil and the IRA aside from a series of meetings between Seán MacBride and de Valera during 1932 and 1933. These meetings lasted several hours and were usually to deal with a specific problem such as the Donamon Castle affair. MacBride tried to raise the question of co-operation between the two organizations but he claimed de Valera constantly avoided dealing with political questions and instead reiterated the need for the maintenance of law and order. He argued that the barriers to the Republic would be removed gradually and that the IRA should recognize majority rule and cease to oppose the government. MacBride's statements of the IRA's position, that in order to carry through the economic war successfully, a united front was needed, and that that would involve sacrifices and compromises on all sides were never addressed by de Valera. MacBride's impression was that, unless the IRA undertook to recognize the authority of the government, de Valera felt that it should disband. As a result no useful or practical purpose came from their meetings, which had ended by the Autumn of 1933.

While the IRA harboured hopes of some form of united front involving Fianna Fáil, the government had no intention of allowing itself to be dragged into something it did not fully control. As its representatives had pointed out in July, there was only one government in Ireland, not two. Despite Aiken's assertion that the two organizations held essentially the same outlook, there were very real differences, which were illustrated in the IRA's belief that the Economic War could be utilized to mobilize the masses into a fight for the republic. At an early stage Twomey realized that Fianna Fáil had no 'desire to rouse up the people'.

The IRA's policy of using 'anti-imperialist' events to up the tempo of anti-British feeling was not unrealistic given the mood of republican supporters in the summer of 1932. Fianna Fáil speakers took part in IRA-organized rallies in Cork, Sligo and Limerick during July. After the government's withholding of the

1 Moss Twomey, November 1926 (courtesy of Maurice Twomey Jr).

2 The Dublin IRA at the 1931 Easter Commemoration, O'Connell Street.

3 IRA prisoners released at the conclusion of the Civil War including *first left standing*: J.J. Rice; *second left seated*: Moss Twomey; *fourth left standing*: Mick Fitzpatrick; *fourth left seated*: J.J. Sheehy (courtesy of Maurice Twomey Jr).

4 Crowds greet the released IRA prisoners at Arbour Hill, March 1932
(National Library of Ireland).

Mr. Maurice Twomey
at
graveside of 1916 men
Glasnevin

5 Frank Ryan, *An Phoblacht* editor speaks to the 30,000-strong rally in College Green to welcome the released prisoners, March 1932 (National Library of Ireland).

6 Moss Twomey at Easter Commemoration, Glasnevin, April 1932, Army Council member Mick Fitzpatrick, *background right* (courtesy of Maurice Twomey Jr).

7 Prisoners released from Arbour Hill and Mountjoy, March 1932 (National Library of Ireland). *From left to right back row*: Michael Sherry (Galway), Sean McGuinness (O/C Offaly), Sean O'Shea (Kerry), Sean Mulgrew (Achill), Thomas O'Driscoll (Kerry), Charles Gilmore (South Dublin), James Hannigan (Dublin), Claude O'Loughlin (Dublin); *middle row*: John O'Connor (Kerry), George Gilmore (Army Council), Brian Corrigan (O/C Achill), Frank Ryan (editor, *An Phoblacht*), George Mooney (Dublin), Sean O'Farrell (O/C Leitrim), T.J. Ryan (O/C West Clare), Thomas Breen (Clare); *front row*: Kathleen Merrigan (Dublin), Richard Stephens (Dublin), Maeve Phelan (Dublin).

8 Peadar O'Donnell, a leading IRA member until 1934, at the 1930 European Peasants Congress in Berlin (courtesy of the Russian State Archive for Social and Political History).

9 Sighle Humphreys, the driving force behind Cumann na mBan in Dublin from 1926 onwards.

10 Twomey gives the oration at Bodenstown, 1933. Cumann na gCailini, *foreground*, Cumann na mBan, *background* (courtesy of Maurice Twomey Jr).

11 The Tralee IRA at Bodenstown, 1934.

AN PHOBLACHT.
THE REPUBLIC.

"Ní Sioccáin
50 Saoirse"
— Pádraic Mac Piarais

"We Shall
Rise Again"
— James Connolly

New Series. Vol. IX. No. 16   SATURDAY, MAY 5, 1934.   PRICE TWOPENCE

I.R.A. POLICY TOWARDS BLUESHIRTS

LOCAL CLASHES CLOUD REAL ISSUE

Two Attempted Murders in the South

FOLLOWING a week-end of speech-making on the part of the President, three Vice-Presidents and lesser chiefs of the Imperial Fascist organisation, arrests have been made in many centres, totalling about thirty. The charges against those arrested are, in the majority of cases, riotous assembly and attacks on Blueshirts.

Another attempted murder follows that of Edward Kinane, reported in last week's issue. James Glynn, residing in the premises at Ennis, part of which is occupied by the I.R.A. club, becoming involved in a fracas with Blueshirts, was shot and as we write lies in a dangerous condition.

He has identified Seán McNamara, leader of the Blueshirts in Ennis, as the man who shot him.

In our editorial we again refer to the attitude of the Republican Army Council towards local clashes, a policy of avoidance of such deeply harmful terrorism and bitterness, of solid work for the realisation of the issue at stake, the subverting of the system which inevitably leads to such incidents.

WAR DANGER IN THE FAR EAST

JAPAN BECOMES TRUCULENT

Japan is far away and the Japanese are one of the "Yellow Races." Because of that, few of us in Western Europe are inclined to take them seriously. The memory of their smashing defeat of the Grand Russian Armies in 1904 is forgotten, or—if remembered—is accounted for by an

I.R.A. POLICY

The booklet "Governmental Policy of Óglaigh na h-Éireann" (third edition), price one penny, twopence by post, can be obtained from AN PHOBLACHT offices.

foreign power." There was more to the effect that "under no pretext"

CHIEF OF STAFF BEREAVED

THE sympathy of Republicans goes out to Maurice Twomey, Chief of Staff, Irish Republican Army, on the death of his mother which occurred on Saturday last at Fermoy Co. Hospital.

Deceased, who was a splendid type of Irishwoman, faced with courage the raids and searches of the Black and Tans during the period when members of her family were on the run, and when division came she never faltered but placed her home and hospitality again at the disposal of the soldiers of the Republic.

The funeral to the family burial ground was very large and included prominent Republican representatives. Domhnall O Domchadha and Jas. Killian represented G.H.Q. of the I.R.A., Sean Mac Swiney, Sean Coughlan and J. O'Donovan, represented Cork No. 1 Brigade.

20 KERRYMEN ARRESTED

Blueshirt Meeting Sequel

There was a sequel to disturbances which occurred at Ballybunion on Sunday, March 4, on the occasion of an U.I.P. meeting addressed by Pro. J. M. O'Sullivan, T.D., and Senator Blythe, when 20 men were charged at a special court in Ballybunion on Monday before Mr. T. Leahy, P.C., with unlawful assembly, conspiracy and disorderly conduct.

Michael Flanagan, The Cashen; Jas.

CRAIGAVON HAS ENOUGH FASCISTS

Blueshirt-Blackshirt Policy Not For Orangemen

CRAIGAVON has declared that with the "Black Brethren" and the B. Specials in "Ulster," there is no need for Fascism in that area. This declaration has been evoked by proposals which have been made to him by British Fascists.

Three months ago we learned through a political correspondent in Britain of overtures made by the Blueshirt organisation here to Mosley, leader of a section of British Fascisti. This was not denied.

THE negotiations touched on a campaign for the establishment of Fascist Governments for the "British Isles." Simultaneously with our publication came "news-items" in Mosley's "Fascist Week," reporting Blueshirt successes here and boosting the idea of Fascist Governments in London, Belfast and Dublin.

The question for the Mosley-Duffy conspirators now resolves itself into an alliance with Craigavon's organisations—which, he alleges, are Fascist. But in the background opposing Fascism in Ulster are the workers among the Orangemen, whose demonstrations recently would lead Craigavon and the Fascists to believe that discretion for the moment is advisable.

'REVOLUTIONARY TACTICS'

POLICE AT NORTHERN FUNERAL

AT the funeral of Sean Sharkey, of Strabane, an I.R.A. officer in that area, whose death is reported on another page, police in uniform and plain clothes attended. These followed the procession of I.R.A. in general public, and during the interment surrounded the Melmount Graveyard.

Shorthand Notes.

Following the interment, at which Rev. G. Ryan delivered a stirring panegyric and at which Sean McCool paid a tribute to the dead Volunteer's faithfulness, the police entered the graveyard and copied the inscriptions on the wreaths which had been placed there by the dead man's relatives and land annuities a sense of defiance seems to have gripped republican Ireland, with county councils and trade union branches proclaiming support for de Valera. The IRA felt that if it could 'develop' this anti-British mood it could arouse enthusiasm for a campaign of non payment, which it feared the government would undermine by relying on legal tactics. With the *Irish Press* enthusiastically reporting Army manoeuvres in the Curragh, the IRA could be forgiven for assuming renewed conflict with Britain was at hand.

In the aftermath of Fianna Fáil's victory there did exist belief among the IRA that the new government might be able to lead the way to a republic. A senior IRA officer, writing in late March 1932, felt that if the oath was removed and the land annuities withheld, the whole basis of the Cumann na nGaedheal party would be removed, leaving it a 'conservative and reactionary' rump. A republican majority could then be easily secured, and a (26-county) republic declared. If this occurred, the IRA might be able to put itself at the disposal of the government.

The IRA felt at this stage that 'aggressive' criticism of Fianna Fáil would only be used by the 'imperialists' to strengthen their position. Twomey expressed the contradictory situation the IRA found itself in later that year. On the one hand Fianna Fáil seemed to be gaining in strength and Twomey felt that if de Valera went to the US he 'would sweep everybody off their feet' and leave the IRA's supporters there isolated. Unless the IRA was careful the same thing would happen to them in Ireland during the next period. The problem was that any successful demonstrations carried out by the IRA seemed to reflect well on the government, but they also benefited republicans generally so the IRA had to continue to organize them. As Twomey exclaimed, 'nobody visualized a Free State which Republicans were not supposed to attack'. But that was what they now faced in the 26 counties. While there were many problems with this state the key issue was that the IRA did not want the return of the 'Cosgrave Imperial Gang' and therefore had to avoid activities that might weaken Fianna Fáil. Over the next year, the IRA initiated or was drawn into conflicts which worsened the relationship between itself and the government. These also had the effect of exacerbating divisions within the IRA itself.

The question of supporting Fianna Fáil in an electoral contest was again put to the IRA by the announcement of a general election in January 1933. An indication of both changed attitudes and circumstances is given in an exchange of letters between Twomey and his old comrade, Senator Bill Quirke. Twomey expressed the view that as much as he 'would hate' to see Cumann na nGaedheal in office again, he was 'not enthusiastic' about supporting the government. He was 'frankly very disappointed' with Fianna Fáil and could not tell what position the IRA would take until a special meeting was held. Quirke replied to Twomey's 'rather depressing letter' by urging him to make every effort to secure co-operation. He raised the spectre of what would happen if Cumann na nGaedheal was returned. The world would look 'on us (the lot) as the greatest bunch of slaves that ever got a chance of liberty and refused to be freed'. British economic warfare would have succeeded and Ireland set back to 'the time of the Act of Union'. Quirke's letter also asserted that whatever difficulty Twomey may have had with the election, if 'left to themselves the Volunteers will decide to co-operate'. This was also implied by Twomey when he explained the fear within the IRA of being seen to help the 'Imperialists' by attacking Fianna Fáil. 'Most' IRA supporters simply expected it to back Fianna Fáil.

The IRA decided to support Fianna Fáil again at an Extraordinary Convention held on 8 January. The tone of the IRA's manifesto made it clear that they were supporting Fianna Fáil reluctantly, as they in no way committed themselves to the policy of that party. They supported Fianna Fáil only to drive out of 'public life a party that has sold itself to the British Empire'. In the event the election saw a record turnout of 80 per cent and the return of 77 Fianna Fáil TDs. The party was then able to form a majority government.

Prior to the IRA's March 1933 Convention the leadership outlined their view of the previous year. Disappointment was expressed that while the IRA had avoided action which could have impeded the government, in return 'to put it mildly, not much assistance' was given by Fianna Fáil. Instead, the police and 'CID' tried to provoke conflict, and IRA members increasingly found themselves in jail. The government's economic policy had 'upheld and bolstered the capitalist system' with the result that they could clearly state that Fianna Fáil policy ran counter to the aims of the IRA. Now for the first time the army council expressed the belief that Fianna Fáil's policies were 'bound to lead to widespread disillusionment among great proportion of its republican supporters, and of the workers and working farmers'. The IRA hoped that the convention could decide how best to harness this discontent.

What the convention did clearly show was that there were growing divisions among the IRA's leadership on how to deal with Fianna Fáil. As early as September 1932 George Gilmore had tried to resign from the army council citing his belief that all anti-Free State opinion in Ireland was now 'hopelessly pro-Dev'. He felt that Fianna Fáil would 'hold the field for a long time to come' and that there was little the IRA would be able to do about it. However, Gilmore was eventually persuaded to reconsider, on the basis that the political situation was actually in a 'very fluid state'. In reality Gilmore's assertion that a revolutionary situation did not exist in Ireland and that the IRA were in for 'a pretty bad time' was more realistic than he probably realized. At the convention his close ally, Peadar O'Donnell, re-iterated that the IRA had supported Fianna Fáil only 'because it was a stick to beat Cosgrave'. But now he felt that some within the movement were 'adjusting themselves to the Fianna Fáil policy'. He implied that Seán MacBride had stated if the oath and the governor general were abolished, then the IRA would have to think seriously about its position as an independent force. MacBride denied this, but O'Donnell would persist with his allegation. Frank Ryan warned that unless the IRA returned to its policies of 1930-31 they would become a 'left wing of Fianna Fáil'. George Gilmore agreed, stating that unless the IRA formed its own political organization and challenged the government, they would simply be a 'safety valve' for de Valera's party. Nevertheless we should not underestimate the existence within the IRA of those who felt that the organization was too critical of the government. Certainly, Tom Barry would have fallen into this category in early 1933 although his attitude was to change later.

The convention admitted attempts by the IRA to involve Fianna Fáil in its 'Boycott British' campaign had been a failure. However despite passing resolutions which indicated a harder line towards Fianna Fáil, the majority at the convention disagreed with Ryan and Gilmore. The IRA decided to make clear its belief that the Fianna Fáil government was not a 'legitimate national authority' and was not entitled to the allegiance of Irish citizens. The IRA demanded the repeal of all 'coercive' legislation as it was the organizations 'right' to drill and hold arms. Furthermore a resolution was passed banning members of 'Free State' parties from speaking at IRA events. This would in theory, exclude Fianna Fáil members from IRA platforms. Most importantly, however the majority at the convention agreed that 'politically the IRA would have to take a back seat for some time as Fianna Fáil held political sway ... owing to their so-called popular National advances'. The majority of the convention decided to leave the matter of separate political organization for the next convention and concentrate on building up the IRA's military expertise.

The disputes over the attitude to Fianna Fáil signalled the increasing disenchantment of O'Donnell, Gilmore and Ryan. O'Donnell would claim that he had been ordered in March 1932 not to criticize Fianna Fáil publicly, and that several articles he submitted to *An Phoblacht* were censored. Shortly after the Convention, Ryan resigned as editor of *An Phoblacht*, and was soon followed by his deputy Hannah Sheehy Skeffington, who told Twomey she was worried that the IRA was moving to the right and becoming a 'Bulmer Hobson-MacNeill wing of Fianna Fáil'. The experience of Fianna Fáil in power was the catalyst for the split in the IRA.

Twomey remained convinced that the IRA's policies were framed correctly to appeal to disillusioned Fianna Fáil opinion, despite relations growing even more hostile during the summer and autumn of 1933. De Valera even took the step of writing to Joseph McGarrity to ask him to use his influence with the IRA to ask not to continue to 'embarrass' the government by their activities. While

Twomey believed that some of the Fianna Fáil leadership hated the IRA more than they did the Blueshirts he remained convinced that 75 per cent of the government's supporters desired some co-operation between Fianna Fáil and the IRA. He had hoped that a 'left-wing' was developing in Fianna Fáil but the emergence of the Blueshirts, had frightened them back into de Valera's hands. Nevertheless he felt it was only the fear of a return to power of the 'imperialist amalgamation' that held Fianna Fáil together. Within the IRA there was now considerable hostility to supporting Fianna Fáil again and increasing demands that the organization challenge them in the 1934 local elections. Twomey believed that the time had come to discuss the formation of a political organization to challenge Fianna Fáil, and take advantage of the discontent both he and MacBride were sure existed among the government's supporters.

The IRA had fundamentally misconceived the political situation confronting it in the Free State. Firstly they could not see that Fianna Fáil's policies might be satisfying the aspirations of most republican voters, rather then simply 'popularising the Treaty' and making the IRA's task more difficult. Because of their belief that they had every right to arm, train and carry out their activities they could not understand how this was not tolerated by a 'republican' government. Their relative lack of violent activities during 1932 was something they thought they should be complimented on rather than something that the government expected of them. When they did find themselves on the wrong side of the government they felt that instinctively the republican rank and file would defend them.

This contradiction shared by all factions within the IRA came to the fore again during the acrimonious 1934 convention. Both those who supported the call for a republican congress and those who stayed loyal to the IRA held that Fianna Fáil had failed and was losing support. O'Donnell, stating that Fianna Fáil could not 'possibly unite the country' used this as an argument for the launch of a political challenge to them. Opponents of any new direction, such as Mick Fitzpatrick, argued that Fianna Fáil claimed the IRA was not the same organization as during the 1919–23 period and that a new departure would give them more ammunition for this claim. The basis of the IRA's constitution had been drawn up by Frank Aiken during 1925 and this made it more difficult for Fianna Fáil to argue that they were a 'new' IRA.

There was general agreement that there was a pronounced difference in the government's attitude to the IRA, with Ryan, MacBride and J.J. Sheehy all noting a new hostility to the organization. This was also used by some to argue against confrontation. MacBride felt that any new initiatives could give the government an excuse to clampdown on the IRA. He also claimed, however, that 'the people who supported them are now leaving Fianna Fáil disappointed' leaving a vacuum in leadership. A supporter of the Congress proposal, Tom

Maguire of Westmeath, used an example of 'whole Fianna Fáil clubs' coming over to the IRA as proof that the government had indeed failed to fulfil its supporters expectations. Following the convention, Donal O'Donoghue also claimed that the IRA had drawn numbers of Fianna Fáil into its organization and too radical a departure politically would only antagonize the people who were gradually realising the government was failing them. Even as late as 1935, with the leadership of his organization on the run and Twomey himself in hiding he could on the one hand admit that it was 'a waste of time' to hope for revolts within Fianna Fáil, but at the same time believe that 'people are being rapidly disillusioned' by the government's policies.

Even as late as 1935 there existed a belief among the IRA leadership that de Valera and the government were still concerned about their opinions. This belief was certainly encouraged by Joseph McGarrity of the Clan na Gael whose long-distance misinterpretations of the relationship between de Valera and the IRA have been much commented on. It was this belief which saw a meeting between Seán Russell and de Valera at Government Buildings during 1934, where Russell pledged that the IRA would not cause the government difficulties if they agreed to declare a republic within five years. De Valera, who continued to demand a hand over of arms from the IRA would not consider the proposal, and indeed there was no reason why a popularly elected leader should defer to suggestions from an organization of declining importance with a contracting base of support.

Why did men as capable, if disimilar in outlook as Twomey, MacBride, O'Donnell and Gilmore envisage the prospect of republicans benefiting from a collapse in Fianna Fáil's support? Partially the answer must lie in the self sustaining nature of their ideology, the belief that they were right and that the Irish people would ultimately realize that. But there were also more practical reasons for believing such an outcome was possible, particularly when one looks at the relationship between the two organizations at rank and file level. For a period it did seem as if the Fianna Fáil government was leading Ireland to a confrontation with Britain. There was also considerable evidence that much of the Fianna Fáil organization found it difficult to sever ties with the IRA.

Incidences of cross over in membership continued to trouble the IRA for a period. In May 1932 two companies in north Clare had to be disbanded because their membership were all 'Fianna Fáil and would not leave it'. A year later Twomey found the IRA in Kilmallock, Co. Limerick, was dominated by Fianna Fáil members. The treasurer of the local Fianna Fáil cumann was also an IRA member. Indeed, in Limerick a local officer complained that there was not enough distinction between Fianna Fáil and his organization. During 1932 at least three IRA members were employed as drivers for government ministers, including Seán T. O'Kelly. More importantly there was a widespread perception that the Fianna Fáil government would take care of republicans who had been discriminated against under the previous government.

The IRA leadership received many requests to use their perceived influence with Fianna Fáil to secure employment for their supporters. One Mitchelstown man, who had heard Twomey enjoyed great influence with Tom Derrig, the new Minister for Education, wrote hoping a position as a teacher could be arranged for his son. A republican from Carrick on Suir wrote hoping to secure compensation for his mother, who had lost her job in 1922 because her sons had fought with the anti-Treaty forces. Local Fianna Fáil supporters had convinced him to write to Twomey, because they believed the IRA had 'tremendous influence' on the new government and their intervention would 'practically ensure its success'. The IRA leadership did urge its officers in Cavan to apply for work at the labour exchanges in Cavan town and Bailieboro, on the basis that local Fianna Fáil TDs had control of appointments there. There were also attempts to use the IRA's influence to prevent Cumann na nGaedheal supporters being appointed, as in the case of a doctor in Carrickmacross, Co. Monaghan. IRA leaders were urged by their local officers to pressurize Frank Aiken to prevent the post going to an ex-Free State officer.

How much real influence the IRA leadership did have is harder to judge. Twomey asked Tom Derrig to help attain a teaching position for the wife of army council member Mick Price, but Derrig, while sympathetic to her case, was not hopeful of being able to help her. Even in the case of a leading figure like Andy Cooney, who had applied for the post of Dublin city coroner, meetings with Derrig and Seán MacEntee failed to secure him the post. However, Derrig does seem to have secured Tomás Ó Maoileóin's registration as a secondary school teacher.

Nevertheless the IRA informed one veteran from Enniskillen who inquired about compensation for civil war service that the organization had 'no intimate connection' with the government at all. There is some evidence of concrete assistance in Kerry, where the secretary of Kenmare Fianna Fáil was instrumental in gaining employment for some local IRA members. Fianna Fáil were later to claim that they had provided numerous 'positions and favours' to IRA members in the county. Indeed, a Westmeath IRA officer complained that men were joining the IRA and Fianna Fáil simply to get jobs. However the IRA leadership had made it clear that while they had no objection to their members in Kerry leading deputations to Fianna Fáil TDs seeking work, they were to do so as civilians, not as IRA officers.

The mood of euphoria among republicans made the Easter 1932 commemorations the largest in many years, conjuring up images of 'the old Sinn Féin and IRA days'. Seán McCool described how Easter 1932 'did one's heart good after all the black years ... the youth are with us and that's everything'. What was notable throughout the year was the participation of Fianna Fáil TDs and councillors in events organized by the IRA. This clearly gave the impression that the two organizations were working in tandem. When Gilmore spoke in Ballymahon, Co. Longford, his meeting was presided over by local councillor Thomas Carter. A talk by Frank Ryan on 'Republicanism and the IRA' in Sligo was chaired by Alderman J. Lynch. TDs Tom McEllistrim, John Flynn and Eamonn Kissane were present at several IRA commemorations in Co. Kerry that spring. Three TDs also attended the Wolfe Tone commemoration at Bodenstown in June. Even with the growing division between the two organizations nationally over the next two years, incidences like these continued to be relatively commonplace; 1933's Easter commemorations saw Fianna Fáil participation in IRA events in Sligo, Kilkenny, Wexford and Offaly.

At Sligo's Easter commemoration in 1934, Alderman Lynch, now Mayor of the town, read the IRA's statement. In Ennis, Councillor Seán Hayes presided over the commemoration and urged young men to 'join the republican army'. Neil Blaney TD marched in the IRA's Drumboe commemoration in Donegal, and in Arklow, Co. Wicklow, there was a strong showing by the local Fianna Fáil cumann at the IRA's Easter ceremony. Even as late as 1935 some Fianna Fáil members from Cork and Wexford were expected to travel to Bodenstown with their local IRA units. Earlier that year when Fianna Fáil attempted to introduce a new badge, the 'Torch,' in place of the lily, there was a backlash from the organization's rank and file. The party's North Leitrim executive condemned the move as a 'weakening from the Republican idea'. Cumainn in Listowel, Co. Kerry, refused to display or distribute the new badges. The party's Roscrea cumann was dissolved for refusing to sell the new emblem. News of the 'great upset' within Fianna Fáil gave heart to Twomey who was on the run following arrests during the Dublin Tram strike.

Much of that could be considered sentimental attachment to republican symbolism. The reaction within Fianna Fáil to the IRA's activities shows that at rank and file level considerable sympathy for the organization continued to exist despite the growing chasm at leadership level. Despite warnings from de Valera that illegal possession of arms would not be tolerated by the government, the November 1932 Fianna Fáil ard fhéis was dominated by calls (22 motions in all) for the disbanding of the 'CID.' Already that month a Fianna Fáil cumann in Ballinrobe had threatened to resign from the party over the jailing of a local IRA member. The year 1932 had been a reasonably peaceful, so perhaps there was little reason to expect a breach between the IRA and the Fianna Fáil rank and file; but 1933 saw increasing violence, and provocative activities by the IRA leading to arrests and jailings. But the Fianna Fáil ard fhéis again heard calls from the floor for the release of republican prisoners, or the granting of political status to IRA men in Mountjoy and Arbour Hill. Delegates raised accusations of ill-treatment and compared government policy to that of Cumann na nGaedheal. The MC of the ard fhéis ceilidhe interrupted the proceedings to inform delegates that he agreed with the actions of Galway IRA men jailed for seizing a British war film. The South East Cork comhairle ceanntair of the party also condemned these arrests. Fianna Fáil cumainn praised the efforts made by Senator Michael Comyn in 'upholding the honour of the IRA' against a 'scurrilous' attack by an opposition senator. Following the arrest and jailing of leading Kerry IRA members after a serious riot in Tralee, the Kerry comhairle ceanntair of Fianna Fáil called for their release. Tralee Fianna Fáil member Ned Drummond claimed that almost all the Kerry Fianna Fáil cumainn had passed resolutions demanding the release of the prisoners.

By 1934 the breach between the IRA and Fianna Fáil should have been complete. *An Phoblacht* was increasingly seized or censored by the authorities and every week brought new cases of IRA prisoners tried before the non jury military tribunal. Pressure from within the IRA meant the organization stood candidates against Fianna Fáil in many areas during the June local elections. Nine were elected as 'Independent republicans', providing evidence of a small base for the IRA electorally. Even then, in some areas, IRA members continued to give assistance to Fianna Fáil candidates. *An Phoblacht* regularly carried reports of Fianna Fáil cumainn who called for the release of IRA prisoners at various stages between 1933 and 1935. The Fianna Fáil Kerry county executive grew exasperated with its members who 'having been silent in the face of brutal attacks on their own supporters' had rallied around the cases of IRA prisoners who had made 'unproven allegations' about ill treatment.

Even so during 1935 both in public and in private Fianna Fáil members continued to attack the government's policies towards the IRA. The Fianna Fáil-dominated Clare county council voted unanimously to call on the government to repeal the Public Safety Act, Seán Hayes describing it as a law designed to keep Ireland 'in subjection'. Fianna Fáil's members on Tralee urban district council backed a motion calling for an inquiry into ill-treatment of IRA prisoners in the Curragh. Similar motions were submitted from cumainn in Tipperary and Kerry. Fianna Fáil members on Donegal county council, including Neil Blaney TD, endorsed the Republican Congress appeal for unity between all republican organizations. A unity meeting also sponsored by Congress was initially endorsed by Fianna Fáil TD Dan Breen and by representatives of four of the party's cumainn. Pleas for the removal of IRA prisoners from the Curragh, or the unconditional release of others were forwarded through Kerry TDs Kissane, McEllistrim and Denis Daly. With that background it is understandable that Twomey could believe in January 1935 that the movement was 'going to gather great strength very rapidly' because Fianna Fáil cumann were 'speaking out openly against the coercion of Republicans'.

The reasons for these motions help illustrate several different reasons for the lingering sympathy within Fianna Fáil for the IRA. Duagh Fianna Fáil in Co. Kerry wanted clemency for local IRA men because they came from 'a badly hit section of the community, who have up to now helped our party'. One of the Tralee IRA prisoners was the son of a Fianna Fáil UDC member. His father expressed the continuing contradiction in rank and file Fianna Fáil attitudes to the state when he claimed his son was only in jail because 'like all young Kerry lads' he refused to give gardaí an account of his movements. Tipperary Fianna Fáil members demanded the release of a local IRA man because in 1931 he had been secretary of their Cumann and had done 'a lion's share' to 'oust the Cosgrave government'. Daly and McEllistrim felt clemency would improve support for the government in Kerry where sympathy for IRA prisoners was 'general' and would also remove a propaganda weapon from the IRA.

Why were Fianna Fáil members so eager to protest on behalf of an organization that was undermining their government? Initially at least, it was because the IRA was not trying to impair the government. Its policy was to support Fianna Fáil in so far as it challenged Britain. Therefore many Fianna Fáil members could happily attend IRA events and cheer speakers who called for a stepping up of pressure against the 'Imperialists'. After all there was nothing in the IRA that was 'inimical to the people of the country' according to Paddy Ruttledge, Minister for Lands and Fisheries. Unlike for example the ACA, Fianna Fáil representatives could argue that the IRA had 'their roots in the sentiments of our people'. In Stranorlar, Co. Donegal, Seán McCool was proposed and seconded as a council candidate by the area's Fianna Fáil cumann, even though he was not a member of the party! Moreover, organizations dominated by Fianna Fáil such as the United Farmers' Association in Cork could pledge 'complete support to the Irish Republican Army'. Given that the IRA was again putting its weight behind Fianna Fáil's re-election effort in January 1933 such pronouncements seemed natural.

The practical value to Fianna Fáil of the IRA's support is illustrated by reports on election work from north Mayo. There 215 IRA men were 'working day and night' on the election campaign. In a show of strength over 100 men had marched in formation to the Fianna Fáil election rooms on 10 January. A week later they had provided stewards for a visit by de Valera and disarmed members of the ACA.

The attitude of many Fianna Fáil supporters to IRA involvement in clashes with the newly formed ACA is not difficult to explain. During 1932 and 1933 supporters of Fianna Fáil were as likely to have been involved in violence against Cumann na nGaedheal supporters as IRA members were. The first major clash between republicans and the ACA occurred in Kilmallock, Co. Limerick on 9 October 1932. Several hours of rioting only ended after the ACA were escorted out of the town by soldiers. During the disturbances the republicans had been addressed by the chairman of east Limerick Fianna Fáil and at court cases following the events gardaí referred to rioters as the 'Fianna Fáil crowd'. As we have already seen the IRA in Kilmallock was dominated by Fianna Fáil members. Twomey argued that violent clashes with the Blueshirts were largely 'spontaneous' and very often carried out by Fianna Fáil supporters.

There were three occasions in late 1932 when the IRA's policy of avoiding conflict with the state forces was put to the test. The first and the most serious occurred in August when Gilmore and T.J. Ryan were arrested in Kilrush, Co. Clare, by detectives and in the process shot and wounded. The IRA's response was to demand the disbandment of the 'CID' but not to allow any 'pretext for armed clashes'. An inquiry found that the detectives were guilty of violation of duty and they were dismissed. The second case involved the training camp established by the IRA for several years in Donamon Castle, Co. Roscommon. Despite there being no problems with the gardaí, the IRA considered that training efforts on that scale made confrontation inevitable and as the 'temper of the enemy forces, as disclosed in Kilrush' made armed conflict likely, they should not be attempted.

Later that year there were serious clashes at a Cumann na nGaedheal meeting in Cork city, and gardaí dispersed republican counter demonstrators with baton charges. The IRA in Cork felt constrained because they were under orders not to confront police and therefore had to stand by as 'some of our men got beaten up'.

During August 1932 Dr T.F. O'Higgins published a list of 12 incidents which he claimed proved that the ACA was needed to protect free speech. Only three were actions carried out by the IRA and two of these were without official sanction. It is difficult to confirm many of the examples often cited of widespread republican intimidation during 1932. What is certainly true is that there was a widespread feeling of euphoria among republicans, with the IRA feeling that they had 'an opportunity now that we have been looking for years'. That confidence among republicans was summed up by one leading IRA officer when he exclaimed that 'the country is splendid just now!' No doubt to their opponents this triumphalism was seen as evidence that the IRA was closer to power than was the reality. To illustrate the disparity in preception, even as late as December 1933 Fianna Fáil supporters in Achill could still conclude that they were more likely to be batoned by gardaí than the Blueshirts and that the law was protecting supporters of the opposition. The intensity of the violence that became associated with republican-Blueshirt confrontations during late 1933 certainly dismayed the government, but not many of its rank and file supporters who were still inclined to engage in physical battles with their 'Free State' enemies. This was certainly the case in Kerry, where civil war bitterness was often sharpest felt. The real turning point for the IRA came when its violence began to be targeted at government supporters. Even then, the reaction was complex and differed from region to region.

There is evidence of a desire on Fianna Fáil's part to put some distance between itself and the IRA as early as the summer of 1932. Firstly the IRA were informed that Fianna Fáil would organize their own Wolfe Tone commemoration unless de Valera was the main speaker at the IRA's event. The IRA refused the demand and in the event Fianna Fáil did not organize a rival commemoration although senior figures did not attend the IRA's rally. From 1933 onwards however there was a separate Fianna Fáil commemoration at Bodenstown. After the first jailing of an IRA member under the Fianna Fáil government it was reported to the IRA that Oscar Traynor TD had complained that the IRA had no right to publicly protest about the arrest and were not giving Fianna Fáil a 'chance to govern'. At this stage divisions seemed to have been more marked at leadership level and in the capital. The IRA had organized a number of rallies under the auspices of the Anti-Imperialist League in an effort to increase the level of anti-British feeling. In Cork, Sligo and Limerick Fianna Fáil sent speakers, but in Dublin they refused to do so. Instead, Fianna Fáil held its own rally, with 30,000 hearing de Valera speak in College Green. In the aftermath of the Kilrush incidents a delegation of Fianna Fáil supporters had visited de Valera and Gerald Boland with demands for the CID's disbandment. They were allegedly told that an 'established body' such as the Special Branch could not be disbanded as easily as people imagined and more importantly that 'delegations such as theirs' could not be allowed to run the government.

During 1933, with Fianna Fáil in office with a secure majority and IRA activities leading to more arrests and jailings the organization's condemnations of the government became shriller. In some areas this led to a definite break in relations between the two organizations. In Dublin the IRA realized as early as April 1933 that ex-members were being utilized by the government to use the ties they maintained with old comrades to collect information on the organization. The actions of the United Farmers' Association in Cork caused distress too for their president, Tom Hales TD, who 'soundly rated' them for their pro-IRA resolution of January and remarked that the IRA leadership were a 'harebrained lot'. In Ballaghadereen, Co. Roscommon, Fianna Fáil members on hearing of an IRA plan to paint slogans before a visit by de Valera, confiscated their paint and brushes and gave the names of the IRA men involved to the gardaí! However, in most areas there was still a good deal of rank and file fraternization. Neither leadership were necessarily happy with this. Twomey complained to one local IRA officer that if 'these Fianna Fáil people are pretending to be friendly' they should support the IRA's Bodenstown commemoration and not the rival Fianna

Fáil event. Personal relationships between individuals suffered increasingly as well, with Twomey objecting to Bill Quirke's interest in a memorial to Liam Lynch, as he was now someone 'doing their best to smash the army' and as such should no longer had 'any rights' in the matter.

Another area where divisions between the IRA and Fianna Fáil became apparent was that of social radicalism. An attempt by the IRA to enlist Fianna Fáil support to prevent an eviction in Offaly helps illustrates this growing division. The case was tailor-made for radical republican intervention. Property in Kinnitty formerly owned by a British Army colonel was granted by the Land Commission to an ex-Free State officer, and a family who had been living on the estate's gate lodge for several years ordered to leave. Local IRA commander Seán McGuinness led 35 men in an occupation of the lodge. His brother Patrick, president of the local Fianna Fáil club, sent a telegram asking for intervention from the Minister for Justice. Official Fianna Fáil circles remained silent on the matter. The IRA leadership too was wary of McGuinness' enthusiasm for this agitation. Eventually the intervention of Fianna Fáil TD Patrick Gorry secured an end to the occupation with the assurance that no eviction would take place until he discussed the matter with the minister. However, the following day the family were evicted; accommodation was secured for them in Tullamore workhouse, while McGuinness attempted to continue the campaign. A rally in Tullamore heard him attack the government for 'spouting and prattling about national unity ... against British Imperialism, but when an old man of 70 years and his wife and family challenge the same Imperialism they are catapulted to the roadside'. The Kinnitty Fianna Fáil club demanded that the government re-instate the family and take them out of the workhouse, an institution that had 'its root in the conquest'. When the Fianna Fáil organization in Tullamore discussed the issue divisions emerged. While one councillor argued strongly for support for the IRA's campaign he was warned that the party should not involve itself in any action that could harm the government, who were 'up against bigger things than an eviction'. The matter was eventually left to rest, disillusioning McGuinness and his allies within the IRA and exposing the limits of Fianna Fáil's commitment to land reform.

The IRA were also accused of being behind an industrial dispute in the *Irish Press* in late 1932. Despite the fact that, as the IRA wryly noted, the paper on occasion liked to 'pretend that everybody employed is a Volunteer', in fact only six IRA members worked there. Nevertheless the organization did support a strike at Fianna Fáil's most important ally and therefore exacerbated tension between itself and the government.

The government's decision to deport Leitrim socialist Jim Gralton in March 1933 also marked a clear shift for Fianna Fáil. The demands to deport Gralton came in the midst of the most sustained anti-Communist campaign in the Free State since the 1931 'Red Scare.' However, this time elements within Fianna Fáil were promoting the campaign, with Leitrim TD Ben Maguire particularly vocal in denouncing Gralton. Only three Fianna Fáil clubs supported Gralton's demand to stay in Ireland, showing a much more marked tendency among the party to adjust to anti-Communist hysteria.

Indeed the occasion of the government's major clampdown on the IRA was one where the organization had intervened in an industrial dispute: the Dublin transport dispute of March 1935. After the government ordered the Army to begin transporting passengers in Dublin city, the IRA denounced this and offered their services to the strikers. The government used the IRA's intervention as an opportunity to round a large number of its Dublin activists, although Twomey, Russell and MacBride evaded capture. Only one Dublin Fianna Fáil cumann came out in support of the strikers, and even that body was divided on the issue.

All of the various political tendencies within the IRA believed that elements with Fianna Fáil were sympathetic to them. After they split from the IRA, O'Donnell and Gilmore's Republican Congress continued to highlight any hint of radicalism from Fianna Fáil's rank and file. Motions at ard fheisanna complaining about the slow pace of land reform, calling for the release of imprisoned IRA members or a ban on Knights of Columbanus membership were seized upon as evidence of grassroots revolt. While motions on these topics appeared regularly at Fianna Fáil gatherings they represented an increasingly marginalized section of the party. Republicans failed to grasp the fundamentally conservative nature of the Fianna Fáil project.

This was apparent too in Twomey's own views on social affairs. In 1933 he argued that Fianna Fáil could be more dangerous than Cumann na nGaedheal because they were encouraging Irish capitalism. Twomey believed that this would inevitably lead to economic chaos. Later that year he criticized the government for yielding to the 'clamour of the Imperialist-rancher-banker-Chamber of Commerce element'. In early 1935 he complained that Fianna Fáil were being dominated by the industrialists who were possibly 'the most powerful menace to republicanism'. Whatever about Twomey's analysis, it is clear that he had expected Fianna Fáil to pursue very different policies. It was not just the IRA left that that held a different vision of 'the republic' from Fianna Fáil's but the IRA 'mainstream' as well.

The IRA's belief in the inevitable disillusionment of rank and file government supporters is a major factor in explaining its decline under Fianna Fáil. Notwithstanding, as we have seen, left to their own devices many Fianna Fáil supporters would have allowed the IRA considerable lee way. How the Fianna Fáil leadership neutralized the IRA, at remarkably little political cost to itself, is the other major factor that must be considered. Again the IRA's own tactics often played into their opponent's hands.

A defining factor in transforming IRA-Fianna Fáil hostility was the launch of the Volunteer Reserve. The reasoning behind the formation of this force was clearly political. The IRA had known and been worried by the possibility of such a development since 1932. Twomey admitted that the launch of such a body would 'impose a great test on young and untried republicans'. At its 1934 convention the organization's leadership had stressed that opposition to the new force should be political rather than military. However, both Leitrim and Kerry delegates had openly forecast a violent reaction in their areas. In Kerry during the winter of 1934–5 there were dozens of violent incidents ranging from assaults on individuals to gun and bomb attacks on Volunteer halls. The IRA representative on Kerry county council proposed that council facilities be denied to the new force, gaining the support of Fine Gael councillors but obviously worsening relations with Fianna Fáil. While it was the case that even after these events there remained reluctance among sections of Fianna Fáil to confront the IRA, the brutality displayed by the organization (with or without leadership sanction) undoubtedly made it easier for the government to isolate them. Some recruitment to the Volunteers seems to have been accompanied by the promise of preferences being given to members in local public works. This would suggest that Fianna Fáil 'bought off' much of the IRA through military service pensions and other preferential treatment. While this cannot be discounted in individual cases, the IRA's shortcomings in strategy combined with an ideological attack from the government were more important factors.

From 1933 onwards Fianna Fáil challenged the IRA's claim to revolutionary legitimacy, claiming that its activities aided the enemies of Irish republicanism, and increasingly appealed to the concept of majoritarian democracy. One important contention was based on the claim that the IRA of 1933 represented a 'new IRA' quite different from the organization of 1919–23. As early as July 1932 this phrase was being used by elements within Fianna Fáil in Dublin, one of whom, an ex-IRA member himself, claimed that the army council were a 'cowardly pack' who had refused to fight during the 'coercion' period. As tension between the organizations increased this argument was expressed more publicly. Fianna Fáil speakers and publications consistently referred to the military record of their leaders, 'nearly all' of whom were 1916 veterans. Contrasting with what he claimed was the liberal regime for IRA prisoners in Arbour Hill, de Valera reminded a Kerry audience that 'prison was never easy' which he could testify having been jailed on several occasions but that both himself and Austin Stack had endured far worse conditions during 1919 but did not 'grumble about it'.

In 1935 Fianna Fáil in Kerry claimed that it contained far more veterans of the civil war in its ranks than the 'new IRA'. What was more this 'new IRA' in many cases contained a 'rabble ... each member of which is a law unto himself' which sheltered behind the 'honoured name' of the IRA.

Fianna Fáil consistently argued that the IRA had departed from its traditional aims. During the Dublin transport strike de Valera contrasted the 'old IRA' which regarded itself as 'the army of the nation ... of the whole people' with the instigators of 'sectional strife' who lent themselves out like some 'racketeering organization'. Fianna Fáil noted too the extent to which 'class propaganda' had supplanted nationalism for the 'new IRA'. Concern was expressed by Fianna Fáil speakers for the young IRA men who were being 'duped' by the 'hot air' talked by their leaders. De Valera warned youngsters not to be seduced by the 'glamour' attached to the title IRA.

The credentials of IRA leaders themselves were challenged. When Frank Aiken was heckled by IRA supporters shouting 'up Tom Barry' he replied that the young men shouting this obviously knew little about the civil war, when while he and others were fighting 'Tom Barry was running around trying to make peace'. Seán MacEntee reminded IRA hecklers that he had fought in 1916, the 'Black and Tan war' and the civil war, before asking them 'can you tell me where you served?'

It was also stressed that whatever their intentions, the actions of the IRA played into the hands of Ireland's enemies. In late 1933 Aiken had referred to the 'foolish friends' of republicanism who unknowingly were doing more damage to it than its enemies. The *Irish Press* in 1935 claimed that the IRA's complaints about Fianna Fáil were being 'greeted eagerly by Ireland's enemies' and contributing to a possible return to power of Fine Gael. The paper was adept at portraying their administration as being under siege 'from three sides' with the IRA playing the worst role of all by undermining the government from the 'left'.

Fianna Fáil also increasingly justified their stance in terms of majority rule. As de Valera warned 'we are either going to have democracy ... or dictatorship of one kind or the other'. Aiken made clear to those who objected to the jailing of IRA members that the government was elected promising to 'protect all citizens and their person and property'. While the use of force may have been justified in the past, now the government had created a situation where 'peaceful ordered progress on the basis of majority decision' was possible. Those within Fianna Fáil who raised objections to government policy towards the IRA or who questioned the government's progress towards republican goals were told to 'get rid of their inferiority complex'. Those who clung to traditional demands were 'too provincial, narrow and small minded' to see the greater strategy the government was employing.

Despite the evidence of rank and file unease Fianna Fáil managed to carry the majority of its supporters with remarkably few losses. Indeed it claimed that even on contentious issues like the Easter 'Torch' the majority of the party had refused to be 'misled by IRA propaganda'. Just one TD, Tom Hales, resigned because of government policy towards the IRA, and republican opponents of the government were trounced in two bye elections during 1936.

Again the IRA's own tactics during 1935 and 1936 played an important role here. The increasingly desperate propaganda about 'Fianna Fáil Fascism' and the violence used against members of the Volunteer Force illustrate how politically bankrupt the organization had become. While the killing of More O'Ferrall in Edgeworthstown did not necessarily widen the gap between the IRA and rank and file Fianna Fáil members, the murders of John Egan and Admiral Boyle Sommerville certainly did so. Fianna Fáil made great play of how these 'callous and cowardly' murders made nonsense of the IRA's claims to patriotism. Frank Gallagher expressed his disgust to Joseph McGarrity at those who believed the way to further their cause was by 'stealing up to an old man's door, calling him out, shooting him down, and running away'.

The IRA's strategy towards Fianna Fáil was based on the belief that once in government it would inevitably disappoint its republican supporters. In fact Fianna Fáil managed to broaden its base of support while maintaining the loyalty of most of its rank and file. While sympathy existed for them at grassroots level in Fianna Fáil, the IRA overestimated the extent of this. The organization's confrontational policies, particularly during 1934, further alienated potential sympathizers within Fianna Fáil. The government's skilful presentation of themselves as both the inheritors of the revolutionary tradition and the defenders of democracy in Ireland forced the IRA onto the defensive politically. The IRA's attempts to deal with this led to the departure of its left wing during 1934 and the dominance of militarism within the organization meant it reacted to its political isolation by belligerent attacks on government supporters, further increasing that isolation. The IRA misjudged not just Fianna Fáil but the extent to which republican supporters in the Free State desired radical change. The evidence suggests that Fianna Fáil satisfied the majority of Irish republican aspirations.

8/The IRA in Northern Ireland

The IRA operated in very different circumstances in Northern Ireland. After 1928 republican Easter commemorations were banned. From 1929 the sale and distribution of *An Phoblacht* was illegal in the six counties. Northern republicans arrested for IRA activity could be deported to the Free State. Republicans were a minority among northern nationalists, most of whom supported the Nationalist Party. All IRA activity took place in the shadow of the origins of the state itself, which had seen almost 500 people killed and thousands driven from their homes. Nationalists remembered these events as pogroms designed to terrorize them into submission. To them, as the IRA was to discover, the fight was 'not so much one of Republic versus Free State' but for their very 'existence'. In contrast to unionists the IRA simply meant 'violence and terror in the name of Irish nationalism'. For them the establishment of the state had not been seen an anti-Catholic pogrom but an attempt to 'strangle Northern Ireland at birth'.

As a result of these influences a consensus exists about the northern IRA. Both supporters and detractors are content to claim that its main role was as a sectarian militia. As Laffan has stated, 'for most of the 1920s and 1930s the Northern units of the IRA saw their role as a defensive one, protecting the Catholic minority against the Protestant majority'. More sympathetic accounts have also described the IRA as the 'only defenders of the Catholic communities in the north, especially in Belfast.' While there certainly existed an element of 'defenderism' that cannot be discounted, for a period during the 1930s, under pressure from its national leadership the IRA made serious efforts to win cross-community support. The key element in this was the industrial unrest of 1932–3, which the IRA believed signalled a breakdown in sectarianism. Even when called upon to 'defend' in this period, the IRA displayed little enthusiasm for that role.

The problems the IRA faced when attempting to reorganise in Northern Ireland during the 1920s cannot be overstated. The majority of the Northern IRA had supported the Treaty, but had engaged in a major offensive in the summer of 1922. A smaller anti-Treaty force had also been involved in conflict with the Northern security forces at this stage. Both were essentially crushed by the autumn of that year, with over 1,000 men going south to join the National Army. During 1924 a report by the IRA's director of intelligence found that there was little enthusiasm for republicanism among most nationalists. Instead they were 'keeping quiet – satisfied that they are allowed to live ... I should say the vast majority look upon the satisfactory solution of the Boundary question as the most that could possibly be achieved. They regard Republicans as attempting the impossible and as a menace to their peace'. IRA strength in Northern Ireland that year was just 628. A year later Twomey himself gained first hand experience of the north when he inspected units in Tyrone and Derry. In Tyrone the IRA's organization was 'exceedingly bad'. There was little civilian support for the IRA and the Catholic population seemed to be 'cowed completely by the Specials'. He also found that nationalists who wanted inclusion in the Free State feared that IRA activity would prejudice their chances of this. In military terms there was no IRA organization in Derry city or county. Most nationalists there too seemed desperate to find some way of being included in the Free State. He also suggested that many northern Catholics seemed to 'slavishly follow' the clergy and that this was a factor in their passivity.

Two years later and the IRA was forced to acknowledge that its northern 'military organization is in a most backward state, and in many areas non-existent ... morale is very low and distrust amongst comrades is widespread'. By November of that year the IRA's strength in the six counties had shrunk to 517 men. All the evidence points towards the IRA in Northern Ireland stagnating for several years. In 1930 the RUC noted the low turnouts for Easter commemorations and felt that in Derry city, for example, there had never been less public sympathy for the IRA. Perhaps because of its own weakness as early as 1924 the IRA was hoping that the Labour movement might make gains which would allow more space for a republican opposition to develop. Just two years later the belief that people were 'flocking' towards Labour and even that the nucleus of a 'Citizen Army' was being formed seemed to give some solace to the Belfast IRA. By 1931 the IRA in that city had just 260 active members; 40 of these men were based in the Ardoyne area and 30 in Ballymacarret and the Markets. Substantial growth in the northern IRA did not occur until after 1932.

Politically the northern IRA was hostile to much of the radicalism espoused by their comrades in Dublin. Unlike in the south, Sinn Féin enjoyed some influence among the northern IRA. Belfast IRA commander Davy Matthews was a member of the party, for example. After the IRA's 1932 convention Matthews informed headquarters in Dublin that his unit were of the 'firm opinion that the army has deviated from the path of nationalism and has taken to the road of materialism through Saor Éire'. Similar attitudes were expressed by IRA units in Down and Armagh, who proposed that Saor Éire be 'absolutely abolished'. An exception was the Derry city IRA who supported the launch of a new radical political organization. This does not mean that the IRA in Belfast was necessarily hostile to activity on social issues however, as we shall see from the events of 1932.

In July of that year the IRA leadership issued an appeal to the Orange Order. At first glance the summer of 1932 would seem an inauspicious time for the IRA to consider issuing an such appeal. The level of inter communal tension was high, following widespread attacks on Catholics travelling to the Eucharistic Congress in Dublin during June. There were assaults on Catholic travellers in several towns including Belfast, Ballymena and Larne, and a mob stormed the railway station at Portadown, where pilgrims were trapped on a train. Early July saw more violence as Catholic homes and businesses were attacked on Belfast's Crumlin Road. There is no doubt that the IRA could have made use of the tense atmosphere to launch attacks on the Orange Order. Seán McCool reported considerable hostility to a planned Orange march in Co. Donegal, springing from the attacks on people travelling to Dublin for the congress, and asked permission to issue a press statement denouncing 'imperialist displays.' Twomey refused the request, telling McCool that 'all our energies should be directed to preventing and discouraging any clashes, even in the face of provocation. Clashes just now would be very bad'. All Ulster units were also issued with these instructions. They were ordered to use their influence with non-IRA members to prevent them engaging in sectarian conflict. Seán Clerkin of the Monaghan IRA responded to rumours of attacks on local Protestants by issuing a statement declaring that 'all Irishmen, Protestant and Catholic ... will condemn the dastardly actions of the hooligans who attacked the six county Catholics while on their way to Dublin for the Eucharistic Congress' but that 'these attacks must not be made an excuse for future conflicts between Catholics and Protestants ... The enemies of Irish freedom are to be found equally within the Catholic and Protestant communities, and their role is to keep the masses of the Irish people divided by sharpening religious antagonisms'.

The IRA issued their 'Address to the men and women of the Orange Order' in July. The 'Address', written by Peadar O'Donnell, was in reality an appeal to Protestant workers and small farmers to unite with their Catholic counterparts in a struggle for 'the transfer of power over production, distribution and exchange to the mass of the people'. The IRA admitted that they were 'mainly Catholics' but reassured their Protestant audience that 'in Southern Ireland the same political and economical interests and voices that tell you we are Catholics, tell the Catholic population of the South that we are Anti-God fanatics'. It concluded with an appeal to the memory of 'your illustrious ancestors and co-religionists, the United Irishmen'. The appeal itself betrays confusion on the IRA's part as to who they were addressing. The terms 'Orange' and 'Protestant' are used interchangeably, if inaccurately. The Order itself had opposed the United Irish radicals of the 1790s, and was not in any way a descendant of theirs. While the IRA in Northern Ireland was also the subject of Catholic clerical condemnation, this did not make it any more attractive to Protestants.

Unionist reaction to the 'Address' was predictably hostile. Captain Chicester-Clark MP, speaking at Kilrea, Co. Derry, denounced the IRA for appealing 'to the small farmer and to the wage earner-whom they claim are being exploited ... they talked about Capitalism – forgetting that it is merely a nickname for civilised life, forgetting that there is no alternative but barbarism and death'. The IRA preached religious toleration , he said, but 'they mean the destruction of all religion, and the return to the barbarism and paganism of the dark ages'. At Ballinderry, Sir Joseph McConnell MP claimed the IRA's statements were 'very similar to those which enticed the Huguenots into Paris on the eve of the slaughter of St Bartholomew'. The *Belfast Newsletter* considered that for 'sheer impudence' it would be difficult to beat the IRA. The *Northern Whig* simply found the 'curious document' a strange example of IRA 'humour'. At Newry, the Revd Canon McGarvey told Orangemen that they had been invited to 'join with the IRA but oil and water could not mix, (and) neither would the Orange colours mix with those of the Pope'. J.C. Crosbie at Aughnacloy asserted that Orangemen would never join hands with republicans until the IRA 'pulled down the tricolour, hoisted the Union Jack, proclaimed the King as sovereign, and sang the National Anthem'. What reaction could the IRA have expected from members of the Orange Order to their arguments? After all they had just 11 months before physically prevented an Orange walk in Co. Cavan, which was widely seen by Protestants as a sectarian action. It should also be noted that the perception of IRA growth in the Free State following the entry of Fianna Fáil into government had caused alarm among northern Protestants.

More important is how the northern IRA itself reacted to the spirit of the 'Address.' All the organization's Ulster units were issued with instructions to both distribute and take note of the reaction to it. The leadership stressed that it wanted the 'Address' posted up in 'Orange districts'. They also wanted 'cuttings from any newspapers' mentioning the 'Address' and they especially wished to hear 'the comments on this Address by Orangemen'. Twomey himself stressed to Matthews that he hoped 'note will be taken of this (Address) in the Falls Road as well as in Sandy Row!' Furthermore all units were put on alert to discourage nationalists from engaging in clashes with Orange marchers. Twomey stressed that he 'hoped that things will pass over' without violence. He instructed Matthews to keep an eye on 'elements on the fringe of our movement' who might be intent on trouble. Matthews agreed to distribute the 'Address' in Belfast, but considered that it would be 'sheer madness' to order his men to post them up in 'hostile areas', so his battalion delivered the appeal door-to-door in Sandy Row. Some were delivered to hairdressers and boot repairers, because these did 'all the talking in their districts'. However, one IRA source reported that recipients of the 'Address' regarded them as 'warning notices'. Among nationalists the reaction was confused. In Derry, the local IRA commander, Terry Ward, reported that the document was 'much resented by the Catholic population who argued (unreasonably I think) that it was a sign of weakness'. Ward also felt that not only were the Orangemen themselves, 'scarcely aware of the appeal' but that 'most republicans, including Volunteers, regard it as a gesture which will not have the least effect'. Nevertheless, his unit distributed the 'Address'. The IRA's Armagh unit on the other hand, refused to, with their commander J.J. Murray telling the 1933 Convention that they had 'burnt them'. The Belfast IRA's intelligence officer was not hopeful of the 'Address' receiving much of a hearing among working class Protestants believing that they were still 'gulled by their leaders ... the IRA and de Valera are thrown up to them in their churches ... (and) the real economic state of the city is glossed over'. In one of the few southern reactions to the 'Address' the *Dundalk Examiner* called it 'an expression of naked and undisguised Communism' and argued that it justified the Catholic hierarchy's condemnation of the IRA. While the 'Address' showed naiveté and political confusion on the IRA's part, the fact that most of its Northern units distributed it would point to the lack of a sectarian mentality among its membership.

The Orange celebrations of that year were an opportunity to test the response of the IRA to the spirit of the address. A concrete example of how the IRA reacted to a potential threat can be seen from their mobilization in the Ardoyne, following rumours that the area was to be attacked after an Orange parade. Matthews mobilized 60 men, and had them order crowds off the streets and away from 'danger points', stressing to them it was their duty to avert trouble. By 6 p.m. the area was deserted, except for IRA units, hidden indoors. Matthews claimed the RUC knew the IRA were in position to defend the area, and kept the Orange marchers well away. However, the 'Greatest Twelfth That Ever Was' did not pass off peacefully. Shots were fired at Catholic homes in Armagh, stones thrown at Catholics on the Falls, and a Catholic was stabbed in Aughnacloy. Catholic ice cream vendors and confectionery sellers were attacked after the traditional sham battle at Scarva, Co. Down. There were also clashes between Catholics and Protestants on the Shankhill and the Falls Roads. There was no suggestion at the time that the IRA was involved in these disturbances, but its members had been mobilised in anticipation of an attack. Two companies of the IRA were undergoing training at camps at Carnlough and Carlingford but when reports were received of mobs gathering near the Falls Road, two sections of 14 men each were recalled to Belfast. The fact that the IRA's Belfast leadership was prepared to allow two companies to leave Belfast at this tense time is evidence of some reluctance, at least, to regard defending Catholic areas as the IRA's primary duty. Even stranger is that while the Belfast IRA informed its superiors that 'sectarian hatred is running high here at present' and that 'several cases of grievous assault' had been reported they did not anticipate serious trouble. Priests had implored mass goers to avoid trouble spots over the coming week. Nevertheless the IRA in Belfast were pleased to report to HQ in Dublin that their orders to 'avert sectarian trouble and at the same time, to stand by and be prepared, if required to take action' had been carried out successfully. The IRA in Belfast had 'kept patrols of Volunteers in all

Catholic districts in the city, to disperse all crowds, and allowing no-one to stand at street corners'. This evidence would point to the IRA wanting to avoid sectarian violence rather than provoke it.

If the IRA leadership were eager for an opportunity to intervene in a struggle which involved both sides of the sectarian divide, then they were soon to be presented with one, in the shape of the Outdoor Relief (ODR) strike of October 1932. The ODR strike is remembered as 'one of the few instances of inter-community action' in Northern Ireland's history. The strike was primarily the result of the effect of mass unemployment, and the low levels of relief open to the unemployed. Anger over the rigorous and demeaning means tests applied to those seeking relief was effectively channelled into action by the organization of a relief workers committee, dominated by members of the Revolutionary Workers' Groups (RWG), the forerunners of the Communist Party of Ireland. The dispute led to two weeks of street demonstrations, rioting and clashes with the police, in which two people (one Protestant and one Catholic) were killed. The RUC came under sniper fire on several occasions.

The IRA's attitude to the ODR strike and the role it played within it, was almost immediately a source of controversy. *An Phoblacht* was ecstatic about the strike, its headline declaring 'Orange and Green United in Belfast' and that the 'Irish Revolution' had begun. Sections of the Unionist Press were anxious to assign a leading role to the IRA in the dispute with one writer claiming 'the Communist element, backed by the local IRA forces, essayed the traditional Red tactics of trench and barricade'. IRA members were certainly involved in the marches, rallies and riots of October 1932. Testimony from veterans of the period confirms this, but also confirms that their involvement was largely as individuals.

The IRA leadership should not have been taken by surprise because its Belfast officers had been providing them with reports on the worsening economic conditions in the city since the early summer. In May they had written that the 'economic situation is gradually becoming worse. The Orange quarters of the city are coming to the point of desperation, as shown in Police reports and court cases ... The unemployment question here is becoming more desperate and confused.' There were reports that the RUC were guarding shops as rumours of looting were current. One reason why the IRA may not have responded quickly enough, was that its Belfast officers feared that this economic discontent was going to exacerbate sectarianism with 'everything pointing to another pogrom in the city'. Later in the summer Dublin were informed that 'discontent is rapidly growing in the city ... Transitional Benefit and Outdoor relief are making matters worse, the working man finding that he cannot hope for any help from either.' Seán MacBride replied that 'it is a pity that some of our people is not close enough to Labour elements to do some propaganda amongst them'. During September it was believed that the unemployed were becoming 'stronger and better organised'. Finally in October a report stated that among the unemployed a 'great deal of talk is going the rounds of action to be taken ... they are very well organised in the various districts and mass meetings have been arranged for all districts in the city.' The IRA also believed that some of the unemployed had access to arms.

The IRA did not take an organized part in the upheavals of October. One of its Belfast officers bemoaned the fact that recruiting had been slow that month. He considered that 'one would have thought the recent trouble in the city would have brought large numbers into the army'. But he also provided a clue as to why that was not the case. While he argued that 'some weeks prior to the strike special men should have been allotted the work of getting on these work-er's committees' he admitted that the IRA did not take part as an organization in the movement. Matthews himself took part in rioting in Sandy Row and attempted to encourage others there to do the same. Two republicans were also jailed for stone throwing. Given that the majority of Belfast IRA members came from working class backgrounds it is not surprising that many were involved in the ODR strike. There was, however, a significant difference between the IRA in Dublin and Belfast. In Dublin many of the small number of Communists were former IRA members and knew the IRA leadership personally. There was also a considerable social interaction between figures such as Hannah Sheehy-Skeffington (the deputy editor of *An Phoblacht*), Seán Murray of the RWG, and IRA members such as Frank Ryan and the Gilmore brothers. This relationship did not exist in Belfast. RWG leaders such as Tommy Geehan and Betty Sinclair had never been republicans. The suggestion by the IRA in Belfast that the unemployed leadership were 'not the right type' points to a suspicion of the communists which made co-operation unlikely. During the strike itself Davy Matthews is alleged to have refused an order from Dublin, because he consid-ered it to be 'Communist philosophy', but his own actions show that he clearly supported the strike, if not all of his leadership's analysis. Indeed, at the 1933 IRA Convention he enthusiastically informed delegates that the masses had united for the first time in the history of Belfast during the ODR strike.

The IRA seem to have decided that following their relative inactivity dur-ing the ODR strike they would not pass up such an opportunity again. Just two months later a bitter dispute broke out on the railways, which partially as a result of IRA action, would become one of the bloodiest in the north's history. During November 1932 the Irish railway companies announced their intention of cutting wages. In the Free State the government stepped in and subsidized the rail workers' pay. However, in Northern Ireland five of the six rail companies went ahead with the cuts. From 31 January 1933 the rail workers' unions began strike action. The rail companies utilized office staff and Queen's University students as strike-breakers and on the first day of the strike a train was derailed at Dromiskin, Co. Louth, and two workers from Dublin killed. As the strike spread, strike-breakers were boycotted, with townspeople in Glenties, Co. Donegal, for example, refusing them refreshments. Trains and buses were routinely stoned and sniper fire was directed at strike-breakers. During February, GNR buses were attacked in Dublin and strike-breakers beaten up in Dundalk. The RUC set up a 100-strong flying squad to patrol the rail network and they too became the target of snipers. The IRA were the driving force behind the widespread use of guns and explosives, with its whole organization involved. As the strike wore on more violent tactics were used to disrupt the rail network and an attempt was made to blow up a railway bridge at Dunmurray. Seán Russell was sent to Belfast to direct the IRA's military intervention. One of his reports confirms the truth of long standing rumours that the IRA co-operated with members of the B Specials during the strike. Russell informed Twomey that it was 'promising to find "B" Specials who are on strike in search of IRA assistance ... they realise that we are the only people capable of assistance - seemingly the only organization that has their confidence and sympathies. What a change to find one group of "Specials" searching the houses of our men, whilst another can be found collaborating with them!' Russell claimed that 'bombs used upon the railway station in Belfast a few days (ago) ... were supplied by the O/C Belfast and thrown by "B" Specials'. He also supplied mines and grenades to the IRA in Newry for use there. During the strike an RUC man was killed in a IRA attack on strike breakers. The young IRA men involved fled south. While four gardaí had been killed by the IRA in the late 20s and early 30s, this was the first time an RUC officer had died at their hands.

That the IRA leadership saw the strike as very significant is again confirmed by Twomey in a letter to a republican who feared sectarian riots in Belfast. Twomey did not believe such strife was likely because 'even if they tried very hard the Orange command would find it almost impossible to work up an atmosphere. There is an amazing change up there ... this railway strike is doing great damage to the Craigavon gang amongst the very people who would in ordinary circumstances, be the pogromists'. The IRA believed there would be a long-term benefit because there had been 'a realignment within the ranks of the Orange population upon a class basis, leading to a partial disintegration of the Orange machine. This tendency has even, in some cases, brought the Catholic and Protestant workers into joint armed conflict with the six-county Government on issues of mutual interest.' The strike itself ended in March, with a compromise involving a wage cut but with the promise of no sackings of strikers. The IRA's intervention had been of a military nature, secretive by necessity, and there is no indication that they gained any Protestant recruits from it. In what may have been a sequel to the strike, Matthews wrote to inform

Twomey that he had been offered ten rifles and ammunition from an 'Orange' source; but, the necessary cash was unavailable to the Belfast battalion and the deal fell through. We do know that the Belfast IRA did contain some Protestant members, such as William 'Liam' Tumilson, who joined the IRA in Short Strand during this period There are also claims from other IRA members that Protestants were involved in the Belfast IRA during the 1930s. The IRA's intervention was not universally approved of in its own ranks. Again the Armagh IRA objected that they had 'no right to take life in a labour dispute' and did not mobilize during the strike.

The experience of the ODR dispute and the Railway strike certainly influenced the IRA's decision to contest the November 1933 Stormont elections. The IRA argued that while the recent withdrawal of Nationalist MPs from Stormont had not meant 'a change of mind' in that party it indicated that 'they realise that their followers are becoming disillusioned, and see the futility of parliamentary methods'. This was leading to increased support for the IRA. The IRA would have to consider how the 'disillusioned elements amongst the Orange workers, and that leaderless section of Nationalist opinion, can be welded into the movement for the overthrow of Imperialism and exploitation'. Matthews told the IRA Convention that the elections offered an 'opportunity of going direct to the people. I understand that the greatest impediment is getting out of the way (Devlin). He has declared in private that he will not oppose the only organization that counts – the organization that has kept up the fight.' This statement confirms that Joseph Devlin, the leading nationalist figure in Northern Ireland politics, had decided to retire in 1933. The IRA leadership were aware of these developments as early as the previous November, when they were informed that there had been contact between Devlin and their members in Belfast. Some IRA officers raised worries about the prospect of electoral defeat. Twomey explained that he did 'not care whether we win or not. We do not expect to win by Parliamentary methods'. The decision to stand was then supported unanimously.

Prior to the elections sectarian tension had been on the increase. On 8 October an RUC officer was shot dead and, in the aftermath of this, 33 republicans arrested though none were charged with the murder. A few days later a Catholic publican was murdered in York Street and angry exchanges followed in Stormont between Nationalists and Unionists over the responsibility for these deaths. For a period after the 'shooting and counter shooting' the IRA leadership feared a 'pogrom' was likely. The elections of November 1933 were contested by four IRA candidates. It had been planned that an IRA prisoner, Arthur Thornbury, would contest Belfast Central, but his nomination papers were not allowed inside the jail. His brother Patrick, living in Westmeath since being deported for IRA activities in 1927, was selected in his place. Also selected to stand were Thomas McGrath in South Down, Seán McCool in Foyle (Derry City) and Patrick McLogan in South Armagh. McGrath was a former republican prisoner and a butcher. McLogan from Armagh, but resident in Portlaoise, was a member of the Army Council and McCool was commander of the IRA's Donegal No. 2 battalion. In a surprise move de Valera was persuaded to contest South Down for the Nationalists. *An Phoblacht* declared that this was the 'last kick of the Hibernians' arguing that the Nationalists had only been pursuing a 'mock opposition' to the Unionist government. The IRA accused de Valera of deliberately splitting the nationalist vote in South Down. His decision to stand was however a massive blow to any Republican hopes of capturing that seat. Devlin also decided to contest the elections, despite his earlier misgivings and the onset of illness. This too was a major blow to the IRA and Thornbury now faced a uphill battle in Belfast.

The contest was a bitter one, and the Nationalist press lost no opportunity to characterize the IRA as outsiders and traitors to the nationalist cause. The *Derry Journal* stated that the IRA were guilty of 'treachery towards the very cause of Irish unity'. Derry Nationalist MP J.J. McCarroll, in an appeal to his 'Catholic and Nationalist Electors' claimed that the IRA was anti-Catholic and that it was more at home with the 'Orange masses whose goodwill it has never tired of courting'. On election day itself the *Journal* advised its readers to 'Vote early, and ensure that these IRA incursionists are sent back to their secret bailiwicks – taught such a lesson that they will never again attempt to sow seeds of disunion in Nationalist Derry'. The *Journal*'s tone is not altogether surprising since its proprietor was McCarroll himself. However, the *Irish News* was if anything more vitriolic. It approvingly quoted Nationalist speakers as claiming the IRA was 'closely associated with Communism', was 'immoral and irreligious' and composed of 'usurpers from Cork'. It asserted that 'Unionists had never stooped so low as the Republicans had done in this election' and that 'Cromwell was the first Republican who came to Ireland, and every school boy knew what his record against the church was'. The *Irish News* stressed that 'Orangeism's one ray of hope in this election is the internal dissension introduced by the IRA'. Nationalist MP Cahir Healy stated that 'no Catholic could vote for the IRA.' The *Irish News* even claimed that the IRA had been given 'freedom of the six counties' by the Unionists.

Far from being given lee-way by the Unionist authorities, *An Phoblacht* claimed republicans were being prevented from campaigning by systematic RUC harassment. By December, 42 republicans were imprisoned in Crumlin Road. One of these was Matthews, who had been republican director of elections. Republican speakers stressed that sectarianism was being used to divide the people of the north. 15,000 people attended a rally for Thornbury in Belfast, and heard Donal O'Donoghue claim that 'the only concessions ever coming from the 'Northern Government' were when Catholic and Protestant stood shoulder to shoulder in the streets of Belfast'. Dublin IRA officer Con Lehane told the crowd that 'the real issue was not Catholic versus Protestant, but the struggle between exploited versus exploiter'. The results of the election were relatively good for the IRA; McLogan was elected in South Armagh and Thornbury was only 2,761 votes behind Devlin in Belfast.

Table 14. Stormont election results, 1933

Belfast Central	Foyle	S. Armagh	S. Down
J. Devlin	J.J. McCarroll	P.J. MacLogan	E. De Valera
(Nat. L) 7,411	(Nat. L) 6,557	(Rep.) 4,803	(Nat.) 7,404
P. Thornbury	S. McCool	J.G. Lennon	
(Rep.) 4,650	(Rep.) 3,031	(Ind. Nat.) 2,211	
		B. O'Neill	J.G. McGrath
		(Nat. L) 1,627	(Rep.) 622

These results were hailed by the IRA as proving that the election bid had been successful. The Belfast vote was seen as the most significant because despite having all the forces of 'Devlin reaction' against him Thornbury secured '1,605 more votes than de Valera secured in 1918 against Devlin' in what was by 1933 a much smaller constituency. Perhaps because of his decision to stand, republican propaganda was very hostile to Devlin and betrayed no hint that there had between discussions between the IRA and him. The Nationalists in Derry were accused of drawing their election workers from the Knights of Columbanus and the St Vincent de Paul Society, and of distributing material claiming McCool was an atheist. The poor result in South Down was put down to the confusion sown by de Valera's candidature. Only 50 per cent of those eligible to do so voted in the constituency, and the IRA attributed this to nationalist disgust at de Valera's last minute recruitment to the 'Hibernians'.

The results were significant. They showed that there was a sizeable urban base for radical republicanism, as well as strength in areas like South Armagh. Obviously the IRA had benefited from its higher profile and activity during the previous year. The results certainly shook the Nationalists with J.J. McCarroll telling Cahir Healy that 'it is a serious business that over 3,000 people voted against us'. The IRA proclaimed that the 'fight in the North has been given new life' and that Protestants now understood that the IRA was fighting for 'equal rights' and not religious bigotry. The IRA's successes were in the contest with conservative nationalism, often so bitterly fought, that young republicans had to depend on the RUC to protect them from enraged Devlin supporters outside the count in Belfast. The elections did not show Protestants were being convinced by the Republican message. Nor did republicans necessarily continue to promote a message of unity after the elections. In May 1934 MacLogan was quoted as telling a rally in Derrycash that 'let those in Ulster or in any part of Ireland who boast of and pride themselves that they are Britons ... clear out of Ireland'. There were distinct regional and personal differences in how IRA leaders interpreted their politics. Armagh was after all the only seat they actually won, and was an area where the local IRA was resistant to the leadership's instructions during 1932. Within a year and a half widespread sectarian warfare would once again be forcing the IRA into its 'traditional' role.

Matthew's IRA career came to a end when he was court-martialled and dismissed from the organization in January 1934. He had given an undertaking to the Northern Ireland authorities to cease membership of the IRA and was accused of attempting to convince other IRA men to do the same. The Communist *Irish Worker's Voice* hoped Matthew's departure signified a new direction for Northern republicans, as they held him responsible for what they called 'anti-working class' policies within the IRA. However, Matthews who attempted to organise rioters on Loyalist Sandy Row during the ODR strike is hardly deserving of that particular label. It is more likely that years of intense underground activity took their toll on him, and worth considering that thousands of young men passed through the IRA in this era and simply left, never having attained sufficient notoriety to be denounced on their departure.

From 1931 onwards loyalist extremism had remerged in the shape of the Ulster Protestant League (UPL). The UPL was involved in attacks on Labour and Communist meetings, as well as assaults on Catholics. Their activities helped create the atmosphere which led to the 1935 riots. Already in September of 1934, a Catholic man had been killed when loyalist mobs attacked Catholic homes in Marine Street. From April 1935 onwards there was a series of violent sectarian incidents. In mid May Catholics were shot and bombs thrown into the Catholic part of Vere Street. The UPL also broke up four Communist meetings. The authorities reacted by imposing a curfew. In June there were several shooting incidents, with both Catholic and Protestant casualties. The Northern government attempted to prohibit all public gatherings, but the Orange Order stated it would break such a ban. In this atmosphere it was obvious there could be serious violence during July, and when clashes broke out between Catholics and Protestants in York Street following an Orange march through there on 12 July, it developed into the worst sectarian violence seen in Belfast since 1922. At first involving rival crowds throwing stones soon firearms were being used and the night of the 12th saw two deaths, that of a Protestant youth, and a Catholic woman. Forty people were hospitalized, 20 with bullet wounds. By Monday the 15th, five people were dead, 58 homes had been looted or burnt out and British troops were called in to back up the RUC. The violence had a profound effect on Belfast's Nationalist population, reviving memories of 1922. The violence continued, although decreasing in ferocity, until two weeks later. Unionist politicians blamed nationalists for the trouble in the city with the *Belfast Newsletter* claiming that an 'unprovoked attack on the Orange Procession' on the 12th had caused the bloodshed. A few days later it attacked Nationalist MPs for petitioning Westminster for aid, when it was really the IRA with its avowed policy of 'using the gun against Ulster,' that was responsible for the 'dreadful bloodshed which is scourging Belfast'. The imperial grand master of the Orange Order claimed that 'Communists and members of the IRA' had attacked the march on 12 July, thus igniting the rioting. However, the RUC suggested that earlier disturbances in York Street had occurred because of Orange bandsmens' conduct.

More Protestants were killed in the violence than Catholics. However attempting to establish who was responsible for the deaths is difficult. At various stages, while thousands rioted, nationalists and loyalists were engaged in gun battles, and the RUC and British troops opened fire on rival crowds at several locations. During 1932 the IRA had noted the formation of 'Catholic Defence' groups, which it believed had access to arms. It is quite possible elements such as these were active in 1935 as well. The majority of those wounded during the disturbances were Catholic, as were most of the 2,000 driven from their homes, and 95 per cent of the compensation was paid out to Catholics. There is no doubt the IRA were active during the July events. IRA members had brought arms into areas where trouble was expected, and had been assigned to defensive duties. It has been claimed that the July riots were the first occasion the IRA used Thompson guns in Belfast. One IRA man claimed his Ballymacarret unit were 'in the thick of it' around York Street for two days. However, as in 1932, a substantial section of the Belfast IRA were not on duty in the city at all, but training outside Dundalk! Indeed the Ballymacarret unit was the only full strength section of the IRA left in Belfast. Over 70 Belfast IRA members were among those present at Giles Quay in the Louth mountains when gardaí raided the camp on 14 July. All of the twelve IRA men arrested were northerners, including several from Belfast. Given the long and violent build up to the July riots, the IRA in Belfast seems to have again been neglecting its duty as defenders. What would the frightened Catholic citizens of Belfast made of the reports in the *Irish News* of 15 July of how in a 'repetition of the terrible happenings of the Pogrom of 1920 to 1922' Catholic areas were being invaded, while elsewhere the paper reported the arrest of 70 of their 'defenders' in Dundalk? While the violence ebbed in intensity after about a week, large numbers of Catholics were forced from their workplaces over the next fortnight. There was ample opportunity for the IRA to wage a sectarian war in July 1935: again it refused to do so. Protestants were not shot at or bombed after the rioting had ceased, while Catholics were.

The riots and their aftermath dominated nationalist politics for the rest of 1935. In November of that year there was a general election in the United

Kingdom. The Nationalist party was in some disarray, following Devlin's death and the bloodshed of that summer. The Nationalists in West Belfast issued a statement explaining why they would not contest the Westminster elections. They outlined what they considered dangerous threats to Catholics and concluded that 'it is not the time to dissipate their energies in a hopeless fight on a register which has a Unionist majority of over 15,000'. The Nationalists made clear that they would not support an IRA candidate as they refused to 'share the title of Irish Nationalists with any element which is ready to fight against its fellow countrymen'. Nevertheless the IRA intervened in the election aiming to stand in four constituencies. Charles Leddy, serving a two-year sentence since his arrest in Dundalk the previous July, was nominated for West Belfast, Patrick O'Hagan, for Down and Charles McGlennon, for Armagh.

The Nationalists ran two candidates, both in the two-seat Fermanagh/Tyrone constituency. This was done after discussions with the IRA, despite Cahir Healy's misgivings about the republicans' ability to run an effective campaign. A reflection of the Nationalist Party's frustration with Northern Ireland's politics was that both these candidates ran on an abstentionist basis. The IRA had also put considerable pressure on the Nationalists to agree to an election pact. The Republican Congress had also planned to back a candidate in North Down, a Protestant farmer who would stand on an anti-partition platform; though the Congress claimed what they called the 'coercive power of his environment' forced him to withdraw from the election. That Cahir Healy was also in correspondence with George Gilmore of the Congress is a reflection of how far the violence of the summer had pushed the Nationalists towards co-operation with republicans. As in 1933 the four Republicans were IRA candidates, Sinn Féin having declared that they would not support them.

Despite the difference in political atmosphere from the Stormont election campaign of two years previously, the IRA attempted to raise similar issues during its campaign. Seán MacBride claimed in Belfast that republicans 'wanted to end (the) system by which the workers were exploited by a handful of capitalists, whether British or Irish'. In Portadown, Seán Russell told his listeners that the 'day (was) fast approaching when the sectarian catch cries, which were dividing the people of the north, would disappear'. Tom Barry spoke to an estimated 10,000 strong crowd in Belfast, warning of an approaching war, in which Britain would attempt to conscript nationalists, and declaring republicans to be believers in religious freedom. He warned 'that if you are tramped down by armed force, the only way to defeat that slavery is with a gun in your hand'. In contrast to 1933, the Nationalist press did not attack the republican campaign. George Gilmore suggested this was because the IRA did not raise strong criticisms of mainstream nationalism during the election. As in 1933, however, republicans complained of RUC harassment. When Donal O'Donoghue and Maud Gonne McBride were arrested in Lurgan, Maud Gonne was deported, while O'Donoghue was jailed in Crumlin Road. More seriously, two people, including a 15-year-old girl, were wounded when shots were fired from a passing car at a republican rally in west Belfast. More violence occurred on polling day itself with the RUC baton charging rival crowds in Lurgan, nationalists in Dungannon attacked at polling stations and a republican election agent injured in Co. Down. The results of the election saw Unionist victories everywhere except Fermanagh/Tyrone where the Nationalists took both seats. In West Belfast, Leddy received 20,313 votes, in Armagh the republican vote was 16,284 and in Co. Down, Patrick O'Hagan won 20,236 votes. Leading Belfast IRA member James (Jimmy) Steele optimistically told supporters at the election count that 'this fight will inevitably bring all creeds and classes to realize that their political spirit, political needs, and economic necessities can best be served in a united Ireland in which every citizen will be given an opportunity to have equal liberty'. Perhaps symbolically Charles McGlennon's post-election address, where he declared 'one day in the near future Orange and Green would unite and their Protestant neighbours would see eye to eye with their Catholic fellow countrymen' was cut short because of the 'pandemonium of Orange drumming'. The *Irish News* reported that many of the voting papers in West Belfast had been spoiled, with slogans mourning the loss of Devlin written on them. Sectarian violence continued, with celebrating Nationalists in Irvinestown, Fermanagh, attacked by mobs, and bombs thrown into Catholic Little Ship Street in Belfast. Nevertheless, a republican statement claimed satisfaction with their effort saying that while they 'recognised that the seats they contested could not be won in this election ... (the) Imperial contention that the six-county area is a satisfied statelet of the British Empire has been challenged'.

Again despite there being potential to exploit sectarian feeling, the IRA avoided the temptation to do so, calling for unity across the divide in circumstances even bleaker than those of 1933. If the IRA were simply a Catholic militia, then surely these election campaigns would have reflected that. But the IRA consistently promoted, rhetorically at least, cross community unity.

What then of Peadar O'Donnell's oft-quoted assertion that the IRA in Belfast were just 'a battalion of armed Catholics?' O'Donnell's statement owes more to the failure of the Republican Congress to make many gains among Belfast republicans than to any objective analysis. The IRA nationally was dominated by Catholics, and as an army council member O'Donnell knew this. All republican commemorations featured the rosary, even though O'Donnell claimed to be shocked at seeing republicans saying it in Belfast. The situation in the north was complicated by the fact that after 1928 all republican commemorations faced bans. On Easter Sunday the RUC would surround Milltown cemetery in Belfast and prevent anything other than a religious service taking place. Unlike in the Free State where political speeches would follow the saying of a decade of the rosary, in Northern Ireland an attempt to do this would lead to arrest. Therefore the religious service was an expression of defiance that republicans could attend in place of a commemoration. While it is quite true that the 'only constituency from which the IRA could realistically hope to draw support in Northern Ireland was comprised by Catholic communities', it was not the case that this meant that it necessarily defined itself 'largely in terms of sectarian rationale'. Neither the national IRA leadership, nor the majority of its northern members can be said to have simply acted as 'Catholic Defenders' in this period. What is true is that the IRA leadership displayed little understanding of Unionist hostility to republicanism. Their impression often seemed to be that once the IRA explained that it was not sectarian Protestants would flock to it. Hence Twomey's assertion that it was the Nationalist Party that had 'knit the Orangemen together and brought things back on sectarian lines'. Had Devlin and his supporters not committed that 'crime' the labour movement and other sectional interests would have combined to oust the Unionist Party.

It is significant that during this period there was no direct Northern influence on the IRA Army Council, MacLogan being resident in Portlaoise since the end of the civil war. The IRA leadership in Dublin directed northern policy. This is not so surprising given the weakness of the IRA in Northern Ireland until 1932. With increased activity and growth, the Northern IRA would begin to demand a greater say in the organization. An example of early tension is well illustrated by messages sent by Belfast to Dublin in late 1932 and during 1933. The first was a complaint about the lack of coverage in *An Phoblacht* for imprisoned Belfast IRA men, the writer claiming that he was 'sick asking publicity for our prisoners'. More serious were Matthew's claims that the three IRA men who had fled south during the railway strike were being neglected, and being given little money and few comforts. He contrasted that with the treatment of Dublin IRA members on the run in Belfast and considered that 'these cases speak well for the manner that HQ treats Belfast when in difficulty'. Wondering how much money was spent on southern IRA matters, he asked if even with a £1,000 reward on their heads 'these boys' might have to return to Belfast. He concluded by asking 'is the north forgotten or is it not worthwhile keeping a promise when a Belfast man is in question?'

The suspicion of the Dublin leadership by the Belfast IRA may well have contributed to the northern IRA's support for the ousting of the remnants of the early 1930s leadership in 1938. While the southern IRA had often displayed a lack of understanding of northern political life, the Belfast IRA's failure to grasp the realities of southern politics eventually led to the absurdity of the Stephen Hayes affair, when the IRA's chief of staff was accused of being a government spy and was kidnapped by Belfast IRA men. However, this should not obscure the fact that the IRA believed that the sectarian divide could be bridged during the early 1930s and did not see itself primarily as a Catholic defence force.

9/The IRA outside Ireland

The two most important areas of IRA activity outside Ireland were the United States and Britain. While there were IRA members and supporters in other countries, in terms of numbers and influence their importance was minimal. By far the most important area was the US, as the IRA depended to a great degree for both financial and military support from its American supporters. It was also to the US that most of those anti-treaty IRA men who emigrated went. The IRA leadership maintained a constant line of communication with its American representatives and leading supporters. They were kept well informed of events in Ireland, and their advice was sought and listened too. Leading IRA officers visited the US on a regular basis. In contrast, the IRA in Britain remained small and did not play a major role in its leadership's calculations.

How to deal with the loss of its members through emigration faced the IRA almost immediately following the civil war. In theory, emigration was tantamount to treachery and the IRA had actually forbidden it during the 1919-21 period, and did so again in July 1922. Initially this view continued to be expressed following the civil war, *An t-Óglách* warning in May 1925 that those who emigrated became 'Ireland's foe'. There was a certain pressure from local officers in hard hit areas to support this view, with one from the west arguing that as only two men out of his 18-strong active service unit were left, the IRA should make clear that those who emigrated were playing 'the enemy's game'. The scale of the situation facing them eventually forced a reassessment from the IRA. In August 1924, the organization was already acknowledging that unemployment was affecting the IRA badly in the west of Ireland. There, it was stated that IRA members could not 'get work' and as a result 'hundreds' had emigrated without informing the IRA. The situation worsened in the following years. In 1925 an officer from Connemara considered that due to poverty, emigration from his area was impossible to prevent, and that soon 'very few who took part in the fight for independence' would be left. The IRA was faced with a choice of prohibiting members leaving Ireland and being ignored, or at least making an effort to maintain some authority among those who left. In order to do this it cancelled its previous ruling on emigration in July 1925.

From that date onwards IRA members were permitted to leave Ireland for treatment of medical problems, provided they supplied a Doctor's Certificate, and for economic reasons provided they agreed to enrol in the IRA's Foreign Reserve. The Foreign Reserve was established to ensure 'that men who were forced to emigrate should be kept in touch' with the IRA, and be kept under its authority. To be transferred to the Reserve, an IRA member had to provide reasons why he wished to emigrate, agree to be bound by IRA discipline while abroad, and be prepared to return to Ireland if so ordered by the IRA. IRA members who had left Ireland after May 1923 and before July 1925 could be retrospectively enrolled in the Reserve.

From the beginning there were problems with this system and an army council member pointed out in 1926 that when the Reserve was formed the IRA leadership did not have a 'decided view' on its function. It was never explained how an IRA member would maintain contact with the organization at home or fellow reservists abroad for example. This, the army council member felt, reflected a deeper confusion about the role of the IRA abroad and more particularly in the US. There was also the added problem that many IRA members must have left Ireland without informing their officers, and began lives abroad without reinvolving themselves in republican politics. Units seem to have been lax in getting the addresses of men who emigrated making it difficult to make contact with the American Clan na Gael. Therefore we can only gain a partial picture of the IRA abroad from the surviving Foreign Reserve lists. The vast majority of those who returned forms went to the US, a smaller number to Britain and a handful elsewhere.

Table 15. Destinations of IRA emigrants, 1924–26

USA	200	Australia	7
Britain	101	New Zealand	2
Canada	9	Others	1

The route that emigrating IRA men took was similar to that of many southern Irish emigrants during the 1920s. The majority of those going to the US went to New York, which remained the most popular destination for Irish emigrants in that period. By the late 1920s however, Irish emigration to the US had begun to decline, mainly due to restrictive Immigration laws and the impact of the Great Depression. As with Irish emigrants generally, IRA men from the same areas tended to travel to the same destinations.

Table 16. Destinations for IRA emigrants in the United States

| New York 130 | Cleveland 29 | Chicago 13 | Boston 8 | Others 20 |

The majority of these men came from Kerry, Mayo, Clare and Leitrim. One reason the figure for Cleveland is relatively high was its popularity with Mayo men, with 20 members of the IRA's Achill company travelling there from 1924-25. During 1926, 27 members of the Carrick-on-Shannon battalion made their way to New York. The most senior IRA figure to emigrate in this period, Michael McLoughlin, was also attached to that unit. The O/C of the Clare brigade, Martin Shanahan, also emigrated to New York, despite the 'very utmost' efforts of the AC to dissuade him. In general however it was mainly junior officers and rank and file IRA members who left Ireland. In the case of at least two IRA men, Seán McGuinness and Jack Keogh, the US was also a refuge following escape from prison.

Of course the US was not important to the IRA simply because its members emigrated there. Since the 1860s, the large Irish-American population had been of importance to revolutionary movements in Ireland. Following the Civil War the base for militant republicanism in the US had shrunk considerably, but it was still a substantial one. The IRA therefore had both military and financial reasons to attempt organization in the US. In 1926 the leading anti-treaty Irish-American organization was the Clan na Gael, originally founded in 1867, whose leading personality was Joseph McGarrity of Philadelphia. The Clan and the IRA had come to an agreement in 1926 that the two organizations recognize each other as the only revolutionary bodies in their respective countries, and that the Clan give undivided financial and military aid to the IRA. Furthermore any changes in policy by either could not take place 'until the party contemplating the change has officially notified the other and their consent obtained'. During 1927 the IRA also appointed a full time representative, Connie Neenan, to be responsible for communication between the army council and the Clan. Neenan, an IRA veteran from Cork was also given responsibility for recruiting IRA members to the Clan, for procuring arms and equipment and collecting funds in the US for the organization. Neenan was the central American link with the IRA for the next decade.

While the IRA did receive arms and ammunition from the Clan, the US was never the source of as much military expertize as they hoped it would be. It was more important in terms of raising finance. At one stage the IRA was claiming it needed at least $1000 a month from the US for it to operate effectively. Clan na Gael camps (branches) existed right across the US from Boston to San Francisco. It was strongest on the east coast and in traditional centres of Irish settlement such as Chicago, Cleveland and Butte, Montana. As might be expected however, New York City was the 'mainstay' of the Clan. Here the organization owned and operated a headquarters, the 'IRA Halls', which functioned as a meeting place and social centre. At the halls Clan supporters could listen to music by the 'IRA Orchestra', purchase *An Phoblacht*, and women supporters could even participate in a yearly beauty contest. Every year a boat trip on the Hudson river was organized to raise funds, and in 1930 the Clan attracted 2,700 people to this fund raiser, making it the 'biggest, best and greatest success' the organization had in fund raising until that date. In that year the Clan had 19 functioning branches in New York. *An Phoblacht* was also available from 17 news stands in Manhattan and Brooklyn.

The Clan was a relatively small organization however, and in 1929 its membership in New York was just 620. The Clan's overall membership is difficult to estimate, but incomplete figures for 1929 add up to just 1,722. In June 1931 only 385 copies of the IRA's journal *An-tÓglách* were being sent to the US. Another rough indicator of the scale of republican support is the number of copies of *An Phoblacht* the Clan recieved from Ireland. During 1930 the Clan was receiving only 480 copies a week. In May 1932 the paper had just 100 subscribers in the entire United States. The Clan in this period was not a mass organization, and this alone would have made it difficult for it to raise the contributions the IRA expected it to.

The Clan's fund raising activities were fairly mundane and unspectacular. Dances and dinners were held at Easter or on St Patrick's Day, collections made and Easter lillies sold. In 1928 a total of just £73 9*s.* shillings and 3*d.* was raised in the US through lily sales. However, nearly $3,000 was raised in New York on St Patrick's Day in 1930 by the holding of three dances. In that case the Clan had been allowed to use the names of the Tipperary, Clare, and Tyrone county organizations in its publicity. This was important, because the majority of Irish Americans did not identify explicitly with any one political organization but often with organizations which brought together emigrants on a regional basis.

More practically two IRA veterans suffering from TB were treated at the Clan's expense in a sanatorium in Chicago during 1930. A Limerick IRA veteran, who had lost his job through ill health, was sent to the US for treatment after his comrades and the IRA in Dublin raised his fare during 1931. By 1932 13 disabled IRA members were receiving medical help in the US, with the Clan again paying for their treatment. Treatment for 'disabled' IRA members was costing the Clan about $6,000 a year in 1932.

As far as political action went, the Clan occasionally held protests during the visits of Free State politicians, such as when they successfully disrupted a speech by Eoin MacNeill to the Ancient Order of Hibernians in Holyoake, Massachusetts, during May 1930.

The Clan did not operate in a situation of mass support for militant republicanism. The majority of Irish Americans had supported the Treaty in 1921. The civil war had then demoralized many former supporters of the IRA. Even the arrival in the US of anti-Treaty veterans did not necessarily lead to a growth in support for the Clan, as many men simply left Irish politics behind them. The IRA were aware of this and with the launch of Comhairle na Poblachta in Ireland during 1929, briefly considered setting up a new open support organization in the US. This was to be called the Councils of the Irish Republic. Former IRA leader Andy Cooney visited the US in the hope of getting in touch with 'those many thousands who gave active support to the Republic in 1922–3 and who have in recent years become inactive'. He also wished to make some contact with the many emigrants who were members of the IRA but had not joined the Clan. He met with considerable hostility from the Clan leadership, who opposed the new organization from the beginning, and Cooney adjudged his mission a failure. The IRA then abandoned their attempt to set up an alternative organization to the Clan.

A year later Twomey himself arrived in America, speaking at the Clan convention in New York and spending the following four months visiting Clan camps in over 20 cities across the US. He was not impressed with the situation he found there. Twomey found an organization seemingly content to remain small, unable to attract recent Irish emigrants and in some cases showing a 'definite inclination to limit the membership'. The Clan, as he found it was 'not suited to embrace the general mass of our people' and its organization in general was 'very poor'. Twomey also noted a tendency among the Clan to associate the IRA entirely with military action with many considering 'that because there are no shootings or military operations at home ... we are not sincere'. This certainly was the case for the Clans most important leader, McGarrity. Throughout the whole period of his involvement with republicanism, he stressed the necessity for military action, pure and simple. For McGarrity, political activity was the 'grave' of militant nationalism. As a result of this belief he clashed with the IRA leadership on numerous occasions, especially about their decision to support Fianna Fáil in the general elections of 1932 and 1933. Fearing a turn to constitutionalism he asked had the IRA become 'spineless and afraid'? McGarrity told Seán Russell that he regarded political activity as a diversion, feeling that 'all energies should be put into the military side'. This attitude was reflected in the Clan more generally, and it was claimed the organization did lose members in New York, Jersey, Boston, Detroit and Chicago when the IRA changed its policy on electoral support for Fianna Fáil. Rumours were also current in the Clan during 1932 that the IRA was going to hand over its arms to the new government.

The most heated debates at the 1932 Clan convention however, centred on the fact that the IRA did not *consult* the Clan before it made these decisions. This, it was argued was a breach of the agreement signed by both organizations in 1926. The Clan felt that the IRA had deliberately kept 'them in the dark' and that they only found out about the IRA's policy through letters to Clan members from Ireland. These suspicions continued with the Detroit Clan demanding an extraordinary convention be held to discuss the support for Fianna Fáil in late 1932. These worries were only finally dealt with by the promptness of the IRA's notification of the Clan of their policy with regard to the 1933 general election and the signing of a new Clan-IRA agreement. However the new agreement made it clear that while consultation and exchanges of viewpoints were necessary, the IRA's convention remained the highest authority. By contrast violent activities, which often cost the IRA support in Ireland, seem to have had the opposite effect in the US. Con Neenan wrote that the raids on garda barracks in November 1926 had given rise to 'great enthusiasm here among all the boys and we believe will gain us new members'. McGarrity continued to argue for offensive action by the IRA at regular intervals. He had warned the IRA in 1929 that money could not be expected unless 'reports of active work are most convincing'. Again in 1934 the Clan leadership were urging that the IRA attack Northern Ireland.

There are grounds for arguing then that one reason why the IRA found it hard to obtain funding from the US between 1927 and 1934 was because of the organization's political direction. The IRA leadership themselves also seem to have occasionally harboured this suspicion. In May 1932 money was withheld from the IRA on the basis that the Clan had not been informed of the launch of Saor Éire and the IRA's decision to support Fianna Fáil in the general election. The IRA's response was to demand the money immediately, and dismiss the Clan's objections. The Clan eventually sent £500 (about $2,000) at the end of May. However, throughout this affair, Pete Kearney, the Clan's treasurer, stressed that the Clan's objection was not to IRA policies themselves, but to the lack of consultation. They claimed that they felt that Saor Éire was a good initiative, and that whatever the IRA did politically within Ireland was not the Clan's concern. Kearney even urged that the IRA make a 'bold attack' on the Catholic bishops' political pronouncements. Opposition to IRA social policies was not voiced at the Clan's 1932 convention. Kearney stressed that in public and to their membership the Clan executive would defend the IRA's position. At the 1933 IRA convention, Clan delegate Tom Magill supported a call for the IRA to develop a social and economic programme. Therefore reasons other than political ones were central to the Clan's failure to adequately fund the IRA.

As in Ireland, republicans in the US were also divided and confused over the issue of Fianna Fáil's entry into Leinster House. Even McGarrity himself maintained correspondence with de Valera until 1936. The Clan found that some of its members left to join Fianna Fáil and others who remained within the Clan were also supporters of the new party. Neenan felt to exclude such men would greatly weaken the organization, so in order to avoid a split they were allowed to remain. De Valera's organization was to prove much more successful at fund raising in the US over the next few years then the IRA would be. However, as in Ireland initially there was a degree of co-operation between both organizations. The main Irish American anti-Treaty newspaper, the *Irish World*, gave coverage to both Fianna Fáil and IRA events. In 1929, Andy Cooney found the Clan in Seattle to be largely 'pro-Dev' and in Minneapolis to be divided on the issue.

In 1932 the Clan admitted that there was still an 'FF tendency' within its ranks. Initially the victory of Fianna Fáil and the release of IRA prisoners in March 1932 generated enthusiasm among the Clan. However, by 1933 the IRA were bemoaning the influence the now strongly pro-Fianna Fáil *Irish World* was having in Irish America, especially as the Clan seemed powerless to resist it, and noted that because of *An Phoblacht's* low circulation it was no surprise that the IRA's policies were so 'badly understood'. Indeed one of the Clan's most high profile members, its attorney, J.T. Ryan, resigned from the organization, after the IRA criticized articles he had written for the *Irish World* as being too pro-de Valera. A measure of the lack of understanding that the Clan sometimes displayed about Irish political realities is shown in their suggestion that the Fianna Fáil government be asked to facilitate the shipment of the arms and ammunition they held for the IRA!

The most important factor in the inability of the IRA to secure large scale funding in the US lies in the nature of its constituency and the period in which it operated. Firstly the IRA had by no means an open field to organize among Irish Americans. Aside from established organizations such as the Ancient Order of Hibernians, there was also a plethora of sporting and local county clubs, which fulfilled the social needs of many Irish emigrants. Politically there remained the remnants of John Devoy's Friends of Irish Freedom and the Fianna Fáil supporting American Association for the Recognition of the Irish Republic. While many of these groups were prepared to endorse resolutions criticising repression under Cosgrave for example, only the Clan was engaged in full time support for revolutionary activity. McGarrity, a businessman who on occasion donated large sums of his personal fortune to the IRA, was not typical of the average Clan member. While middle class Irish Americans such as J.T. Ryan, were also active in the Clan, the majority of its membership were working class or lower middle class. In Butte, for example, almost the entire Clan membership worked as miners. In New York many Clan members were employed in work in the transit industry, whose workforce was at least 50 per cent Irish-born during the 1930s. While by the 1920s Irish Americans were moving steadily upward in comparison to newer immigrant groups, the Great Depression in 1929 seems to have had a devastating effect on the majority of them. After 1929 the Clan na Gael faced a situation where large numbers of its members were out of work and were unable to contribute to its fund raising efforts. Even McGarrity himself was reduced to relying on his teenage daughters' wages from waitressing for support by 1933.

There is widespread evidence of this from 1929 on. Only one third of the funds the IRA claimed it needed to function was supplied to them in that year. At the 1930 Clan convention, McGarrity admitted that the organization had failed to raise funds they had pledged to the IRA. He put this down to 'the depressing economic conditions prevailing in the country at large'. Earlier that summer Clan activists in Chicago had reported that 'working conditions were never as bad here' and that most of their membership were unemployed. During that autumn Twomey was able to assess the state of the US for himself as he travelled from coast to coast. He found 'things are awful at present – such unemployment and uncertainty among those who have jobs'. In Butte nearly all the Irish miners were out of work and American people in general seemed to be facing the winter 'with a feeling of despair'. The economic situation continued to worsen and by 1932 the Clan's contributions to the IRA were a fraction of what was demanded. From November 1931 to June 1932 just £500 was sent from the US. Following that donation Pete Kearney informed the IRA that the Clan 'treasury was depleted'. He later explained that the depression had affected 'our people much more than the average' and that the unemployment rate was exceptionally high among Clan members, most of whom had not 'put anything by for a rainy day'. The prospects of getting any more money did not look good as Neenan informed Twomey in August that 'New York is broke'. Furthermore he claimed that many unemployed IRA veterans would return home if they could. Seán Russell arrived in the US that month and the IRA hoped that Russell's visit would lead to some arrangement with the Clan whereby they would be spared 'recurring nerve wracking experiences' about money.

While in some respects Russell was happy with his American tour, principally with how military training was going ahead, in general he found the Clan in a poor state. Membership was decreasing, and the majority of members were unemployed. New York was 'in a bad way', Philadelphia 'just paddling', Chicago 'finding it very hard', Detroit was 'very bad' and Butte 'gloomy'. In December the IRA leadership were forced to accept that 'owing to the terrible economic conditions in the USA, no money can be expected until next year'. The same month Neenan informed *An Phoblacht* that most of their debts in the US could not be paid, and that in the case of some areas they 'may as well forget them'. *An Phoblacht* had earlier been told that Chicago could not pay their bills, due to 'old man depression'. Their major annual source of income, a fund raising picnic, had only just broken even that year. In late December the IRA received just £150 from the Clan, with a note saying that this would 'practically drain' the organization's treasury. Late in 1933 McGarrity informed Twomey that with half the Clan out of work it was now 'well nigh impossible' to collect money.

In early 1933 the IRA attempted to convince the Clan of a scheme to secure more funds. The episode would illustrate that while the Clan often misunderstood the situation in Ireland, so too could the IRA misjudge American affairs. During 1920 de Valera had succeeded in securing nearly 6 million dollars in the US, through the issue of 'republican bonds'. Some $3 million of this money was left in the US, and became tied up in the wrangling between pro and anti-

Treaty factions. Both the Free State government and de Valera made efforts to recover the money, but finally in 1927 the courts in the US ruled that the money should be returned to its original Bond holders. De Valera made an audacious appeal to the bond-holders to subscribe their shares towards the setting up of a republican newspaper, the *Irish Press*. In government by 1932, de Valera announced that the bond-holders in the US were to be repaid. The IRA seem to have believed that the bond-holders could be convinced to assign their Bonds 'for the benefit of the Army'. They wanted the Clan to set up a committee to appeal for bond-holders to subscribe to the IRA, and draw up a list of bond-holders to be written to. The IRA demanded that the 'whole weight of the Clan' be thrown behind the project as 'money is vital to progress here' and this scheme was considered 'one of the few means offering by which it can be secured'.

In a detailed reply the Clan explained that they believed the whole idea to be seriously misjudged. They estimated that here were about 400,000 bond-holders, and it was 'inconceivable' that they would turn their share over to the IRA as most of them were 'destitute' and desperately needed the money. The Clan stated that they would not 'get a DOLLAR in such an appeal'. They also felt that such an appeal would antagonize the bond-holders, as it would be perceived as an attack on de Valera. Most of the bond-holders believed that the IRA were supporting Fianna Fáil and did not understand the internal politics of the Free State. The appeal would not 'bring any fruitful results' and indeed would embarass the IRA later on. The IRA were forced to drop the plan.

As was the case with the IRA, the Clan also contained members who were eager to promote action on social and economic issues. The James Connolly club of the Clan in New York included among its members former Meath IRA man Gerald O'Reilly, Charles MacGinnitty, who was *An Phoblacht*'s distributor in the city, and Michael Quill, from Co. Kerry. For a period McGinnitty had also sold the communist *Irish Worker's Voice* from the Clan's halls at Columbus Avenue, until he received orders from Dublin to cease doing so. When the IRA split in 1934 these men remained members of the Clan, while supporting the new Republican Congress. A similar situation existed in Chicago with the Irish American Labour League. It was not until July 1935 that a branch of the Congress was officially launched in New York. A cross-over in membership with the Clan seems to have continued until Twomey wrote to McGarrity to complain about it. In late 1934, George Gilmore visited the US on behalf of the Congress and spent eight months there, mainly in New York. He also travelled to Boston, Buffalo, Chicago and Philadelphia. Gilmore claimed that Congress knew little money would be forthcoming from the US, so he concentrated on trying to win political support there. He managed to convince a number of republican supporters in the US to sign an appeal for unity between the IRA, Fianna Fáil and unaffiliated republicans in order to avoid another civil war in

Ireland. The appeal was vague enough to be supported by a broad range of Irish Americans, but largely fell on deaf ears in Ireland.

In the longer term Quill and O'Reilly, along with at least two dozen former IRA veterans who also worked on the subways, successfully built the Transport Workers Union as a major force in New York labour politics, with over 30,000 members. The union took a strongly Irish republican stance while also opposing anti-Semitism at a time when there was considerable Irish-Jewish conflict. Quill's support for IRA internees during World War Two *and* his denunciation of de Valera's visit to the German legation in 1945 made him the subject of much criticism in Ireland. One author has argued that the Clan, though largely unknown outside Irish circles played a 'crucial role in the creation of modern transit unionism'. The views of this group were not representative of the majority of the Clan, however.

The views the IRA expressed publicly on American politics deserve some attention. From 1926 onwards *An Phoblacht* was highly critical of many aspects of American society. Support was expressed for anarchists Sacco and Vanzetti in 1927 and for the Scottsboro Boys about to be 'burned alive by American "justice"' in 1932. A long campaign was waged by the paper for the release of Tom Mooney, an Irish-American labour radical. Strikes and labour agitation in the US were supported, while US foreign policy was criticized, most notably in Nicaragua. In 1927 the chairman of the army council had asked if the US was pursuing an 'imperialist policy' in Nicaragua, arguing that as far as he could see they were. *An Phoblacht* referred to US marines in Nicaragua as 'America's Black and Tans' and congratulated nationalist leader Sandino on 'winning his war'. While the US circulation of *An Phoblacht* was low, these articles placed it on the left of American politics. However, by 1934 *An Phoblacht* was also publishing articles praising the right wing populist Fr Charles Coughlin.

There was no immediate recovery in fortunes for the Clan, and in 1935 Twomey expressed the view that the organization seemed to have 'ceased to exist outside of New York'. Sales of *An Phoblacht* in the US had almost completely collapsed by that time. Ironically despite the Clan's decline, the connection with the US became crucial to the IRA following the clampdown by the Fianna Fáil government in 1936. McGarrity and Russell developed a plan for a bombing campaign in Britain which had far reaching consequences for the IRA. The ending of the Depression in the US had encouraged Twomey to hope that the Clan would revive again. During the preparations for the bombing campaign, Russell again toured the local branches of the Clan, and there certainly seems to have been a new enthusiasm within them. The McGarrity-Russell relationship is primarily important in how it was used to deceive and actually disrupt the plans of Russell's rivals in the IRA leadership after 1936.

Unlike the United States, the IRA in Britain was directly under the control of its Dublin leadership. It was organized into three regional areas in England, and one in Scotland. The No. 1 Area covered London and the Home Counties, No. 2 Manchester, Salford and parts of Yorkshire and No. 3 Liverpool and the surrounding region. Despite Britain being the main destination for Irish immigrants during the 1920s, and the IRA being based in areas where there was a large Irish population, its organization remained tiny. In late 1926 it claimed just 189 members in Britain. Between 1926 and 1927 only 93 IRA members requested transfers to the British organization. Most settled in the English north west.

Table 17. British destinations of IRA emigrants

| London 28 | Manchester 31 | Liverpool 34 | Scotland 20 |

In 1926 an army council member had asked whether any serious thought had been given to the function of the IRA in Britain. He felt militarily it was incapable of carrying out offensive action against the British state and that it was possibly better to disband the British units and replace them with tightly organized cells. His proposals were not acted on. Nor did the IRA dramatically increase its strength in the following years. In 1930 the Manchester region's strength was still only 38. Two years later it had declined to just 20. However there was a larger constituency for republicanism among the Irish in Britain than these figures would suggest. Both Sinn Féin and the Cumann na mBan organized in England and Scotland also, and in many ways these organizations fulfilled a social function for a section of the Irish in Britain. Activists like Joseph Fowler carried on the work they had begun in the Irish Self-Determination League during the early 1920s into Sinn Féin. Large numbers attended events organized by Sinn Féin's Roger Casement club in London, the Cathal Brugha club in Manchester, or by the Manchester Martyrs committee in that city. During the early 1930s several thousand people were drawn to republican commemoration events in the north of England. Dances and social events were organized regularly at premises like the Shamrock Hall in Manchester's Rochdale Road, under the direction of that city's leading republican personality, Seamus Barrett.

Until 1930 there were still four IRA prisoners held in British jails and the IRA instructed its British organization to organize campaigns among the Irish community to raise their case, and put pressure on the Labour party. In January 1930 a delegation of IRA supporters actually met J.R. Clynes, the Secretary of State for Home Affairs, in Manchester. Clynes 'was very nice' to the delegation, but warned them he could not speak for the cabinet as a whole on the prisoners issue. In May of that year, however, two IRA members, Bernard Iago and J. Foley, jailed for a bank raid in Manchester during 1922, were released from Maidstone prison. A welcome rally was held for them in Manchester in late

May, at which two Labour councillors, J.P. Mannion of Wigan and George Hall of Manchester, spoke. Iago resumed activity with the IRA in Manchester, becoming its intelligence officer, and within two years had embroiled it in a serious factional dispute with Seamus Barrett and the Manchester Martyrs committee. During this dispute the tiny IRA unit was split in half, with Iago and the adjutant opposing the unit's commander and quartermaster. There were accusations of assaults on Seamus Barrett and of drunken young IRA men causing disorder in the Shamrock Hall. Barrett was sent a forged letter dismissing him from the IRA, and both sides appealed to Dublin for backing. Eventually the IRA ordered Iago's faction to cease interfering with Barret's supporters, who had 'served (the) movement faithfully for years'. The IRA also warned Iago that the setting up of a rival Manchester Martyrs committee would not be tolerated. That such a inconsequential dispute was able to take up almost a year of the Manchester IRA's time is evidence of the impotence of the IRA in Britain. Indiscipline seemed to have been a feature of the IRA in Scotland as well. The Glasgow IRA was badly affected by a violent feud during 1925.

While the police in Britain maintained a watch on republican activities there, the IRA was in no way a serious threat for most of this period. Nor does the Dublin leadership seem to have paid a great deal of attention to it. There was no discussion of its British organization at either of the IRA's 1933 or 1934 general army conventions. A veteran of the period described how a handful of IRA men would meet weekly in a trade union hall in Blackfriar's Road in London, but carried out no activity because 'GHQ had over the years no policy as to what role the organization was to fulfil'. The majority of IRA members worked in construction and therefore travelled from place to place to where ever work could be found. Contact between them was often very tenuous. After the IRA split in 1934 the Republican Congress also organized in Britain, publishing the *Irish Front* newspaper, edited by the Tyrone poet Charles Donnelly. Communist initiatives such as the Irish Anti-Imperialist League also courted IRA support, but its Dublin leadership remained suspicious, and its British organization aloof, from participation in them.

As early as 1926, there had been suggestions that the IRA should concentrate on military operations in Britain itself. The IRA's attention at the time was concentrated on opposition to the Free State government. This changed in the late 1930s with the acceptance of the Russell-McGarrity plan for a bombing campaign in Britain. It is a measure of how desperate the IRA was at this stage that this plan was embraced with enthusiasm, when an inspection of the British units by Twomey had shown them to be 'poor and loose, and militarily ... almost elementary'. Twomey found that the IRA in Britain had few links with the Irish community at large, and most IRA men who had emigrated there avoided the IRA, whose central activity appeared to be 'the running of dances and ceilidhthe'. Nevertheless the IRA leadership pushed ahead with its campaign which eventually led to the deaths of seven civilians, the execution of two IRA members and the jailing or deportation of over 200 republicans.

Only a handful of IRA members who completed the Foreign Reserve list emigrated to Australia and New Zealand. In 1931, just 90 copies of *An Phoblacht* were being sent to Australia and 15 to New Zealand. Again, by the mid 1930s many were cancelling their orders claiming that 'the exiles are very apathetic – due no doubt to the very keen economic struggle'. Others suggested that more mainstream Irish publications had achieved dominance among immigrants.

Most of the IRA's other international contacts were from anti-colonial movements in Aisa or left wing organizations in Europe. *An Phoblacht* gave extensive coverage to the movement for independence in India during the late 1920s and early 1930s. Indian speakers were a regular feature of republican rallies in Ireland. During 1931 the organization even attempted to bring Mahatma Gandhi to Ireland for a speaking tour. The presence of Indian speakers was thought by the IRA to have been useful when promoting the 'Boycott British' campaign during 1932. The support given seems to have been largely rhetorical however. But in the case of the Chinese revolution from 1926 there does seem to have been an effort by the IRA to secure practical help for the rebels. As well as *An Phoblacht*'s enthusiastic coverage, the IRA leadership asked Con Neenan in New York to organize pro-Chinese demonstrations if it were possible. Neenan was already attempting to use Clan influence on behalf of a Chinese representative in the city. He asked the *Irish World* to give prominence to the Chinese fight for independence, as the rest of the US 'Government and Press (was) Imperialistic'. Even more interestingly, the IRA leadership actually discussed the possibility of sending volunteers to aid the Chinese rebels, and it was agreed to do so if 'conditions for service, (and) cost for travelling were satisfactory'; though this proposal does not seem to have gone any further. One other example of practical solidarity was the claim that in October 1930 Clan na Gael members in Detroit helped guard an Indian independence march against a threatened attack. Among the marchers was Captain Robert Monteith, a member of Roger Casement's Irish brigade in 1916. This activity was possibly the result of IRA criticism that the Clan was not making contact with other anti-colonial organizations in the US.

By the late 1920s the IRA was also rethorically very pro-Soviet Union. Contacts had been established during between the IRA and the Russian government during 1925, when Seán Russell along with Gerald Boland and 'Pa' Murray had visited Russia. By the late 1920s the contacts were largely political in nature. Leading IRA members visited the Soviet Union on several occasions. Mick Fitzpatrick was in the USSR as a delegate to congresses of Friends of the Soviet Union in 1927 and 1932. David Fitzgerald and George Gilmore visited the country in 1930. Seán McCool recieved medical treatment from the Soviets during 1931. Individual IRA members such as Nixie Boran of Kilkenny also visited Russia during those years, but in his case without notifying his superiors. The IRA leadership also sent delegates to Comintern supported organizations such as the League against Imperialism. Frank Ryan and Donal O'Donoghue attended one such conference in Brussels during 1927, and Peadar O'Donnell and Seán MacBride represented the IRA at the League's second conference in Frankfurt. Within Ireland, the gardaí considered the Friends of the Soviet Union to be an IRA, rather than a communist, front organization. Indeed, three of the major Comintern-sponsored international organizations, the League against Imperialism, the Labour Defence League and the Irish Working Farmers' Congress, were largely run by the IRA in Ireland.

It is worth noting, particularly in the light of later events, that the IRA's press was completely hostile to Nazi Germany from the beginning and to Fascist Italy after 1926. In 1933 *An Phoblacht* attacked those 'rather foolish people' who had admiration for Hitler's 'reactionary regime'. Three years later it argued that every 'genuine' Irish person should have sympathy with Abyssinia then under Italian invasion. However, there was contact during the early 1930s between a group of German nationalists studying at Trinity College and the IRA in Dublin. Two of these students, Jupp Hoven and Helmut Clissman, became Abwehr (German military intelligence) agents during the Second World War and played a significant role in Germany's policies towards the IRA.

Despite the dependence of the IRA on American funding, the Clan na Gael was never able to adequately fulfil this function, largely for reasons beyond its control. Even with the huge Irish American population and the post-civil war exodus of republicans to the United States the Clan na Gael was never a dominant force in *émigré* politics. In Britain the IRA was a marginial force, largely fulfilling a social function. The IRA's international policy was governed by hostility to Britain although support was expressed publicly for anti colonial revolts in other parts of the world. During the planning of the British bombing campaign the IRA's leadership established operational and ideological links with Nazi Germany which are discussed in the final chapter.

10/The IRA and Irish society, 1926–1936

The politics of the IRA were influenced by a variety of political currents, both Irish and international, and its leadership formulated their ideas in response to developments within Ireland and abroad. Within the IRA there existed support for very contradictory ideas and this was reflected in the stances the organization took on particular issues. IRA policies reflected the fact that it was largely composed of men from the urban and rural working and lower middle classes. However, the overriding belief that held the IRA together was that military force was the most effective means to achieve its aims.

The central feature of the IRA's politics was that belief in the use of force to bring about political change. As Twomey argued, the two governments in Ireland had been 'imposed by force' then it was the duty of Irishmen to over-throw them by that method. This belief was shared by all the factions repre-sented within the organization and was the aspect of the IRA best known to peo-ple outside its ranks. This belief in armed force informed the IRA's attitude to almost all its activities, from involvement in nation-wide industrial disputes to arguments between neighbours. Without the belief that the IRA was preparing for war the organization would have found it even more difficult to hold its dis-parate factions together. While there may have been differences in attitude as to how that force would be used the belief that it eventually would be was central to the IRA.

This expressed itself in the widespread attachment within the IRA to the idea that social and political campaigns interfered with preparation for war. The belief in 'physical force as the only means of securing freedom' and that politics would divert 'our mind and divides our energies' were raised consistently against arguments for new political departures. Tom Barry could argue that the IRA had a 'moral right to make war and kill when necessary' but only in a strug-gle for national freedom and not for a social policy. To maintain unity within the organization the IRA repeatedly shelved political initiatives in favour of concentrating all its effort on the 'perfection of the IRA as an efficient military force'. There was a distinct feeling that entering politics itself was compromis-ing and that those involved were only interested in 'what they can get'. The IRA's main argument against the Republican Congress departure was not that they disagreed with the politics of the new group but that it would lead to par-ticipation in Leinster House. Even those who did agree with political initiatives accepted the need for physical force whether to make the IRA a 'bully' for strik-ing workers or a new Citizens' Army.

While the militarist ethos may have helped hold an organization together it also meant that frustration developed when years passed and the organization did not go to war. Decisions to concentrate 'all effort and energy' into the training of the IRA as a military force prepared to 'take the field' within a short period of time simply raised expectations only to dash them again. One of the factors behind the IRA's stagnation between 1927 and 1931 was the complaint from members that if the organization was not going to fight then what was the point of parading, drilling, and recruiting. This accelerated disputes between those who favoured a political direction to break the deadlock and those who argued for military action.

The IRA during this period contained several competing factions, not all of whom put forward coherent viewpoints and many IRA members did not necessarily support any of them. In his perceptive study of *An Phoblacht*, James McHugh noted the existence of four separate tendencies within the IRA – apolitical militarists, conservative supporters of Sinn Féin, socialists and a broad layer committed to armed force but receptive to radical policies. The reality is even more complex. For example, Seán Russell openly admitted having to 'no liking for political parties'. Yet he organized IRA intervention during the northern railway strike and enthused about the prospect of co-operation with Protestant strikers. Tom Barry could argue that the IRA should have no social policy at all during 1932 but make a nod towards radicalism two years later by declaring that he had not fought at Crossbarry so that Irish workers could be exploited by employers. J.J. Murray of Armagh belonged to the faction of the IRA which endorsed Sinn Féin policy. He argued that the IRA had no right to take armed actions during labour disputes and refused to distribute the appeal to the Orange Order. Another northern officer and member of Sinn Féin, Belfast's Davy Matthews, both circulated the appeal and intervened personally in the ODR and railway strikes. Individuals prominent on the left of the IRA during the late 1920s such as Seán McCool and Mick Fitzpatrick remained loyal to the organization when it split in 1934, while Frank Ryan and Michael Price who were not sympathetic to socialism during the early 1930s would help found the Republican Congress.

The IRA's politics are best understood as attempts to respond to conditions within Ireland by developing policies drawing on contemporary native and foreign influences with the hope that these would attract popular support. Many of these policies faced intense political and clerical censure and provoked internal dissension with the IRA. Twomey's own political evolution offers a guide to shifts within leadership thinking. Initially Twomey expressed the traditional militarist distrust of politics. In 1924 he complained that most of those holding positions within the IRA had no 'military outlook' but were 'politicians'. Three years later he gave a conventional republican explanation as to how British 'intrigue' and the weakness of Irish negotiators had allowed the Treaty to be signed, but by 1931 he was arguing that the 'lack of an economic and political policy' was more responsible for defeat in the civil war than treachery. He now argued that the republican movement would be inevitably composed of the poor in the countryside and towns, as the wealthy would never favour real national independence. At the 1933 convention Twomey warned the militarists that it was dangerous to 'preach that we are soldiers only. We are revolutionaries'. As Twomey later explained to Joseph McGarrity, the organization could not expect to convince people to support it by simply repeating that it wanted 'the Republic'. To succeed the IRA needed to have its policies understood as widely as possible and the 'active sympathy' of a civilian political party.

Why did Twomey arrive at these conclusions? Undoubtedly his close association with the left within the IRA meant that he was familiar with their arguments, but the key factor was the impact of the Great Depression on Irish society. As he noted during 1931, the ending of emigration was leaving large numbers of young people looking for alternatives to their plight. The IRA's growth after several years' stagnation was obviously related to this as the organization represented the most radical, if confused, opposition to the Free State. Twomey saw conditions in Ireland as 'very bad and worsening' with those with wealth frightened and the poor hoping 'that out of the breakdown something better' would emerge. He believed that the more people thought about their economic plight the better for the IRA, as long as it took an interest in economic and social conditions. To win wider public support and avoid its military organization becoming isolated the IRA decided to launch a 'Civil Revolutionary Organization' in early 1931. This was the background to Twomey's endorsement of the Saor Éire initiative, which was necessary for it to gain the support of the majority of the IRA leadership. Saor Éire was not 'forced' upon a reluctant IRA leadership. Neither was Twomey opposed to it, because if he had been it would not have been launched.

Outside of the economic background what were the ideological influences on the IRA's politics? One clearly evident strain was the rejection of majoritarian democracy. The IRA did not believe 'national feeling, sentiment, and desires' could be judged by election results. What is more the organization claimed for itself the right to hold power in Ireland until such time as it was ready to give way to a republican government. At its most extreme IRA members believed that their organization should have the 'supreme power over life and death'. This could lead to farcical situations such as the IRA seriously demanding that de Valera release a prisoner arrested for arms possession, on the basis that his membership of the IRA meant he was entitled to be armed. The fact that de Valera was the elected head of the Irish state and that the IRA leadership represented 10,000 men at most did not strike the authors of this letter as ironic. Their reasoning was that while Ireland was ruled by puppet governments north and south, the IRA could not be 'bound by election results on the issue of sovereignty'. Seán MacBride argued that 'majority rule might be a good rule for people in a free country but ... it could not be enforced as a rule of morality in a country which was not free'. In fact, for the IRA progress towards freedom could not be made through majority rule as they believed the 1916 Rising and support for the Treaty had proven. However, the contradictions inherent in holding this view and claiming to desire freedom forced the IRA to explain that 'there was no question of forcing the people against their will' to accept IRA policy. Instead, when the IRA had governed for 'a reasonable length of time' they would then allow an election. Interestingly those within the IRA who questioned this view were often conservatives who feared the imposition of socialism under an IRA regime. Another attempt to work around an essentially undemocratic viewpoint was to argue, as Twomey did, that the IRA really did represent the Irish people but their policies had been so 'misrepresented' that the people themselves were unaware of that fact.

The reality of political life meant that the IRA had to attempt to win public support by the launch of support organizations or by standing in elections. As early as 1927 the IRA leadership had accepted the need for a 'civilian' revolutionary organization. However, their dismissal of majoritarian democracy meant that IRA leaders often displayed disdain for the opinions of the population at large. Arguing against attempts to call a congress of republicans in order to galvanize popular support MacBride declared that he had 'very little faith ... in the opinion of the mass of the people'. Donal O'Donoghue described how Tom Barry had the 'utmost contempt for what the phrasemongers describe as the masses'. O'Donoghue then confessed that he shared this contempt with Barry, but while Barry believed there was no point in trying to win popular support, O'Donoghue thought it was possible to educate the 'non-thinking persons of no property'. Frustration at failure to achieve their aims was easily transferred into a belief that the Irish people themselves had let the IRA down. This in turn could lead to justifying dictatorship on the basis that 'Ireland intellectually, morally and physically requires discipline'. This opposition to democracy was not the preserve of the militarists within the IRA. It was Frank Ryan and Peadar O'Donnell who signalled in November 1932 the beginning of the 'no free speech for traitors' campaign. Supporters of the left within the IRA also argued that there was a limit to 'tolerance' and that O'Duffy and his supporters should be 'swinging from lampposts' rather than allowed freedom to organize.

Opposition to the parliamentary system helps partially explain how the major European political trends which reflected opposition to democracy found an echo within the IRA. By far the most important for the IRA in this period was communism. Between 1928 and 1932 communist ideas had influence within the IRA and interaction with Irish and foreign communists was tolerated by the IRA leadership. Army council members visited the USSR and these liaisons were approved of by the leadership. Added to this was the public association of lead-ing IRA members with Comintern-affiliated organizations such as the League against Imperialism in Ireland during the same period. The Comintern bypassed the Irish communists and instead Mick Fitzpatrick became their main link to Irish politics for a period. Communist membership of the IRA was tol-erated with nearly half of the membership of the Workers Revolutionary Party in Dublin also IRA members. Leading IRA figures were not afraid to confront charges of being communist sympathizers. MacBride argued to allow private capitalism to exist in any form guaranteed social inequality. More significantly Twomey replied to charges of communism by arguing that if it was communism 'to undo the conquest ... to destroy landlordism ... to end robbery and exploita-tion by a privileged minority, then Tone, Emmet, Mitchel, Lalor, Connolly, Pearse and Mellows were Communists, and the Irish Republican Army is a Communist organization'. The important point is that two years later Twomey would reply to charges of communism in very different terms. Indeed by 1933 membership of the IRA by communists would be outlawed by the army coun-cil and a number of communists left the IRA following its 1933 Convention.

Between 1931 and 1933 significant changes occurred in the general political atmosphere in Ireland. Before 1931 communism was hardly popular but was not subject to the same level of denunciation that it would be from that year onwards. The scale of the economic crisis facing Ireland made radical solutions seem reasonable to a section of the population. During 1930 two communist candidates had been elected to Dublin city council. The fact that Fianna Fáil councillors joined organizations affiliated to the Comintern meant that there was a certain insulation to attack from anti communists. This also helps explain the IRA leadership's decision to launch the 'emphatically socialist' Saor Éire. As the largest revolutionary organization in the country, with a section of its lead-ership already sympathetic to socialism, the IRA was receptive to the rhetoric of communism particularly when embellished with references to republican heroes of the past. Twomey, MacBride and Jim Killeen among others were not ideologically committed to socialism but were open to policies which not only addressed social injustices but which also might reinvigorate a stagnant IRA.

The intensity of the Church's condemnation of Saor Éire undoubtedly helped force a rethink among the IRA leadership about association with such an openly socialist body. They themselves noted that an organization on 'purely nationalist lines' might have escaped censure. What was key, was the hostile reaction to Saor Éire by large sections of the IRA itself, which intensified as anti – communism became a more central feature of Irish politics during 1933. In late 1931 the Belfast IRA were already complaining that *An Phoblacht* had become 'too communistic' and asking why Sinn Féin had not been chosen as the IRA's political voice instead of Saor Éire. In the aftermath of Fianna Fáil's election victory during 1932 the IRA committed itself to supporting Saor Éire's ideals without publicly organizing Saor Éire. Only a few officers, such as Offaly's Seán McGuinness were in favour of openly re-launching the latter body.

By 1933 the hostility of broad sections of the IRA to Saor Éire, communism and even politics in general was apparent. Twelve units put forward motions to that year's convention arguing that the IRA concentrate on military affairs and avoid social policy while several called for the organization to disassociate itself from communism. During discussion on these issues delegates expressed the belief that the IRA was thought to be 'anti-religious' and that its social policies were keeping recruits out of the organization. Seán MacSwiney, a former secretary of the Irish section of the Comintern's League against Imperialism, now argued that no Christian could be a communist. The constant attempts by IRA left-wingers like O'Donnell and McCool to gain support by claiming the mantle of Liam Mellows were now contested. Tom Barry pointed out that Mellows was not infallible and reminded delegates that in 1922 most of the IRA had rejected his ideas. There is no doubt the IRA's decision to stand aside from the mob attacks on Connolly House just a week after their convention was influenced by their junior officers' hostility to association with communism.

At Bodenstown that June, Twomey signalled the IRA's intention to disassociate itself from communism by denying it was the movement's policy and stating there was no alliance with the Communist movement. *An Phoblacht* made public the order forbidding dual membership of the IRA. However, Twomey's speech did not mark a retreat from radicalism *per se*. He stressed that the 'communist label' was being used to smear anyone who was against 'existing social and economic conditions'. He suggested that everyone bar those 'who gain by robbery and by sweating the very bones of the people' should oppose the economic and social system in Ireland. While those on the republican left were disappointed by Twomey's speech they too were affected by the new atmosphere within the Free State. Such was the hostility to communism following 1933 that even Republican Congress supporters would deny being associated with it. As Twomey himself admitted, the Saor Éire project had been 'engineered from the top' and local officers had been inclined to shy away from defending it. More importantly the clerical and political attacks on Saor Éire had made it more difficult to recruit to the IRA. The aftermath of the 1933 convention marked the IRA's abandonment of openly socialist policies. Those within the IRA with an *ideological* commitment to these policies would either reavaluate them or leave the organization.

However, an element of communist rhetoric remained in use among the IRA's propaganda. During the early 1930s the Comintern was arguing that capitalism had entered a 'Third Period' of crisis during which even social democratic and liberal parties were preparing the ground for fascism. During 1934 the IRA was labelling both Roosevelt's New Deal and Fianna Fáil's economic policies as fascist attempts to reform capitalism. Outside of international communism the IRA was possibly unique in those interpretations.

An easy assumption would be to imply that the IRA rank and file had no understanding of, still less sympathy for, any of these radical policies. There is some evidence for this view. J.J. Sheehy claimed his men in Kerry had just 'their own local thought – sometimes Fianna Fáil thought'. Others stressed that the 'ordinary Volunteer' had no understanding for political documents issued by the leadership. However, others claimed their men did ask 'What are we fighting for – is it just to put up another flag?' In contrast reports from the large Leitrim unit in early 1933 stress how slow ordinary members were to voice opinions and how they had to be prompted to answer questions by their commanding officer. On questions of radicalism the IRA leadership were generally more radical then their junior officers and certainly more so then their rank and file. This obviously impacted on how far they promoted these policies. This is reflected in the internal IRA reaction to the Gralton case. There was widespread disquiet within the IRA with leadership statements and *An Phoblacht* articles defending Gralton. At the 1933 convention a committee of inquiry into the Gralton case stated that while deportation without trial went against the 'first principles of liberty' that the IRA's interests would be best served by avoiding further statements on the matter. While Twomey had personally supported Gralton the local IRA in Leitrim not only refused to do this, but were probably responsible for a gun attack on his dance hall! The IRA were not unique in facing these problems, as the Labour Party was forced to drop its commitment to the slogan of the 'Workers' Republic' because of both internal and external pressure after 1936.

However, after 1933 the IRA continued to promote radical economic policies. These actually reflected more the thinking of Twomey, MacBride and O'Donoghue than that of O'Donnell or Gilmore. These policies were also influenced by European trends as well as by the experiences of IRA members at local level. They were outlined in the 'Constitution of Governmental Programme for the Republic of Ireland'. This was a slightly updated version of a constitution adopted at the IRA's 1931 convention. In a further reflection of internal hostility to communism additions to the constitution made it clear that the IRA was not 'irreligious'. The 'Constitution' *was* a radical document. It outlined plans for decentralized government through local assemblies, free education, a minimum wage and unemployment benefits. Private property would be allowed to exist only as long as it was not 'detrimental to the common good'. Land not being used productively would be seized and redistributed and the majority of Irish farm land would be used for producing food rather than grazing. The judicial system would be modernized and legal aid available to all, with a penal system geared towards 'reforming' offenders rather than punishing them. Landlordism would be abolished in cities and towns, with housing provided for all by the state, although private ownership of individual housing would be encouraged. The transport system would be state run. The state would also encourage manufacturing and regulate private industry. Industry would run a distributive system through co-operatives ensuring goods were supplied throughout the whole community. Finally the banking system would be taken over by the state and wealth and credit of the nation used to benefit the community. This programme was much further to the left of anything the Irish Labour Party advocated in that period.

The influence of Patrick Pearse's 'communalist' ideas in this programme have been noted. While the ideas were radical they did not suggest any practical steps to achieve them through class struggle for instance. However, there were also other influences apparent in the IRA's programme. Elements within the IRA were influenced by theories of Distributism developed by the English Catholic intellectuals G.K. Chesterton and Hiliare Belloc. There was also a pronounced interest in the ideas of Social Credit, popularized by Clifford Douglas. These beliefs stressed community rather than class, allowed for private property but were highly critical of capitalism. They had some influence during the Depression among those who shied away from socialism or communism. Distributism also had the advantage of claiming Christian, especially Catholic, roots. The IRA too increasingly referred to the capitalist system as 'pagan and unchristian'. There was also a great emphasis on the need to control credit and the banking system. Twomey believed that banking was 'the corner-stone of the Imperialist system' and he was for 'knocking it down'. He outlined his own ideas of how a republican government would deal with the Free State's economic difficulties during 1932. Tillage farming should replace grazing land as much as possible, with land redistribution in favour of the small farmers and rural poor. Cheap milk and food should be provided to city dwellers and manufacturing industries developed to provide work and increase prosperity. Since industrialists were hostile to republicanism, the government would have to take control of credit and the banks. In an Ireland with increasing Catholic social power and strong popular anti-communist feeling these ideas offered the IRA a chance to promote radical views without being associated with socialist class struggle. The IRA's involvement in land agitation and the Dublin Tram strike were in part justified by the ideas outlined in the 'Constitution'.

It was not the case that the IRA's politics reflected 'fantasies' rather than the needs and concerns of any social strata. The politics of the 'Constitution' reflect both the ideas of the leadership and the concerns of the strata most heavily represented within the IRA. Outside Dublin the IRA's officer corps was largely lower middle class or from small farming backgrounds. During 1932 there was a desire for social change among this section of the population which is reflected in communications between local officers in the west of Ireland and the IRA leadership. A Dingle officer remarked on how because of 'capitalistic swindling' the small farmers and fishermen of the Gaeltacht were suffering but had nobody to voice their grievances. He felt that the local IRA could become the vehicle for a movement to improve conditions in the area. In north Mayo the IRA reported that the farmers were in a 'bitter mood'. Small farmers in particular were impatient with the pace of change and desired industrial development so that there would a large urban population for them to feed. The IRA leadership in turn encouraged their officers to take up agitation on these issues but stressed that rural demands be linked to those of the unemployed and urban poor. Twomey warned that much of the discontent among larger farmers was aimed at destabilizing the Fianna Fáil government and that republicans should encourage the poorer farmers to make their demands heard instead. These ideas were reflected in the demands the IRA made to conferences of farmers in Tipperary and Limerick during 1932 and in *An Phoblacht* articles on the land situation. Demands for tillage rather than 'bullock raising' and appeals to small farmers and 'landless men' who made a living in 'bogs and hills' to rally against the 'ranchers' did have a basis in real grievances. Similarly the demands that food be provided to the urban poor and work found for the unemployed were hardly the stuff of fantasy.

There was a strong sense of impending crisis in much of the IRA's analysis of Irish society in that period. It was continually stressed that there was 'no hope of improvement' in economic conditions and that capitalism was facing an inevitable collapse. This was allied to a belief that if the Fianna Fáil government would only 'harness all this discontent' they would have popular backing for carrying through major reforms. However, the IRA were hamstrung by their desire not to be seen as antagonistic to Fianna Fáil by leading agitation themselves and also by their belief that the government would disillusion its supporters in the longer term anyway.

It should be noted that even these amended policies came under internal attack by militarists within the IRA who still believed the leadership was 'too communistic' and who suspected 'confiscation' of land lay behind the idea of 'co-operative redistribution'. While many of these policies were based on the experience of the IRA nationally the IRA membership was not generally consulted about them. It was pointed out by one IRA officer that all the organization's political initiatives had been 'handed down by the Army Council' and that the rank and file had never had a say in their formulation. The accusation of having communist sympathies followed even those sections of the IRA who went 'constitutional' during the 1940s.

These ideas were also highly ambiguous politically, appealing to a sense of radicalism which was not necessarily left-wing. The obsession with banking and control of credit led the IRA to champion opponents of the 'International

Bankers' like Fr Charles Coughlin, the phenomenally popular US 'radio priest'. Coughlin, one of the 'great populist demagogues' of American history had a mass audience in the US for his appeals for social justice and attacks on big business. By the late 1930s, Coughlin had become one of the foremost defenders of Nazism within the US and a virulent anti-Semite. Some enthusiasts for Social Credit in Ireland took the same route, but the IRA did not in this period transfer its hostility to banking and sloganeering against capitalism into support for fascism. There were elements within the IRA, as early as 1926, who suggested forming an Irish 'Milesian Legion' in a conscious emulation of Italian fascism. The legion, which would serve 'God and Ireland' would be hostile to 'destructive and despotic Communism' but would also be democratic. The fear was expressed that unless the IRA formed an Irish 'Fascisti' some other political force would get there before them. However, these suggestions were not acted on. Given the disregard for majority rule which existed within the IRA and its militarist ethos, there was certainly a potential for fascist influence. Nevertheless, whether because it had already successfully applied that label to its enemies the Blueshirts, or because of the hostility to fascism promoted by the left within the organization, IRA sympathy for fascism was marginal in this period. Twomey worried that if Fianna Fáil disappointed its supporters there was an 'awful possibility' that they would 'lose heart' and fling themselves into 'the arms of re-action' as had happened in Germany. *An Phoblacht* published the German Social Democrats' verdict on the 1934 elections in Germany and commented that 'Nazi terrorism' had guaranteed an outcome favourable to Hitler. Republican hostility to fascism contained distinctive appeals to Irish conditions. After describing in detail how Hitler and Mussolini had destroyed women's rights, Eithne Coyle then argued that fascism would also be 'alien to our Celtic nature'. Elements within the IRA's last political initiative of this period, Cumann Poblachta na h-Eireann argued that members of the 'Fascist' Irish Christian Front should be forbidden from joining the party.

However, by 1940, a younger IRA leadership would no longer have a political problem with fascism and they too would couch their rhetoric in terms of 'Christian Justice'. This has been difficult for republicans to accept. There is no doubt that many within the IRA saw their alliance with Nazi Germany as simply tactical and favoured neither 'King nor Dictator'. However, by 1940 the IRA were publicly making clear that the Nazis would be welcomed in Ireland as 'Liberators'. The IRA claimed to be giving active assistance to German bombing missions and to have influence with the Nazi leadership. Open anti-Semitism surfaced in republican publications with allegations of Jewish machinations in both the Irish and British governments. In 1941 the IRA's *War News* would refer to Jews as 'human lice' who the 'cleansing fire' of the Nazi armies was finally driving from Europe. By that year IRA members were engaging in bizarre alliances with former Blueshirts and Irish Nazi supporters. Rather than see the explanation for this in some republican original sin the acceptance of Nazi ideology by the IRA reflects both the confused nature of republican radicalism and also the organizations marginality by 1940. By that year most of its pre-1936 leadership had left the IRA, hundreds of its members were interned and it numbered less than a thousand. At rank and file level utter confusion seems to have reigned, with only the Kerry IRA maintaining anything like a functioning organization. Politically the organization could contain former members of the International Brigade such as Mick O'Riordan, ex-members of the British Social credit 'Greenshirts' like Tarlach Ó hUid and men who would canvass for the Irish Labour party in the 1943 general election! Ascertaining which members of the IRA were most enthusiastic about the Nazi connection is extremely difficult.

The IRA did not devote nowhere near as much attention to partition as it did to social and economic matters. When *An Phoblacht* became the IRA's newspaper 'north east Ulster' ranked seventh in a list of subjects it would focus on. Indeed, in 1933 the paper had admitted that the IRA not 'spoken specifically of partition as often as other sections in the country'. Furthermore it suggested that it was only when 'unscrupulous' politicians were meeting political problems in the south that they resorted to 'maudlin sentiment' about the border. At both the 1933 and 1934 conventions only a fraction of the discussions involved events in Northern Ireland. These largely concerned the possibility of political advances among the Protestant working class following the 1932 and 1933 strikes and the IRA's decision to stand candidates against the Nationalist Party, rather the issue of reunification. In 1933 the IRA leadership considered that how to weld a movement from 'disillusioned elements amongst the Orange workers' and the 'leaderless section of Nationalist opinion' was the most important aspect of its northern policy. Just two motions at that Convention, both from northern units, suggested military operations in the north should be a priority. The fact that the majority of the IRA, leadership and rank and file, was southern based obviously had some bearing on their attitude to the north. Their organization in the north did not really begin to expand until after 1932 and then it remained the subject of perspectives about the area developed in Dublin. The IRA leadership regarded unionism as having a very fragile basis which was dependent to a large degree on the activities of the Nationalist Party. Again and again the IRA stressed that 'Devlin and company will only play into the hands of Craigavon' or that the Nationalists had united 'the loyal elements' by talking 'nothing except religion'. This was also reflected in the propaganda the IRA used during its northern election campaigns which was very much centred around calls for unity across sectarian lines. The IRA leadership did not want to have to face the implications of Joseph McGarrity's statement that 'every second man, woman and child' in the north was an 'enemy'. In many ways the IRA leadership had little understanding of the culture of its organization in the north, especially in Belfast. For the southern IRA the overthrow of the Free State was very much its principal focus. This is not to ignore that there were often sectarian implications in IRA assumptions about the north but to stress that the issue of partition came second in the IRA's world view anyway.

This changed when the growth of the IRA in the north coincided with growing difficulties for the organization south of the border. The suggestion of a campaign in the six counties as a method of winning wider support and regaining the initiative in Irish politics seems to have originated with the Clan na Gael. It was taken on board partially out of desperation by an increasingly marginalized southern IRA. A last echo of the older IRA perspective was given by Twomey at Bodenstown in 1938 when he warned the IRA not to believe partition was the 'only obstacle before them'. In reality from that period onwards ending partition became the *raison d'être* of the IRA in the south.

The IRA's attitude to the southern state also needs re-examinination. It appears that for a period it believed that the Fianna Fáil government could declare the 26 counties a republic, and that the IRA would have accepted this. Prior to the 1932 convention a senior officer put forward a series of alternative policies in the event of this occurring including handing over IRA arms to the government, becoming part of a volunteer force or forming a new republican party. In the case of a republic being declared the IRA would then be free to concentrate its attention on Northern Ireland but not necessarily in terms of military operations. This points to a pragmatic tendency among many of the IRA about political affairs which perhaps explains how so many of the organization were eventually able to make the transition to democratic politics. The majority of the IRA officer corps who remained politically involved were to become members of a party that was in government when an Irish republic was declared. Even Tom Barry confessed during 1935 that if de Valera declared a republic he would have no right to oppose it militarily. Peadar O'Donnell consistently claimed that MacBride's position was that if Fianna Fáil removed the oath of allegiance and the governor generalship then he would have no problem with the southern state. The fact that long standing officers like Seán Buckley and Michael Hilliard could as late as the mid 1930s leave the IRA and become elected Fianna Fáil politicians would point to there being a section of the organization which did not differ politically very much from Fianna Fáil.

What strategy, if any, did the IRA have between 1926 and 1936? Peter Berry of the Department of Justice, an astute if hostile observer, believed the IRA leadership felt they had a 'prescriptive right' to their positions as inheritors of the physical force tradition. Their strategy was simply to preserve this tradition and hand on the torch to another generation. In the meantime the tradition was maintained by speeches, parades, commemorations and by 'letting a few of their supporters go to gaol from time to time'. This echoed comments of Peadar O'Donnell's that the problem with the IRA was not that they were not socialist, but that they were not 'taking steps to get the Republic'. There is some evidence to support these assertions. The IRA continually avoided having to set up a political wing from 1932 to 1935, every year deferring on the basis of perfecting their military organization. This was partly because of the reaction to their launch of Saor Éire during 1931 but it also reflected a desire to avoid political confrontation with the government. The key impulse for the IRA leadership was survival and avoiding costly schisms. The preparation for 'war' would help prevent internal fracturing. Training and drilling was to take place until an 'opportune time' arrived to begin an insurrection. However, as the years went on and the IRA did not 'take the field' frustration and a desire for action meant some members indulged in unofficial violence or were caught up in local feuds, while others left disillusioned for personal or political reasons. Richard English has characterized republicans during this period as 'solipsists' acting as if their own beliefs were the only really existent ones. This certainly is apparent in the ability of republicans to deny to themselves as well as to others their responsibility for unpopular actions. Maud Gonne could blame 'secret detectives' of the government for the murder of Albert Armstrong and Donal O'Donoghue was still denying IRA involvement in the Somerville and Egan murders over a decade later. What mattered of course, was not whether or not non republicans would believe these statements, but that the faithful would.

Not only was the IRA's ideology self sustaining, but much of its activity was as well. The IRA could mount an attack on a pub selling Bass providing excitement and activity for its members. The arrest of IRA men for this attack would then lead to protest marches, postering, wall painting and another round of activity. In the longer term this would achieve nothing concrete but would keep the membership busy and maintain the facade that they were preparing for war.

While the solipsist characterization is useful there was also a material basis to the IRA's existence in this period. If their only attraction was their quaint belief that they represented the legitimate government of Ireland they would have remained as isolated as Sinn Féin. However, over this period they recruited several thousand members, many of whom were talented and capable individuals. One attraction was obviously the appeal to the Irish physical force tradition. There is nothing particularly surprising in this as Irish society had seen an intense militarization between 1900 and 1914, then participation in the greatest human conflict to that date, followed by a revolution and civil war. The use of force was not beyond the life experience of a substantial section of the Irish people in this period. Whats more the dominant political culture of the Free State looked back to its violent origins with pride. The appeal to this tradition was important, which is why it was so heavily contested between the main political forces in the Free State. Fianna Fáil, the Blueshirts and the IRA would all claim to be the legitimate inheritors of the revolutionary tradition. The attraction to young men (and women) of military organization is no mystery then. This must be put in context however. From 1917 to 1923 an estimated 3,269 people died in political violence in Ireland. Between 1926 and 1936 just 38 people died because of violence linked to politics. Compared to contemporary European events this figure reflects that however dramatic they seemed domestically, political violence in post-revolutionary Ireland was a fraction of that in much of Europe. It is significant that none of the republican schisms of the period produced any serious bloodshed for example. It may even be the case that the majority of the IRA leadership, having had experience of serious guerrilla conflict desired, if at all possible, to avoid such a conflict again.

While the IRA was often very wrong in its analysis of developments within Ireland there was a real basis for many of their calculations. There was still in the late 1920s a substantial section of the Free State's population who felt alienated from the new state and who regarded its institutions with less than respect. This resentment fed into toleration and among a section of the young, admiration, for those who completely rejected the Treaty settlement. The Great Depression did produce both despair and radicalisation in Ireland and the IRA benefited from this. The Outdoor Relief rioting and the rail strike did seem to signal a breakdown in sectarian division within Northern Ireland. The IRA's belief that the tension between the Free State and Britain would lead to armed conflict during 1932 was not wildly unrealistic given the atmosphere of the time. Elements within the state forces did consider attempting to prevent Fianna Fáil's asscession to power and had they acted then the IRA could possibly have benefitted from a republican backlash. The IRA only began to founder when the Fianna Fáil government began to solidify its support rather than disillusion it, and the frustration of the IRA's own members began to express itself in political disagreement or violence. While a sizeable number of people remained estranged from the Free State, the IRA had a base from which to recruit, but that base had shrunk by 1935. The progress of Fianna Fáil in government allied to the violently anti-left wing atmosphere after 1931 seriously diminished the attraction of the IRA's social policies. North of the border, however, conditions for the Catholic minority meant there remained a constituency for militarist conspiracy.

What other factors could have drawn men towards the IRA in this period? Unfortunately the motivation of ordinary IRA recruits is hard to assess. There are few documentary sources which point towards anything more concrete than a desire to 'obtain Irish Freedom'. Therefore we can only speculate on other factors. For most of the decade in question the IRA was not an attractive option for young men who sought advancement in society. Membership meant giving up time for largely boring parades and having to take orders and obey rules which had no formal basis. It could mean imprisonment and certainly harassment by the police, although it was unlikely to lead to great physical danger for most of this period. The exception to this was the period between 1932 to 1934 in the Free State where there was relative freedom to organize and some prestige in association with the republican movement. There may also have been some sense of status that went with IRA membership in strongly republican areas before 1932. There was the social element that parading and drilling provided, as well as attendance at 'Aeridheacht.' The clashes and street fighting of the Blueshirt period were attractive and having access to arms and the potential to use them was no doubt also a factor. We have seen that the IRA was wracked by disputes over its allegedly communist nature. Its members were obviously affected by the broader political atmosphere in Ireland. However, the IRA's radicalism was also an attractive feature for some, appealing to a belief that injustice and inequality should not exist in an Irish republic. A less admirable attraction may have been the ability to bully which membership of an armed group gave to some young men. The IRA was capable of including those who joined to fight Blueshirts, to be seen parading on Easter Sunday, to get to fire a rifle, to defy the local police or to attack strike breakers. It could appeal to those for whom the republican ideal was a 'spiritual' one and also those who believed unless the republic brought change for 'the man in the street' then it would have failed. It is quite possible that all of these things could at different stages, appeal to the same individual.

When W.T. Cosgrave wrote to ask Cardinal McRory for support for the clampdown on the IRA during 1931, he outlined his analysis of how the organization was gaining support. As well as their claim to the revolutionary nationalist tradition, Cosgrave argued that the IRA appealed to the 'poverty of the poor ... the cupidity of the dishonest and the envy of the unsuccessful'. Despite his patronizing tone, Cosgrave was more correct than he probably realized, as discontent was the motor of IRA support. The IRA was made up largely of those who did not believe they had benefited from the revolution of 1917-21 and who sensed that the revolution was unfinished. By 1933 this belief was only going to appeal to a minority of the Irish population, generally those who lacked any concrete stake in society or felt they deserved more. Therefore the IRA after 1926 became more radical politically, but less violent than their predecessors of 1919-23. Most of its members came from humbler backgrounds than the 'Old IRA' and their organization identified with workers and small farmers in a way the IRA had never done before. They drew their revolutionary legitimacy from the conflicts of 1916-23 but most of their members had not been involved in these events. In many ways confused and contradictory as they were, the IRA represented some of the losers of Ireland's revolution, the republican section of the population who only began to see positive changes occurring during the post 1932-period. However, the majority of their constituency were satisfied by the limited constitutional and economic reforms carried out by Fianna Fáil rather than the revolutionary vision of the IRA. The IRA's successors too would claim legitimacy from the revolutionary period, but differ significantly from the IRA of 1926-36 by their single minded obsession with partition and narrower social vision. The IRA during the 1930s represented the last fading embers of the revolutionary period.

Appendices

APPENDIX 1 / **Biographical notes:**
IRA leadership, 1933

Tom Barry

Barry who became the IRA's chief of staff in 1937 had only rejoined the organization during 1932 after several years outside it. His reputation as one of the most successful IRA commanders during the War of Independence masked the fact that he was distrusted by the organization for a long period. In 1923 he proposed that the IRA destroy all its arms and ammunition. Following the rejection of this proposal he had left the organization. He became active again during 1932, although he continued to have reservations about the IRA's social policies. Barry was born in 1897 in Bandon, Co. Cork, the son of a former RIC officer who had become a shopkeeper. He was educated for a period at Mungret College, Co. Limerick. In 1915 he joined the British Army and served in Mesopotamia. On his return to Cork he was involved with ex-servicemen's organizations. During 1919 he joined the IRA and eventually led the west Cork flying column, which was involved in two of the best known engagements of the period at Kilmichael and Crossbarry. During 1921 he married Leslie Price, the director of organization of Cumann na mBan. In 1927 he became a superintendent of Cork Harbour Commission and held this post until 1965. Barry was given to threatening violent retribution against the IRA's enemies. This sometimes belied a more compassionate side to his nature. A leading figure in the IRA by 1934 he was jailed that year and again in 1935. He succeeded MacBride as C/S in 1937. Barry became embroiled in a conflict with the supporters of Seán Russell and claimed that they sabotaged a planned IRA offensive in Northern Ireland. Barry would assert in later life that he opposed both the bombing campaign in Britain and IRA contacts with Nazi Germany. He briefly joined the Irish government's defence efforts during 1940. In 1941 he was denounced by the IRA for writing for the Defence Force's journal. Barry was an unsuccessful candidate at the 1946 Cork Borough bye-election. His account of the War of Independence, *Guerrilla days in Ireland*, was published in 1949. Barry has been claimed as a supporter by Provisional Sinn Féin but evidence suggests he was disillusioned by the killing of civilians in Britain and Northern Ireland by the mid 1970s. He died in 1980.

David Fitzgerald

A little-known figure outside republican circles, Fitzgerald was credited by Peader O'Donnell as a key figure in the radicalization of the IRA during the late 1920s. A native of Tipperary, Fitzgerald was active in the 1916 Rising and the War of Independence. An engineer by profession, he was jailed during 1925. In 1930 he visited the Soviet Union as a guest of the FOSR. He was a member of the National Executive of Saor Éire and author of its *Indictment of capitalism in Ireland.* After a long period of illness Fitzgerald died of cancer in 1933.

Michael (Mick) Fitzpatrick

Fitzpatrick was a central figure in the IRA leadership between 1926 and 1937 when he eventually became its chief of staff. Born in Wexford in 1893 he was one of the 'driving forces' behind the anti-Treaty IRA in Dublin during the civil war. He was briefly the O/C of the IRA's Dublin Brigade and was interned in 1923. During this period he was also involved with the first Irish Communist Party. Fitzpatrick was a full-time official of the Grocers' trade union and secretary of its social club at the Banba Hall in Dublin's Parnell Square. He also managed the Balalaika Ballroom in the same area. Fitzpatrick was the key figure in IRA contacts with the Soviet Union during the late 1920s. In 1927 he attended the first International Congress of the Friends of the Soviet Union in Moscow. In 1928 he helped establish the Irish branch of the FOSR. During 1929 he was involved in launching the Irish Labour Defence League and the Workers Revolutionary Party. He visited Russia again in 1932. Fitzpatrick chaired the 1933 IRA GAC. At the 1934 Convention he disagreed with the call for a Republican Congress and remained within the IRA. His union was involved in a strike with O'Mara's Bacon Shops in late 1934 in which the IRA intervened violently. During 1935 he was involved in the IRA's intervention in the Dublin transport strike. In 1936 he was an unsuccessful candidate for Cumann Poblachta na h-Éireann. Fitzpatrick succeeded Barry as IRA leader in 1937, only to be ousted by Russell at the 1938 convention. He was involved in the launch of Clann na Poblachta in 1946 and a member of its national executive. Fitzpatrick was elected as a TD for Dublin North West in 1948 and held his seat until 1951.

George Gilmore

One of the best known IRA leaders of the period, Gilmore was born in Dublin in 1898. He played a minor role in the 1916 Rising and was active in the South Dublin brigade of the IRA from 1920. He was jailed in Mountjoy during the civil war. In November 1925 he helped organize the mass breakout of IRA prisoners from Mountjoy. He was imprisoned on several occasions during the late 1920s and early 1930s. His two brothers, Harry and Charlie, were also active in the

Dublin IRA. Gilmore was O/C of the Dublin brigade for a period and was believed to be responsible for at least one murder. He visited the Soviet Union in 1930. Gilmore was arrested and jailed during the winter of 1931–32 after the discovery of an arms dump near his family home in Killakee, Rathfarnham. He was wounded in a clash with gardaí in Kilrush in August 1932. Gilmore was a popular figure within the IRA but was not a comfortable public speaker or agitator. He was cynical about the prospects of revolutionary change and attempted to resign from the AC in late 1932. At the 1933 convention he warned that the IRA was becoming a 'safety valve for Fianna Fáil.' He supported Mick Price's proposal at the 1934 convention and after the failure of the convention to endorse the Congress idea he left the IRA. He was subsequently a member of the AC of the Irish Citizens Army. Gilmore collaborated closely with Peadar O'Donnell for whom he had a high regard. He was active in the Republican Congress from 1934, visiting the US to raise support in 1935. He continued to work with O'Donnell on left republican projects into the 1940s. By the 1960s his advice was sought by sections of the IRA who were moving towards the left. Gilmore died in 1985.

James (Jim) Killeen

Killeen was appointed adjutant general of the IRA in 1927 and held that position until 1933. Born in Westmeath in 1893, Killeen had joined the Irish Volunteers in 1918. He was arrested in Britain during 1926 and jailed for attempting to smuggle arms. Killeen was not prominent in the political debates within the IRA but closely worked with Twomey and MacBride. He was arrested in Belfast in 1936 and jailed for four years in Crumlin Road. He did not resume IRA activity on his release but was involved in re-organization talks among republicans in 1945. In 1946 Killeen became a member of the national executive of Clann na Poblachta and was active in that party until the late 1950s.

Seán MacBride

MacBride was widely believed to have been the IRA's adjutant general during the late 1920s and early 1930s. While he may not have actually held this position, he certainly was a key figure within the IRA and effectively Twomey's closest collaborator. He was IRA director of intelligence in 1933. The son of Major John MacBride and Maud Gonne, he was born in Paris in 1904. MacBride was involved in the Irish Volunteers from 1918 and in the Dublin brigade active service unit from 1920. He was attached to IRA GHQ staff and served as an aide-de-camp to Michael Collins during the Treaty negotiations. Jailed during the civil war, he escaped with Mick Price in 1923. He married Catalina (Kid) Bulfin in 1926. MacBride was arrested in connection with the Kevin O'Higgins assassination in 1927 but successfully defeated the state's case. During that period his official occupation was managing director of the Roebuck Jam Company, operating from the family home at Roebuck House, Clonskeagh. In 1929 he was arrested at an IRA meeting in Tullamore. MacBride attended the congress of the Anti-Imperialist League in Frankfurt during 1929. He was arrested in Listowel during 1931 and found to have documents relating to Saor Éire. He was a member of the national executive of that body. MacBride was involved in IRA negotiations with Frank Aiken in the summer of 1932 and later met de Valera on behalf of the IRA. He was briefly editor of *An Phoblacht* during 1933 and also worked for the *Evening Press* for a period. He was firmly against the Congress proposal at the 1934 convention and was bitterly disliked by Congress supporters such as George Gilmore. He was involved in IRA intervention in the Dublin transport strike and went on the run following the government clamp-down during March 1935. He was the secretary of Cumann Poblachta na Éire-ann during 1936. He became IRA C/S following Twomey's arrest in May that year. He handed over this post to Barry in 1937. MacBride was called to the Bar that year and to the Inner Bar in 1943. He defended all the IRA members tried for murder by the Special Criminal Court and Military Court from 1940 to 1946. The gardaí suspected that he maintained links with the IRA despite hav-ing signed an undertaking not to do so in 1940. He founded Clann na Poblachta in 1946 and was elected a TD for Co. Dublin in 1947. He became Minister for External Affairs in the 1948-51 Inter-Party government. MacBride remained a TD until 1957. He was a founder and chairman of Amnesty International and a winner of both the Nobel and Lenin Peace prizes in 1974 and 1977 respective-ly. MacBride maintained a deliberate vagueness about his political positions in later years, claiming that he was not involved in Cumann Poblachta na h-Éire-ann and had left the IRA because he supported the 1937 Constitution. He also denied having had any contact with Nazi Germany while the IRA's leader.

Patrick McLogan

The only member of the IRA leadership to come from what became Northern Ireland, McLogan was born in Markethill, Co. Armagh, in 1894. After a period in Scotland he returned to Ireland and joined the Irish Volunteers in 1917. In the post civil war period he settled in Portlaoise where he owned a public house. McLogan opposed IRA involvement in land agitation in Laois-Offaly during 1932. He was elected as an MP for Armagh in the Stormont elections of November 1933. He chaired the 1934 IRA convention and was involved in Cumann na Poblachta h-Éireann during 1936. He was interned from 1940 to 1941. McLogan remained active within the IRA during the 1940s and was later President of Sinn Féin from 1950 until his death in 1964.

Peadar O'Donnell

Possibly the best known, after MacBride, of the IRA leadership from this period is O'Donnell, largely due to the volume of literature produced by or about him. Born in 1893 in Dungloe, Co. Donegal, O'Donnell became a school teacher in 1913. He was active in the Irish National Teachers Organization and later became a full time organizer for the ITGWU in 1918. He joined the Irish Volunteers in 1918. Despite retrospective claims that he was 'not the military type' O'Donnell was O/C of 2nd brigade of the IRA's Ulster Division and amember of the anti-treaty executive by 1922. He was elected a TD for Donegal in 1923. A member of the IRA executive from 1924, he became editor of *An Phoblacht* in 1926 and held this post until 1929. He married Lile O'Donell during 1924. He was jailed in 1929 for assaulting a garda. From 1927 O'Donnell attempted to organize a mass anti-annuities campaign. In 1929 he attended the Frankfurt anti-imperialist congress with MacBride. In 1930 he was a delegate to the congress of the European Peasants Movement, the Krestintern. He established an Irish section of the Krestintern called the Irish Working Farmers Committee. He was a member of the national executive of Saor Éire in 1931. O'Donnell authored several novels and pamphlets during this period. He was disillusioned from an early stage by the refusal of the IRA to undermine Fianna Fáil. He wrote the IRA's 'Appeal to the Orange Order' during 1932. O'Donnell considered the IRA to be the 'most intense form' of the working-class movement. He complained of censorship of his views by the IRA and left the organization after the 1934 convention. He was then court-martialled and dismissed by the IRA. He was involved with the Republican Congress from 1934 until 1936. O'Donnnell was in Spain at the beginning of its civil war in 1936. He then helped edit and produce the *Irish Democrat* in 1937. O'Donnell also established and edited *The Bell* from 1940 until 1954. He was active in the Campaign for Nuclear Disarmament and against the Vietnam War during the 1960s. With Gilmore he was involved in giving advice to republicans during the 1960s. With age, he became the 'grand old man' of the Irish left, active in various causes until his death in 1986.

Donal O'Donoghue

O'Donoghue became the IRA's adjutant general in March 1933. Born in Cavan in 1897 he had been a member of the 5th Battalion (Engineers) of the IRA's Dublin brigade. He was interned during the Civil War. O'Donoghue was jailed in connection with the IRA's moneylending raids during 1926. He attended the 1928 congress of the Anti-Imperialist League in Brussels. He was director of the Boycott British Campaign during late 1932 and later editor of *An Phoblacht*. He was arrested during the Dublin transport strike and jailed in the Curragh in March 1935. He married Cumann na mBan activist Sighle Humphreys that year. Later that year he was arrested in Lurgan during the 1935 Westminster elections and jailed in Crumlin Road. O'Donoghue left the IRA in 1938. He edited *Republican Review* from 1938 to 1939. He worked as an accountant for An Solus Teo and was a founding member of Clann na Poblachta in 1946. A member of that party's executive he was an unsuccessful candidate in Dublin South West in 1948. He died in 1957.

Séan O'Farrell

A commander of one of the IRA's strongest battalions in the west midlands and Leitrim, O'Farrell was a former Sinn Féin TD for the area. He remained active in that party until the late 1920s. He was also a member of the provisional committee of the Irish Working Farmers movement during 1930. O'Farrell did not agree with informing recruits to the IRA about the movement's social policies and he favoured neutrality on the Gralton issue during 1933. He was a member of the Gaelic League and active in its anti-jazz campaign in Leitrim. He was jailed following a clash with Blueshirts in 1934 and was elected to Leitrim county council after topping the poll in Carrick on Shannon that year. He resigned his position on the council later that year and left the IRA shortly afterwards.

George Plunkett

Plunkett served as the IRA's director of engineering in 1933. Born in Dublin in 1896 he was the son of Sinn Féin's Count Plunkett and the brother of executed 1916 leader Joseph Mary Plunkett. He fought in the 1916 Rising and from 1919 to 1923. His privileged background meant his occupation was listed as 'gentleman' by the gardaí. He was hostile to the IRA's involvement in politics during this period. He supported Russell in 1938 and became a member of his army council. Plunkett was interned briefly during 1940 and died in an accident in 1944.

Michael (Mick) Price

Price was the IRA's director of training in 1933, having previously been a director of intelligence for the organization. He was born in Dublin in 1896. He served in the British Army during World War One and joined the Irish Volunteers in 1918. He was jailed in Belfast later that year, and took part in a hunger strike there. He was a staff officer in west Cork by 1921. Three of his brothers and a sister were involved in the republican movement during that period. During the civil war, Price was QM and then O/C of the IRA's 1st Eastern Division. He escaped from prison along with MacBride in October 1923. He became the O/C of the Dublin brigade and was one of those pushing for more militant activity during 1925. He was jailed after the moneylending raids in 1926. He was regarded by the gardaí as one of the 'most dangerous' IRA activists in Ireland during that period. Price was arrested on the eve of the Bodenstown commemoration in June 1931 and was sent to the US later that year during the government's clampdown. Twomey felt that there was no one in the IRA 'more sincere' or 'prepared to make sacrifice' than Price. Price was a member of the executive of Saor Éire but had been hostile to radical ideas within the IRA until 1931. He voted against setting up a political organization in 1933. However, at the 1934 convention he put forward a motion calling for the IRA to commit itself to remaining in existence until a Workers Republic was achieved. When this was rejected, he left the convention and was court-martialled and dismissed from the IRA. He helped found the Republican Congress. He was also a member of the AC of the ICA. He left the congress over its failure to form an openly socialist party in late 1934 and led his own faction of the ICA. He was jailed in the Curragh during the Dublin transport strike of 1935. He led his followers into the Labour Party later that year. Price was elected to the Labour Party's administrative council in 1937 and later became secretary of its constituencies council. He died in 1944.

Seán Russell

Of all his colleagues on the 1933 army council Russell had held the highest position in the IRA prior to the civil war. Born in Dublin in 1893 Russell joined the Irish Volunteers in 1913. He took part in the Easter Rising, as an officer in Dublin Brigade's 2nd Battalion. Following the Rising he was interned in Frongoch and Knutsford. From 1919 he was attached to the IRA's headquarters staff and became director of munitions in 1920. Russell travelled to the USSR on an arms buying mission in 1925. Later that year he was jailed in Mountjoy but escaped in November in a breakout he helped organize. Russell was one of those within the IRA pushing for more militant activities in 1926. He was appointed QMG in 1927 and held that position until 1936. He travelled widely within Ireland reorganizing the IRA during 1929–31. Russell was due to give the oration at the 1931 Bodenstown commemoration but was arrested on its eve. He visited the US in the autumn of 1932. During the Northern Ireland rail strike of 1933 he organized IRA intervention from Belfast. Russell remained aloof from the IRA's political debates and following the split of 1934 chaired the court-martial of Price and O'Donnell. He met de Valera at Government Buildings during 1934. While in the US during 1936 seems to have conceived along with Joseph McGarrity, the plan for the bombing campaign in Britain. He was accused of misappropriating funds by the IRA leadership and was court martialled. Along with McGarrity and elements among the IRA in Northern Ireland colluded in a take over of the IRA in 1938. After becoming C/S he put into motion the bombing campaign and contacts with Nazi Germany. His letters to both McGarrity and German contacts betray astonishing political

naiveté. Arrested in the US during 1939, Russell was released on bail and spir-
ited to Europe. He arrived in Nazi Germany during 1940 and agreed to return
to Ireland with Frank Ryan. He became ill on board a U-boat and died at sea.
Russell became the idol of traditionalist republicanism during the 1950s and a
memorial to him was unveiled in Dublin's Fairview Park during 1951.

Frank Ryan

Ryan remains a recognizable figure in Ireland both politically and in popular
culture. He was born in Limerick in 1902 and joined the IRA in 1921 too late to
take part in the War of Independence. During the civil war, he was interned in
the Curragh where he edited an Irish language journal, An Giorrfhiodh. Ryan
had won a scholarship to UCD which he took up when he was released from jail.
There he was an active member of An Cumann Gaedhealach and won their gold
medal for oratory. Ryan was active in the UCD Republican Club and in the
Dublin IRA. He worked briefly as a teacher and at the Irish Tourist Association
but was a full-time IRA activist by 1928. He was arrested on several occasions
after clashes with the gardaí. Ryan attended the 1928 Brussels anti-imperialist
congress. In 1929 he became editor of An Phoblacht and also an IRA inspection
officer. Ryan visited the US during 1930 and spoke at the New York Easter commemoration. He was jailed twice during 1931, once for assaulting a Garda and
again during the clampdown of winter 1931–2. He refused to wear prison uniform or obey regulations and his health may have begun its long-term decline
in this period. During 1932 he became increasingly dissatisfied with the IRA's
policies towards Fianna Fáil and moved politically towards a socialist position.
At the 1933 Convention he expressed dissatisfaction with the IRA's failure to
become a 'Citizens Army.' He resigned as editor of An Phoblacht and from the
IRA executive in April 1933. Ryan was further alienated by an IRA investigation
into his alleged presence at a communist meeting that year and he always
denied being a communist. Twomey described Ryan as a 'bad man in a team' but
he was a popular figure even among his political opponents within the IRA. At
the 1934 convention he sided with O'Donnell and Gilmore and became editor
of the new Republican Congress paper in May of that year. Ryan helped organize alternative Armistice Day parades in November 1934 and 1935 and also
stood as a congress candidate in the 1936 Dublin municipal elections. With the
outbreak of war in Spain in 1936 Ryan decided to aid the Spanish Republic
directly as a volunteer. He made it clear that he still regarded himself as a
Catholic despite criticism from the Irish Church during that year. He was the
highest ranking Irish officer in the International brigades and was wounded at
the battle of Jarama in 1937. Ryan returned to Ireland to convalesce and was
involved in anti-Coronation protests alongside the IRA. He also ran as an 'anti-
Fascist' candidate in the 1937 elections. Ryan returned to Spain and was cap-

tured by Italian troops in 1938. He was imprisoned under harsh conditions at Calaceite and eventually sentenced to death. Ryan refused to give the fascist salute or co-operate with his captors and his health declined further while in captivity. An international campaign succeeded in having his death sentence commuted. In 1940 German military intelligence negotiated his release into their custody and he was taken to Germany. He intended to travel back to Ireland with Russell but the latter's death saw him returned to Germany. Ryan suffered a stroke in 1942 and died in Dresden in 1944. Almost all shades of republicanism claim Ryan as a hero, but his co-operation with the Nazis means his legacy remains controversial.

John Joe Sheehy

The gardaí regarded J.J. Sheehy as being 'chiefly responsible' for the existence of the IRA in Kerry during the 1920s and 1930s. Born in Tralee in 1899, Sheehy joined the IRA in 1920 and was an officer in Tralee's Boherbee Company. He became commandant of the Kerry No. 1 brigade during the civil war. As an outstanding Gaelic footballer he won four All-Ireland medals, twice captaining his county to the title. Sheehy used his prominent position with the Irish National Assurance Company to help secure work for IRA members. He was regarded by the gardaí as a moderating influence on the IRA in Kerry. A member of Sinn Féin, Sheehy was wary of, if not completely hostile, to the IRA's social policies. He resigned from the IRA in 1938 in protest at the take-over by Russell's supporters. However, he became active again during the 1940s, aiding German spy Hermann Goertz in Kerry, although the gardaí still felt his leadership in Kerry was preferable to that of a more militant activist. He was interned during 1944 and jailed again in 1946. Sheehy remained supportive of the republican movement during the 1950s and maintained his prominence within the GAA. The road which runs alongside the Kerry GAA headquarters in Tralee is named after Sheehy, who died in 1980.

Maurice (Moss) Twomey

Twomey and MacLaughlin had two children both born in the early 1930s. Following his arrest in 1936 Twomey served over a years imprisonment in the Curragh. During his period of imprisonment his family depended heavily on money sent to them by McGarrity of the Clan na Gael. On his release Twomey became adjutant general on Russell's army council. He travelled to Britain and inspected the IRA's units there. Twomey concluded that the IRA was in no position to launch a campaign and withdrew from IRA activity. In 1939 he opened a newsagents and confectioners in Dublin's O'Connell Street. He was interned for two weeks during 1940. He remained close to the IRA, giving assistance to republicans deported from Britain and mediating in disputes between IRA factions. He was not active in politics after the 1940s, although he did speak at a number of commemorations, most notably at the restoration of Wolfe Tone's grave at Bodenstown in 1971. He never claimed an IRA pension or gave an account of his record to the Bureau of Military History. Twomey considered writing a memoir of his period in the IRA but felt that much of the memoirs published were 'myths and legends' which he had no wish to add to. He was badly injured in an accident in 1971 and was deeply affected by the death of his wife in April 1978. Twomey himself died in October of that year. The presence at his funeral of members of both Fianna Fáil and Fine Gael, Official and Provisional Sinn Féin, the labour movement and old comrades from the 1930s was evidence of his enduring popularity.

APPENDIX 2 / **IRA weaponry captured in the Free State from 1923 to 1931**

Firearms

Year	Rifles	Revolvers	Pistols	Shotguns	Machineguns
1923	31	53	12	38	
1924	63	155	24	127	
1925	244	306	54	1190	
1926	273	299	47	1243	
1927	112	102	21	42	5
1928	86	72	16	22	1
1929	92	81	5	6	2
1930	47	61	-	8	
1931	37	27	6	3	1
Total	985	1156	185	2979	9

Ammunition and explosives

Year	Rifle	Revolver	Shotgun	Bombs	Mines	Explosives
1923	6916	1587	52	72		114
1924	1814	1198	7108	24		37
1925	1426	11766	5025	206		2897
1926	10487	40766	8055	588		6578
1927	12274	5174	21	21	1	66
1928	6181	2324	276	98	2	74

1929	3896	2020	-	190	1	41
1930	1724	422	-	12		133
1931	2533	2232	3	51	1	262
Total	47261	67499	20540	1262	5	10200(lbs)

'Return of "Dumped" Arms, Ammunition and War Material Discovered and Seized by the Police from Year 1923 to July 1931.' Source: D/T S 5864 A NAI.

APPENDIX 3 / **IRA training course at Donamon Camp, August 1932.**

Sunday. Reveille 6 a.m. Parade (Physical jerks) 6.30–7 a.m.
Breakfast 7–8 a.m.
Parade 8 a.m.–12.30 p.m. (5 minutes rest each hour).
Company Drill – without arms.
Dinner 12–2 p.m.
Parade 2–5.30 Company Drill.
Tea 5.30–6.30 p.m.
Lecture 6.30–7.15 p.m. (Discipline).
Football 7.15–9p.m.
Lights out 9.30 p.m.

Monday. Reveille 6a.m. Parade 6.30 a.m. (Close Order Drill).
Breakfast 7–8 a.m.
Parade 8 a.m.–12.30 p.m. (Extended Order Drill).
Dinner 12.30–2 p.m.
Parade 2 p.m.–5.30 (Extended Order Drill, Musketry instruction).
Tea 5.30–6.30 p.m.
Lecture 6.30–7.30 p.m. (Care of arms, theory of rifle fire, direction of fire).
Football 7.30–9 p.m.
Lights out 9.30 pm.

Tuesday. Parade 8–12.30 a.m. (Extended order).
Dinner 12.30–2 p.m.
Parade 2–5.30 p.m. (Close and extended order drill).
Tea 5.30–6.30 p.m.,
Lecture (Open air). 6.30–7.30 p.m. (Judging distance).
Football 7.30–9 p.m.
Lights out 9.30 p.m.

Wednesday. Reveille 6 a.m. Parade 6.30 (Company drill).

Breakfast 7–8 a.m.

Parade 8 a.m.–12.30 p.m. (Extended order 2 hours; musketry instruction 2 hours)

Dinner 12.30–2 p.m.

Parade 2 p.m.–5.30 p.m. (Company drill – usual rest).

Tea 5.30–6.30 p.m. Lecture 6.30–7.30 p.m. (Duties of sentry and sentry groups, telling off and posting of sentries).

Football 7.30–9 p.m.

Lights out 9.30 p.m.

Thursday. Reveille 6 a.m. Company Drill 6.30–7 a.m.

Breakfast 7–8 a.m.

Parade 8–12.30 p.m. (Extended order 3 & half hours; 1 hour lecture 'Section in attack.').

Dinner 12.30–2 p.m.

Parade 2–5.30 p.m. (Extended order 2 and a half hours; 1 hour lecture 'Section in defence').

Tea 5.30–6.30 p.m.

Lecture 6.30–7.30 p.m. (Use of cover–open air).

Football 7.30–9 p.m.

Lights out 9.30 p.m.

Friday. Reveille 6 a.m.

Parade 6.30–7 a.m.

Breakfast 7–8 a.m.

Parade 8am–12.30 p.m. (Extended order 1 hour; lecture – use of cover 2 hours; musketry 1 and a half hours).

Dinner 12.30–2 p.m.

Parade 2–5.30 p.m. (Attack and defence of an agreed post).

Tea 5.30–6.30 p.m.

Lecture 6.30–7.30 p.m. (Thompson or grenade).

Night operations 10–12 midnight.

Saturday. Reveille 6 a.m.

Company Drill 6.30–7 a.m.

Breakfast 7–8 a.m.

Parade 8–11.30 a.m. (Company drill and lecture on Lewis Gun).

Class dismissed 12 noon.

Source: MTUCDA, P69/54 (156-158).

APPENDIX 4 / **The Coercion Act –
our attitude and tasks**

27 October 1931 A/G to Commander
of each Independent Unit

A Chara,

1 The Army Council directs that the following statement be communicated to
all Volunteers: –

The Army Council believe that the party in power in the 26 Counties aims
at using the Coercion Act to reap the greatest possible party advantage from it.
The prime motive is to enable them to retain and extend their period of office.

They believe it would serve their aims if a state of war and turmoil could be
provoked, so that they may be afforded a pretext for a great onslaught on
Republicans, especially on Volunteers. In other words, they wish to promote
another civil war now, and so prevent us from developing the full strength of the
Army, or from securing an organized mass backing of the people.

On no account must we fall into the trap which is being laid for us. Any violence or sporadic outbursts now on our part would supply the pretext our enemies desire.

At the present time, discipline and cohesion are of vital importance. It may
be expedient, in Units which have been very active, to curtail training activities,
in public, but Companies and Sections must continue to parade frequently, for
orders and instructions.

Recruiting should not be relaxed. The present excited and roused state of
feeling is favourable to recruiting, and the fullest advantage must be taken of
these circumstances.

As regards the pronouncement of the Hierarchy this must be regarded as
inspired by the desire to rescue the Free State Government from its difficulties,
political and economic, and to attempt to check the organising of the people
against Imperialism and the chronic conditions arising out of it. Again, as in
1922 the Hierarchy are lending their sanction to brutal and repressive measures
against Republicans. They are taking advantage of the religious feelings and
scruples of our people, to promote certain interests and political opinions that
they hold. The role of the Hierarchy should be exposed, when necessary.

In the present situation there is a considerable amount of useful work which
Volunteers can do, working amongst the people. They can use their influence to
steady those who may feel nervous in the face of the threats and penalties of the

Coercion Act. They must calm those inclined to be stampeded by the pronouncement of the Hierarchy.

The enemy wishes to deprive Republicanism of public expression. Where possible local meetings should be held. At those meetings demands should go forth for the resignation of those who voted for the Coercion Act. Local publicity could be very useful at the present time, and Units are asked to take up this activity.

We must fight the campaign of misrepresentation and calumny directed against us from so many directions. The best method is for Volunteers to get amongst neighbours and friends and let them know exactly what it is we stand for. The campaign will be fought down as the days go by.

The worsening of the economic crisis must inevitably deprive the present Government party of support, but we must not be content with this, we must work to attract the greatest measure of support to us. Concrete programmes must be put forward dealing with the immediate problems and hardships under which the mass of the people are suffering in the countryside and town. The enemy is trying to rob us of the initiative which we had recovered and to isolate us once more so that we could be crushed. We must not allow this, and it will not occur if Volunteers in their own localities not only use their influence but supply local leadership.

The future is with us: the spirit of National revolt and discontent will collect around the most courageous minds, and a free Ireland will become the clear ideal and hope of salvation for the enslaved people of the country. In God's name then let us build and wait confidently for the day that is coming when the Irish people will again take the road of revolt against British rule and Imperialism, and call on the youth of Ireland to get to the front to clear the way."

2. It is very important that every Volunteer should be acquainted with the policy of the Army Council just now. You will therefore arrange without delay to have copies of the above statement circulated, with definite orders that it is to be communicated to every Volunteer.

3. Please acknowledge receipt of this communication.

D_____
Adjutant General._____

Source: D/T S 5864 C NAI.

APPENDIX 5 / **National Pilgrimage to Bodenstown, June 19, 1932**

Orders of Procession from Sallins to Bodenstown.

'Fall-in' will be sounded at 2.30 by Fianna Trumpeters.

(1) Advance Guard, O'Rahilly Brass and Reed Band (Dublin)
(2) Contingents Irish Republican Army.

    (a) Dublin Brigade (2nd, 3rd, and 4th Battalions). Fintan Lalor Pipers' Band.
    (b) South Dublin Battalion.
    (c) Clare Battalion.
    (d) Clann na Gaedheal (*sic*) USA. Cork Volunteers Pipers' Band.
    (e) Cork Brigade.
    (f) Tralee Battalion. Killarney Pipers' Band.
    (g) Killarney Battalion.
    (h) Listowel Battalion.
    (i) Castlegregory and Castleisland Battalions.
    (j) Dingle Battalion.
    (k) Galway Battalion.
    (l) Belfast Battalion.
    (m) Kilkenny Battalion. Wexford Pipers' Band.
    (o) Wexford Battalion.
    (p) Leitrim and Longford Battalions.
    (q) Roscommon Battalion.
    (r) Louth Battalion. St Mary's Band, Limerick.
    (s) Limerick Battalion
    (t) Meath Battalion
    (u) Mayo Battalion
    (v) Tipperary and Clonmel Battalions.
    (w) Mid. Tipperary, Nenagh, Ciamalta Battalions. Kilmeade Fife and Drum Band.
    (x) Offaly Battalion.
    (y) Monaghan Battalion.
    (z) Waterford Battalion. Monasterevan Fife and Drum Band.
    (aa) Kildare Battalion. Clonaslee Pipers' Band.
    (bb) Leix Battalion. Baltinglass Pipers' band.
    (cc) Carlow Battalion.
    (dd) Cavan Battalion. Ballynoggin Fife and Drum Band.
    (ee) Westmeath Battalion.
(3) St Laurence O'Toole Pipers' Band.
(4) Cumann na mBan.

(5) Clann na nGaedheal (Republican Girl Scouts)*

(6) Fianna Eireann.

(7) American Friends of the Irish Republic.
   Nenagh Castle Brass and Reed Band.

(8) Fianna Fáil.

(10) People's Rights Association.+

(11) Revolutionary Workers' Party. St. Kevins' Fife and Drum Band.

(12) 1916 Club. (13) Labour Bodies. (14) General Public.

* Later Cumann na gCailíní.
+ Women's Prisoners Defence League.
Source: *An Phoblacht*, 18 June 1932.

APPENDIX 6 / **Fatalities caused and suffered by the IRA, 1926–36**

Fatalities caused by the IRA, 1926–36

Name	Date	Location	Description
James Fitzsimons	14 Nov. 1926	Cork City	garda sergeant
Hugh Ward	14 Nov. 1926	Tipperary	garda
Kevin O'Higgins	10 Aug. 1927	Dublin	Minister for Justice
Albert Armstrong	20 Feb. 1929	Dublin	insurance agent
Patrick Murray*		Clare	IRA member
Tadgh O'Sullivan	11 June 1929	Clare	garda detective
Patrick Carroll	30 Jan. 1931	Dublin	IRA member
Seán Curtin	31 Mar. 1931	Tipperary	garda superintendent
John Ryan	20 July 1931	Tipperary	IRA member
John Ryan	28 Feb. 1933	Belfast	RUC Constable
Hugh O'Reilly	29 Oct. 1933	Cork	Blueshirt
Mrs Frances McGrory	11 Feb. 1934	Dundalk	civilian
Richard More O'Ferrall	9 Feb. 1935	Longford	civilian
Vice-Admiral Henry Boyle Somerville	24 Mar. 1936	Cork	civilian (retired Royal Navy)
John Egan	26 Apr. 1936	Waterford	IRA member
Dan Turley	4 Dec. 1936	Belfast	IRA member

* Missing presumed dead. *Sources*, Murders and Principal Outrages Committed By Irregulars since the 'Cease Fire' Order, April 1931, in D/T S 5864 A NAI; Notes on Events, 1931–41, in MacEntee Papers, UCDA, P67/534; *Irish News*, 1 March 1933.

Fatalities suffered by the IRA, 1926–36

Name	Location	Date	Cause of death
Timothy Coughlan	Dublin	28 Jan. 1928	Shot by garda agent
Michael McLaughlin	New York		
	(ex Roscommon)	Jan. 1931	Shot by robbers
James Vaugh	Leitrim	25 Dec. 1931	Died following release from garda custody
James Glynn	Ennis, Co. Clare	29 Apr. 1934	Shot by Blueshirt
William Brett	Kilkenny	14 Aug. 1936	Accidental shooting
Seán Glynn	Arbour Hill Prison		
	(ex Limerick)	13 Sept. 1936	Suicide

APPENDIX 7 / **IRA executive election**

General Army Convention, 14–15 November 1925

Name	Votes	Placing
Cooney	32	1
Kilroy	31	2
Twomey	30	3
Maguire	28	4
O'Donnell	26	5
Daly	25	6
Murphy	23	7
Derrig	22	8
Aiken	20	9
Price	20	10
Murray	20	11
Plunkett	20	12
Sheehy	18	Not elected
Ruttledge	18	Not elected
MacSwiney	17	Not elected
Lemass	15	Not elected
Hyde	13	Not elected
Mangan	12	Not elected
Reilly	11	Not Elected
Corvin	6	Not Elected

Source: MTUCDA, P69/179 (190).

APPENDIX 8 / **General Order No. 28. Volunteers as Parliamentary Candidates**

Dept. A/G 21 October 1926.

To Commanders of all independent Units.

1. The Army Council has directed that the following statement and order be circulated:

> "Oglaigh-na-hEireann was created and is being maintained primarily for the following object:
> To establish and uphold a lawful government in sole and absolute control of the Republic."

The primary, and it is believed by the Army Council, the only effective means by which this object can be achieved are:

1. Force of arms
2. Organising, training and equipping the manhood of Ireland as an effective military force.

The Army Council is decidedly of opinion that these means can best be promoted when a volunteer is free to concentrate is free to concentrate on them and is not distracted by holding the responsible position of T.D. and endeavouring to fulfil the duties attaching to it. Further and especially bearing in mind late experiences, there is the danger of military discipline being impaired by actions taken by T.D.'s who are also volunteers.

To ensure that the energies of volunteers are concentrated on volunteer activities and on promoting the means outlined and in the interests of military discipline the Army Council hereby order:

> "That a member of Oglaigh-na-hEireann shall not permit himself to be put forward or accept nomination as a candidate in any constituency for which Teachtai are being elected, and that this order be transmitted to all ranks."

2. You are hereby ordered to have the above transmitted to all ranks in your area at once.

Adjutant General

Source: MTUCDA, P69/149 (38).

9 / I RA officers standing in general election, June 1927 in contravention of General Order No. 28.

Candidate	Unit	Constituency	Party
Denis Allen	North Wexford	Wexford	Fianna Fáil
Frank Aiken	GHQ	Louth	Fianna Fáil*
Neil Blaney	Tirconnaill	Donegal	Fianna Fáil*
Michael Cleary	North Mayo	Mayo North	Fianna Fáil
Daniel Corkery	Cork No. 1	Cork North	Independent*^
Seamus Colbert	Limerick	Limerick	Fianna Fáil*
Michael Corry	Cork No. 1	Cork East	Fianna Fáil*
Tom Derrig	GHQ	Carlow	Fianna Fáil*
Seán Hayes	Tipperary	Tipperary	Fianna Fáil*
Patrick Houlihan	East Clare	Clare	Fianna Fáil*
Mark Killilea	South Galway	Galway	Fianna Fáil*
Michael Kilroy	North Mayo	Mayo South	Fianna Fáil*
T Mac'Ellistrim	Kerry No. 2	Kerry	Fianna Fáil*
Dr J.A. Madden	North Mayo	Mayo North	Sinn Féin*
Tom Maguire	Claremorris	Mayo South	Sinn Féin+
Eamonn Moane	North Mayo	Mayo South	Fianna Fáil
Seán O'Farrell	C. on Shannon	Leitrim-Sligo	Sinn Féin
Tom Powell	Claremorris	Galway	Fianna Fáil*
Tim Sheehy	Tipperary	Tipperary	Fianna Fáil
Mick Sheridan	Cavan	Cavan	Fianna Fáil
Patrick Smith	Cavan	Cavan	Fianna Fáil*
Dr S. Tubridy	Claremorris	Galway	Fianna Fáil*
Dick Walsh	Claremorris	Mayo South	Fianna Fáil

* Elected.
+ Withdrew.
^ FF September 1927
Sources: Disobeyal of General Order No. 28, May 1927, in MTUCDA, P69/149 (6).
Michael Gallagher (ed.), *Irish elections, 1922-44: results and analysis* (Limerick, 1993).

APPENDIX 10 / **Suspension of**
General Order No. 28

Ard Oifig, Ath Cliath.
12 January 1932.

A/G, *B.B. 48*

To:

The Commander of each Independent Unit.

A chara,

The following has been ordered by the Army Council to be communicated to all ranks: –

(1) At the General Army Convention, January 1929, an order was made forbidding Volunteers to work or vote at Elections for membership of the so-called Northern Ireland or Free State Parliaments.

(2) The Army Council is aware that there is throughout the Army a feeling that this order should be reviewed and that those who are at present in control of the 26 counties should be deprived of power.

In the present circumstances it is not feasible to hold a General Convention before the Elections in the 26 Counties take place. This question of the General Election was considered by the Army Executive who advized that the order be suspended.

The Army Council made the following decisions: –

(a) That the order be suspended which forbids Volunteers to work or vote at elections for membership of the so-called Northern Ireland or Free State Parliaments.

(b) That the pending election in the 26 counties Volunteers and supporters are recommended to vote against the candidates of the Cumann na nGaedheal party and other candidates who actively support the policy support the policy of that party.

(c) That while volunteers and supporters are recommended to vote it must be clearly understood that Oglaigh na h-Eireann do not accept or approve of the policy of any of the parties contesting the elections.

(d) Volunteers shall not become candidates nor shall they speak on the platforms of any of the parties.

3. It is strongly recommend that the Election campaign be availed of for the holding of meetings in every unit. At these meetings the policy of Oglaigh na h-Eireann shall be put before the people from our own platforms.

4. Realising the natural urge to end the rule of a party which has been responsible for so much national disaster and economic distress, the Army Council would, however, emphasize to Volunteers that while advocating voting at these elections, our objects cannot be achieved by the methods or policies of the parties seeking election.

This fact should be borne in mind by Volunteers throughout the Elections.

5. Please acknowledge receipt.

Source: copy in D/T S 5864 C NAI.

APPENDIX 11 / **Application for transfer to Foreign Reserve List**

To
The Adjutant General

I am forced to leave Ireland through extreme economic distress in order to obtain a livelihood (or for reasons stated in attached sheet). I wish to be transferred to the Foreign Reserve List for a period of five years: I promise to return at the end of that time if I do not get an extension, and to abide by the conditions set out hereunder:

1. To be bound by the same disciplinary code as active Volunteers, i.e. all my actions to be sober and upright and a true soldier of the Republic.
2. To save up as soon as possible and keep intact the price of a return journey to Ireland.
3. To return to Ireland immediately General Headquarters informs me that my presence in Ireland is necessary and orders me to return.
4. To keep the Adjutant General informed of my address through the prescribed channels.
5. To endeavour to increase my efficiency as a soldier and as a citizen in order to be of greater use in defending and building up the country when I return.
6. To do my utmost to promote the interests of the Republic and to help all organizations working for that object in the country to which I go.

7. Not to organize or join any organization into which it is proposed to admit only Foreign Reservists of the Irish Republican Army.

(Signed)_____
Unit and Appointment_____

I, the undersigned, hereby declare that the statements in above application are true, and I believe the applicant will, as he has promised, abide faithfully by above conditions.

(Signed) Unit and Appointment_____
Date_____

Source: MTUCDA P69/167 (49).

Notes

ABBREVIATIONS USED

A/G	Adjutant General
Adjt	Adjutant
ACA	Army Comrades Association
AOH	Ancient Order of Hibernians
Batt	Battalion
Bdge	Brigade
Coy	Company
C/S	Chief of Staff
D/I	Director of Intelligence
D/J	Department of Justice
D/T	Department of the Taoiseach
GAA	Gaelic Athletic Association
GAC	General Army Convention
GHQ	General Head Quarters
ICA	Irish Citizen Army
IRA	Irish Republican Army
ITGWU	Irish Transport and General Workers Union
MTUCDA	Moss Twomey Papers University College Dublin Archives
O/C	Officer Commanding
QMG	QuarterMaster General
PP	Private Papers
UCDA	University College Dublin Archives
NAI	National Archives of Ireland
NLI	National Library of Ireland
PRONI	Public Record Office of Northern Ireland
T/O	Training Officer

Introduction
PAGE 9 critiques of its politics The two major general studies are J. Bowyer Bell's *The secret army. The IRA, 1916–1979* (Dublin, 1979) and T. P. Coogan's *The IRA* (London, 1995). On the organization's politics see R. English, *Radicals and the Republic – socialist republicanism in the Irish Free State* (Oxford, 1994) and H. Patterson, *The politics of illusion. Republicanism and socialism in modern Ireland* (London, 1989). **decisions were made** B. Bell,

Secret army, p. 447; J.P. McHugh, 'Voices of the rearguard. A study of *An Phoblacht* – Irish republican thought in the post-Revolutionary era, 1923–1937' MA thesis (UCD, 1983). **leader** Deposited by M. Twomey Jr in University College Dublin Archives (UCDA) in 1985. **Cumann na nGaedheal** All held at the UCD Archives, I have made extensive use of the *Departmental Notes on Events*, Jan. 1931–Dec. 1940 in MacEntee papers, UCDA, P67/534.,written by Peter Barry of Department of Justice. **playing with politics** The *Last Post* is published by the National Graves Association. It lists republican dead since 1916. 1976 edition (Dublin) p. 54.

Chapter One

PAGE 11 IRA members Bell, *Secret army*, p. 57. **estimate of members** General Report for Executive Meeting, 10 Aug. 1924, in Moss Twomey papers, University College Dublin (MTUCDA) P69/179 (104–9). **an Army together** General Report for Executive, MTUC-DA, P69/179 (109). **it shrank drastically** The November 1925 General Army Convention saw the IRA withdraw its allegiance from the Second Dáil 'Republican Government' and replace Frank Aiken as chief of staff with Andy Cooney. Bell, *Secret army*, p. 53. **declined to** Notes for Statement by C/S, 1 Nov. 1926 in MTUCDA P69/181 (5).

PAGE 12 strengths AC Report to GAC, Autumn 1925, in MTUCDA P69/181 (91). **rank and file level** Many of the Fianna Fáil-aligned officers would not be forced out of the IRA until after they stood as candidates in the June 1927 general election. See p. 113. **in the near future** AC report, P69/181 (91). The extent of the emigration and the IRA's response to it is examined in Chapter Nine. **aggressive activities** A/Commandant Dan Bryan, to Irish Army Chief of Staff, 2 Dec. 1925, in Desmond FitzGerald papers, UCDA, P80/849 (11).

PAGE 13 land annuities to Britain The IRA leadership endorsed this campaign in Jan. 1928. A/G to O/C Tirconnaill Batt, 12 January 1928, in MTUCDA, P69/149 (70–1). **Donegal** All figures from MTUCDA. All from 1930 except Kerry. Northern Ireland, 29 July 1930, in P69/153 (237), Kerry, 18 Jan. 1931 in P69/153 (19–20). Dublin, 17 Nov., in P69/153 (76–9). Tipperary, 6 Nov., in P69/153 (99–104). Sligo, July, in P69/153 (228). Donegal, 22 Sept., in P69/153 (181–183). Limerick, 25 Nov., in P69/153 (70–2). Galway, Connemara and Claremorris, July, in P69/153 (229). Drogheda, 31 Oct., in P69/153 (86). Clare, 25 Nov., in P69/153 (64–7) South Dublin, 11 Sept., in P69/153 (202). **training being carried out** 'Q' report (Seán Russell), July 1930, in MTUCDA, P69/153 (231).**Westmeath** 'M' report, Mar. 1930, in MTUCDA, P69/151 (193–7). **resume the fight again** Staff Captain 'Jones' report on South Tipperary, 6 Nov., 1930, in MTUCDA, P69/153 (101). **could not be trusted** 'J.J.' report on Kerry, 18 January 1931, in MTUCDA, P69/153 (14–18). **Comintern** Report on Anti-State Activities, September 1931, in D/T S 5864 B NAI. **membership** The estimate is of 1,300 officers and 3,500 rank and file. D/T S 5864 A, NAI. **would not survive** See for example the garda chief Superintendent of Kerry, October 1931 'If the Soviet comrades are not dealt with more determinedly at once the state will perish', in D/T S 5864 B NAI. **present year** *An t-Óglách*, July 1931, copy in D/T S 5864 A, NAI.

PAGE 14 Volunteer movement Twomey to McGarrity, 26 June 1931 in McGarrity papers, Ms 17,490 NLI. **conditions** Twomey to McGarrity, 9 December 1931, in McGarrity papers, Ms 17,490 NLI. **morale of men** Twomey to McGarrity, 26 June 1931, in McGarrity papers, Ms 17,490 NLI. **recruiting meeting** C/S to A/G, QMG and D/I, 29 May 1931 in MTUCDA, P69/51 (9). **29** *An t-Óglách*, March 1931, in MTUCDA, P69/263 (7). **local people** Staff Captain 'McAuley', 26 November 1930, in MTUCDA, P69/153 (63–72). **benefit the IRA** Twomey to McGarrity, 23 June 1931, in McGarrity papers, Ms 17,490 NLI. **death penalty** D. Fitzpatrick, *The two Irelands, 1912–1939* (1998). pp 164–5 & 189; English, *Radicals*, pp 138–46. For government perspectives see J.M. Regan, *The Irish counter revolution, 1921–1936* (Dublin, 1999) pp 287–304. **difficulties** Twomey to McGarrity, 9 December 1931, in McGarrity papers, Ms 17,490 NLI. See pp 36–37 for discussion of these difficulties. **morale of our organization** A/G to Adjt Tralee Battalion, 22 June 1932, in MTUCDA, P69/155 (113).

PAGE 15 **in some areas** O/C South Dublin Batt to A/G, 25 Sept. 1932 in MTUCDA, P69/156 (105–6) and report on North Tipperary Batt, 30 June 1932, in MTUCDA, P69/155 (98). **enthusiasm** Adjt Leitrim Batt to A/G, 24 May 1932, in MTUCDA, P69/155 (217) and Adjt, Dingle Batt, to A/G, 26 Oct. 1932 in MTUCDA, P69/156 (50). **recruits** Russell to C/S, 10 Jan. 1932 (*sic*), in Frank Aiken papers, UCDA, P104/2835 (1–2). **first half of 1933** *Notes on Events*, General Survey, MacEntee papers, UCDA, P67/534, p. xvi. **Bodenstown events** Mike Cronin states incorrectly that only the Blueshirts held open rallies in Ireland during this period. *The Blueshirts and Irish politics* (Dublin, 1997) p. 49. **hurling competitions** For example in Ballymahon, Co. Longford, during Oct. 1932, AC member George Gilmore spoke after a march featuring the Ballymore and Kellinure fife and drum bands. The meeting which was followed by a football tournament with teams from Ardagh and Tubberclair. *Longford Leader*, 1 & 15 Oct. 1932. **libel** *An Phoblacht* usually referred to Twomey as chief of staff. See issue of 13 Oct. 1934 **Free State** Coogan, *The IRA*, p. 79. See also E. O'Halpin, *Defending Ireland.* (Oxford, 1999), p. 108. **truce of July 1921** Twomey to Connie Neenan, 15 September 1932, in MTUCDA, P69/155 (196). Neenan was the IRA's representative within the Clan na Gael. See Chapter Nine. **by the year's end** C/S to O/C Dublin Bdge, 17 December 1932, in MTUCDA, P69/54 (21).

PAGE 16 **Table 4** IRA reports, 1932, Dublin (April), Ulster No. 1 (October), Leitrim, Sligo, Tirconaill (June), Connemara (November), Waterford (September), North Clare (June), Tipperary (July), Clonmel (October), North Cork (June), Caherciveen (August), Dingle (October), Killarney (September), Tralee (October), Roscommon (June), in MTUCDA, P69/155 (116–21), P69/156 (25–38), P69/155 (95), P69/155 (95), P69/156 (3), (95), P69/155 (179), P69/156 (69), P69/155 (154–6), P69/156 (75), (78), (54), (56), P69/155 (59). **membership** Adjt Dublin Bdge to A/G, 14 June 1932, in MTUCDA, P69/155 (115). **47** Dublin Report, Jan., West Cork report, 9 July, in Frank Aiken papers, UCDA, P104/2822 (1–7) & P104/2852 (9). Leitrim, 10 Mar., Tirconaill, 11 Mar., Laoghis, Feb., and Offaly (nd) 1933, in MTUCDA, P69/187 (17–20). **total membership** 'The 12,000 men is the material on which we have to work'. Notes of Mar., 1933 GAC in MTUCDA P69/187 (95) and 'We have about 12,000 people in the IRA'. Notes of 1934 GAC, in MacEntee papers UCDA, P67/525. **Bodenstown** *An Phoblacht*, 23 June 1933. **Blueshirt movement** Figure quoted in M. Cronin, *Blueshirts and Irish politics,* p. 115. **under severe pressure** See Notes of 1933 GAC, in MTUCDA, P69/187 (114–115) and Notes of 1934 GAC, MacEntee papers, UCDA, P67/525. See p. 141. **rise of the Blueshirts** Twomey to Neenan, 15 Sept., 1932, in MTUCDA, P69/185 (195–9).

PAGE 17 **'clerical opposition'** Notes of 1933 General Army Convention (GAC), in MTUCDA, P69/187 (90–117). C/S to Secretary Clan na Gael (Clan), 21 March 1933, in MTUCDA, P69/185 (55). **'put before the people?'** C/S to O/C Tralee No. 1 Batt, 17 May 1933, in MTUCDA, P69/53 (12). **Table 6** Belfast figure from report of Belfast delegate, 1934 GAC, MacEntee papers, P67/525 UCDA. Adjt Caherciveen to A/G, 29 October, 1934. Adjt, East Limerick to A/G, 7 November 1934. Adjt West Clare to A/G, 9 December, and Adjt North Clare to A/G, all in Jus 8/319 NAI. **continuing to 'flourish'** Garda Detective Branch, 16 Nov. 1934 in Jus 8/319 NAI. **attendance to that date** Garda report, 20 June 1934 in Jus 8/310 NAI. **Congress** See AC Correspondence Book entries, West Clare 27 Apr., Dublin Brigade, 15 May and 6 June, South Dublin, 6 Sept. and West Mayo 26 May 1934 in Aiken papers, UCDA, P104/2854 (7–27). **IRA's strength** S. Cronin, *The McGarrity papers* (Tralee, 1972) p. 166. Cronin's figures are based on those he found in McGarrity's papers. However, he does not give a reference for these important statistics. Cronin has 'no doubt at all that the figures are correct', but could not help with an exact reference. Seán Cronin to author, 3/8/1999.

PAGE 18 **great enthusiasm** Twomey to McGarrity, 7 Oct. 1935, in McGarrity papers, Ms 17,490 NLI. **organization** Garda report, 18 May 1936, in Jus 8/881 NAI. **civil war** Cronin, *McGarrity*, p. 166. **campaign in Britain** Report from outgoing AC to GAC, 1938, in Aiken papers, UCDA, P104/2833 (1–3). **bombing campaign** Barry to Humphreys, 12 June 1976, in Humphreys papers, UCDA, P106/839. **jailed or inactive** 1,944 members according to a Military Intelligence estimate, Oct. 1940, in G2/X/0058, Military Archives, Cathal Brugha Barracks, (MA). **General Army Convention** IRA executive election, Nov. 1925 in MTUCDA P69/179 (190). See also Appendix 7. **imprisonment in 1936** Cooney was active on IRA business in the US during 1926. M. MacEvilly, 'IRA chief – a life of Dr Andy Cooney' (unpublished manuscript) pp 138–47. Twomey's jailing in *Irish Independent*, 20 June 1936. **Fermoy in Co. Cork** He was born 10 June 1897. **Irish Volunteers** Information from Maurice Twomey Jr, 26 Feb. 1999; Peter Hart, *The IRA & its enemies* (Oxford, 1998), p. 210. **Brigade area** F. O'Donoghue, *No other law* (Dublin, 1996), p. 60. Also E. O'Malley Notebooks, UCDA, P17b/96,107.

PAGE 19 Bill Quirke W. Quirke 'Escape from Spike Island' in N. Hartnett, *Prison escapes*, (Dublin, 1945). pp 33–9, and 'Second escape from Spike Island' in F. O'Donoghue, *Sworn to be free* (Tralee, 1971), pp 179–83. **civil war** M. Hopkinson, *Green against Green* (Dublin, 1988), pp 103 & 109; L. Deasy, *Brother against Brother*(Dublin, 1999), p. 46. J.P. Duggan, *A History of the Irish Army* (Dublin, 1991) p. 46. Twomey's own account of the death of Lynch was published in the *Wolfe Tone Weekly*, 9 Apr. 1938 and *Evening Herald*, 2 Feb. 1972. **units during 1925** Inspection reports, 10 Aug. 1924 and 10 May 1925, in MTUCDA, P69/179 (104) & P69/47 (242–3). **An Phoblacht** Often under the pen name 'Manus O'Ruairc'. See *An Phoblacht*, 29 Nov. 1930 & 14 Feb. 1931. There is a vivid description of the social circle frequented by MacLaughlin and her friends during the mid-1920s in C.S. Andrews, *Man of no property* (Dublin, 2001), pp 26–31. Other women who moved in this circle included 'Kid' Bulfin who would marry Seán MacBride and Mary McCarthy who married George Plunkett. Twomey's biography is continued in Appendix 1, p. 252. **lazy assumptions** Twomey was 'a tower of strength ... an excellent organizer, a man trusted by all, with an almost faultless intuition'. B. Bell, *Secret Army*, p. 57. P. O'Donnell described how Twomey 'listened in on the organization breathing'. O'Donnell, *There will be another day* (Dublin, 1963) p. 104. **radicalism within the IRA** Coogan, *The IRA*, p. 59. Also P. Murray, *Oracles of God* (Dublin, 2000), p. 318. **late 1920s** Patterson, *Politics of illusion*, p. 46. **political strategy** Notes of 1933 GAC, in MTUCDA, P69/187 (100). **seeing another's viewpoint** Hannah Sheehy Skeffington to Twomey, 2 Apr. 1933, in MTUCDA, P69/53 (167–9). **'reactionary' views** Twomey to Con Neenan, 21 & 28 Mar. 1933, in MTUCDA, P69/185 (48) & (21–5). **Table 7** Notes of 1933 GAC, in MTUCDA, P69/187 (86–7). Twomey to Neenan, 28 Mar. 1933, in MTUCDA, P69/185 (21–5). **training** In the case of local officers this was done with the recommendation of the local O/C and the IRA's inspecting officer. Notes on leadership positions (N/D) in MTUCDA, P69/146 (17–18).

PAGE 20 rival organizations Notes on leadership positions, in MTUCDA, P69/146 (17–18). **Executive** 'Army Council' in MTUCDA, P69/181 (100).

PAGE 21 universally white collar See Appendix 1 pp 244–53. **social background** Peter Hart, 'The social structure of the Irish Republican Army, 1916–23' in *Historical Journal* 42:1 (1999), 207–31. **'workers and peasants'** 'Mr. Ambrose' Outline of the Present Movement, 1927, in MTUCDA, P69/72 (3–14). **'Volunteer officer'** Adjt Connemara to A/G, 3 Nov. 1930, in MTUCDA, P69/153 (105). **case in 1933** Joost Augusteijn, *From public defiance to guerrilla warfare* (Dublin, 1996), pp 358–9. **Table 8** Oglaigh na h-Éireann, General Headquarters Staff, Jan. 1933 (IRA GHQ Staff) in Aiken papers, UCDA, P104/2822 (1–7). * 6 printers, 3 electricians, 2 fitters, 2 painters, 2 sign writers, 1 fireman, 1 baker. + 1 shopkeeper, & 1 'Fish and Chip Saloon owner' Leo Burdock. **Dublin brigade** RUC report, 22 May 1936, in Home Affairs (HA) File 32/1/628 in the Public Record Office of Northern Ireland (PRONI). **Table 9** Sample spans 1929–36. David Matthews File, HA/5/2361, in PRONI. T.J. Ryan, O'Duffy report, 5 July 1929, in Blythe papers, UCDA, P24/477 & *Dáil Debates*, Vol. 31, 31 July 1929. J. O'Connor, Notes of 1933 GAC in MTUCDA, P69/187 (74) and P. O'Connor, *Soldier of Liberty* (Dublin, 1996), p. 1. M. Ferguson, *Irish Independent*, 2 July 1935, J. McAdams & M. Gallagher, HA/32/1/628 in

PRONI, P. McKeon, O/C N. Rosc to C/S, 28 Mar. 1933, in MTUCDA, P69/53 (77–9). T. Ó Maoileóin, Secretary Dept of Education, 4 Jan. 1933, in MTUCDA, P69/53 (356). J.J. Rice, *Kerry Champion,* 16 Dec. 1933, P. Fleming, 8 Jan. 1935, in Jus 8/201 NAI. M. O'Kane, A/G to CRC, 13 Feb. 1930, in MTUCDA, P69/152 (136). M. Kyne, A/G to Adjt, Galway City Batt, 2 July 1932, in MTUCDA, P69/155 (92). Kyne later gaelicized his name to Máirtín Ó Cadhain. For T. Lynch, S. McCool, B. Corrigan & T. Ward see text. **local shopkeepers** O/C North Mayo to C/S, 1 March 1933 in MTUCDA, P69/53 (114). 'Cases of Distress' 1926, in MTUCDA, P69/175 (4). O/C N. Mayo to A/G, January 1932, in MTUCDA, P69/155 (284).

PAGE 22 a place to live O/C Offaly Batt to A/G, 17 May 1932, in MTUCDA, P69/157 (34). **for the newspaper** Application for job as editor, *An Phoblacht,* 29 Mar. 1933, in MTUCDA, P69/53 (235). Garda report, 19 June 1933, in Jus 8/716 NAI. **experiences of these men** T. Garvin, *Nationalist revolutionaries in Ireland, 1858–1928* (Oxford, 1997), pp 24–9. **IRA in 1932** Tom Barry to Twomey, 13 May 1932, in MTUCDA, (63–4). **USSR** *Notes on Certain Individuals,* in Appendix IX, Departmental Notes on IRA Activities, 1941–7, in MacEntee papers, UCDA, P67/550, pp 159–60. **imprisoned on several occasions** Matthews File, HA/5/2361 in PRONI. **'Sean Forde'** For Rice see O'Malley Notebooks, UCDA, P17b/102,139 & also T.R. Dwyer, *Tans, terror and troubles* (Dublin, 2001). For O'Maoileoin, O'Malley Notebooks, UCDA, P17b/106,124, S. Malone, *Alias Seán Forde* (Dublin, 2001) and MacEoin, *Survivors,* pp 75–104.

PAGE 23 prominence within the organization Fleming was born in 1904 and joined the IRA in 1925. Lehane was born in 1905 and joined the IRA in 1929. *Notes on certain individuals,* pp 156–7. **risks or responsibility** See O/C North Wexford to A/G, 22 Feb. 1930, in MTUCDA, P69/152 (193–196). The officer, a veteran of 1916 and 1919–23 resigned because he feared the consequences of arrest now that he had a family. 'My wife and kiddies have made a coward of me'. **1916 leader** See Officers' Meeting, 9 Apr. 1927, in MTUCDA, P69/48 (152–162). **mayor of Cork City** Notes on Certain Individuals, p. 159. See O/C Cork No. 1 to C/S, 14 Dec. 1932, in MTUCDA, P69/54 (26–7). **October 1920** *Notes on Events,* in MacEntee papers, UCDA, P67/534 p. 52. **Michael Mallin** *An Phoblacht,* 14 Oct. 1933 and Notes of 1934 GAC, in MacEntee papers, UCDA, P67/525. **Black and Tans** *An Phoblacht,* 14 Oct. 1933 and P. O' Farrell, *Who's who in the Irish War of Independence and Civil War, 1916–1923* (Dublin, 1997). p. 119. **Gilmore brothers of Dublin** George Gilmore was an AC member. Harry and Charles were variously O/C and QM of the South Dublin Battalion. George Gilmore Notes, Private papers, held by Anthony Coughlan. See also IRA GHQ Staff in Aiken papers, UCDA, P104/2822 (1–2) & *Irish Press,* 1 Apr. 1933. **Protestant IRA members** For Bradshaw see Chapter Three p. 33. Fagg was I/O of the South Westmeath Battalion, in MTUCDA, P69/54 (150–55). For Mitchell, see MacEoin, *Survivors,* pp 379–92. **South Armagh in 1933** See Chapter Eight p. 154. **during 1933** Notes of 1933 GAC, P69/187 (87) and *Westmeath Independent,* 30 June 1934. **1934 local elections** *Leitrim Observer, Longford Leader, Kerry Champion,* 30 June 1934. *Cork Examiner,* 29 June 1934. **Fianna Fáil** I/O Kenmare Batt to I/O (D/I), 18 Apr. 1934, in Jus 8/319 NAI. **electoral intervention** See C/S to O/C Tirconaill No. 2 Batt, 13 May 1933, in MTUCDA, P69/53 (16). **IRA were unemployed** 310 out of 460 men according to their O/C. Notes of 1934 GAC, MacEntee papers, P67/525. **out-of-work in 1932** Adjt South Carlow to A/G, 20 May 1932, in MTUCDA, P69/157 (14–15). **were now idle** Adjt Cork City to A/G, 3 July 1930, in MTUCDA, P69/151 (216). Seán MacSwiney and Michael Burke, Cork IRA officers, both worked in Fords during 1929. O'Duffy report, 5 July 1929, in Blythe papers, UCDA, P24/477 **some of the proceeds** Adjt Drogheda Coy to A/G, 16 Mar. 1931, in MTUCDA, P69/151 (178–179).

PAGE 24 Tralee Hospital Adjt Tralee Batt to A/G, 28 Oct. 1932, in MTUCDA, P69/156 (56–58). **Scotland** Garda report, 27 July 1931, in D/T S 5864 B NAI. **labourers in Britain** Adjt North Mayo Bdge to A/G, 2 Aug. 1932, in MTUCDA, P69/158 (238). **summer and autumn** O/C North Mayo to C/S, 23 Aug. 1932, in MTUCDA, P69/54 (194). **away in**

England Jack McNeela to Seán MacBride, June 1935, in Sighle Humphreys papers, UCDA, P106/2106 (39). **'corner-boy type'** Garda report, 27 July 1931, in D/T S 5864 B NAI. **two clerks** Garda report, 21 Apr. 1934, in Jus 8/108 NAI. **father and brother** *Clare Champion*, 5 & 12 May 1934. The locally based union had been involved in a general strike in early 1934. Garda report, 1 Mar. 1934, in Jus 8/337 NAI. **doctors or solicitors** Farrell Leddy of the Belfast IRA was a doctor. *Irish News*, 29 July 1932 and O/C Ulster No. 1 to A/G, 7 Aug. 1932, in MTUCDA, P69/158 (218–22). **Cearbhall Ó Dálaigh** For UCD Republican club see report, 27 Nov. 1929, in D/T S 5864 A NAI. Also see C.S. Andrews, *Man of no property*, pp 48–60. For TCD see Bob Clements in MacEoin, *Twilight years*, pp 463–70. For St Patrick's Training College, AC Correspondence Book, 6 February 1934, in Aiken papers, UCDA, P104/2854 (11). **Peadar O'Donnell** Notes of 1933 GAC, in MTUCDA, P69/187 (104). **'poor working men'** Twomey to McGarrity, 9 Dec. 1931, in McGarrity papers, Ms 17,490 NLI. **extra contributions** Notes of 1934 GAC, MacEntee papers, UCDA, P67/525. **greatly restricted** See Chapter Nine. **over the summer** 'M' report on Offaly, Apr. 1930, in MTUCDA, P69/151 (101–05). **civil war** C/S to Count Plunkett, 19 Jan. 1932, in MTUCDA, P69/52 (242–4). *An t-Óglách*, Oct. 1931, in MTUCDA, P69/263 (9). **'heart and soul'** Adjt Dingle Batt to A/G, 26 Oct. 1932, in MTUCDA, P69/156 (50). **newer recruits** Tom Barry to Twomey, 13 May 1932, in MTUCDA, P69/52 (63–4).

PAGE 25 training camp O/C Ulster No. 1 to C/S, 30 July 1932, in MTUCDA, P69/54 (224–30). **soldier of the IRA** *An Phoblacht*, 12 Nov. 1932. **by peacetime** *Cork Examiner*, 20 Dec. 1932. **'not even in the cradle'** *Northern Standard*, 27 July 1936. **convincing credentials** For example a Clare Blueshirt wanted in connection with the death of James Glynn had lost his father and brother during the War of Independence and another brother in the Civil War. *Clare Champion*, 29 Sept. 1934. **republican support** Mick Fitzpatrick at the 1934 GAC, Notes of 1934 GAC, UCDA, P67/525. **Dubliners** See for example the transfer of two men from Laois who had gained employment in the city to the Dublin Brigade. A/G to Adjt Dublin Bdge, 18 June 1932, in MTUCDA, P69/155 (70). **violence between 1917 and 1923** 39.1 per cent of the entire violence of that period took place in Cork. Peter Hart, 'The geography of revolution in Ireland, 1917–1923', in *Past and Present*, 155 (May 1997) 143–76. **the IRA** The Blueshirts in Cork had 9,955 members by Mar. 1934. According to S. Cronin the entire IRA may only have had 8,036 members by Oct. of that year. Mike Cronin, *Blueshirts and Irish politics*, p. 115. S. Cronin, *McGarrity papers*, p. 166. **demoralized shell** During 1922 1,685 IRA members had left to join the Free State Army. Enda Staunton, *The nationalists of Northern Ireland, 1918–1973* (Dublin, 2001), p. 71. The IRA claimed only 240 members in the city by 1924. See above p. 11.

PAGE 26 electoral politics Clare, Kerry, Mayo and Leitrim-Sligo figured among the highest FF voting constituencies in 1927 and 1933. M. Gallagher (ed.), *Irish elections, 1922–44* (Limerick, 1993). pp 115 and 176. **revolutionary period** *Kerry Champion*, 4 Feb. 1933. **civil war** Chief Superintendent's report, 10 Jan. 1935, in Jus 8/201 NAI. **Tralee** Military Intelligence report, 31 Aug. 1940, in G2/X/0093 MA. **residual support** Military Intelligence report, 26 Feb. 1942, in G2/X/0058 MA. **indiscipline** See Chapters Two & Four.

Chapter Two

PAGE 28 Easter lily sales Ist Batt, Dublin Bdge report, 31 Mar. 1932, in MTUCDA, P69/155 (134). **roads across Ireland** See Garda report from Kilkenny, 20 Mar. 1935, in Jus 8/206 NAI. See A/G to Adjt Dublin Bdge, 9 Oct. 1930 on painting slogans at Croke Park and Adjt Dub. Bdge to A/G, 5 Aug. 1930, on painting the windows of Arnotts shop in MTUCDA, P69/153 (161) & (217–19). **republican candidates** See Chapter Six p. 124. **jailed members** See C/S to mother of George Gilmore, 14 Mar. 1927 and 9 Jan. 1928 for grants of £20 and £10 respectively. MTUCDA, P69/48 (243) & P69/60 (4). **medical care** C/S to Seán O'Carroll, 19 Sept. 1927, for grant of £15 towards cost of operation, in

MTUCDA, P69/60 (11–17). **relatives in the city** A/G to Run Onorach, CRC, 26 Mar. 1930, for instructions to organize visitors to Clare man in hospital in Dublin, in MTUCDA, P69/152 (142). **force of arms** Constitution of Oglaigh na h-Éireann, Mar. 1932, in MacEntee papers, UCDA, P67/524 (10–14). **arms available to the organization** Cooney had been appointed QMG that month. C/S report to Executive, 10 Aug. 1924, in MTUCDA, P69/179 (126–9). **1,400 handguns** Report, July 1924, in MTUCDA, P69/179 (115).

PAGE 29 weapons in dumps 'Q' report, July 1930, in MTUCDA, P69/153 (228–34). **under IRA control** Report, 20 May 1925, in MTUCDA, P69/47 (242–3). **left the organization** See for example inspection report on west Limerick, 25 Nov. 1930, in MTUCDA, P69/153 (72). **in north Cork** QMG, Report, 10 June 1932, in MTUCDA, P69/155 (154–7). **local dump was lost** Adjt Connemara Batt, to A/G, 24 June 1930, in MTUCDA, P69/153 (254). A/G to O/C, North Kilkenny Batt, 6 Mar. 1931, in MTUCDA, P69/153 (2). **in dumps for long periods** Report by 'McAndrews' to A/G, 21 Jan. 1928, on condition of guns in Dundalk, in MTUCDA, P69/149 (62).

PAGE 30 safe to use them *An t-Óglách*, Dec. 1924, in Aiken papers, UCDA, P104/1277. **useless through neglect** A/G to O/C NE Batt Cork, 22 July 1929, in D/T S 5864 A NAI. **seized by the gardaí** Over 114,000 rounds of ammunition had also been captured. 'Return of 'dumped' arms, ammunition and 'war material' discovered and seized by the Police from year 1923 to July 1931, in D/T S 5864 A NAI. See Appendix 2. **Killakee in 1931** At St Enda's 61 weapons were captured, along with over 7,000 rds of ammunition. *Irish Independent*, 3 Feb. 1926. At Killakee the IRA lost 47 guns and 3,000 rds of ammunition. Notes on Events, MacEntee papers, UCDA, P67/534 p. 6. **Thompson gun** Staff Captain 'Jones' report on Tipperary, 6 Nov., Adjt. South Wexford Batt, to A/G, 13 May , and 'M' to A/G, 16 Oct., 1930 in MTUCDA, P69/153 (104), P69/152 (17) & P69/153 (160).

PAGE 31 rifle of unspecified type Report to A/G, List of arms in units, 1930, in MTUC-DA, P69/152 (66). **Lee Enfield rifles** Adjt, Connemara Batt, 24 June 1930, in MTUCDA, P69/153 (255–6). **Nationalist and Unionist use** The Mauser 98 was the standard rifle of the German military from 1898 to 1918. I. Hogg, *Jane's guns recognition guide* (Glasgow, 2000). p. 252. **into the 1950s** The Lee Enfield Mk III was the model most common in that period. About 3 million were produced between 1907 and 1943. Hogg, *Jane's*, p. 269. **Parabellum and 'Peter' automatics** Reports on training with these weapons from Dublin Bdge, 30 Apr. 1932, in MTUCDA, P69/155 (116) and Belfast Batt, 30 September 1932, in MTUCDA, P69/156 (110–22). The British Webley .45, and American Colt .45 and Smith and Wesson .38 & .45 had been widely used in World War One. Automatic pistols were rarer with the German Parabellum and the 'Peter the Painter' a Mauser pistol, available in smaller quantities. Hogg, *Janes*, pp 137, 145, 162, 48 & 45. Also *An t-Óglách*, Apr. and June 1925, in MTUCDA, P69/44 (360) and Aiken papers, UCDA, P104/1282. **First World War** 40,000 had been used by the British, Commonwealth, Italian and French armies. J. Ellis, *The social history of the machine gun* (London, 1993), pp 74–6. **military use** Ellis, *Social history*, pp 149–64. The use of the 'Tommy gun' in Ireland has spawned its own history industry. See Bowyer Bell, 'The Thompson sub machine gun in Ireland, 1921,' in *Irish Sword* 31 (1967); P. Hart, 'The Thompson sub machine gun in Ireland revisited' in *Irish Sword* 77 (1995) 160–70 and P. Jung, 'The Thompson sub machine gun during and after the Anglo-Irish War. The new evidence' in *Irish Sword* 84 (1998). 190–218. **the best known** 'Irish Cheddar' contained Potassium Chlorate, Di-nitrotoluene and castor oil. Once this was mixed it could be used as a 'heaving explosive' against buildings, for example. Jim O'Donovan, IRA director of chemicals in 1921, is credited with inventing this explosive. O' Farrell, *Who's who*, p. 79. 'Paxo' contained a mixture of Potassium Chlorate and Paraffin wax which could be mixed when heated in a pan. *An t-Óglách*, Apr. 1925, in MTUCDA, P69/44 (360). **coup d'etat** Motion from South Dublin Batt, at 1925 GAC, in MTUCDA, P69/179 (189). **during the 1919–21 period** 'Lessons from 1922' in *An Phoblacht*, 12 Aug. 1927. **mass popular movement** *An t-Óglách*, Mar. 1931, in MTUCDA, P69/263 (7).**'military movement'** Twomey to Neenan, 28 Mar. 1933, in MTUCDA,

P69/185 (21–5). **over the Treaty** IRA Officer's meeting, 9 Apr. 1927, in MTUCDA, P69/48 (152–62).

PAGE 32 seizure of power Twomey to McGarrity, 23 June 1931, in McGarrity papers, Ms 17,490 NLI. **conflict was in the offing** See p. 127, **unleash revolution** AC to Secretary, Clan, 8 Nov. 1932, in MTUCDA, P69/185 (153). **next twelve months** Notes of 1933 GAC, in MTUCDA, P69/187 (95). **'take the field within a year'** Clan to AC, 8 October 1934, in McGarrity papers, Ms 17,539 NLI. **trained than it was** In 1925 the Irish Army had access to 42,500 rifles, although only 8,000 were serviceable, and 1,002 machine guns of various types. J.P. Duggan, *History of the Irish Army* (Dublin, 1991), p. 163. The IRA of course had no mortars or artillery. **between 1923 and 1931** 'Return of "dumped arms",' July 1931, in D/T S 5864 A NAI. **arms raids** See Adjt Ulster No. 1 to A/G, 6 April 1930, in MTUC-DA, P69/151 (43) & O/C Ulster No. 1, 16 Mar. 1931, in MTUCDA, P69/151 (166–7). **in 1932** The raid was on the home of an ex-National Army officer in Castlebar. The raid itself is examined below. *Notes on Events*, MacEntee papers, UCDA, P67/534, p. 10. **to bear arms** Notes of 1933 GAC, in MTUCDA, P69/187 (90). **later that year showed** Notes on Events, MacEntee papers, UCDA, P67/534, p. 13. **Martin Corry** Notes on Events, MacEntee papers, UCDA, P67/534, pp 48–9. **successful this was** QMG to O/C Galway City Coy, 2 July 1932, in MTUCDA, P69/155 (91). **killed one of his livestock** O/C Clonmel Batt to A/G, 29 July 1932, in MTUCDA, P69/158 (242). **private disputes** C/S to A/G, QMG & D/I, 29 May 1931, in MTUCDA, P69/51 (9–11).

PAGE 33 if they persisted Reports by O/C North Clare & West Clare, 4 & 9 Nov. 1932, in MTUCDA, P69/116 (1–20). **Antwerp and Southampton** Comdt Officer, Finance and Accounts to C/S & QMG, 16 April 1925, in MTUCDA, P69/210 (13–17). **officials and consuls** It would mean bribing these officials, which one of the German arms dealers was in a position to do. Briscoe and McGuinness had worked for IRA HQ purchases during the 1919–23 period. **manufacture ammunition** Machine guns at £20 each, rifles at £2 each and revolvers at 13/ each. **any future deal** The late director of purchases had also left a young lady stranded in Antwerp with no fare back to Ireland after his last trip there. **ended this route** AC Minutes, 26 May 1926, in MTUCDA, P69/69 (2). Killeen served only six months for that offence. *Notes on certain individuals*, MacEntee papers, UCDA, P67/550 p. 155. **agents of theirs** Deciphered document found in Killakee Dump, in FitzGerald papers, UCDA, P80/869 (1). **his own particular line!** Twomey to Neenan, 8 Nov. 1932, in MTUCDA, P69/185 (165–7). **Galway, Cobh and London** AC to Secretary Clan, 27 Mar. 1933, in MTUCDA, P69/185 (32). These Thompsons were the remains of a shipment of 495 captured by the US authorities at Hoboken, New Jersey during 1921. They were released to the Clan's Attorney, J.T. Ryan in 1925. Hart, 'The Thompson sub-machine gun revisited', pp 160–70.

PAGE 34 examined by Customs Not all the sympathizers were necessarily Irish, indeed one was a Spanish fisherman who regularly visited Valentia, Co. Kerry. Dublin Bdge Intelligence report, 20 Aug. 1932, in MTUCDA, P69/199 (94) & A/G to QMG, 18 June 1932, in MTUCDA, P69/155 (153). **smuggle in weapons** Chairman AC to Secretary Clan, 15 Sept. 1932, in MTUCDA, P69/185 (184). **to fight for more than a day** AC to Secretary Clan, 8 Nov. 1932, in MTUCDA, P69/185 (153). **reacted angrily too** Clan to Chairman AC, 24 Mar. 1933 and AC to Secretary, Clan, 24 Apr. 1933, in MTUCDA, P69/185 (45–6). **March 1937** Receipt in McGarrity papers, Ms 17,544 (2) NLI. **Cork in late-1936** *Notes on Individuals*, in MacEntee papers, UCDA, P67/550 p. 162. **US in 1938** G2, Southern Command, 30 June 1941, in G2/X/0093 MA. **contemporary reports** During 1931 gardaí had reported that arms were being landed in Ballybunion, Co. Kerry, 31 June 1931, in D/T S 5864 A NAI. See *Evening Standard*, 19 Oct. 1932, for reports of 'Gun running by night'. **Fianna Fáil government** Twomey to Neenan, 15 Sept. 1932, in MTUCDA, P69/185 (195–199). **military training** AC to An Timthire, Clan, 25 Feb. 1930, in McGarrity papers, Ms 17,535 (2) NLI & Memorandum to Members of AC on USA Organization, 11 Feb. 1926, in MTUCDA, P69/181 (62–4). **air school in Chicago** Neenan

to M. Hayes, 10 July 1930, in McGarrity papers, Ms 17,467 (50) & (8) NLI. **need such men** 'Q' to C/S, 4 Oct. 1932, in MTUCDA, P69/185 (173–5).
PAGE 35 IRA possessed 'Q' to C/S, 20 Aug. 1930, in MTUCDA, P69/153 (211). **local IRA** McCool used the code name 'McAuley', C/S to O/C Tirconaill No. 1, 16 Mar. 1933, in MTUCDA, P69/53 (248). **even more apparent** 'Q' to C/S, 10 Jan. 1933, in Aiken papers, UCDA, P104/2835 (1–2). **countryside at weekends** D/T to C/S, 18 May 1933, in MTUCDA, P69/53 (9–10). **RUC officer in Belfast** Bob Bradshaw Interview, courtesy of Eunan O'Halpin. Bradshaw and Seamus Mallin would leave Dublin on Saturdays and undertake training in a rural area on Sunday mornings. **place outside** Premises controlled by the republican movement such as Kevin Barry Hall in Dublin's Parnell Square. MacEoin, *Twilight Years*, pp 418–20. **Crumlin and Rathfarnham** Garda reports, 30 May & 23 Aug. 1933 and 11 Feb. 1934, in Jus 8/713 NAI. **Dundalk in 1935 showed** Belfast Batt report, July 1932, in MTUCDA, P69/158 (228–33) and *Irish News*, 20 July 1932. Notes on Events, in MacEntee papers, UCDA, P67/534 p. 44. **Kerry during 1930** 'M' to A/G, 20 Oct. 1930, in MTUCDA, P69/153 (159). See also report on north Cork Batt, 18 Sept. 1930, in MTUCDA, P69/153 (200). **in Leix** Staff Captain 'W' to A/G, 29 Sept. 1930, in MTUCDA, P69/153 (177). **forced its abandonment** 'M' to A/G, Aug. 1930, in MTUCDA, P69/153 (212–15). This camp was made up of men from Athlone, Mullingar and north Meath. **Russell himself** 'Q' to C/S, 20 Aug. 1930, in MTUCDA, P69/153 (211). **shot from a rifle** 'M' to A/G, 29 Aug. 1930, in MTUCDA, P69/153 (208–9). **shot with the rifle** O/C west Cork Batt to C/S, 18 May 1933, in MTUCDA, P69/53 (7). **two shots a month** Acting T/O to D/T GHQ, 29 Oct. 1934, in Jus 8/319 NAI.
PAGE 36 was not always the case See instructions on rifle training in *An t-Óglách*, Oct. 1931, in MTUCDA, P69/263 (9). **'rather ordinary cover'** Report on OTC, Westmeath Batt, Aug. 1930, in MTUCDA, P69/153 (212–15). **in its ranks** Staff Captain 'W' to A/G, 11 Oct. 1930, in MTUCDA, P69/153 (148–9). **members in musketry** Staff Captain 'McAuley' to A/G, 25 Nov. 1930, in MTUCDA, P69/153 (63–7). **a major difference** As in Leitrim during 1932 where an ex-British soldier was helping train the local IRA. Adjt Leitrim to A/G, 6 Oct. 1932, in MTUCDA, P69/156 (62–5). **Sunday mornings** Lectures were held on the Saturday night and firing practice on Sunday mornings. Adjt Dub Bdge to A/G, 7 Oct. 1930, in P69/153 (162). **attend a camp** Leix report, 29 September 1930, in MTUCDA, P69/153 (177).**'further exertion'** 'Q' to A/G, 27 Apr. 1931, in MTUCDA, P69/151 (33–4). The IRA complained too of members turning up for training in 'light shoes and their best clothes' and without bringing 'rations.' *An t-Óglách*, Oct. 1931, in MTUCDA, P69/263 (9). **obedience can be instilled** A/G to Ajdt, Ulster No. 1, 17 Apr. 1931, in MTUCDA, P69/151 (68). **absolutely vital** *An t-Óglách*, July 1931, in Jus 8/681 NAI. **fight when necessary** A/G to Adjt Connemara Batt, 3 July 1930, in MTUCDA, P69/153 (253). **to the membership** See Garda report, 10 Sept. 1933, on IRA parade at Tullyvin, Co. Cavan, in Jus 8/725 NAI. **in the presence of their peers** Prospective recruits were invited to a meeting and had the 'Aims and Objects' of the IRA explained to them. They were then sworn in front of their unit, 'drawn up and standing to attention.' *An t-Óglách*, July 1931, in Jus 8/681 NAI. **commitment to the IRA** See A/G to Adjt South Carlow, 20 May 1932, in MTUCDA, P69/157 (13), Ulster No. 1 report, 31 October 1932, in MTUCDA, P69/156 (26–36) and Adjt Ulster No. 1 to A/G, 6 Apr. 1930, in MTUCDA, P69/151 (41) for report of 20 dismissals for non-attendance. **attendance at its parades** In South Galway during Apr. 1930. 32 out of a possible 58 was the parade strength. Report in MTUCDA, P69/151 (36–7). In Dublin out of a potential 198 members parading, 57 were excused and 40 absent from parades during June 1930. Dublin report, June 1930, in MTUCDA, P69/153 (224–5). **sparsely attended** Adjt Drogheda to A/G, 29 Dec. 1930, in MTUCDA, P69/153 (35–6). **during 1930** Outside of Belfast most of the northern IRA was judged 'poor.' 'J.J.' reports, 29 July 1930, in MTUCDA, P69/153 (235–40). Many units in both Galway and Mayo were 'absolutely untrained' and some never paraded. Report, 16 July 1930, in MTUCDA, P69/153 (246–50).

PAGE **37** **weapons training** See Garda report, 4 June 1933, on drilling at Elphin, Co. Roscommon, in Jus 8/715 NAI. **secluded area** See Donegal Garda reports, 31 Aug. 1933 on unarmed IRA parade at Convoy, and 30 Nov. 1933 on smaller armed parade at Annagry, Thor, in Jus 8/723 NAI. **interest in parading** Adjt Tralee Batt to A/G, 27 Apr. 1931, in MTUCDA, P69/151 (13–14). **practice was promised** 'M' to 'Mr. B', 2 Mar. 1930, in MTUCDA, P69/151 (191–2). **intensified training** A/G to Commander of Each Independent Unit, 18 Feb. 1933, in MTUCDA, P69/187 (1–3). **August 1932** Nearly 40 officers from Roscommon, Leitrim, Mayo, Westmeath, Sligo and north Galway took part in the camp. Details in MTUCDA, P69/54 (150–5).] **'lights out' at 9 p.m.** In MTUCDA, P69/54 (156–158). See Appendix 3. **Mick Price** Garda report, 21 Aug. 1932, in D/T S 6328 NAI. **similar events elsewhere** 'Q' to C/S, 10 Jan. 1932 (*sic*), in Aiken papers, UCDA, P104/2835 (1–2) *Irish Times*, 22 Aug. 1932. C/S to O/C Cork No. 1 Bdge, 10 Sept. 1932, in MTUCDA, P69/155 (39). The IRA feared a 'pitched battle' if the gardaí had attempted to retake the castle from them. **within the IRA itself** A/G to Commanders, 18 Feb. 1933, in MTUCDA, P69/187 (1–3). **'voluntary and for Ireland'** Notes by Frank Aiken, undated, in MTUCDA, P69/144 (96–97).]**'very special' cases** Restatement of General Order No. 24, 12 Jan. 1932, in D/T S 5864 C NAI. An exception was where the death penalty was a possibility.

PAGE **38** **with the police** C/S to O/C Dublin Bdge, 1 Nov. 1927, in MTUCDA, P69/50 (13). **legal defence** A/G to O/C Dundalk, 2 Dec. 1929, in MTUCDA, P69/151 (296–90). **during 1930** Garda report, 8 Nov. 1930, in FitzGerald papers, UCDA, P80/851 (24). **in the Dublin area that year** O'Duffy to Members of the Executive Council, 27 July 1931, in FitzGerald papers, UCDA, P80/856 (6). **to a nearby pub** Report on Causeway parade, 'J.J.' to A/G, 18 Jan. 1931, in MTUCDA, P69/153 (22–3). **to the gardaí** A/G to O/C Carrick on Shannon Batt, 24 Feb. 1931, in MTUCDA, P69/151 (151). **possession of** *An Phoblact* A/G to Adjt, Ulster No. 4, 6 Dec.1932, in MTUCDA, P69/158 (5). **operate with gardaí** Adjt Dundalk to A/G, 19 Nov. 1932, in MTUCDA, P69/158 (16–20). **officer to the gardaí** Garda report, 30 Sept. 1933, in Jus 8/715 NAI. **activity in early 1934** *An Phoblacht*, 3 Feb. 1934 & *Northern Whig*, 23 Dec. 1933. **information when questioned** Notes of 1934 GAC, in MacEntee papers, UCDA, P67/525. **was occurring in Kerry** A/G to O/C Listowel Batt, 17 December 1934, in Jus 8/319 NAI. According to the Gardaí, Twomey had lectured the IRA in Tralee on their record of indiscipline earlier that year. *Notes on Events*, MacEntee papers, UCDA, P67/534 p. 20. **participate in the trial** To the evident delight of the gardaí who believed it would effect IRA morale. Report, 8 Nov. 1930, P80/851 (24). **induced him to do so** Adjt Dundalk to A/G, 19 Nov. 1932, in MTUCDA, P69/158 (16–20). **taught him otherwise** Adjt Ulster No. 4 to A/G, 27 Nov. 1932, in MTUCDA, P69/158 (6). **possible imprisonment** A/G to O/C Dundalk, 2 Dec. 1929, in MTUCDA, P69/151 (296–300) **directives by 1934** A/G to O/C Listowel Batt, 17 Dec. 1934, in Jus 8/319 NAI.

PAGE **39** **display of indiscipline** 'J.J.' to A/G, 18 Jan. 1931, in MTUCDA, P69/153 (22–23). **132** For various aspects of this see English, *Radicals*, pp 143–6; Regan, *The Irish counter revolution, 1921–1936*, pp 288–91, & O'Halpin, *Defending Ireland*, pp 79–80. **provoked into violence** A/G to the Commander of each Independent Unit, 27 Oct. 1931, in D/T S 5864 C NAI. See Appendix 4. **similar assurances** *Irish Press*, 1 Dec. 1931. Mulgrew was not actually an IRA member at the time of his arrest, but was in Saor Éire. AC to Clan, 30 July 1932, in MTUCDA, P69/185 (266). **connection with the IRA** *Irish Press*, 15 Dec. 1931. **garda undertaking** O/C Roscommon Batt to A/G, 27 Apr. 1932, in MTUCDA, P69/155 (211–12). **arms dumps in the area** Garda report, 7 Nov. 1931, in D/J 93/3/14 (7–8) NAI. **denounced the organization** *Irish Press*, 11 Feb. 1932. **solitary confinement** Over the winter of 1931–2 Frank Ryan, George and Charles Gilmore, T.J. Ryan, Seán O'Farrell and Seán McGuinness were among the most prominent of the 34 IRA members jailed. T.J. Ryan had expressed the fear that only 'the two Gilmores and the two Ryans' would remain loyal to the IRA while in Arbour Hill. Captured communication to F. Ryan, 11 Jan. 1932, in FitzGerald papers, UCDA, P80/496 (2). **type of young men** Twomey to McGarrity, 9 Dec. 1931, in McGarrity papers, Ms 17,490 NLI. **meetings were being held** AC correspondence book, 7 Nov. & 15 Dec. 1931, 11 & 13 Feb. 1932, in MTUCDA, P69/71. **damaged the organization** See resolutions condemning the treatment of IRA prisoners from county councils in Youghal, Mountmellick, Sligo, Nenagh and Dublin City Council in FitzGerald papers, UCDA, P80/497. **induced their discipline** A/G to Adjt Ulster No. 4, 15 Nov. 1930, in MTUCDA, P69/153 (83).

PAGE 40 pleaded 'not guilty' O/C North Mayo Batt to A/G, 26 Mar. 1932, in MTUCDA, P69/155 (271–4). **re-admitted to the IRA** Adjt Leitrim to A/G, 6 Oct. 1932, in MTUCDA, P69/156 (64). **conclusion of a concert!** Adjt Ulster No. 1 to A/G, 31 Oct. 1932, in MTUCDA, P69/156 (26). **case was refused** P.J. Cleary to C/S, 19 Apr. & C/S to Cleary, 29 Apr. 1927, in MTUCDA, P69/48 (87–88). **Roebuck Jam Company in 1929** MacBride to Secretary, Department of Justice, 20 Apr. 1929, in D/T S 5864 A NAI. **helped IRA morale** Three Dublin IRA men spent 14 months in solitary confinement from late 1929 to 1930. See A/G to all ranks, Dublin Brigade, 9 Dec. 1930, in MTUCDA, P69/153 (51). **before they had** O/C Dundalk to C/S, 10 Jan. 1933, in MTUCDA, P69/55 (35–38).

PAGE 41 in early 1933 I/O Dublin report, 21 Dec. 1932, in MTUCDA, P69/53 (252–4). **1934 convention** Notes of 1933 GAC, in MTUCDA, P69/187 (78–79). RWG Members included Bill Gannon, Jack Nalty and Donal O'Reilly, all later members of the Communist Party of Ireland. **to carry arms** Garda reports, 27, 29 & 30 Mar. 1933, in Jus 8/711 NAI. An anonymous account of the attack on Connolly House is contained in Humphreys papers, UCDA, P106/1421 (2–7). **IRA weapons** *Irish Press*, 1 Apr. & *An Phoblacht*, 8 Apr. 1933. **the Dublin Brigade** C/S to O/C Dublin Bdge, 29 Apr. 1933, in MTUCDA, P69/53 (87–8). **'in constant dread'** Adjt Ulster No. 1 to A/G, 6 Apr. 1930, in MTUCDA, P69/151 (43). **strike-bound merchant** O/C West Clare to D/I, 13 May 1932, in MTUCDA, P69/199 (179). **her husband's will** O/C North Roscommon Batt to A/G, 5 Sept. 1932, in MTUCDA, P69/158 (188).

PAGE 42 a neighbour's drains! Adjt North Clare Batt to A/G, 15 June 1932, in MTUCDA, P69/155 (150–2). **image locally** Adjt Kildare Batt to A/G, 19 August 1929, in MTUCDA, P69/151 (268). **robbery during 1930** A/G to O/C Dublin Bdge, 6 Feb. 1930, in MTUCDA, P69/151 (231–2). **to be arrested** Correspondence on the affair between O/C South Mayo and A/G, Sept. 1932, in MTUCDA, P69/158 (151–62). **members were demoted** A/G to O/C West Clare, 16 July 1932, in MTUCDA, P69/158 (267–71). **involvement in the dispute** IRA Statement to the press, 15 Aug. 1932, in MTUCDA, P69/158 (217). **Ireland in this period** See examples in *Kerry Champion*, 20 Jan.1934, *Westmeath Independent*, 14 Apr. 1934 and *Dundalk Examiner*, 28 Apr.1934. **denials were probably genuine** A/G to Dr FitzGerald, Mental Hospital, Clonmel, 16 Apr.1931, in MTUCDA, P69/151 (63). A/G to Adjt Kildare, 5 September 1932, in MTUCDA, P69/156 (152). **ACA provocation** See p. 139, below. **severely lectured** O/C South Mayo to A/G, 19 Sept. 1932, in MTUCDA, P69/158 (151–62). **from a local woman** *Irish Press*, 11 Feb. 1932.

PAGE 43 tank almost empty Statements from Thomas 'Sonny' Breen and Mick Silver to C/S, 14 May 1932, in MTUCDA, P69/155 (239–41). **with ignominy** *Republican File*, 5 Mar. 1932. **to prove counter-productive** O/C Kildare to A/G, Sept. 1932, in MTUCDA, P69/156 (127). **gates as punishment** A/G to Adjt Ulster No. 4, 18 June 1932, in P69/155 (158). **a regular army** Notes by Aiken, in MTUCDA, P69/144 (96–7). **wilfully ignored** See pp 83–9. **the 'big fist'** Notes of 1934 GAC, in MacEntee papers, UCDA, P67/525. **no practical effect** A/G to Commanders of Each Independent Unit, 17 Apr. 1934, in Jus 8/319 NAI.

PAGE 44 procedure was 'futile' Fianna Fáil members in Kenmare pointed this out to the local IRA. I/O Kenmare Batt to I/O (D/I), 18 Apr.1934, in Jus 8/319 NAI. **violent attacks** See also pp 89–90. **repayment of £70** A/G to O/C Connemara Batt, 27 July 1932, in MTUCDA, P69/158 (261) & O/C Connemara Batt to A/G, 5 Nov. 1932, in MTUCDA, P69/156 (7). **misappropriated money** Ex-O/C West Clare to A/G, 30 Oct. 1934, in Jus 8/319 NAI. *An Phoblacht*, 17 Nov. 1934. **Ballinamore, Co. Leitrim** *Leitrim Observer*, 28 Jan. 1927. **of an IRA gang** *Dáil Debates*, Vol. 20, 26 June 1927. See also Conor Brady, *Guardians* *of the peace* (London, 2000) p. 138. **the civil war** *The Nation*, 6 Aug. 1927. **against those involved** C/S to O/C Carrick on Shannon Bdge, 2 Apr. 1926, in MTUCDA, P69/44 (224–5). **with his unit** O/C North Roscommon Batt to A/G, 5 Sept. 1932, in MTUCDA, P69/158 (188). **into IRA coffers** Report by O'Duffy on Clare, 6 Apr. 1929, in FitzGerald papers, UCDA, P80/851 (5). **an IRA operation** Plant was executed for the murder of Michael Devereux, an IRA member accused of being an informer in 1942. M. Mooney, *George Plant and the rule of law* (Tipperary, 1989) p. 3. **on behalf of the IRA** Report by Chief Superintendent J. Hannigan, 16 May 1929, in FitzGerald papers, UCDA, P80/851 (15). **after the robbery** Report by Chief Superintendent Hannigan, 23 Apr. 1929, in FitzGerald papers, UCDA, P80/851 (7). See also *Tipperary Star*, 27 Apr. 1929. **of its organization** *Tipperary Star*, 15 June 1929.

PAGE 45 **could be addressed** See names for dispatch of communications to Wexford IRA, 22 Feb. 1930, in P69/151 (219–21) or Donegal, 13 Feb. 1931, in MTUCDA, P69/151 (228). **Mrs Kelly in Marino** C/S cover address, 8 Feb. 1933, in MTUCDA, P69/53 (303) & 4 Feb. 1933, in MTUCDA, P69/55 (35–8). **system was employed** See A/G to O/C Derry, 12 May 1932, complaining that the posting of sensitive material could have led to the arrest of officers, in MTUCDA, P69/158 (27–8). **finally to Dublin** A/G to O/C No. 2 Ulster, (nd) in MTUCDA, P69/151 (85). **interception by the gardaí** Garda report, 22 Feb. 1933, in Aiken papers, UCDA, P104/2845 (1–6). **their mail** O'Duffy to Ministers, 5 July 1929, in Blythe papers, UCDA, P24/477. **a local IRA man** I/O No. 2 Ulster to A/G, 14 Dec. 1929, in MTUCDA, P69/151 (276). **known to the gardaí** List of Dublin safe-houses, (nd) in MTUCDA, P69/157 (44–9). **in several ways** A/G to Editor, *Irish Times*, 22 Aug. 1932, in MTUCDA, P69/158 (204).

PAGE 46 **could always be found** *An t-Óglách*, Mar. 1931, in MTUCDA, P69/263 (7). **military manuals and maps** *An t-Óglách*, Oct. 1931, in MTUCDA, P69/263 (9). **Killakee arms find** Although most of the documents were 3 years old and relatively unimportant. Inventory of documents captured in Killakee dump, in MTUCDA, P69/154. **estimate local support** See Garda report, 10 Dec. 1933, on 'Four Martyrs' Commemoration at Castleblaney for example, in Jus 8/725 NAI. Bob Bradshaw felt the IRA was slow to realize the 'advantage' it was giving to the gardaí in holding open parades. Bradshaw tape. **the local ACA** A/G to Adjt Caherciveen Batt, 19 Sept. 1932, in MTUCDA, P69/158 (176). **during 1922** I/O Ulster No. 1 to D/I, 25 Nov. 1926, in MTUCDA, P69/193 (86–94). **land them by plane** Adjt Leitrim Batt to A/G, 2 Nov. 1932, in MTUCDA, P69/156 (10–11). **on Curragh camp** D/I to I/O Kildare Batt, 26 Nov. 1927, in MTUCDA, P69/196 (32). **British garrison there** I/O Ulster No. 2 to D/I, 10 Sept. & 6 Nov. 1927, in MTUCDA, P69/196 (29–30). **was scrutinized** I/O Dublin Bdge to D/I, 5 July 1932, in MTUCDA, P69/199 (125). **and their armament** 'J.J.' to C/S, 19 Feb. 1931, in MTUCDA, P69/51 (14–15). **of some help** C/S to O/C Dublin Bdge, 11 March 1931, in MTUCDA, P69/51 (12–13). **based in Omagh** Inspection Officer report, 20 May 1925, in MTUCDA, P69/47 (242–3). **IRA during 1924** His name was Stephen Lally. Interview by Niall C. Harrington of Military Intelligence, 5 Feb. 1942, in G2/X/0058 MA. Lally's account of the Mutiny in MTUCDA, P69/59 (14–49). **family's political links** 'William' to C/S, (nd) in MTUCDA, P69/196 (61).

PAGE 47 **watching the premises** 'J' to D/I, 13 Dec. 1927, in MTUCDA, P69/196 (18). **help collect information** List of alleged Touts, (Nov. 1927?), in MTUCDA, P69/196 (34). **paranoia about informers** Bob Bradshaw remarked that 'every ejit' in the IRA discovered at least 'half a dozen' informers. Bradshaw tape. **being an informer** A/G to O/C North East Cork Batt, 26 Aug. 1932, in MTUCDA, P69/158 (197). **informer being discovered** Q/M Ulster No. 2 to C/S, 4 July & A/G to Q/M Ulster No. 2, 14 July 1932, in MTUCDA, P69/158 (273–5). **Fianna Fáil CID** C/S to O/C Dublin Bdge, 29 Apr. 1933, in MTUCDA, P69/53 (87–8). **during 1928** Superintendent William Geary of Kilrush, whose name was cleared in 2000. Brady, *Guardians*, p. 153. **split the jury** I/O Belfast Batt to D/I, 10 July 1932, in MTUCDA, P69/199 (126). **both men were jailed** *An Phoblacht*, 21 Oct. 1933. **was** occasionally effective O'Halpin, *Defending Ireland*, p. 66. **IRA ruse was successful** Adjt Ulster No. 1 to A/G, July 1932, in MTUCDA, P69/158 (228–233). **location to the gardaí** O/C Dublin Bdge to C/S, 10 July 1926 and Inquiry into Capture of St Enda's Dump, in P69/57 (2–9).

PAGE 48 Clonmel working for them O'Duffy to Ministers, 5 July 1929, in Blythe papers, UCDA, P24/477. **work for the gardaí** I/O Dublin Bdge to D/I, 12 Dec. 1927, in MTUCDA, P69/196 (19). **area during 1930** Adjt North Cork to A/G, 18 Sept. 1930, in MTUCDA, P69/153 (200). **never seen again** O'Duffy to Ministers, 5 July 1929, in Blythe papers, UCDA, P24/477 & Garda report, 7 June 1929, in D/T S 5864 A NAI. **organization was death** *An t-Óglach*, Mar. 1931, in MTUCDA, P69/263 (7). **former Dáil courier** I/O Dublin Bdge to D/I, 12 Dec. 1927, in MTUCDA, P69/196 (19). O'Halpin, *Defending Ireland*, p. 67. **but denied it** I/O Dublin Bdge to D/I, 27 Oct. 1927, in MTUCDA, P69/196 (37). **Timothy Coughlan** Gabriel Doherty, 'A Star Chamber affair – the death of Timothy Coughlan' in *History Ireland*, Spring 1993. **to the gardaí** Inquiry into capture of St. Enda's Dump, March – May 1926, in MTUCDA, P69/(5–9). **he was not harmed** Report in O'Duffy to Ministers, 24 June 1931, in FitzGerald papers, UCDA, P80/856 (18). **'valuable information'** O'Duffy to Ministers, 24 June 1931, in FitzGerald papers, UCDA, P80/856 (18–19). **of these as well** 'Every phase of activity in the ... Communist party is known through an agent within'. O'Duffy, 5 July 1929, in Blythe papers, UCDA, P24/477. **within the organization** O/C North Monaghan to A/G, 1 Mar. 1931, in MTUCDA, P69/151 (157–160). **his neck during 1929** O/C Midland Batt to A/G, 25 Nov. 1929, in MTUCDA, P69/151 (319–22) & *Westmeath Examiner*, 23 Nov. 1929. **involved with the IRA** Inquiry into capture of St. Endas Dump, March – May 1926, in MTUCDA, P69/57 (5–9).

PAGE 49 imprisonment in Belfast *An Phoblacht*, 16 July & 1 Oct. 1932. **period in Southampton** *Northern Whig*, 21 Sept. 1945. **shot dead by the IRA** *Irish News*, 4 Dec.1936. **with pliers and a poker** *Irish News*, 21 Sept. 1945. Turley's family are still adamant that he was not an informer. See Raymond J. Quinn, *A rebel voice* (Belfast, 1999), pp 49–51. Jack McNally, a Belfast IRA member of the period, claimed that brutal methods were being used to discipline Belfast members routinely by the mid 1940s. J. McNally, '*Morally good – politically bad*' (Belfast, 1989), pp 112–3. **about the affair** *Dáil Debates*, 29 (9 May 1929) and Cabinet Document, 22 May 1929, in FitzGerald papers, UCDA, P80/851 (13). **'as a mystery'** Garda report, 14 Apr. 1930, in FitzGerald papers, UCDA, P80/916 (3). **Michael Price** I/O Dublin Bdge to D/I, 12 Dec. 1927, in MTUCDA, P69/196 (19). **the assassination** O/C Dundalk to 'Q', (nd), in MTUCDA, P69/196 (75–6). Information originally from Waterford. Obviously an extremely busy man, Dalton has also been linked to the killing of Michael Collins. J.M. Feehan, *The shooting of Michael Collins* (Dublin, 1981) pp 91–4. **Communist Party of Ireland** Gannon had served in Michael Collin's 'Squad' during the 1919–21 period. He claimed the killing was a spontaneous action on seeing O'Higgins walking alone. Gannon Statement in 999/591 NAI. **IRA for robbery** A/G to O/C Dublin Bdge, 12 Feb. 1930, in MTUCDA, P69/151 (231–2). Doyle too was an associate of the 'St Enda's gang.' **some time before that** Garda report, 13 Sept. 1929, in D/T S 5864 A NAI. **during the 1940s** Garda report, (nd) D/T S 11552 B NAI. Doyle was suspected of the robbery from the Player Wills factory in 1943.

Chapter Three

PAGE 50 supporting organizations See Appendix 5. Speakers at Bodenstown from 1926; Dr. Madden TD, 1927; Art O'Connor, 1928; George Gilmore, 1929; Seán Buckley, 1930; Tom Maguire, 1931; Peadar O'Donnell (in place of Seán Russell), 1932; S. Russell, 1933; Moss Twomey, 1934; Patrick McLogan, 1935; Seán MacBride, 1936 – Banned. *An Phoblacht*, 1926–36. **Belfast and Derry** See 'GNR Annual Pilgrimage to the Grave of Wolfe Tone at Bodenstown, on Sunday 23 June. Special Train will run from Belfast to Dublin and Sallins.' in Humphreys papers, UCDA, P106/2104 (2). **to travel with them** *Irish Independent*, 22 June 1931. **1934 commemoration** Garda report, 19 June 1934, in Jus 8/310 NAI.

PAGE 51 Tyrone and Derry Wolfe Tone Commemoration Committee to Traffic Manager,

Great Southern Railways (GSR) 19 June 1935 and 10 July 1935, in Humphreys papers, P106/2102 (3) & (7–8) & P106/2106 (26). **damage to their property** Frank Driver to Seán MacBride, 13 June 1936, in Humphreys papers, UCDA, P106/2114 (5–6).**members in each area** Report of Officers Meeting, Sligo (286 members), Leitrim (330), Roscommon (180) and Tirchonaill No. 1 & 2, May 1932, in MTUCDA, P69/155 (94–7). **for the event as well** Addt. Tralee to A/G, 2 May, and O/C N.E. Cork Batt. to A/G, 7 May 1932 in MTUCDA P69/155 (214–215) & (223). **a retreat sermon instead** Entry, Rosamond Jacob Diaries, 19 June 1932, in Ms 32,582 (69) NLI. **1933 onwards** See condemnation of FF in *An Phoblacht*, 1 July 1933. **on several occasions** See Sinn Féin to S. MacBride, 17 May 1935, in Humphreys papers, P106/2113 (15). **by the IRA** *Irish Workers' Voice*, 24 June 1933. **a year later** See pp 176–7. **back to Sallins** Garda reports, 19 June and 20 June 1934, in Jus 8/310 NAI. **Bodenstown** Secretary Wolfe Tone Commemoration Committee to Traffic Manager GSR, June 1935, in Humphreys papers, UCDA, P106/2102 (49–50). **Hotel in Naas** *An Phoblacht*, 18 June 1932. **on several occasions** List of bands to Traffic Manager GSR, 13 June 1936, in Humphreys papers, UCDA, P106/2126 (17). **play at the event** The WUI Band planned to march in 1936 to show the 'parasites in power' that 'coercion will not work'. Tony Brack to Secretary, Bodenstown Committee, 9 June 1936, in Humphreys papers, P106/2126 (19); 130 tickets were issued to bands from Dublin in 1935. P106/2102 (3). **Bodenstown commemoration** *Irish Press*, 15 June 1935. **following the event** One reason buses were favoured by northern visitors in 1935 was because they could attend the Mansion House event and travel home later. Secretary's note, 12 June 1935, in Humphreys papers, UCDA, P106/2106 (24–6). **17,000 attending** *Irish Press*, 18 June 1934. The gardaí estimated 17,000 marchers and 4,000 onlookers. Report, 20 June 1934, in Jus 8/310 NAI.

PAGE 52 between 8,000 and 10,000 *Irish Press*, 25 June 1934. **rally in Dublin** Notes on Events, P67/534 p. 55. **a half-hearted affair** Tom Barry gave the oration. Garda report, 22 June 1937, in Jus 8/475 NAI. **largely risk free** The IRA's estimate for 1931 was 10,000. *An Phoblacht*, 27 June 1931. The *Irish Independent* estimated a crowd of 9,000 attended the 1935 ceremony. *Irish Independent*, 24 June 1935. **militant republicanism** In 1938 1,400 heard Twomey address the rally. Garda report, 20 June 1938, in Jus 8/475 NAI. In 1942 numbers had fallen to just 280. Garda report, 23 June 1942, in Jus 8/900 NAI. **Dublin Brigade** Garda report, 13 March 1932, in Jus 8/698 NAI. **in a particular area** C/S to O/C Dublin Bdge, 31 Mar. 1931, in MTUCDA, P69/51 (26). **publicizing its views** The paper's first editor P.J. Little had joined Fianna Fáil. Notes of Army Council meeting, 21 Apr. 1926, in MTUCDA, P69/181 (46). **to its policies** A/G to Adjt. Connamara Batt, 3 July 1930, in MTUCDA, P69/153 (253). **their assistants were** O'Donnell was succeeded by Frank Ryan in May 1929. Ryan's assistant editor was Geoffrey Coulter. In 1931 Coulter was replaced by Hannah Sheehy Skeffington. Ryan and Sheehy Skeffington resigned in Apr. 1933 and were temporarily replaced by Seán MacBride. From the summer of 1933 the paper was edited by Terry Ward and Liam McGabhainn. Donal O'Donoghue was editor for a period in 1934 and 1935. **a similar publication** During Dec. 1926 a one page edition was published because of censorship. Between Apr. and May 1929 it was replaced by a typed sheet called *Dublin News*. From November 1931 to Mar. 1932 the paper was banned and was replaced by *Republican File*. As Ryan was jailed during this period Sheehy Skeffington edited this paper. In Dec. 1933 it was seized for the first time under Fianna Fáil. When it was published for a brief period from March to July 1936 it was officially the organ of Cumann Poblachta na h-Éireann. During 1937 *An Phoblacht* was allowed publish four special issues in the run up to the referendum on the new Constitution. **Republican Press Ltd** The Republican Press Ltd was established on the 10 May 1929. Ryan and Sheehy Skeffington were directors and Aine O'Farrelly was secretary. In July 1933 Seán MacBride and Michael Fitzpatrick took over as directors and O'Farrelly remained secretary. Report, 8 Jan. 1934, in Jus 8/68 NAI. **such as Easons** Easons distribution, in P69/55 (55) and A/G to Adjt. Leitrim, 19 Sept. 1932, in MTUCDA, P69/156 (129). See also *An*

Phoblacht, 1 Apr.1927 **Electricity Supply Board** See *An Phoblacht*, 11 March 1933 for the ESB advert. From 1926 onwards the most consistent advertiser was the New Ireland Assurance Company. At various stages McBirney's furniture store, Guiney's clothes stores and HB Dairies advertised in the paper. **An Phoblacht** Staff Captain 'W' to A/G, 11 October 1930, in MTUCDA, P69/153 (148). **'lack of interest' in it** Inspecting Officer to A/G, 16 July 1930, in MTUCDA, P69/153 (246; 250) **close it down** A/G to Adjt. Tralee, 22 June 1932, in MTUCDA, P69/155 (111).

PAGE 53 could not be sold O/C Ulster No. 1 to A/G, 5 Oct. 1929, in MTUCDA, P69/151 (337). **Dublin and Belfast** Note to An Phoblacht, 11 Dec. 1933, in MTUCDA, P69/243 (29). **youth of Kerry** Garda reports from Kerry and Tipperary, in Commissioner O'Duffy to Secretary Dept. Justice, 27 July 1931, UCDA, P80/857 (41). **a sale of 8,000** Ryan to McGarrity, 25 Jan. 1930, in McGarrity papers, Ms 17,535 NLI. **10,000 a week** Report, 1 Oct. 1932, in MTUCDA, P69/55 (55). **sold 27,727 copies** Sales for May 1932, in MTUC-DA, P69/52 (175). **relatively limited circulation** The *Irish Press*, by contrast, had a daily circulation of around 100,000. J. Horgan, *Irish media* (London, 2001), p. 30. *An Phoblacht* Cost of printing, March to Nov. 1932, in MTUCDA P69/55 (59) **closing it down** Chairman AC to Editor, AP, 28 Sept. 1932, in MTUCDA, P69/55 (53; 64) and C/S to 'Jack Jones' 1 October 1932, in MTUCDA, P69/54 (36). However, it should be noted that Frank Ryan felt that economics were being made a cover for political disagreements with him. See P. Ó Rian to Chairman AC, 1 October 1932, in MTUCDA, P69/55 (54). **were being print-ed** 11,120 copies were seized at the printers. Garda report, 18 Jan. 1934, in Jus 8/68 NAI. **articles missing** Garda report, 1 January 1934, in Jus 8/68 NAI. See *An Phoblacht*, 5 Jan. and 2 Mar. 1935 for missing articles. The paper was printed in Longford by the Longford Printing and Publishing Company. **to settle accounts** AP to Secretary, T. MacSwiney Club, Massachusetts, 26 March 1936, in MTUCDA, P69/225 (1). **in July that year** Longford Printing and Publishing Company, 30 May 1935 & 8 May 1936 in MTUCDA, P69/244. **to support it** AC Statement to GAC 1938, in Aiken papers, UCDA, P104/2833 (1–3). For the issues produced in order to oppose the 1937 Constitution the IRA leadership had to borrow from personal friends. **younger leadership** This was not the case between 1919 and 1923. See for example, *English radicals*, pp 29–52 & D. Fitzpatrick, *Politics and Irish life* (Cork, 1998) pp 209–30.

PAGE 54 the working class Tom Daly at the 1933 GAC, Notes of GAC, in MTUCDA, P69/187 (99). **and small farmers** 'Lines on which paper is to be run' AC meeting 29 Apr. 1926, in MTUCDA, P69/181 (41). **attacking strike breakers** Commandant CJ O'Donohue to I/O Eastern Command, 22 Oct. 1925, in FitzGerald papers, UCDA, P80/847 (117).

PAGE 79 anti-Treaty forces 'Mr Ambrose' (James Killeen) 'General Outline of the Present Movement' August 1927, in MTUCDA, P69/72 (3; 14) and 'Mr Holmes' (Peadar O'Donnell) 'Notes on the Irish Labour Movement' in MTUCDA, P69/72 (15; 18). **gen-uine labourism** 'Notes' P69/72 (16). Johnson was one of the founders of the Irish Labour Party. He had been president of the Irish Trade Union Congress and was a TD and leader of the Labour Party from 1922 to 1927. The phrase was O'Donnells, who always nursed a particular dislike of Johnson. See also O'Drisceoil, O'Donnell, pp 28 & 32. **their own organization** O/C Kerry No. 1 Batt. to A/G, 8 February 1930, in MTUCDA, P69/152 (217). **O'Farrell in 1934** *Leitrim Observer*, 30 June 1934. **local Labour Party** The local Labour Party and the EULA Band had taken part in the Ennis Easter Commemoration. *Clare Champion*, 7 Apr., 5 & 12 May 1934. **Fianna Fáil government** Twomey to Neenan, 15 Sept. 1932, in MTUCDA, P69/185 (195–9). **attacked by the IRA** An exception being a debate between Frank Robbins, formerly of the ICA, and the IRA in *An Phoblacht*, 28 Mar. 1936. **the best situation** At the beginning of the 1930 IOC strike *An Phoblacht* explicitly rejected claims that the NUR was a foreign union. By the strike's conclusion, however, it was claiming that the fact that the NUR was British-based had contributed to the strikes defeat. *An Phoblacht*, 24 May and 2 Aug. 1930. **trade unions' to join** Garda report, 19 June 1929, in FitzGerald papers, UCDA, P80/851 (20). **Labour Defence League** Garda report, 16 July 1929, in FitzGerald papers, UCDA, P80/907 (2).

IRA commemorations Donation from IRA GHQ Staff to Greenmount Mill strikers, 5
May 1931, in MTUCDA, P69/151 (4; 5). The Greenmount Mill strikers took part in
Dublin's Easter Commemoration in 1931. *An Phoblacht*, 11 Apr. 1931.
PAGE 55 over wage cuts O/C North Mayo to A/G, 2 Aug. 1932, in MTUCDA, P69/158
(235). clashes with Blueshirts *Kerry Champion*, 16 Dec. 1933. Armagh and Down Notes of
1933 GAC, P69/187 (113). in Sligo town Reports in *Irish Independent*, 4 June 1930, most of
these incidents See O/C North Wexford to A/G, 23 July 1930, in MTUCDA, P69/153
(186). attacks on buses commenced 'D' to A/G, 27 June 1930, in MTUCDA, P69/153
(255–6). three years later See p. 151. smashed equipment inside *Irish Times*, 22 Dec. 1934.
Notes on the Republican Congress Movement, MacEntee papers, UCDA, P67/527 p. 15.
on the streets *Notes on Events*, MacEntee papers, UCDA, P67/534 p. 37. strike in protest *An
Phoblacht*, 23 Mar. 1935. Strike Committee *Irish Times*, 25 Mar. 1935. helped ease relations
Garda report, 27 Mar. 1935, in Jus 8/405 NAI. army lorries Garda report, 26 Mar. 1935,
in Jus 8/405 NAI. under Fianna Fáil *Notes on Events*, P67/534, pp 38–9.
PAGE 56 only national paper O'Donoghue to Sighle Humphreys, 30 Aug. 1934, in
Humphreys papers, UCDA, P106/1644 (1–4). its regular paper See *An Phoblacht*, Special
Edition by Consent of Strike Committee, 11 Aug. 1934. the union's efforts Garda report,
26 Sept. 1934, in Jus 8/365 NAI. co-operate with it The IRA claimed to be supplying
strikers with explosives in Belfast during the rail strike. See p. 151. Three rail workers
were charged with bomb attacks during the strike. *Irish News*, 30 Mar. 1933. Two of those
arrested in connection with the Bacon Shop attacks were strikers. *Irish Times*, 31 Dec.
1934. Two men arrested after shots were fired at gardaí during the Dublin Tram strike
were bus drivers. *Irish Independent*, 25 Mar. 1935. of those sacked *Notes on Events*, P67/534
p. 48. *Kerry Champion*, 23 Mar. 1935 & 8 Feb. 1936. a local employer O/C West Clare to
D/I, 13 May 1932, in MTUCDA, P69/199 (179). the 1919–21 period 'Mr. Holmes', Notes
on the Labour Movement, MTUCDA, P69/72 (15–18). against land annuities See pp
119–20. republican support anyway O/C South Carlow to A/G, 8 July 1932, in MTUC-
DA, P69/158 (285–6). the rural population Down from 300,000 in 1911 to 150,000 in 1936.
Lee, *Ireland*, p. 159. See also Paul Bew, 'Sinn Féin, agrarian radicalism and the War of
Independence, 1919–1921' in D.G. Boyce, *The revolution in Ireland, 1879–1923* (Dublin,
1988) pp 217–34.
PAGE 57 to Irish property Adjt. Leitrim to A/G, 24 Aug. 1932, in MTUCDA, P69/156
(134). a local school Adjt. Tralee Batt. to A/G, 28 Oct. 1932, in MTUCDA, P69/156
(56–58). allowed to take action O/C Sooey Unit to O/C Sligo Batt., 6 Oct. 1932, in
MTUCDA, P69/158 (65). in this case See p. 37. were responsible Garda report, 25 May
1929, in FitzGerald papers, UCDA, P80/851 (16). the civil war Adjt. North Mayo Bdge
to A/G, 7 Sept. 1932, in MTUCDA, P69/158 (182–6). was evicted O/C Offaly to A/G,
28 May 1932, in MTUCDA, P69/155 (171). on its own A/G to O/C Tipperary Batt. 21
Sept. 1932, in MTUCDA, P69/158 (128). using violence C/S to O/C Sligo Batt, 26 Oct.
1932, in MTUCDA, P69/158 (62–9). IRA leadership A/G to O/C Offaly, 19 May 1932,
in MTUCDA, P69/157 (32) and A/G to O/C Offaly, 9 June 1932, in MTUCDA,
P69/155 (169). Article in *Worker's Voice*, 14 May 1932.
PAGE 58 undermine their organization A/G to O/C Limerick, 18 Oct. 1932, in MTUC-
DA, P69/54 (32). land for tillage C/S to Jack Jones, 1 Oct. 1932, in P69/54 (34–5). *An
Phoblacht*, 1 Oct. 1932. in the towns Report on Thurles Conference, 2 Oct. 1932, in
MTUCDA, P69/54 (37–41). in May 1934 F. Columb, *The shooting of More O'Ferrall*
(Monaghan, 1996), pp 3–16. *Longford Leader*, 5 & 12 May, 2, 9 & 30 June 1934. to Captain
Montague MacEoin allegedly told the tenents that if he was still 'leading soldiers' their
fight would be over in '24 hours'. *Longford Leader*, 23 Mar. 1935. to help them *Longford
Leader*, 29 Sept. 1934. evictions were threatened *Notes on Events*, P67/534 pp 32–3. against
'Landlordism' Devine had asked IRA HQ for help on 21 Oct. AC correspondence book,
in Aiken papers, UCDA, P104/2839 (2). of the association *Longford Leader*, 10 Nov. & 8
Dec. 1934, *An Phoblacht*, 8 Dec. 1934. was fatally wounded *Longford Leader*, 16 Feb. 1935.

PAGE 59 as republican representatives *Longford Leader*, 27 Mar. 1935. in June 1935 *Longford Leader*, 22 June 1935. These terms included a 25 per cent reduction in rent and re-instatement of evicted tenants. back to Edgesworthstown *Irish Times*, 16 Dec. 1935. on their support See *Republican Congress*, 1 June 1935. at Dublin port *Irish Independent*, 21 Mar. 1927. O/C Dub Bdge to C/S, 21 Mar. 1927, in MTUCDA, P69/48 (205) and *Notes on events*, P67/534 p. 6. control of it A/G to Secretary, British Boycott Committee, 6 Sept. 1932, in MTUCDA, P69/158 (191–3). Independence League 'Boycott British' National executive minute book, 14 Sept. 1932, in Humphreys papers, UCDA, P106/2101. suggested as alternatives 'Boycott British' League, National Executive, Deire Foghmhair 1932, in MTUCDA P69/247 (2–4). Urney's were owned by a Fianna Fáil supporter Henry Gallagher, see McGarrity papers, *Irish Press* subscriptions, 1928, in Ms 17,441 NLI. Urney's Chocolates and O'Connell's Ale were both regular advertisers in *An Phoblacht*. See *An Phoblacht*, 25 Mar. 1927 and 1 July 1933. 'very disappointing' Chairman AC to Army Executive, 18 Nov. 1932, in MTUCDA, P69/155 (30). most energetic area Reports from Con Lehane, Secretary BBL to A/G, 22 Nov. 1932, in MTUCDA, P69/247 (10–22).

PAGE 60 of British goods Chairman AC to Army Executive, MTUCDA, P69/155 (30). of ale smashed Garda report, 13 Dec. 1932 in D/T S 5864 D NAI & *Irish Press*, 14 Dec. 1932. on people's imagination AC Memorandum on Boycott British Campaign, 21 Dec. 1932, in MTUCDA, P69/54 (14). a 'sufficient boycott' O/C South Mayo to A/G, 17 Nov. 1932, in MTUCDA, P69/157 (7). ignoring the campaign AC Memorandum, P69/54 (14) and Con Lehane to A/G, MTUCDA, P69/247 (10–22). *Irish Press*, 19 & 21 Dec. 1932. Fianna Fáil supporters Tom Barry at the March 1933 GAC, MTUCDA, P69/187 (109). not in Dublin O'Donoghue at the 1933 GAC, MTUCDA, P69/187 (110). Waterford report, 22 Nov. 1932, in MTUCDA, P69/247 (10–22). with the campaign March 1933 GAC, MTUCDA, P69/187 (110). See also O'Connor, *Soldier of Liberty*, p. 2 and Byrne *Republican Congress revisited*, p. 10. While the Republican Congress would later ridicule the 'squabble over Bass bottles' none of its future members spoke against it at the 1933 GAC. *Republican Congress*, 29 June 1935. pay decent wages C/S to Chairman Boycott committee, 20 Oct. 1932, in MTUCDA, P69/247 (5–6). a serious campaign Notes for defendants in Boycott case, Dec. 1932, in MTUCDA, P69/53 (361–4) in six counties Adjt Ulster No. 4 to A/G, 27 Nov. 1932, in MTUCDA, P69/158 (7). built up beforehand Notes 1933 GAC, MTUCDA, P69/187 (110). to Dublin pubs *Notes on Events*, P67/534 pp 16–17. support for a boycott Despite bravado about the Bass firm being 'broken' in Ireland. *An Phoblacht*, 16 Sept. 1933. an effective campaign De Valera to McGarrity, 6 Sept. 1933 (care of S.T. O'Kelly), in McGarrity papers, Ms 17,441 NLI.

PAGE 61 was quietly abandoned Notes of 1934 GAC, MacEntee papers, UCDA, P67/525. of the Irish people Constitution of Oglaigh na h-Éireann, MacEntee papers, UCDA, P67/524 (10–14). platform and press' *An Phoblacht*, 14 Mar. 1931. revival of the language Saor Éire Constitution and Rules, Sept. 1931, in D/T S 5864 A and Cumann Poblachta na h-Éireann, Fundementals of Political and Economic System, 7 & 8 November 1936, in Jus 8/68 NAI. among the leadership Ryan was so upset by an article critical of Irish by Frank O'Connor in the left-wing *Irish People* that he almost resigned from the paper. Entry, Jacob diaries, 17 Feb. 1936, Ms 32,582 (78) NLI and Cronin, *Frank Ryan*, p. 69. the available candidates Cumann na mBan Convention Notes, 4 May 1926, in Humphreys papers, UCDA, P106/1144 (6). where 'practicable' Notes of 1933 GAC, MTUCDA, P69/187 (118). always in English See Garda report on IRA mobilization at rally in Dublin, 13 Mar. 1932, in Jus 8/698 NAI. would be of use Adjt. Dingle Batt. to A/G, 9 October, and A/G to Adjt Dingle, 24 Oct. 1932, in MTUCDA, P69/156 (77–9). received in Dublin Adjt Connemara Batt to A/G, 25 Nov. 1932 & reply 5 Dec. 1932, in MTUCDA, P69/155 (7–12). 'not to speak Gaelic' *Irish Independent*, 7 Nov. 1932. another district justice *An Phoblacht*, 22 Oct. 1932. He could not understand the questions the Judge put to him in Irish. 'grim realism' Margaret Ward, *Hannah Sheehy Skeffington* (Cork, 1997). pp 273–8. *An Phoblacht*, 23 Sept. 1933. As early as 1928 O'Casey was being praised in *An Phoblacht*. See issue of 9 Jan. 1928. **an oppressed race** *An Phoblacht*, 6 Jan. 1934. Seán O'Farrell's involvement in the local Gaelic League may account for the appearance of this article. Robeson review in *An Phoblacht*, 23 Feb. 1935.

PAGE 62 GAA correspondent McHugh, *Voices of the rearguard*, pp 348 & 354. **followed this game** The IRA's Dublin membership was predominantly working class in a city with a strong soccer tradition. Certainly some prominent Fianna Fáil members such as Oscar Traynor and Todd Andrews were very enthusiastic soccer fans, sometimes to the discomfort of the GAA. Marcus de Burca, *The GAA* (1999) pp 171–2 & Andrews, *Dublin* pp 45–7 & *Man of no property*, p. 41. There is an intriguing hint of non-GAA support for republicans in the claim that 'even Rugby clubs' in Tralee cancelled games in protest at the jailing of IRA members. *Kerry Champion*, 24 Feb. 1934. Parts of Kerry, like Limerick, have a popular rugby tradition. **'foreign' games** 'Mutius' *An Phoblacht's* GAA correspondent for 1925–31 went on to *Republican Congress*. **imprisonment of republicans** De Burca, *GAA*, pp 129–30. J.J. Barrett, *In the name of the game* (Bray, 1997), pp 68–9. **respective counties** A/G to O/C Divisions and Independent Brigades, 20 June 1924, in MTUCDA, P69/145 (231). **gaining influence in it** Twomey to A/G, 25 Sept. 1924, in MTUCDA, P69/141 (32). Report for IRA Executive, 10 Aug. 1924, in MTUCDA, P69/179 (111). **in the IRA** Draft notes on the GAA (1931) in MTUCDA, P69/73 (73–4). **four were 'neutral'** C/S to O/C North Mayo, 28 Apr. 1932, and list in MTUCDA, P69/52 (199). **IRA sympathizers** Chairman AC to secretary Clan na Gael, 8 Nov. 1932, in MTUCDA, P69/185 (154–56). **executive in 1927** An Timthire, Clan na Gael, 15 Jan. 1927 in MTUCDA, P69/183 (134). **in America** Neenan to Twomey, 21 Mar. 1933, in MTUCDA, P69/185 (26). **during 1932** Brosnan was involved in the killing of an RIC district inspector during 1921. Dwyer, *Tans, terror and troubles*, pp 270–2. An unsuccessful Cumann na Gaedheal candidate in 1933, he resigned from the ACA after the election, *Notes on Events*, P67/534, p. 12 and *Kerry Champion*, 4 Feb. 1933. **in the GAA there** Barret, *Name of the game*, pp 150–8. **Connaught council** A/G to Adjt Killarney, Sept. 1932, in MTUCDA, P69/158 (166).

PAGE 63 affected the association De Burca, *History of the GAA*, pp 151 & 154. **organization's activities** A defendant in the More O'Ferrall case, John 'Nipper' Shanley, was a Leitrim footballer. *Longford Leader*, 6 Apr. 1935. Future Chief of Staff Stephen Hayes was secretary of the county board in Wexford. The unfortunate John Egan, murdered in 1936, was also a member of his local GAA club in Dungarven. *Irish Press*, 28 Apr. 1936. **Leitrim or Roscommon** Officers meeting, May 1932, in MTUCDA, P69/155 (94–7). **in the competition** Tomás Ó Maoileóin to A/G, 14 Sept. 1932, in MTUCDA, P69/156 (139–40). Ó Maoileóin was later a member of the North Tipperary board and the Munster council. Malone, *Alias Seán Forde*, p. 99. **in the GAA** Sheehy was also treasurer of the GAA's Munster council. Fleming was a member of Killarney's Legion club and Powell of John Mitchels. *Kerryman*, 27 Jan. 1934, *Kerry Champion*, 24 Feb. 1934 & 1 June 1935. **by the government** *Kerry Champion*, 24 Feb. 1934, *Kerryman*, 9 & 16 Feb. 1935. **allow games to resume** T. McEllistrim TD, 4 Feb. 1935, and D. Daly TD, 5 Feb. 1935 to Frank Aiken, in Aiken papers, UCDA, P104/2801 (80–3). **on the streets' too** *Kerry Champion*, 9 Feb. 1935. **and games anyway** *Kerry Champion*, 2 Mar. 1935. **to resume play** *Kerry Champion*, 25 May 1935. **confrontational tactics** *Kerryman* & *Kerry Champion*, 24 Feb. 1934.

PAGE 64 it could chew *Kerry Champion*, 25 May 1935. **if necessary'** *Kerry Champion*, 15 June 1935. **in Kerry itself** 'Liam' GAA columnist, *Kerry Champion*, 11 Jan. 1936. **'murder before God'** Murray, *Oracles of God*, pp 75–80. **now dominates Russia** Quoted in *English Radicals*, p. 144. **denounced the organization** *An Phoblacht*, 17 Feb. 1934, *Irish Press*, 12 Feb. 1934, *Irish Press*, 4 Mar. 1935. **belong to the IRA** *Irish Press*, 4 Mar. 1935. **'good' effect locally** Eoin O'Duffy to Government ministers, 5 July 1929, in Blythe papers, UCDA, P24/477. **anti-Treatyite republicanism** Murray, *Oracles of God*, pp 137–242. **of its influence** 'Mr Ambrose' General outline of the present movement, Aug. 1927, in MTUCDA, P69/72 (3–14). **influenced by it** Twomey to McGarrity, 9 Dec. 1931, in McGarrity papers, Ms 17,490 NLI.

PAGE 65 political influence Twomey to Count Plunkett, 26 Oct. 1931, in Jus 10/93/3/14

(3) NAI. **clerical condemnation** Notes of 1933 GAC, P69/187 (95). **'against religion'** See for example, *Irish Press*, 11 Feb. 1932. **to the IRA** Notes of 1933 GAC, P69/187 (77). **from the Church** C/S to Secretary, Clan na Gael, 21 Mar. 1933, in MTUCDA, P69/185 (55). **to its support** Notes of 1933 GAC, P69/187 (106–7). **from communism** *Irish Times*, 19 June 1933. **leader Brian Corrigan** A/G to O/C North Mayo Bdge, 12 Jan. 1932, in MTUCDA, P69/155 (287). **to leave the organization** AC Correspondence book, 5 Nov. 1931, in MTUCDA, P69/71. **a place to stay** 'R' to C/S, 3 June 1932, in MTUCDA, P69/155 (183–6). **or the IRA** O/C Tipperary Batt. to A/G, 3 July 1932, in MTUCDA, P69/158 (284). **from the area** P. Carrig to C/S, 6 Dec. 1932, in MTUCDA, P69/54 (67). **socialist James Gralton** O/C North Roscommon Batt. to C/S, 28 Mar. 1933, in MTUCDA, P69/53 (77–9). **similar accusations** For Waterford see Notes of 1933 GAC, P69/187 (107). Offaly in Garda report, 27 December 1933 in Jus 8/733 NAI.

PAGE 66 extended to McKeon O/C North Roscommon to C/S, P69/53 (77–9). **about him** Twomey to Mary MacSwiney, 27 June 1933, in MacSwiney papers, UCDA, P48A/199 A. **Friends of Soviet Russia** Seamus Ó Maoileóin, 12 May 1932, in MTUCDA, P69/52 (138–48). Ó Maoleóin produced an impressive set of references to prove he was a competent teacher. Interestingly his only job offer came from a Protestant school. **subject of communism** Twomey to Con Neenan, 28 Mar. 1933, in MTUCDA, P69/185 (21–25). **'burning your churches'** Notes recorded by Ms Connolly O'Brien, (ND) in MTUCDA, P69/53 (236). **Connolly House** Garda Commissioner report, 30 Mar. 1933, in Jus 8/711 NAI. **rioting at Connolly House** 'Such a gang of rowdies' Twomey to Neenan, 28 Mar. 1933, in MTUCDA, P69/185 (21–25). **to defend them** Unsigned representative for *An Phoblacht* to G. Griffen, 24 Aug. 1933, in MTUCDA, P69/224 (24). **within the IRA** See *An Phoblacht*, 8 Apr. and *Irish Press*, 1 Apr. 1933. Harry Gilmore argued that Patrick Pearse would have gone to James Connolly's aid in a similar situation. The former co-editor of *An Phoblacht*, Geoffrey Coulter told Twomey that the IRA's attitude would 'make a dog vomit'. Coulter to C/S, 3 Apr. 1933, in MTUCDA, P69/53 (239). **by these bodies** *Irish Times*, 14 Mar. 1932. **to clerical influence** *Catholic Herald*, 2 Apr. 1932. Garda report, 27 Dec. 1933, in Jus 8/733 NAI. **Holy Catholic Church** *An Phoblacht*, 23 Dec. 1933.

PAGE 67 in either were slim C/S to O/C North Roscommon, 25 Apr., O/C N. Rosc to C/S, 13 Apr., statement from neighbour, 27 Apr. 1933, in MTUCDA, P69/53 (69–80). **could be utilized** A/G to O/C Tipperary Batt. 12 July 1932, in MTUCDA, P69/158 (281–2). **as priests** Twomey to MacSwiney, 27 June 1933, in MacSwiney papers, UCDA, P48A/199A. **out of the church** Garda report, 19 Jan. 1935, in Jus 8/323 NAI. **'very responsive'** Garda report, 24 Sept. 1934, in Jus 8/342 NAI. **in the protest** Edwards was a teacher at Mount Sion Christian Brother's School. *Notes on Events*, P67/534 p. 32. *Irish Press*, 28 Jan. 1935. **the late 1920s** The phrase is from a Comhairle na Poblachta leaflet of May 1929. Copy in D/T S 5864 B NAI. See also B.S. Murphy, 'The stone of Destiny: Fr John Fahy (1884–1969) Lia Fail and smallholder radicalism in modern Irish society' in G. Moran (ed.), *Radical Irish priests* (Dublin, 1998), pp 185–218. **the local commemoration** Garda report, 8 May 1931, in D/T S 5864 A NAI. **and his killers** Garda report in Eoin O'Duffy to Ministers, 27 July 1931, in D/T S 5964 B NAI. **we have – England** O/C Kildare to A/G, 14 Sept. 1932, in MTUCDA, P69/156 (128). **towards the IRA** Adjt, Waterford City Unit to A/G, 20 Sept. 1932, in MTUCDA, P69/156 (95–6).

PAGE 68 parishioners following this Carrig to C/S, 6 Dec. 1932, C/S to O/C West Clare, 7 Dec. 1932, O/C West Clare to C/S, 12 Dec. 1932, in MTUCDA, P69/54 (67–71). Interestingly there was a suggestion that George Gilmore address an after-Mass meeting to refute the priest's allegations. However, Gilmore himself thought this a bad idea; whether for political reasons or because he was a Protestant is unclear. **in his parish** Garda report, 27 December 1933, in Jus 8/733 NAI. **de Valera's party** O/C North Mayo to A/G, 22 Jan. 1933, in MTUCDA, P69/53 (121). **Fr John Fahy** O'Duffy to Minister for Justice, 5 July 1929, in Blythe papers, UCDA, P24/477. **were important** *An Phoblacht*, 17 Dec. 1932. **increasingly after 1933** Mick Price argued that Saor Éire's policies were ones 'all

Christians' could support. *Irish Independent*, 28 Sept. 1931. **teachings of Christianity** IRA reply to Bishop Kinnane of Waterford, *An Phoblacht*, 19 Jan. 1935. **capitalist policies** *Irish Citizen Army Bulletin*, 4 Dec. 1934, in Humphreys papers, UCDA, P106/3814 (1).

PAGE 69 the Dublin Brigade See motions from College Company and 4th Battalion Dub Bdge and 2nd Batt Dub Bdge in Clár, 1933 GAC, in MTUCDA, P69/53 (273–86). **aims of the IRA** Notes of 1933 GAC, MTUCDA, P69/187 (103). **Eucharistic Congress of 1932** See Gillian McIntosh, 'Acts of "national communion": the centenary celebrations for Catholic Emancipation, the forerunner of the Eucharistic Congress' in Augusteijn (ed.), *Ireland in the 1930s*, pp 83–95. **ordinary Irish Catholics** O/C Belfast to C/S, 10 July 1932, in MTUCDA, P69/52 (87). Twomey attended at least part of the Congress, C/S to P. Whelan, 1 July 1932, in MTUCDA, P69/54 (250) **attempt to recruit them** AC Minutes, 13 June 1932, in MTUCDA, P69/71. **within this milieu** Coogan's claim that Twomey was 'scrupulous in his religious practice' tells us little about the relationship or lack of it between his political beliefs and his religion. Coogan, *IRA*, p. 59. Peadar O'Donnell remained a Catholic all his life while espousing radical politics. Ó Drisceoil, *O'Donnell*, p. 129. **rosary at commemorations** See 'Training Notes' in *An Phoblacht*, 8 Apr. 1933. **were very isolated** *An Phoblacht*, 12 Jan. and *Republican Congress*, 5 Jan. 1935. The mayor of Waterford, the local INTO, and several FF Cumainn supported Edwards. *An Phoblacht* reported that the local UIP and the Waterford Pig Buyers' Association passed resolutions supporting the Bishop. *An Phoblacht*, 19 Jan. 1935. **'anti-God doctrines'** Twomey thought the campaign against Gralton was a 'damn shame'. Twomey to Neenan, 3 Mar. 1933, in MTUCDA, P69/185 (78–79). Leitrim Batt Convention report, 1933, in MTUCDA, P69/187 (4–14). Delegates at the Battalion Convention voted 27 to 4 to remain neutral. **his IRA membership** *Notes on Events*, P67/534 p. 64. Local IRA members beat up Ó Cadhain's replacement during May 1937. **the Orange Order** *An Phoblacht*, 21 July 1934. **if they wished** A/G to Adjt Ulster No. 4 Bat, 15 Nov. 1930, in MTUCDA, p 69/153 (83). **within Fianna Fáil** C/S to 'Thomais', 23 Mar. 1933, in MTUCDA, P69/53 (268–70). **by the Knights** Twomey to Neenan, 3 Mar. 1933, in MTUCDA, P69/185 (78–9). **were members** Among them Lemass, MacEntee and O'Kelly. E. Bolster, *The Knights of Columbanus* (1979) p. 70.

PAGE 70 the civil war M. Farry, *The aftermath of revolution, Sligo 1921–23* (Dublin, 2000), pp 19–20, 23–4, 29–30. **supporter in 1932** He was the main speaker at the 1933 Easter commemoration in Roscommon. *An Phoblacht*, 15 Apr. 1933. **and replaced him** *An Phoblacht*, 17 June 1933. **seem to have been** *An Phoblacht*, 21 Apr. 1934. Bolster suggests Bradshaw's IRA sympathies rather than his religion was the key factor in the affair. *Knights*, pp 71–3. **the job was dismissed** *An Phoblacht*, 5 June 1937. **within Fianna Fáil** *An Phoblacht*, Christmas edition, 1930. See Lee, *Modern Ireland 1912–1985*, pp 161–6. **industrial school system** 'The Industrial School scandal' *An Phoblacht*, 4 Sept. 1934. **'fellow Christians'** 'Seachránaidhe' (Frank Ryan), *Irish emancipation* (Dublin, 1929) Foreword. **republican participation** *Irish Press*, 31 Aug. & *Cork Examiner* 21 Sept. 1936. Indeed those involved in protesting against the Front later on seem to have been more likely to have been republicans. Garda reports, 28 Feb. & 5 Apr. 1937, in Jus 8/448 NAI.

Chapter Four

PAGE 71 in 1924 Jane Leonard, 'The twinge of memory – Armistice Day and Remembrance Sunday in Dublin since 1919' in G. Walker and R. English (eds), *Unionism in modern Ireland* (Dublin, 1996), pp 99–114. **anti-Poppy Day platforms** Garda reports on Anti-Imperialist League (AIL) demonstrations, 10 Nov. 1933, 10 Nov. 1931 and 10 Nov. 1930 in Jus 8/682 NAI. **in 1932** Garda reports, 7 Nov. 1931 (an account of the previous year's protest) in Jus 8/682 and 10 Nov. 1932 in Jus 8/684 NAI. **the British Legion** See for example *Irish Independent*, 12 Nov. 1930. A graphic account of one such clash is given in Jacob Diaries, Entry, 11 Nov. 1926, Ms 32,582 (58) NLI. **occupants assaulted** Garda reports, 7 November 1931 in Jus 8/682 and 11 November 1932 in Jus 8/684 NAI. **co-ordinate these activities** Communication, 26 Mar. 1927, in MTUCDA, P69/48 (67). **an unfree Ireland** *An Phoblacht*, 8 Nov. 1930.

PAGE 72 to England's king *An Phoblacht*, 11 Nov. 1933. **imperialism in Ireland** Irish Anti-

Imperialist League, aims and objects, 26 Mar. 1927, in MTUCDA, P69/48 (68). **entire Dublin IRA** See reference to order for Dublin Brigade to assemble, unarmed, at Foster Place on Armistice night. O/C 4th Battalion to C/S, 3 Dec. 1926, in MTUCDA, P69/47 (22). **Free State's police** A poster for the AIL featured a map of Ireland with sites of British reprisals in the period 1919–21 highlighted. See *An Phoblacht*, 4 Nov. 1933. **after Poppy Day** Jacob described Ryan and others as 'awful babies really' for their eager plans for conflict on Poppy Day. This activity was not risk free however and in 1930 she described how Ryan 'had his face battered in'. Entries, Jacob Diaries, 24 Oct. 1926, Ms 32,582 (58) & 11 Nov. 1930, Ms 32,582 (61) NLI. **in Dublin** Garda report, 7 Nov. 1931 in Jus 8/682 NAI. The attendance at an indoor AIL rally was also described by the gardaí as being mostly 'working class'. Report, 25 Sept. 1930, in Jus 8/682 NAI. **'imperialist bunting'** Among those listed were Hayes, *Conyhgam* and Robinson, Weirs, Brown Thomas and Wests in Grafton St and Trinity College, Prudential and Scottish Insurance companies in College Green. Sinn Féin Anti-Imperialist Committee, September 1928, copy in Humphreys papers, UCDA, P106/2090. **Trinity College** *Irish Times*, 11 Nov. 1932. **into the next decade** Jacob mentions 'women of the separation allowance kind' among the marchers. Entry, 11 Nov. 1930, Jacob Diaries, Ms 32,582 (61) NLI. The gardaí noted an incident where women 'of the street dealing class' objected to the burning of a Union Flag at an AIL rally. Report, 20 Aug. 1928, in Jus 8/682 NAI. **largely meant Protestants** According to one source in 1936 53 per cent of bank officials in the Free State were from Anglo-Irish backgrounds. B. Kissane, 'The not-so amazing case of Irish democracy' in *Irish political studies* 10 (1995) 43–68. **anti-imperialist rallies** *Irish Independent*, 11 Nov. 1930. **every 11 November** *Irish Times*, 11 Nov. 1932. **(and) unemployment** An Open Letter to Ex-Servicemen in *An Phoblacht*, 14 Nov. 1931.

PAGE 73 **'torn down'** *An Phoblacht*, 10 Nov. 1928. **on Remembrance Day** Gilmore claimed to have had a very cordial meeting with Hickie at the Kildare Street Club. Hickie allegedly agreed to move the parades assembly point to the quays so as to avoid passing Trinity College. The Legion had moved its rallying point to Phoenix Park after 1926 to prevent clashes in College Green but Gilmore gives no date for this meeting and violence continued up until 1933. Gilmore Notes, and Leonard, *'Memory'*, p. 102. **to the government** A/Commandant Dan Bryan to C/S, 2 Dec. 1925, in FitzGerald papers, UCDA, P80/849 (11). **'God save the King'** Eoin O'Duffy to Minister for Justice, 21 Sept. 1932, in Jus 8/684 NAI. TCD students had done this since 1919. Leonard, *Memory*, p. 101. **by the commemorations** Chief Superintendent David Neligan to Commissioner, 7 Nov. 1928, and O'Duffy, 21 Sept. 1932. A garda superintendent in Ennis expressed the opinion that 'Imperialistic display' was 'hateful to nine-tenths' of the Irish people, report 12 Nov. 1928. All in Jus 8/684 NAI. **men and fascists** *Irish Independent*, 19 Nov. 1926 **from the gardaí** The organization was formed during the mid 1920s and existed largely as a social club, confining its activities to Remembrance Day. See Jus 8/719 NAI. See *Irish Independent*, 5 Nov. 1928 for photograph of Fascists at Poppy Day parade. **Poppy Day protests** During Oct. 1930 a revolver was taken from a Blackshirt by the IRA in Dublin. Adjt. Dublin Bdge to A/G, 1 October and A/G to Adjt. 9 October 1930, in MTUCDA, P69/153 (161–4). Gilmore later claimed that most of the IRA's Poppy Day activity was focused on the Fascists. This however was simply not the case. Gilmore Notes, **to the event** Eamon Broy, garda commissioner after Feb. 1932, wished to prohibit all but church services. The Department of Justice replied that the government did not wish to give offence to 'the large body of ex-servicemen in this country' and permission should be granted for the march on November 11. Broy to D/J 18 Oct. & Sec. D/J to Broy, 19 Oct. 1932, in Jus 8/684 NAI. **featuring ex-servicemen** See *Republican Congress*, 17 Nov. and *An Phoblacht*, 10 Nov. 1934. **concentrated in Dublin** Garda report, 21 Nov. 1928, in Jus 8/684 NAI. **Imperialist display** A/G to Adjt. Dub. Bdge 9 Oct. 1930, in MTUCDA P69/153 (161) PAGE 74 **'in no way aggressive'** Adjt Drogheda, to A/G, 19 Nov. 1930, in MTUCDA, P69/153 (38). **Kilkenny during 1928** Garda report, 21 Nov. 1928, in Jus 8/684 NAI. **all tar-**

geted The cinema was showing a film called 'Ypres'. *Notes on Events*, in MacEntee papers, UCDA, P67/534 p. 211. **in their areas** A/G to O/C Sth. Dub. Batt., 11 Sept. 1930, in MTUCDA, P69/153 (201). **of the European war'** O/C Dub. Bdge. to Corinthian Cinema, 1 Mar. 1927, in MTUCDA, P69/48 (275). **potential strike breakers** The IRA were not alone in these beliefs about the Boy Scouts. See editorial in *The Nation*, 22 Sept. 1928. O'Duffy also expressed his opposition to the Scouts, to Dept. of Justice, 8 Nov. 1928, in Jus 8/684 NAI. Their role during the General Strike in Britain was described in *An Phoblacht*, 4 Mar. 1927. **in Wicklow and Dublin** Garda reports in Dept. Justice File H 280/37 NAI. The gardaí also believed that the IRA planned to bomb Elvery's sports shop in Dublin because it had a window display for the World Scout Jamboree! Garda report, 7 Dec. 1929, in D/T S 5864 A NAI. **in Herbert Park** *Notes on Events*, P67/534 pp 214–16. **ranks of the IRA** See editorial in *The Nation*, 17 Nov. 1928. **near their target** D/J report, 31 Oct. 1930, in D/T S 5864 A NAI. **Baden Powell version** Letter objecting to Catholic Scouts from Fianna Eireann, in *Irish Independent*, 14 Aug. 1926 and *An Phoblacht*, 14 Oct. 1933. **in the Free State** *An Phoblacht*, 6 June 1931. **from his offices** *Notes on Events*, P67/534 p. 216. There is a file on the Armstrong case in FitzGerald papers, UCDA, P80/851 (8). See also Appendix 6.

PAGE 75 Knights of Columbanus I/O Ulster No. 1 to D/I, 25 April 1926, in MTUCDA, P69/163 (86–94). The British Fascists were a rather more formidable organization north of the border. During 1933 and 1934 they engaged in a number of serious attacks on Catholics in Kilkeel and Belfast. See James Loughlin, 'Northern Ireland and British fascism in the inter-war years' in *Irish Historical Studies*, 116 (Nov. 1995) and *Irish News*, 25 May 1934. **these type of activities** One exception being the destruction of a war memorial in Armagh in 1934, believed to be in retaliation for permission being refused to construct a republican memorial at Carrickmore. See *Northern Whig*, 7 May 1934. **11 November 1929** Adjt. No.1 Area to A/G, 6 Apr. 1930, in MTUCDA, P69/151 (39–41). **widespread casualties** Belfast Telegraph, 11 Nov. 1929. **to produce fatalities** Had the IRA leadership authorized the bombing of people at a memorial service than they surely would have attempted it again, in Belfast or elsewhere. There is no reply to this report in the Twomey papers so it is difficult to judge the context of this plan. Of course 'bomb' could have referred to smoke bombs or other disruptive but non fatal devices. **through violent activity** Col. Dan Bryan and Col. Costello to C/S, 2 & 4 Dec. 1925, in FitzGerald papers, UCDA, P80/849 (11) and (12) **notes of transactions** *Irish Independent*, 8 & 30 July, 18 Aug. and 2 Sept. 1926. **'poorest citizens'** *An Phoblacht*, 16 July 1926 and IRA statement, *Irish Independent*, 18 Aug. 1926. **in the campaign** *Irish Independent*, 8 July, 18 Aug. and 2 Sept. 1926. **in early 1927** Text of undertaking given by moneylenders in Notes of Army Council meeting, 27 Jan. 1927, in MTUCDA, P69/181 (3). **IRA's motivation** Coogan, *The IRA*, pp 47–8. Roughly 6 out of 12 of those raided were Jewish. **not religious prejudice** *An Phoblacht*, 23 July and 13 Aug. 1926.

PAGE 76 'this rotten trade' *An Phoblacht*, 16 July 1926. In a later letter Briscoe informed *An Phoblacht*'s readers that a Liberal Jewish synagogue in London refused membership to moneylenders. 3 Sept. 1926. **carrying out the raids** Figures from *Dáil Eireann report of select committee on the Moneylenders Bill*, 1929, in D/T S 5943 NAI. Briscoe had attempted to introduce a Private Member's Bill to regulate moneylending in 1929. In 1933 he sponsored the Moneylenders Act. *Dáil Report*, p. 2. See also D. Keogh, *Jews in twentieth-century Ireland* (Cork, 1998), pp 89–90. **as far worse** See Kevin C. Kearans, *Dublin tenement life* (Dublin, 1996), pp 31, 146–148, 172, 205 & 215. Also see statement of witness to Dáil Committee above, 'I have no edge on Jewmen, because Irishmen are worse'. p. 55. **anti-Semitic themes** See 'Usury' leaflet distributed by Political Prisoner's Committee in support of IRA members jailed in connection with the raids. The leaflet seems to have been written by Maud Gonne MacBride, who would become more obsessed with this theme during the 1930s. Copy in Humphreys papers, UCDA, P106/1663. **for the raids** It was not until the Second World War that IRA publications began to stress this theme. See for

example *War News*, in Jus 8/752 NAI. There was also a garda suggestion however, of IRA involvement in the launch of the Anti-semitic newspaper *Aontas Gaedheal* during 1935. The evidence however, is vague. See report, 18 June 1935, in Jus 8/406 NAI. **in this period** Kernoff was involved with IRA members in Friends of Soviet Russia during 1930. Garda report, 9 Nov. 1930, in FitzGerald papers, UCDA, P80/905 (8). He also contributed sketches to republican publications and leaflets. See 'Who is George Gilmore?', 1931, in Humphreys papers, UCDA, P106/2430. Gardaí reported that there were two Jewish members along with several IRA figures in the James Connolly Worker's Club. Report, 6 Apr. 1930, in FitzGerald papers, UCDA, P80/916 (2). **Dublin during 1933** See 'Dublin's Hitlerites' in *An Phoblacht*, 1 July 1933. **lenders and debtors** Text of undertaking, 27 Jan. 1927, in MTUCDA, P69/181 (3). **in February 1927** Battn. Council, 4 Batt. Dub. Bdge. to C/S, 3 Dec. 1926, in MTUCDA, P69/47 (22–23). *An Phoblacht*, 11 Feb. 1927. **for it to do so** Instructions to check if moneylenders were still charging exorbitant rates of interest. C/S to O/C Dub Bdge, 16 Mar. 1924 (7) in P69/48 (178). See *An Phoblacht*, 14 June 1930 and motion from South Dublin Battalion to 1933 GAC, in MTUCDA, P69/187 (41). **little actual physical violence** *Irish Independent*, 13 Aug. 1931. **convent was attacked** D. Kennedy, *The widening gulf* (Belfast, 1988), pp 164–5 and *Donegal Vindicator*, 22 Aug. 1931. **from local people** *An Phoblacht*, 15 Aug. 1931.
PAGE 77 were not sectarian *An Phoblacht*, 8 Aug. 1931. **victimization of Protestants** *Irish Independent*, 24 Aug. 1931. **government supporters** *Leitrim Observer*, 18 July 1931. **widespread consternation** *Meath Chronicle*, 18 July 1931. **reinforcements arrived** *An t-Óglách*, Oct. 1931. **'contemptible blackguards'** *Leitrim Observer*, 22 Aug. 1931. **names of the IRA** *An t-Óglách*, Oct. 1931, in MTUCDA, P69/263 (9). **of the IRA** Five men were lured from their homes, and then blindfolded and chained to the City Market's Gates in Armagh for 'using the name IRA to which they have no connection.' RUC report, 11 Sept. 1931, HA/32/1/584 in PRONI. **by these events** *An t-Óglách*, Oct. 1931, in MTUCDA, P69/263 (9). **sectarian clashes** O/C Tirconaill No. 2 to C/S, 4 July and reply, 6 July 1932, in MTUCDA, P69/52 (112–3). Also p. 146 below. **IRA intervention** P.J. Neary to C/S, 27 Oct. 1932 & C/S to Neary, 5 Jan. 1933, in MTUCDA, P69/53 (343–55).
PAGE 78 covered with posters *Irish Press*, 18 July 1932. **hall was targeted** *An Phoblacht*, 2 Feb. 1935. For republican attitudes to Freemasons see Murray, *Oracles of God*, pp 274–80, 307 & 415. **never physically targeted** Indeed Twomey himself did not adhere to conspiracy theories about the power of the Freemasons. See p. 68 below. **'force of arms'** Constitution of Oglaigh na h-Éireann, Mar. 1932, in MacEntee papers, UCDA, P67/524 (10–14). **in the civil war** There were an estimated 150 unofficial killings of anti-Treatyites during the civil war. O'Halpin, *Defending Ireland*, pp 35–6. **attitude towards them** D/I report, 9 Aug. 1924, in MTUCDA, P69/179 (122).
PAGE 79 within the IRA Draft document on IRA policy within the GAA, 1925, in MTUCDA, P69/73 (73–4). **by IRA members** *An t-Óglách*, Jan. 1929, in Jus 8/681 NAI. **with the IRA** *An Phoblacht*, 16 May 1931. **republicans arrested** *Irish Independent*, 16, 17 and 18 Nov. 1926. Garda Hugh Ward was killed in Tipperary and Sergeant James Fitzsimons in Cork. See Appendix 6. **had not resisted** *Irish Independent*, 24 Nov. 1926. **Volunteers and arms'** 'Mr Ambrose' (Jim Killeen), 'General outline of the present movement', Aug. 1927, in MTUCDA, P69/72 (3–14). **down on the IRA** *Irish Independent*, 17 and 19 Nov. 1926. **to be satisfactory** The Battalion Council of the Dublin 4th Batt. threatened to resign. O/C 4th Batt. to C/S, 11 Dec. 1926, in MTUCDA, P69/47 (22–3).
PAGE 80 exploit this publicity *Notes on events*, P67/534, pp 212–13. Maud Gonne MacBride produced a detailed report on the Waterford events for the IRA see MTUCDA, P69/197 (43–9). **complaints signalled** Garda Commissioner report, 6 April 1929, in FitzGerald papers, UCDA, P80/851 (5). **violence being used** O/C West Clare to D/I, 3 Dec. 1926, in MTUCDA, P69/193 (80–3) **in west Clare** Report on west Clare by Staff Captain 'McAuley', 25 Nov. 1930, in MTUCDA, P69/153 (67). **response to this** The garda killed was Det. Tadg O'Sullivan. O'Duffy to Ministers, 5 July 1929, in Blythe papers,

UCDA, P24/477. **by local factors** The atmosphere of hatred that existed between the IRA and the gardaí in west Clare is described by Brady, *Guardians*, pp 152–4. **of their members** D/J report, 8 Nov. 1930, in D/T S 5864 A NAI. **to their plight** A/G to O/C Dublin Bdge. 17 Feb. 1930, in MTUCDA, P69/152 (203).

PAGE 81 a month later Garda reports in O'Duffy to Secretary Department of Justice, 27 July 1931, in D/T S 5864 B NAI and *Kerry Champion*, 18 July 1931. **sports day in Letterkenny** *Donegal Vindicator*, 15 Aug. 1931. **against their officers** O'Duffy claimed that superintendent Seán Curtin had, by getting IRA members to give evidence, accomplished 'something a Irish policeman has not done for at least one hundred years'. O'Duffy to Ministers, 27 July 1931, FitzGerald papers, UCDA, P80/856 (16). **the IRA** See reports from chief superintendents in Kerry and West Cork, 24 June 1931, in FitzGerald papers, UCDA, P80/857 (37). **gardaí nationwide** Garda report, 1 Sept. 1931, in S 5864 A NAI. **garda resolve** Twomey to McGarrity, 26 June 1931, in McGarrity papers, Ms 17,490 NLI. **Easter Sunday** Commissioner O'Duffy to Ministers, 27 July 1931, in FitzGerald papers, UCDA, P80/856 (22). **amongst its members** AC to Commander of each Independent Unit, 27 Oct. 1931, in D/T S 5864 C NAI. **by gardaí** AC correspondence book, 16 Oct. 1931, 21 Jan. 1932, in MTUCDA, P69/71 & O/C North Clare to A/G, 29 Feb. 1932, in MTUCDA, P69/155 (277). **congestion of the lungs** *Notes on events*, MacEntee papers, UCDA, P67/534, p. 8. **through ill-treatment** A/G condolences to T. Vaugh, 16 Feb. 1932, in MTUCDA, P69/155 (296). **behaved as it liked** Brady, *Guardians*, pp 172–5. O'Halpin, *Defending Ireland*, pp 112–13.

PAGE 82 such searches Adjt. Leitrim to A/G, 6 Oct. 1932, in MTUCDA, P69/156 (62–5). **were in power** Entry in Jacob Diaries, 19 June 1932, Ms 32, 582 (69) NLI. **to be dissolved** Twomey to Neenan, 15 Sept. 1932, in MTUCDA, P69/185 (195–9). **to avoid conflict** C/S to O/C Cork No. 1 Bdge, 10 Sept. 1932, in MTUCDA, P69/155 (39). **'bad battering'** C/S to O/C Cork No. 1 Bdge, 16 Nov. 1932, in MTUCDA, P69/155 (33–4). **his head at home'** Garda reports, 11 & 15 Nov. 1932, in Jus 8/684 NAI. **was fired on** *Notes on events*, P67/534 pp 12 and 17. **local IRA members** Garda report, 16 July 1933, in Jus 8/213 NAI. **rail strike** *Notes on events*, P67/534 p. 12. **officers in the town** A detective sergeant was wounded in Tralee on 17 Mar. Two uniformed gardaí were shot in Grafton Street on 23 Mar. Another uniformed guard was shot by the IRA in Leeson Street during May 1935. *Notes on events*, P67/534, pp 35–7 & 41.

PAGE 83 occasions See 'Protect your prisoners' (nd) in D/T S 5864 A NAI. **around his neck** *Notes on Events*, P67/534 pp 214 & 217. **during late 1930** A/G (National Army) to Minister for Defence, 26 Nov. 1930, in FitzGerald papers, UCDA, P80/851 (27). **in 1931 and 1936** *Notes on Events*, pp 17 and 55. *Irish Independent*, 22 June 1931, *Kerry Champion*, 14 Oct. 1933, *Irish Press*, 22 June 1936. **during 1934** *Limerick Leader*, 31 Dec. 1934. **'Black and Tans'** 'To the soldiers of the Free State Army' 1931, in D/T S 5864 C NAI. **rail strike** See p. 151 below. **during 1934** HMS *Tenedos* was fired on with rifles on 19 May, allegedly by Tom Barry among others. *Notes on Events*, MacEntee papers, UCDA, p. 53. **against imperialism** *Irish Press*, 26 Mar. 1936. Seán Russell subsequently claimed Sommerville was 'executed' by the IRA. *New York Daily News*, 15 Aug.1936, in Jus 8/802 NAI. An account of the affair, from a relative of one of the IRA men involved is given in Joseph O'Neill's *A blood dark track* (London, 2000) **allies of the Blueshirts** See M. O'Riordan, *Connolly column* (Dublin, 1979) pp 34–5. Manus O'Riordan, 'The struggle against fascism in Dublin', in H.G. Klaus (ed.), *Strong words, brave deeds* (Dublin, 1994) p. 220. G. Gilmore, *The Irish Republican Congress* (Cork, 1978) p. 58. Contemporary accounts in letters by Frank Ryan and George Gilmore to *Irish Press*, 1 May 1936 and Brian O'Neill, 'Dublin Strike Episode' in *Left Review*, June 1935. **than is often allowed** Garda reports on the storming of Connolly House in Mar. 1933 stress that the 5,000 strong crowd who assembled was "made up of persons of different walks of life in the city, including a very large percentage of respectably dressed young women." Report, 30 Mar. 1933, in Jus 8/711 NAI. **alternately as thugs** Kearns, *Dublin tenement life*, pp 55–7, 66–8, 77–8, 126, 153. **autumn of 1934** See p. 54 below.

PAGE **84 Dublin city centre** *An Phoblacht*, 29 Sept. 1934. Kearns, *Dublin Tenement Life*, pp 66–8. **used by both sides** Garda report, 12 Sept. 1934, in Jus 8/67 NAI. See also *Cork Examiner*, 12 Sept. 1934. *Irish Press* **dispute** Report on *An Phoblacht* sales, May 1932, in MTUCDA, P69/52 (175). *An Phoblacht*, 25 Oct. 1932. See also *Republican File*, 5 Dec. 1931. **challenge themselves** Garda report, 12 Sept. 1934, in Jus 8/67 NAI. **not to be ruled out** Entry in Jacob Diaries, 6 Sept. 1934, Ms 32,582 (26) NLI. **with the Blueshirts** Because of the rapid number of name changes forced upon the movement, largely through official suppression I have used the term ACA until 1933 and then Blueshirts to describe the organization. Founded as the Army Comrades Association in February 1932, the organization adopted the blueshirt as a uniform in February 1933. In July 1933 it was re-named the National Guard. In September that year, the United Ireland Party (Fine Gael) was founded and the National Guard became the Young Ireland Association. In December 1933 this became the League of Youth See Cronin, *Blueshirts and Irish politics*, pp 17–27. **of the IRA** See F.S.L. Lyons, *Ireland since the Famine* (London, 1971) pp 527–36. Lee, *Ireland*, pp 179–81, and Regan, *Irish counter-revolution*, pp 325–72. **in every local area** D/I to O/C Offaly, 17 Sept. 1932 in P69/199 (65–8). A/G to Adjt, Caherciveen Battn. 19 Sept. 1932 in MTUCDA, P69/158 (176). **as the irregulars** See for example Adjt Caherciveen to A/G, 10 Sept. 1932, in MTUCDA, P69/158 (178). Chief Superintendent, Tipperary, June 1932, in Jus 8/446 NAI. The information contained in IRA intelligence reports on the ACA is of value to anyone studying the emergence of the Blueshirt movement.

PAGE **85 would 'fizzle out'** Twomey to Con Neenan, 15 Sept. 1932, in MTUCDA, P69/185 (195–9). Twomey described many ACA members as the 'shopkeeper's son type', many of whom had never been 'in any army!' **Killmallock, Co. Limerick** See p. 137 below. **ACA's membership** *An Phoblacht*, 10 Sept. 1932. **for their activities** *An Phoblacht*, 15 Oct. 1932. **conflict was avoided** *Irish Press*, 13 Dec. 1932. **later that month** Ryan was speaking at the Anti-Imperialist League rally of Nov. 1932. *Irish Independent*, 11 Nov. 1932. Chairman AC to IRA Executive, 18 Nov. 1932, in MTUCDA, P69/155 (30). **the ACA was finished** Chairman AC to Secretary Clan na Gael, 13 Feb. 1933, in MTUCDA, P69/185 (88). **the ACA at all** Statement, 18 Feb. 1933, in MTUCDA, P69/187 (1–3). **in dealing with them** Notes of 1933 GAC, in MTUCDA, P69/187 (82–3). **a mass movement** Cronin, *Blueshirts and Irish politics*, p. 21 and M. Manning, *The Blueshirts* (1972) pp 77–9. **mass march in Dublin** Regan, *Irish counter-revolution*, pp 336–7. **on the brink of collapse** *An Phoblacht*, 26 Aug. 1933. **come to power** Although *An Phoblacht* had referred to the 'Fascist or white army' as early as 10 Sept. 1932. **had used tear gas** *Notes on Events*, P67/534 p. 17 and *Kerry Champion*, 14 Oct. 1933.

PAGE **86 with the Blueshirts** Tom Barry, quoted in *An Phoblacht*, 9 Dec. 1933. **no 'local feuds'** Twomey to McGarrity, 26 Oct. 1933, in McGarrity papers, Ms 17,490 NLI. **to the disorder** *Kerry Champion*, 10 Feb. 1934. **not the way forward** *An Phoblacht*, 17 Feb. 1934. **of the capitalist system** *An Phoblacht*, 5 May 1934. **financiers of the organization** Garda report, Roscommon, 22 May 1934, in Jus 8/313 NAI. **challenge to 'imperialism'** *Kerry Champion*, 28 July 1934. **had declined perceptibly** Much of the violence was directed against rate collectors, and occasionally gardaí and Fianna Fáil members. Reports in Jus 8/355 NAI. **received from Dublin** O/C Kildare to A/G, Sept. 1932, in MTUCDA, P69/156 (126). **'hunt them out of the place'** Adjt. Castlegregory to A/G, 7 Nov. 1932, in MTUCDA, P69/156 (16). **against the government** Adjt. North Mayo to A/G, 2 Aug. 1932, in MTUCDA, P69/158 (238).

PAGE **87 of the local ACA** Adjt. Caherciveen to A/G, 10 Sept. 1932, in MTUCDA, P69/158 (178). **the work of the ACA** O/C Sligo to C/S, 27 Oct. 1932, in MTUCDA, P69/158 (67–9). **one of its members** O/C Mayo to A/G, 19 Sept. 1932, in MTUCDA, P69/158 (151–62). See also Chapter Two. **came from the ACA** Robert Briscoe TD and Frank Fahy TD were the source of this information. Dub. Bdge. I/O to D/I, 28 Sept.1932, in MTUCDA, P69/199 (35). **Blueshirt activities** *Notes on Events*, P67/534. p. 11. **a year later** *Offaly Independent*, 1 Apr. 1933 and p. 139. **in early November** Chairman AC to

Secretary Clan, 8 November 1932, in MTUCDA, P69/185 (154–6). **two local youngsters** O/C North Mayo to A/G, 20 and 22 January 1933, in MTUCDA, P69/53 (121–4). **and rather aggressive** Chairman AC to Secretary Clan na Gael, 21 Mar. 1933, in MTUCDA, P69/185 (55). **to defend his men** Notes of 1933 GAC, in MTUCDA, P69/187 (114–15). **PAGE 88 in December** Hugh O'Reilly of Bandon. *Notes on Events*, P67/534 pp 17–18. *An Phoblacht*, 4 Nov. 1933 for original case. **accepted as fact** See Bowyer Bell, *Secret army*, pp 107–8 & M. Cronin, 'The Blueshirts in the Irish Free State, 1932–1935: the nature of socialist republican and governmental opposition' in Kirk and McElligot, *Opposing fascism* (Cambridge, 1999), pp 80–96. **for mass carnage?** Twomey writing to McGarrity some weeks later gives no indication that the IRA had planned a major armed operation for 12 August. Twomey to McGarrity, 26 Oct. 1933, Ms 17,490 NLI. Neither do the discussions at the 1934 GAC, MacEntee papers, UCDA, P67/525. **of stones on the day** See claim by Senator Michael Staines, *Seánad Debates*, 22 Aug. 1933, Vol. XVII, pp 1137–39. **larger groups of people** Garda report, 9 Feb. 1934, in Jus 8/108 NAI. **resulted from it** Garda report, 16 Aug. 1934, in Jus 8/36 NAI. **seemed rather abstract** Orders given to meeting of IRA unit commanders, Oct. 1933, see Twomey to McGarrity, 26 Oct. 1933, in McGarrity papers, Ms 17,490 NLI and *An Phoblacht*, 17 Feb. 1934. **due more to accident than design** Michael Laffan argues that the Blueshirts were 'basically defensive and harmless ... less violent than republican extremists, and – with one exception they never killed anyone'. *The resurrection of Ireland* (Dublin, 1999), p. 448. **involving firearms** James Glynn of Ennis, see *Clare Champion*, 5 May 1934. See reports of 30 cases of violence by Blueshirts during 1934 in Jus 8/355 NAI. Blueshirts also carried out sectarian attacks on Protestants in Kerry and Tipperary during July 1935. Garda estimate of gun attacks in Jus 8/446 NAI. **PAGE 89 local Blueshirts** Secretary, Ballynoe FF Cumann, East Cork, to Department of Justice, 10 Oct. 1933, in D/J H306/31 NAI. **a trade union march** Garda report, 23 July 1934. 18 of 20 men arrested were Blueshirts. The gardaí also felt that a fair trial would not occur because the local district justice was of 'Blueshirt tendencies'. Jus 8/167 NAI. **anti-Blueshirt rallies** *Leitrim Observer*, 16 June 1934 and *Kerry Champion*, 16 Dec. 1933. The British Ex-Servicemen's Association in Kerry also condemned the Blueshirts, after O'Duffy referred to Tralee protesters as ex-British soldiers and 'cornerboys'. *Kerry Champion*, 21 Oct. 1933. See also Garda report of Fianna Fáil members joining an IRA parade to a Blueshirt meeting in Dunlavin, Co. Wicklow, 9 Apr. 1934, in Jus 8/315 NAI. **have been spontaneous** See Garda reports, Feb. and Mar. 1934, in Jus 8/258 NAI. **and their enemies** Cronin, *Blueshirts and Irish Politics*, pp 156–8 **to attack the IRA** De Valera in Tralee, *Kerry Champion*, 23 Dec. 1933 and Twomey to McGarrity, 26 Oct. 1933, Ms 17,490 NLI. **against the Blueshirts** Gilmore, *Irish Republican Congress*, p. 15. **in their localities** O'Farrell led 200 IRA men into Mohill where they burnt a platform erected for a Blueshirt rally. *Leitrim Observer*, 5 May 1934. **crush the IRA** Notes of 1934 GAC, in MacEntee papers, UCDA, P67/525. **conflict with them** Kerry IRA leader Seán Ryan, quoted in *Kerry Champion*, 2 Dec. 1933. 'How Fascism must be Fought' in *Republican Congress*, 27 Oct. 1934. In many cases the arguments that the Blueshirts were both fascists and the old enemy from the Civil War were used interchangeably.

PAGE 90 for rapprochement A disgusted Blueshirt prisoner complained that his superior officer in Arbour Hill was co-operating with the IRA inmates. K. Holland to Director General, League of Youth, 3 June 1935, in Aiken papers, UCDA, P104/2801 (67–8). **already unlikely alliance** Despite garda speculation after the appearance of 'up the IRA' and 'up O'Duffy' graffiti in Ballaghdeeren in 1933. Garda report, 13 October 1933, in Jus 8/715 NAI. O'Duffy also told his followers in July 1934 that there were 'some good men in the IRA'. *Kerry Champion*, 7 July 1934. See also McGarry, *Irish Politics and Spanish Civil War*, pp 20–1. **it was disowned** Mrs Frances McGrory was injured when a mine was thrown into her house in February 1934. She died in April. Her son, a Fine Gael supporter, had been involved in a dispute with the local IRA. *An Phoblacht* 'unhesitatingly' condemned the 'deplorable' outrage in Dundalk. *AP*, 17 Feb. 1934. **in July 1932** Confidential record of

meetings with Fianna Fáil, sent to O/C Cork No. 1 Bdge, 19 July 1932, in MTUCDA, P69/52 (54–7). **would be behind it** Twomey to McGarrity, 26 Oct. 1933, in McGarrity papers, Ms 17,490 NLI. **into its ranks** Barry at the 1933 GAC, MTUCDA, P69/187 (113). **1933 Convention** Notes of 1933 GAC, MTUCDA, P69/187 (82) and (114). **launched in 1934** There was a long period of financial wrangling as Aiken's ambitious original plan of Nov. 1932 was considered too costly See Dept of Finance memorandum, 25 Sept. 1933, in D/T S 6327 NAI. **burn their halls'** Notes of 1934 GAC, MacEntee papers, UCDA, P67/525 The gardaí believed the IRA were planning to do this in Roscommon during late 1934 Garda report, 14 Dec. 1934, in Jus 8/144 NAI. **to the IRA** Seán O'Farrell and Tom Barry, Notes of 1934 GAC, in MacEntee papers, UCDA, P67/525. **promoters of the volunteers** 'Young Irishmen beware', Jan. 1934, copy in Jus 8/738 NAI.
PAGE 91 members in Longford Listed in AC Correspondence Book, in Aiken papers, UCDA, P104/2854 (1), (4), (23), (24) and Garda report, 27 Nov. 1934, in Jus 8/68 NAI. **raided in Roscommon** Notes on Events, P67/534 pp 29 and 31. **local IRA** Notes on Events, P67/534 pp 27–31 and *Kerry Champion*, 10 Nov. and 1 and 8 Dec. 1934. **armed men** *An Phoblacht*, 29 Sept. 1934 and Notes on Events, P67/534 pp 26 and 29. **attacks on volunteers** See Notes on Events, P67/534 pp 26–31. **violence of their own** The Blueshirts also occasionally attacked the Volunteers, see report of Nov. 1934 in Jus 8/355 NAI. **had been disobeyed** Their former comrades in the Republican Congress denounced the IRA's 'silly attacks' on the 'neighbourhood lads' of the Volunteers. *Republican Congress*, 26 June 1935. **to bear this out** A/G to O/C Listowel 17 Dec. 1934, in Jus 8/319 NAI. **concentrated in that county** See Chapter One pp 28–29 and garda report, 8 Jan. 1935, in Jus 8/201 NAI.

Chapter Five

PAGE 93 the Second Dáil See Bowyer Bell, *Secret Army*, pp 52–3, and English, *Radicals*, pp 66–71. **Fianna Fáil's resistance** See p. 116 below. **to hold his seat** Gallagher, *Irish elections*, pp 57–94. List of officers who disobeyed General Order No. 28, May 1927, in MTUCDA, P69/149 (6) and Appendix 9. Tom Maguire explained his standing down in R. Ó Brádaigh, '*Dílseacht' – the story of General Tom Maguire and the Second Dáil* (Dublin, 1997) p. 30. **lost their seats** Gallagher, *Irish Elections*, pp 92–3. The absence of Traynor and Stack from the list of IRA officers indicates that they had left the organization before 1927. **out of Sinn Féin** See *An Phoblacht*, 24 Sept., 5 and 29 Oct. 1927 for debate on these issues between Peadar O'Donnell and Mary MacSwiney
PAGE 94. in political circles Garda report, 15 Dec. 1927 in Jus 8/675 NAI. **with the IRA** J.J. O' Kelly was Sinn Féin president from 1926 until 1931. He had been editor of the *Catholic Bulletin*, president of the Gaelic League and Minister for Education in the First Dáil. Brian O'Higgins became president in 1931. He had been a TD for Clare from 1918 to 1927. In 1923 he received the lowest ever first preference vote (114) for a successful candidate in a Dáil election. He ran a newsagents in Dublin which specialized in republican greeting cards. O'Higgins was succeeded as president by Fr Michael O'Flanagan in 1933. **in *An Phoblacht*** MacSwiney to Twomey, 8 June 1933, in Mary MacSwiney papers, UCDA, P48a/59 (30). Three years earlier Sinn Féin had complained that the editor of *An Phoblacht* 'just publishes what suits him'. SF to MacSwiney, 16 Dec. 1930, in P48a/46 (3). **to publicize its view** The Kerry-based Honourable Albina Broderick, sister of the earl of Midleton, who gaelicized her name and became a fiercely orthodox republican. She was also a member of Cumann na mBan until 1933. **anti-imperialist protests** Count Plunkett and Austin Stack apparently believed that it was a breach of honour to withhold the Annuities. See MacEoin, *Survivors*, p. 396. **had betrayed it** Mick Price, Seán MacBride and Frank Ryan attended the 1929 ard fhéis but did so only as observers. Garda report, 8 December 1929 in Jus 8/675 NAI. **mix with people** *Irish Independent*, 1 Dec. 1930. **Free**

State election See MacEoin, *Survivors*, p. 52. **in 1931** SF claimed to have 71 Cumainn in Ireland and Britain in 1929. Garda reports, 10 Dec. 1929 and 5 Oct. 1931 in Jus 8/675 NAI. **'Free State' organizations** Sinn Féin Standing Committee to MacSwiney, 25 June 1931 in MacSwiney papers, UCDA, P48a/48 (25–6) and *Irish Freedom*, June 1931. **to that idea** O/C Dublin Brigade to A/G, 14 Mar. 1931 in MTUCDA, P69/151 (174). 17 Garda report, 2 Nov. 1931 in Jus 8/675 NAI. **of proclaimed organizations** Garda report, 6 Oct. 1931 in Jus 8/675 NAI. **road of abstention'** *Irish Freedom*, Feb. 1932.

PAGE 95 citizens are concerned Twomey to Count Plunkett, 19 January 1932 in MTUC-DA, P69/52 (242–4). **in the west** O/C South Mayo to A/G, 1 Aug. 1932, in MTUCDA, P69/158 (161–2). Maguire occupies an exalted position for republican legitimists, as the only survivor of the Second Dáil who refused to endorse any moves towards constitutional politics, in 1946, 1969 or 1986. In reality he was an inactive, marginal figure during the 1930s. **'gone Fianna Fáil'** C/S to MacSwiney, 8 Apr. 1933, in MTUCDA, P69/53 (160) **not their party** MacSwiney to C/S, 12 Apr. 1933, in MTUCDA, P69/53 (157–8). **'added insult to injury'** Brian O'Higgins to MacSwiney, 12 Apr. 1933, in MacSwiney papers, UCDA, P48a/49 (3). **beyond reason** Cumann na mBan Convention Notes, 10 and 11 June 1933, in MacSwiney papers, UCDA, P48a/17. **militant republicanism** *Irish Freedom*, July 1933. **government of the Republic** MacSwiney to J.J. O'Kelly, 20 Nov. 1933, in MacSwiney papers, UCDA, P48a/59 (32). **its own dictatorship** Seán O'Deorain to MacSwiney, 4 June 1934 in MacSwiney papers, P48a/246 (3). **any concrete result** SF Meeting with IRA, 4 Oct. 1935 in MacSwiney papers, UCDA, P48a/51 (2). **play this role** The Cumann Poblachta na hÉireann, launched in March 1936. See *Notes on Events*, MacEntee papers, UCDA P67/534 p. 49. **republican principles** *Irish Independent*, 11 Nov. 1935. **by that stage** MacSwiney to J.J. O'Kelly, 19 Nov. 1935, in MacSwiney papers, P48a/60 (16a). **to hold theirs unhindered** Garda report, 10 Aug. 1936, in Jus 8/1053 NAI.

PAGE 96 bye-election there Report in Blythe papers, 5 July 1929, UCDA, P24/477. **the party in 1933** Standing Committee, Sinn Féin Ard Fheis, 1 Oct. 1933, in MacSwiney papers, P48a/49 (8). **Sinn Féin instead** O/C Monaghan Batt, 16 Mar. 1931, in MTUCDA, P69/151 (155). **its 'political arm'** Clar, General Army Convention 1933, in MTUCDA, P69/53 (276). **party was boycotting** *An Phoblacht*, 2 Dec. 1933. **one Holy Catholic Church** SF Standing Committee, 'A remonstrance to Pope Pius XI', 16 Dec. 1929, copy in Jus 8/675 NAI. **spiritual and unselfish'** O'Higgins to SF meeting, quoted in *Irish Press*, 2 Nov. 1931 and Padraig O'Tuile, *Life and times of Brian O'Higgins* (Navan, nd) p. 21. **Eucharistic Congress** Garda report, 5 Oct. 1931 in Jus 8/675 NAI. **'unscrupulous Jews'** J.J. O'Kelly, *The Sinn Féin outlook* (Dublin, 1930) p. 15. In later years O'Kelly's racism would grow more vicious. See, for example, his praise for Hitler rescuing Germany from the 'Jewish white slave trade' in O' Kelly, *Stepping stones* (Dublin, 1939?) p 23. **president in 1933** See Denis Carroll, *They have fooled you again* (Dublin, 1993) & *Unusual suspects* (Dublin, 1998), pp 205–46. **interference in politics** Garda report, 5 Oct. 1931, in Jus 8/675 NAI. See also Murray, *Oracles of God*, pp 306–10. **party in protest** See Carroll, *Unusual suspects*, pp 236–8. MacSwiney explained her resignation, 10 Dec. 1937, in MacSwiney papers, P48a/53 (3). **January 1936** Carroll, *Unusual suspects*, p. 241.

PAGE 97 influence of the left See also McHugh, *Voices of the rearguard* pp 493–4 **in their image** *Irish Freedom* ceased publication in August 1937 to make way for the *Wolfe Tone Weekly*. See also Pat Walsh, *Irish republicanism and socialism* (Belfast, 1994), p. 37. **of its exponents** Marie Comerford found Brian O'Higgins a 'bitter little man ... always ready with a graveside speech, yet he scarcely volunteered himself'. MacEoin, *Survivors*, p. 53. Twomey was less scathing, allegedly calling O'Higgins just an 'old fogey'. Military Intelligence File, 5 Feb. 1942 in G2/X/0058, MA **for their authority** The seven were Tom Maguire, Mary MacSwiney, J.J. O'Kelly, Count Plunkett, Professor Stockley, Brian O'Higgins and Cathal Ó Murchadha. See Bell, *Secret army*, pp 154–5 and English, *Radicals*, pp 257–9. The republican legitimist view of this event is given in O'Bradaigh, *Dílseacht*, pp 37–43. **whatever way possible** Cumann na mBan Constitution, 1934, in Sighle

Humphreys papers, UCDA, P106/1126 (5). **Table 12** Cumann na mBan Convention, 18 Nov. 1925, in Humphreys papers UCDA, P106/1136 (1136). **the following year** Margaret Ward, *Unmanageable revolutionaries* (London, 1995). pp 201–2. **as vice president** Cumann na mBan Convention, 4 and 5 Dec. 1926 in Humphreys papers, P106/1144 (1–10).

PAGE 98 for the next decade Coyle (1897–1985) was from Donegal. She was involved in Cumann na mBan from 1917. She was imprisoned and escaped from Mountjoy during 1921, and endured a hunger strike during the civil war. She worked in the Irish Hospital Sweep Stakes. She married Saor Éire activist Bernard O'Donnell. Humphreys (1899–1994) came from a Kerry republican family. She was jailed after the capture of Ernie O'Malley in her family home in November 1922, and endured a 31-day hunger strike. She was imprisoned on three occasions between 1926 and 1932. She was joint treasurer of Saor Éire, and on the executive of the Boycott British committee. She married IRA officer Donal O'Donoghue in February 1935. See O'Malley *Notebooks*, UCDA, P17b/91. See also MacEoin, *Survivors*, for Coyle, pp 151–60 and Humphreys pp 331–53. *An Phoblacht* Just 3 branches out of 74 at the 1935 convention, in Humphreys papers, UCDA P106/1152 (1–8). Donnelly edited the first edition of *The Last Post* in 1932. **just 50 members** Cumann na mBan report, 27 Feb. 1928 in Humphreys papers, UCDA, P106/1147 (1–2). **within 12 months** Suggestions for future activities of Cumann na mBan, (N/D) captured by gardaí in raid on Humphreys home, 30 January 1929 in FitzGerald papers, UCDA, P80/879 (2). **during 1931** List of Revolutionary Organizations, Apr. 1931, in D/T S 5864 A, NAI. Cumann na mBan members were allowed attend the IRA convention that year. Humphreys memoir, Humphreys papers, UCDA, P106/1426 (8). **military tribunal** Maeve Phelan and Kathleen Merrigan were jailed along with Humphreys. See *Republican File*, 9 Jan. 1932. **Cumann na gCailíní** Cumann na mBan Convention, 10 and 11 June 1933 in MacSwiney papers, UCDA, P48a/17. **organization's strength** Draft Constitution for Mná na Poblachta, in MacSwiney papers, UCDA, P48a/11 (3). **by the gardaí** Garda reports, 1933 and 1934 in Jus 8/317 and Jus 8/717 NAI. **27 branches** Cumann na mBan Convention, 15 and 16 Sept. 1934, in Humphreys papers, UCDA, P106/1152 (1–8). **marched in uniform** Garda superintendent's estimate, 19 June 1934, in Jus 8/310 NAI. **showing off a uniform'** Cumann na mBan Convention, 1936, in Eithne Coyle O'Donnell papers, UCDA, P61/7 (a).

PAGE 99 interested in this Cumann na mBan examination entrants, June 1936, in Humphreys papers, P106/1239. **'the domestic servant type'** Chief Superintendent, Thurles, 30 Apr. 1934, in Jus 8/317 NAI. **republican colours'** Fiona Plunkett and Sighle Humphreys to all Branch Secretaries, 15 Mar. 1926, in Humphreys papers, UCDA, P106/1138 (1). **Poppy Day** Cumann na mBan to An Timthire, Clan na Gael, 23 Dec. 1929, in McGarrity papers, Ms 17,534 (3) NLI. The extent to which the Easter Lily campaign was consciously emulating the sale of poppies is emphasized in *An t-Óglách*, Mar. 1931, in MTUCDA, P69/263 (7). **do little at Easter** HQ Cork No. 1 Brigade to A/G, 5 Feb. 1930 in MTUCDA, P69/152 (221). **west Limerick 5,000** Staff Officer 'J.J. to C/S', and O/C west Limerick to A/G, Easter 1930 reports in MTUCDA, P69/152 (153–61) and (163). **impressive figures** See report to Inspector General RUC, 20 Mar. 1929, for the police attitude to the sale of 'Republican poppies' in HA/32/1/465 in PRONI. **in the Free State** See letter from Fianna Fáil TDs and senators to Minister for Justice, asking that permits be granted for lily sales, letter of 16 Mar. 1932 in Jus 8/699 NAI. **for Ireland's dead'** The profit made from these sales amounted to £648.3.9, which was divided equally with the IRA. Cumann na mBan Convention 1934, Humphreys papers, UCDA, P106/1152 (5). **sold most of them** Cumann na mBan Convention 1933, in MacSwiney papers, UCDA, P48a/17. **administration of justice** Memorandum from W.T. Cosgrave to Bishops, 17 Sept. 1931 in D/T S 5864 B NAI. **(and) Police'** Cumann na mBan Convention, 1926, in Humphreys papers, UCDA, P106/1143. **fellow country men** 'To the Shopkeepers of Ireland' Oct. 1930, in Humphreys papers, UCDA P106/2419.

PAGE 100 be set free 'Ghosts' to each member of the jury panel, Dublin, 20 Apr. 1931, in FitzGerald papers, UCDA, P80/893. **country of the world** Copy in D/T S 5864 B NAI.

written from 'irritation' A/G to Runaidhte Onoracha Cumann na mBan, 30 Nov. 1927, Cumann na mBan to A/G, 2 Dec. 1927, Sighle Humphreys to C/S, 5 December 1927 and C/S to Humphreys, 9 Dec. 1927 all in MTUCDA, P69/67 (1–4). **in 1929** See O'Halpin, *Defending Ireland*, pp 66–8. **some of the leaflets** Report on Ryan, 26 Mar. 1928 and on Humphreys, 23 Aug. 1928 in FitzGerald papers, UCDA, P80/851 (1) and P80/879 (5). **in the legal sphere** Suggestions for future activities of Cumann na mBan, FitzGerald papers, UCDA, P80/879 (2).

PAGE 101 day of the trial Garda report, Bray 22 Nov. 1933 and Detective Branch report, 7 Dec. 1933 in Jus 8/717 NAI. **the prisoners' dependants** Cumann na mBan, Ard Oifig, 11 Oct. 1935, in Jus 8/326 NAI. **a military appearance** Garda report, 22 Mar. 1934, in Jus 8/317 NAI. **on the beret** Cumann na mBan, circular to Branch Secretaries, 2 Nov. 1934, in Humphreys papers, UCDA, P106/1158 (1–2) and 25 May 1935, in Jus 8/326 NAI. **through ballads'** Cumann na gCailíní, Rules in Humphreys papers, UCDA P106/1243 and 1934 Convention report, in Humphreys papers, UCDA, P106/1152 (4). **could train with firearms** Cumann na mBan Convention 1926, in Humphreys papers, UCDA, P106/1143 and P106/1144. **'care and use of arms'** Cumann na mBan Report Form in Humphreys papers, UCDA, P106/1250 (2).

PAGE 102 a Capitalist Republic' Notes for instructors on economics, May 1934 in Humphreys papers, UCDA, P106/1231 (1–3) and Convention 1934 op cit. P106/1152 (7). **factories and shops** Monthly report form in Humphreys papers, UCDA, P106/1250 (2) and 1933 Convention, P48a/17. **1934 convention** Cumann na mBan Convention, 1934, in Humphreys papers, UCDA, P106/1152 (1). **over and done with'** Cora Hughes of UCD. 1933 Convention notes, MacSwiney papers, UCDA, P48a/17. **before the convention** Mary MacSwiney to Eithne ni Cumaill, 13 June 1933, in Coyle O'Donnell papers, UCDA, P61/7 (4). **earned the Fainne** Circular, 11 Oct. 1935 in Jus 8/326 NAI. Although this did not mean that Cumann na mBan leaders were all able to speak Irish themselves. See Chapter Three p. 59. **a common social policy** Cumann na mBan Convention, 1934, in Humphreys papers, UCDA, P106/1152 (6). **Coyle and Humphreys** Call for Congress, 9 Apr. 1934 in Humphreys papers, UCDA, P106/1480 (4). **among others** Meeting between Executive Cumann na mBan and Donal O'Donoghue, Seán MacBride and Jim Killeen (IRA) 18 April 1934 in Humphreys papers, UCDA, P106/1153 (1–4).

PAGE 103 Cumann na mban executive Blathnaid Ni Charthaigh and Sighle Nich an Airchinnigh to Each Branch, 18 May 1934 in Humphreys papers, UCDA, P106/1157. **on both sides** Humphreys would marry IRA A/G Donal O'Donoghue in 1935. Letters from O'Donoghue to Humphreys written while jailed in the Curragh, reveal deep affection and also respect. See O'Donoghue's apology for fellow prisoners use of the term 'Donal's wife'. 12 Apr. 1934, in Humphreys papers, UCDA, P106/1746 (1) **Free State commemorations** Coyle and Humphreys, 18 July 1934, in Humphreys papers, UCDA, P106/1490 (1–2). **'headless' activities** *Republican Congress*, 11 Aug. 1934. **Coyle and Humphrey's decision** There were 12 motions supporting the IRA and 5 supporting Congress at the 1934 Convention, Humphreys papers, UCDA, P106/1152 (1–8).

PAGE 104 *Republican Congress* See Mary Cullen and Maria Luddy (eds), *Female activists, Irish women and change, 1900–1960* (Dublin, 2001) for chapters on Jacob, Molony and Sheehy Skeffington. **and demonstration** Twomey to Joseph McGarrity, 23 June 1931 in McGarrity papers, Ms, 17,490 NLI. **in early 1933** Margaret Ward, *Hannah Sheehy Skeffington*, pp 306–12. **during this period** See MacEoin, *Survivors*, pp 33–55. **IRA prisoners** Ward, *Unmanageable revolutionaries*, pp 190–2. **20 members at most** List of Revolutionary Organizations, Apr. 1931, D/T S 5864 A NAI. **by the gardaí** Usually matters of Maud Gonne's preoccupation's such as 'Financial Freedom' or the conditions in Industrial Schools, Garda report, 10 June 1934. See Jus 8/316, Jus 8/387 and Jus 8/425 NAI. **played at the paper** McHugh, *Voices of the rearguard*, p. 240. **political development** Meeting between IRA and Cumann na mBan, 18 Apr. 1934, Humphreys papers, UCDA, P106/1153 (1–4).

PAGE 105 **during 1930** See *An Phoblacht*, 7 Feb. 1931. **Bodenstown in 1933** Entry, 18 June 1933 in Rosamond Jacob Diaries, Ms, 32,582 (72) NLI. **he decided to remain** Notes of 1934 GAC, in MacEntee papers, UCDA, P67/525. **by the army council** Meeting between O' Donnell and Mick Price with Cumann na mBan Executive, 20 Apr. 1934 in Humphreys papers, P106/1154 (1–5). **army council permission** Notes of 1934 GAC, in MacEntee papers, UCDA, P67/525. **being nationally known** He received 28 votes for the IRA Executive at the 1934 GAC, not enough to secure a place. Notes of 1934 GAC, MacEntee papers, UCDA, P67/525. **September 1932** Gilmore to Chairman, Army Council, 16 Sept. 1932, in MTUCDA, P69/53 (367–9). **social policy** Twomey to Neenan, 28 March 1933, in MTUCDA, P69/185 (21–7). **the Irish communists** Entries, Jacob Diaries, 9 January 1934, 14 August 1934, 26 May 1936. Ms 32,582 (74), Ms 32,582 (75), Ms 32,582 (78) NLI. **leaving the IRA!** He received 36 votes. Notes of 1934 GAC, MacEntee papers, P67/525. **in early 1933** For dispute over *An Phoblacht*, see Ryan to Chairman, AC 1 October 1932 in MTUCDA, P69/55 (54). On communist meeting see A/G to Staff Captain 'O'Reilly' 13 May 1933 and 'O Reilly' to A/G, 14 May 1933, in Humphreys papers, UCDA, P106/2038. **to the GAC** O'Donnell to Cumann na mBan Executive, 20 April 1934, hand-written version, in Humphreys papers, UCDA, P106/2040. **to discuss his plan** Entry, 10 March 1934, Jacob Diaries, Ms32, 582 (74), NLI. **Galway and Mayo** Appeal for Congress, Humphreys papers, UCDA, P106/1480. Officers from list for Donamon training camp, July 1932, MTUCDA, P69/54 (150–155). Seán McGuinness, Offaly O/C, Tom Maguire, North Westmeath O/C, Patrick Norton, South Westmeath O/C, Charles Reynolds, Séamus de Búrca, O/C and Adjutant, Galway, Brian Corrigan, O/C North Mayo. 2nd Lieutenant Patrick Gralton and Section Leader J.J. Hoey, Leitrim. The former Derry City O/C Seamus McCann also endorsed the call. **its quartermaster** George Gilmore Notes, the records of the 1934 GAC list Kelly as O/C of South Dublin. **an overestimation** Coogan mentions a figure of 4,000 defections, *The IRA*, p. 79. Patrick Byrne, former joint secretary of Congress put the number of Congress recruits from the IRA at 'about 6,000 to 8,000' quoted in English, *Radicals*, p. 208. Both these figures are serious overstatements. The number of defectors would certainly be in the hundreds rather than thousands.

PAGE 106 **a new IRA** O'Donnell at meeting with Cumann na mBan Executive, 20 April 1934, in Humphreys papers, UCDA, P106/1154 (4). **Frank Purcell** The organization still had about 200 members with access to 90 firearms in Dublin during 1922. Adjt to Assistant C/S, 26 July 1922, in Humphreys papers, UCDA, P106/1954 (8). McGowan, a 1916 veteran, was one of those who held the organization together through activity in the James Connolly Workers Club. See report of ICA activities during the Civil War in Cowan papers, UCDA, P34/D/45. **ICA army council** Price to Humphreys, 13 and 19 July 1934, in Humphreys papers, UCDA, P106/1489 and P106/1491 (1–2). **in Congress** *Republican Congress*, 18 August 1934. **in October 1934** Notes on Events, P67/534 p. 27. **in June 1934** *Republican Congress*, 23 June 1934. **to the IRA** Patrick Byrne, *The Irish Republican congress revisited* (London, 1994) pp 15–16. Gilmore's *Republican Congress* argues that the ICA enabled men 'used to military formations to keep their units intact', p. 44. **would use them too** Garda report, 24 Sept. 1934, in Jus 8/342 NAI. **not to resist them** O'Donnell to Cumann na mBan Executive, 20 Apr. 1934, in Humphreys papers, P106/1154 (4). **to the town** *Kerry Champion*, 1 Sept. 1934. These men were members of the Republican Labour Party which was the Kerry section of Congress. **from their allegiance** De Búrca to Michael Price, 12 Apr. 1934, in Jus 8/319 NAI. **from the IRA** IRA to the Commander of each Independent Unit, 17 Apr. 1934, in Jus 8/319 NAI.

PAGE 107 **within its ranks** For Hoey see MacEoin, *Twilight Years* pp 607–16. For Mitchell, MacEoin, *Survivors*, pp 379–92. **units lost heavily** Stephen Hayes, 'My Strange Story' in *The Bell*, July 1951 pp 11–16. However, it is possible Peadar O'Donnell may have ghost-written this article and therefore retrospectively given Congress more weight. **members to Congress** *Notes on the Republican Congress Movement*, in MacEntee papers, UCDA,

P67/527 pp 2–3. **lost many members** Garda estimate, 20 June 1934 in Jus 8/310 NAI. See also *Irish Press*, 18 June 1934. **less than 70** Around 50 in Belfast, 10 in Tyrone and 6 in Derry. E. Staunton, *Nationalists of Northern Ireland, 1918–1973* (Dublin, 2001) p. 116. **on Volunteers** I/O Kenmare Battalion to I/O (sic) 18 April 1934, in Jus 8/319 NAI. **in Westmeath and Dundalk** Four Congress members stoood as 'Worker's Republicans.' Tom Maguire took a seat in North Westmeath. The other successful candidate was John O'Byrne. *Notes on Republican Congress*, p. 7 and *Republican Congress*, 30 June 1934. **Twomey and Ryan** 'Fianna Fáil at heart' was Gilmore's judgement on MacBride. He also claimed MacBride was pro-Nazi for a period. Twomey, however, was 'a good man ... always a good friend ... even after we split'. Gilmore Notes **to smash the army** O'Donoghue to Humphreys, 12 April 1935, in Humphreys papers, UCDA, P106/1746 (1). **in the fracas** *An Phoblacht*, 23 June 1934. **to Tone's grave** See Foley, *Legion of the rearguard*, p. 140. and Byrne, *Revisited*, p. 24. **attending the event** Garda report, 19 June 1934, in Jus 8/310 NAI. **was just 36** Detective Branch estimate, 18 June 1934 in Jus 8/310 NAI. Byrne, *Revisited* p. 23. *Northern Whig*, 18 June 1934. **for the task** *Republican Congress*, 23 June 1934. **a role in the attack** 'It was sectarianism but not of the religious kind'. Byrne, *Revisited*, p. 24.
PAGE 108 cause the IRA Entry, Jacob Diaries, 18 June 1934, Ms, 32,582 (75) NLI. **one of the recipients** *Irish Press*, 18 June 1934. **September of 1934** *Republican Congress*, 29 June 1935. **'pleasure to hurt them'** Entry, Jacob Diaries, 23 June 1935, Ms, 32,582 (77) NLI. **republican movement generally** Ryan and Gilmore to Run Onor, Wolfe Tone Commemoration, 13 May 1936, in Humphreys papers, UCDA, P106/ 1864 (9). **a peaceful if uneasy one** Twomey to Humphreys, 11 June 1934 in Humphreys papers, UCDA, P106/2120 for Castlecomer incident and *Republican Congress*, 17 Nov. 1934 for the Belfast affair. **condemned the incidents** Entry, Jacob Diaries, 14 Apr. 1936, in Ms 32,582 (78) NLI. *An Phoblacht*, 18 Apr. 1936. **it would be unarmed** *Notes on Events*, p. 51. Bill Gannon, Jack Nalty, Larry O'Connor and Bill Scott were among the members of the 'Defence Corps'. Nalty died fighting with the International brigades in Spain. **Bacon shops strike** *Notes on Republican Congress Movement*, pp 7–8. **in their locality** A/G to Commander each Independent Unit, 31 August 1934 in Jus 8/319 NAI. See *An Phoblacht*, 8 Dec. 1934 for list of prisoners. Reporting even the existence of prisoners from an organization that had split from the IRA would subsequently be unheard of in republican publications. **protest in Dublin** *Notes on the Republican Congress movement*, MacEntee papers, UCDA, P67/527, p. 14.
PAGE 109 his political views *An Phoblacht*, 12 and 19 Jan. 1935. MacEoin, *Survivors*, p. 10–11 and Murray, *Oracles of God*, pp 337–8. **left in Congress** Various accounts in *Notes on Republican Congress*, pp 12–14, English, *Radicals*, pp 216–31, and Bowyer Bell, *Secret Army*, p. 117. **to which he belonged** ICA *Army Council Bulletin*, Nov. 1934. **armed force in Ireland** Garda report, 7 May 1929, in FitzGerald papers, UCDA, P80/906 (2). **magic wand'** R.J. Connolly, A/G ICA, 20 Nov. 1934, in Jus 8/320 NAI. **Irish Worker's Voice** *Republican Congress*, 8 Dec. 1934, *Irish Worker's Voice*, 1 Dec. 1934. **by his followers** ICA *Army Council Bulletin*, 16 Jan. 1935 in Jus 8/322 NAI. **in handling explosives** A/G ICA to Adjutant, Kilkenny, 5 December 1934, in Jus 8/320 NAI. **on the docks** Memoirs of Liam MacGabhann, *Sunday World*, 27 Apr. 1975.
PAGE 110 director of finance Garda report, 18 Nov. 1934, in Jus 8/320 NAI. **to the 'enemy'** ICA GHQ, 4 Sept. 1934, in Jus 8/320 NAI. **the Free State** A/G ICA to Adjutant Kilkenny City Company, 5 Dec. 1934, in Jus 8/320 & ICA GAC, 13 June 1935 in Jus 8/322 NAI. **in Belfast** See Peter Carleton in MacEoin, *Survivors*, pp 304–10. **November 1934** ICA GHQ, 17 Nov. 1934 in Jus 8/320 NAI. **and Russia** ICA GHQ, 4 Apr. 1935 in Jus 8/322 NAI. **Table 13** ICA report, 31 Jan. 1935, in Jus 8/322 NAI. **'which nobody reads'** C/S ICA to Kilkenny City Company, in Jus 8/322 NAI. **unemployment agitation** ICA GAC 13 June 1935, and ICA GHQ to Kilkenny City Company, 23 June 1935 in Jus 8/322 NAI. **workers' republic** Garda report, 6 Nov. 1935 in Jus 8/322 NAI. **as an objective** See Dunphy, *Fianna Fáil power*, pp 200–1. Connolly was a Labour TD for Louth 1943 to 1951 and later Chairman of the party. He supported coalition with Fine Gael and bans on

republican commemorations of the 1916 Rising in 1976. He died in 1980. Browne & Farrell, *Magill*, p. 271. Nora Connolly O'Brien remained a supporter of the republican movement, siding with the Provisionals, and also being associated with the IRSP, until her death in 1981. See N. Connolly O'Brien, *We shall rise again* (London, 1981). **into Labour politics** See his obituary, *Irish Press*, 17 Jan. 1944. **on armed force'** Neither did short lived organizations such as the 'Irish Republican Worker's Guard' four members of whom were charged with riot and possession of firearms in Cork during early 1934. Garda report, 9 Feb. 1934 in Jus 8/318 NAI. **mutiny of 1924** D/I to C/S, 1 May 1926, in MTUC-DA, P69/44 (65).

PAGE 111 involvement with them C/S to IRA Executive, 9 Aug. 1924, in MTUCDA, P69/179 (126–9). **keep away from them** *An t-Óglách*, Apr. 1927, in Jus 8/681 NAI. **Clann Eireann** Army Intelligence had noted the close co-operation between Clann Eireann and the 'Old IRA' during 1926. Eastern command intelligence report, Feb. 1926, in FitzGerald papers, UCDA, P80/847 (174). **March 1924** Regan, *Irish Counter-Revolution*, pp 166–70. **Jim Killeen** A/G to O/C Cork No. 1, 27 September 1930, in MTUCDA, P69/153 (122). **Truce of 1921** *An Phoblacht*, 2 and 9 May 1931. **pre-Truce era** *An Phoblacht*, 16 May 1931 **'National Guard'** C/S to MacSwiney, 25 Mar. 1933, in MTUCDA, P69/53 (95). **in the past** C/S to Dr J.A. Madden, 27 Mar. 1933, in MTUCDA, P69/53 (99). **Donoghue-Deasy clique** Twomey to Con Neenan, 15 Sept. 1932, in MTUCDA, P69/185 (199).

PAGE 112 IRA' bodies C/S to O/C Limerick City Batt, 14 Dec. 1932, in MTUCDA, P69/54 (28–29). See also p. 56 below **as Bodenstown** Clann na nGaedheal National Executive to army council IRA, 6 May 1933, in MTUCDA, P69/53 (60–1). **election rallies** See *Irish Press*, 8 and 15 of May and 8 June 1934 for reports of Old IRA participation in IRA election and anti-Blueshirt meetings. **towards the Republic** Garda report, 17 Dec, 1933 in Jus 8/718 NAI. **Volunteer Reserve** *Irish Independent*, 2 Apr. 1934. **to the IRA** Garda report, 18 Feb. 1934 in Jus 8/718 NAI. Garda report, 30 Nov. 1934 in Jus 8/319 NAI. See also letter in *Irish Independent*, 29 Nov. 1934. The Clann also produced occasional publications such as *Sean Oglach* and *The Sentry*. **from the republic** *Irish Independent*, 30 June 1937. **a potential threat** Several Old IRA members such as Seán Fitzpatrick and Simon Donnelly would later be involved along with their IRA contemporaries of the 1930s in Clann na Poblachta. See Eithne MacDermott, *Clann na Poblachta* (Cork, 1998) pp 10–11.

Chapter Six

PAGE 113 new departure Notes of Statement by C/S, 9 Apr. 1927, in MTUCDA, P69/48 (154). **within the organization** Aiken to Chairman of army council, 18 Nov. 1925, in MTUCDA, P69/181 (77–8). Aiken came ninth in the election for the Executive. See Appendix 7. The IRA were still unsure about Aiken's status within the organization as late as Apr. 1927. See Notes of Army Executive, 27 April, 1927, in MTUCDA, P69/48 (104–5). **council was disbanded** 'Mr Ambrose', General outline of the present movement, August 1927, in MTUCDA, P69/72 (3–11). **the IRA leadership** Agenda for Convention, 1925, in MTUCDA, P69/179 (185–9). **after 1926** Executive membership 1925: T. Derrig, E. O'Malley, M. Kilroy, P.J. Ruttledge, J. O'Connor, S. Robinson, S. MacSwiney, F. Aiken, P. O'Donnell, L. Pilkington, S. Hyde, T. Maguire, C. Maloney, P. Whelan, P. O'Brien, S. Moylan. List in MTUCDA, P69/179 (184). **IRA members arrested** See p. 78 above **with their predicament** QMG to C/S, 4 May 1927, in MTUCDA, P69/48 (47). **IRA's actions** *Cork Examiner*, 23 Nov. 1926.

PAGE 114 to the raids Acting Secretary, AC to Murphy, 8 Dec. 1926 and IRA Executive report, 27 Apr. 1927 in MTUCDA, P6948 (104 5) and (318). **of Fianna Fáil** This trend was already apparent to Military Intelligence in late 1925. See Dan Bryan to C/S, 2 Dec. 1925 in FitzGerald papers, UCDA, P80/849 (11–12). **parliamentary candidates** G.O. 28, 21 Oct. 1926 in MTUCDA, P69/149 (38). See Appendix 8. **Neil Blaney** Disobeyal of General Order No. 28, May 1927 in MTUCDA, P69/149 (6). See Appendix 9. **to stand down** Ó Bradáigh, *'Dílseacht'* p. 30. **its public image** W.T. Cosgrave had quoted G.O. 28 in the Dáil following the capture of IRA documents in November 1926. See *Irish*

Independent, 10 Nov. 1926. A/G to O/C South Galway, (Mark Killelea) 17 May 1927 in MTUCDA, P69/149 (23). **rejoin the IRA** Patrick Houlihan to A/G, 6 May 1927 in MTUCDA, P69/149 (28). **not lost faith** Patrick Smith to A/G, 13 May 1927 in MTUC-DA, P69/149 (22). **were elected** Houlihan lost his seat in 1932, regained it in 1933 and lost again in 1937. Smith held his seat until 1973, and twice served as Minister for Agriculture and as Minister for Local Government. Browne and Farrell, *Magill* p. 43 and p. 57. **in early July** O'Higgins had been described by the IRA as 'the brains of the government'. 'Mr. Ambrose' Outline of the present movement, MTUCDA, P69/72 (14). **to avoid arrest** *An Phoblacht*, 22 July 1927. C/S to local commanders, 29 July 1927 in MTUCDA, P69/50 (27). **Fianna Fáil TD** Staff Commandant 'J. O' Neill' to C/S, 28 July and C/S to Frank Kerlin, 29 July 1927 in MTUCDA, P69/49 (7–8). Kerlin's election in Gallagher, *Irish Elections*, p. 101.

PAGE 115 to Fianna Fáil Report for A/G, 17 Feb. 1930, in MTUCDA, P69/151 (225–27). **Fianna Fáil members** Limerick report, 26 Nov. 1930, in MTUCDA, P69/153 (70–2), Donegal report, 18 Sept. 1930, in MTUCDA, P69/153 (178–83), Kerry report, 18 Jan. 1931, in MTUCDA, P69/153 (18–20). **Fianna Fáil cumann** AC Correspondence book, 11 Jan. 1932, in MTUCDA, P69/71. **and inactivity** Fahy was prosecuted before the military tribunal in early 1932 see *Irish Press*, 11 Feb. 1932. Limerick report, 26 Nov. 1930, in MTUCDA, P69/153 (73). **bring about this** See *Honesty*, 19 Mar. 1927 and statement by C/S, 9 Apr.1927 in MTUCDA, P69/48 (154). **power bloodlessly** C/S to officer's meeting, 9 Apr. 1927 in MTUCDA, P69/48 (152–62).

PAGE 116 about successfully All quotes, C/S, O/C Boyne Batt, O/C Carrick on Shannon, Jack and George Plunkett from officer's meeting, P69/48 (152–62). **carry out a coup** IRA membership had fallen from 14,541 in 1924 to 5,042 in 1926. See pp 9–10 above. **of 31 to 9** Russell voted against the proposals but made it clear he would not work against them if they were accepted. Officers' meeting, P69/48 (152–62). **British government** Memorandum of suggested basis for co-operation between Republican bodies for general election and after if a majority of Republicans are elected, Apr. 1927, in MTUC-DA, P69/48 (35–6). **of a united effort** Joint meeting of representative members of Sinn Féin and representatives of the army council, 14 Apr. 1927, in MTUCDA, P69/48 (116).

PAGE 117 made at the meeting Joint meeting of representative members of Fianna Fáil and of representatives of the army council, 15 April 1927, in MTUCDA, P69/48 (115). **by his executive** Secretary Army Council (AC) to Run Onoracha, Fianna Fáil, 28 Apr., reply, 29 Apr. Secretary AC to Run Onoracha, FF, 3 May, reply 4 May. Secretary AC to de Valera, 11 May, reply, 13 May 1927. All in MTUCDA, P69/48 (29–34). **'Vote Solidly Republican** *An Phoblacht*, 3 June 1927.**repression of republicans** *An Phoblacht*, 19 Aug. 1927. **general election** Although an unamed FF TD did approach the IRA to ascertain their attitude on a possible FF led coalition government. C/S to President, Cumann na mBan, 7 Sept. 1927, in MTUCDA, P69/67 (5).

PAGE 118 friendly political party C/S, 25 Aug. 1927, in MTUCDA, P69/72 (27–8). **reluctantly tolerated** At the 1929 GAC the IRA revised G.O. 28 to outlaw working or voting for parties that entered the Free State or Northern parliaments. See A/G to Commander of each Independent Unit, 12 Jan. 1932 in D/T S 5864 C NAI. **to Fianna Fáil** Garda Commissioner report to Ministers, 5 July 1929, in Blythe papers, UCDA, P24/477. **during elections** Report by 'J.J.', 18 Jan. 1931, in MTUCDA, P69/153 (14–18). **'trumped up charges'** *Irish Independent*, 26 Nov. 1926. **in the country** *Dáil Debates*, Vol. 29, 8 May 1929. **to smear republicans** *Dáil Debates*, Vol. 22, 15 Feb., 1928. **by the CID** *Dáil Debates*, Vol. 29, 9 May 1929. **of the gardaí** *The Nation*, 24 Sept. 1927. The paper was edited by Seán T O'Kelly until July 1929 when he was relaced by Frank Gallagher. **form of humanity'** Andrews, *Man of no property*, p. 71. **IRA detainees** See for example *The Nation*, 15 Oct. 1927, 28 Jan. and 11 Aug. 1928. **not die out** *Dáil Debates*, Vol. 26, 2 Nov. 1928. **and Mick Price** *Dáil Debates*, Vol. 28, 21 Mar. 1929.

PAGE 119 to Briscoe annoyance Complaint about Briscoe by Superintendent J. O' Gorman to Commissioner, 9 Nov. 1929 in Jus 8/682 NAI. Complaint by Briscoe in garda report on speech at WPDL meeting, 24 Oct. 1930 in D/T S 5864 A NAI. **discuss his case**

D/I to O/C Prisoners, Maryboro', 5 Dec. 1927, in MTUCDA, P69/197 (58). **in early 1928** See p. 46. **in his honour** Lemass, Boland, O'Kelly, Briscoe, MacEntee and Aiken were among the mourners. *Irish Independent*, 2 Feb. 1928. For naming of Cumann, *Dáil Debates*, 29, 17 May 1929. **to unpunished** *The Nation*, 4 Feb., 1928. **harassment of Ryan** *Dáil Debates*, 29, 24 Apr. 1929. **in Clare** *The Nation*, 16 Mar. 1929. **his own cows!** *The Nation*, 27 July 1927 and *Dáil Debates*, 31, 31 July 1929. **Ireland was free** *Dáil Debates*, 29, 8 and 9 May 1929. **'illegal acts'** Garda report, 11 Nov. 1929, in FitzGerald papers, UCDA, P80/904 (5). **of the IRA** O'Duffy to Minister for Justice, 27 July 1931, in FitzGerald papers, UCDA, P80/856 (2). **PAGE 120 to the gardaí** Report by O'Duffy, 6 May 1929, in FitzGerald papers, UCDA, P80/851 (5). **the local population** Garda report, 25 May 1929, in FitzGerald papers, UCDA, P80/851 (16). **its electorate by this stand** Garda reports from 1931 cited areas of west Cork where '75%' of the people allegedly supported the IRA and few spoke to gardaí, especially 'none in public'. The entire population of Carnew village in Co. Wicklow apparently refused to speak to gardaí. See reports in D/T S 5864 C NAI. **in Ireland** *The Nation*, 22 Sept. 1928. **day was passing** *The Nation*, 9 Nov. 1929. **was a success** Seán Lemass and Gerald Boland, Fianna Fáil, to Seán MacBride, Irish section of the League against Imperialism, 5 Nov. 1930 in Jus 8/682 NAI. **their victim** Garda report, 2 May 1929, in FitzGerald papers, UCDA, P80/851 (8). **the ceremonies** See p. 72. **Senator Seamus Robinson** Report on revolutionary organizations, 4 Apr. 1930, in FitzGerald papers, UCDA, P80/916 (3). The report stressed that Briscoe should be investigated further as 'it is often suggested that the Irish was not his first venture in revolutionary activities'. **with this grouping** Eoin O'Duffy's description, report to the Executive Council, 27 July 1931, in FitzGerald papers, UCDA, P80/856.
PAGE 121 brought about Notes on the Irish labour movement by Mr. Holmes, (O'Donnell), Aug. 1927, in MTUCDA, P69/72 (15–8). **land annuities** Hegarty, *O'Donnell*, p. 167, *An Phoblacht*, 8 Apr. and *The Nation*, 23 Apr. 1927. **in January 1928** A/G to O/C Tirconaill Battalion, 12 Jan. 1928, in MTUCDA, P69/149 (70–1). **Co. Galway** *An Phoblacht*, 18 Feb., 1928. **with O'Donnell** Hegarty, *O'Donnell*, pp 178–9. **not their abolition** See English, *Radicals*, pp 86–95, Patterson, *Politics of illusion*, pp 35–43 and R. Dunphy, *The making of Fianna Fáil power in Ireland* (Oxford, 1995) p. 97. **money in Ireland** Garda reports, (Dungloe) 12 Feb. and (Kinsale) 16 May 1929, in FitzGerald papers, UCDA, P80/916 and P80/856 (10). **in that district** O'Duffy to Government Ministers, 5 July 1929, in Blythe papers, UCDA, P24/477.
PAGE 122 for the campaign Staff Officer 'Jack Jones' to A/G, 22 September 1930, in MTUCDA, P69/153 (178–3). **during 1931** O'Duffy to Government Ministers, 24 June 1931, in FitzGerald papers, UCDA, P80/856 (10). **it does not deserve** See O'Donnell, *There will be another day*, and Michael McInerney, Peadar O'Donnell (Dublin, 1974) pp 119–30. **been widely discussed** See Dunphy, *Fianna Fáil power*, pp 39–49, English, *Radicals*, pp 95–108, Paul Bew, Ellen Hazelkorn and Henry Patterson, *The dynamics of Irish politics* (London, 1989) pp 41–7. **playacting and posing** Eoin O'Duffy, 6 Apr. 1929, in FitzGerald papers, UCDA, P80/851 (5). **the state forces** Claims of gardaí beating up Fianna Fáil canvassers were raised by P.J. Ruttledge in the Dáil. See *Dáil Debates*, 21, 12 Oct. 1927. See *Tipperary Star*, 20 Apr. 1929 for claims of ill-treatment of Fianna Fáil members by the gardaí in Cahir. **Irish section there** Report on Revolutionary organizations, (1931) in MacEntee papers, UCDA, P67/522 (7) and report on Galway conference, 27 Mar. 1930 in FitzGerald papers, UCDA, P80/909 (2). **was actually neither** Fahy had taken part in the raid on the State Solicitor's office in Ennis discussed in Chapter Two. For his earlier remarks see *An Phoblacht*, 12 Jan. 1929. For trial see *Irish Press*, 11 Feb. 1932. **utter cowardice'** *The Nation*, 28 Mar. 1931. In reply *An Phoblacht* accused *The Nation* of 'felon-setting.' AP, 25 Apr. 1931.
PAGE 123 to criminal status' *Dáil Debates*, 40, 15 Oct. 1931. **Free State** *The Nation*, 1 Aug. 1931. **not politically biased** *Dáil Debates*, 26, 1 Nov. 1928 and de Valera at republican rally in Dublin, garda report, 8 Nov. 1929, in D/T S 5864 A, NAI. **a housing programme** *Dáil Debates*, 40, 14 Oct. 1931. **of private property** Quoted in Murray, *Oracles*, p. 257. See also

Dermot Keogh, 'De Valera, the Catholic Church and the 'Red Scare', 1931–32' in J.P.O'Carroll and J.A. Murphy (eds) *De Valera and his times* (Cork, 1983) pp 134–57. **to begin with** *Dáil Debates*, 40, 14 Oct. 1931. Mullins did not name which four organizations but one was the Irish Friends of the Soviet Russia. He was TD for Cork West but did not stand for re-election in 1932. He remained active in Fianna Fáil and became a Senator and Secretary of the party. Ironically Mullins was chosen as FF candidate for Co. Dublin in 1948 in an attempt to prevent Seán MacBride holding that seat. Gallagher, *Irish elections*, p. 153 and Doherty and Hickey (eds), *A dictionary of Irish history, 1800–1980* (Dublin, 1987) pp 378–9, MacDermott, *Clann na Poblachta*, pp 51–2. **and other matters** Although Mayo Fianna Fáil member John Mulgrew was on the Saor Éire national executive, he left the party for the IRA after his imprisonment during late 1931–2. AC to Clan, 30 July 1932, in MTUCDA, P69/185 (266). **that was foolish** *The Nation*, 3 Aug. 1929.

class war *Irish Press,* 29 Oct. 1931. **electorate report** For a discussion of this see Lee, *Ireland 1912–85*, pp 167–8. **the middle ground** See Twomey, in *The Nation*, 10 Aug. 1929.

PAGE 124 defied the ban Twomey to Joseph McGarrity, 23 June 1931 in McGarrity papers, Ms 17,490 NLI. **to Tone's grave** See *Irish Independent*, 22 June 1931. **could take advantage** Twomey to McGarrity, 23 June 1931 and Army Council to Secretary Clan na Gael, 7 May 1932, in MTUCDA, P69/185 (298–302). **Cumann na nGaedheal party'** A/G to Commander of each independent unit, 12 Jan. 1932, in D/T S 5864 C NAI. See Appendix 10 pp 365–7. **as simply tactical** Twomey to McGarrity, 9 Dec. 1931, in McGarrity papers, Ms 17,490 NLI. **Cumann na nGaedheal** Army council to Secretary Clan na Gael, 7 May 1932, in MTUCDA, P69/185 (298–302). **they have now** C/S to Count Plunkett, 19 Jan. 1932, in MTUCDA, P69/52 (242–44). **election effort** IRA members were permitted to work for other genuinely anti-government parties, so Waterford City IRA Adjutant Frank Edwards supported his local Labour party candidate. MacEoin, *Survivors*, p. 6.

PAGE 125 Fianna Fáil election effort Dublin Brigade reports, Feb.–Mar. 1932, in MTUCDA, P69/155 (130–7). **come to pass** Garda report, 9 Feb. 1932, in D/T S 8878 NAI. **of some writers** Bowyer Bell claims the IRA received lists of absent voters and its members used them to vote up to 50 times each. *Secret army*, p. 93. Conor Foley claims an IRA officer named David Fitzpatrick organized this with Lemass. Presumably this character is a combination of Michael Fitzpatrick and David FitzGerald. *Legion of the rearguard*, p. 102. **the new administration** See T.P. Coogan, *De Valera, long fellow, long shadow* (Dublin, 1993) pp 433–5. **the released men** This figure is a garda estimate. Report, 13 Mar. 1932, in Jus 8/698 NAI. **republic was achieved** *An Phoblacht*, 19 Mar. 1932. **for republicans** Entry in Jacob Diaries, 13 Mar. 1932, Ms 32,582 (69) NLI. **returned home** See for example *Kerry Champion*, 19 Mar. 1932 for report of 2,000 people welcoming Seán O'Shea to Cahirciveen. **by the gardaí** See next chapter for details of commemorations. Fianna Fáil TDs and Senators had lobbied the Minister for Justice to allow the sale of Easter lillies. See P.J. Little, B.M. Maguire, M.J. Corry, Wm. Quirke and S. Robinson to Minister, 16 Mar., 1932, in Jus 8/699 NAI. **working hand in hand** See Regan, *Counter-revolution*, pp 279–304.

Chapter Seven

PAGE 126 to recruit and train A/G to O/C Limerick City Batt, 12 May 1932, in MTUCDA, P69/155 (228). **for these suggestions** Aiken to Twomey, 19 Feb. 1932, in Aiken papers, UCDA, P104/1322 (1–2). **army or government** There were persistent claims that commissions in the National Army were offered to IRA officers. See Tomás Ó Maoilóin and Seán MacBride in MacEoin, *Survivors*, pp 100 and 123.

PAGE 127 discussing the matter AC to Secretary Clan na Gael, 7 May 1932 in MTUCDA, P69/185 (298–302) and Twomey to Aiken, 1 Mar. 1932, in Aiken papers, UCDA,

P104/1322 (9). **towards them** AC to Secretary Clan, 7 May 1932, in MTUCDA, P69/185 (298–302) **land annuities** Barry had been out of the IRA since the conclusion of the civil war but was considering rejoining in the summer of 1932. See Barry to Twomey, 13 May 1932, in MTUCDA, P69/52 (63–4).

PAGE 128 support the government All details of the meetings are contained in Confidential record of meetings with Fianna Fáil (nd) enclosed in communication from C/S to O/C Cork No. 1 Bdge, 19 July 1932, in MTUCDA, P69/52 (54–57). Twomey felt that Barry had left Dublin agreeing more with the IRA than Fianna Fáil but 'then one never knows!' **part of its militia** Twomey to Joseph McGarrity, 26 October 1933, in McGarrity papers, Ms 17,490 NLI. **during 1932 and 1933** The IRA claimed in late 1932 that it 'no regular direct contact' with the Fianna Fáil leadership. Chairman AC to Secretary, Clan na Gael, 8 November 1932, in MTUCDA, P69/185 (158). **Donavon castle affair** Explained in p. 35. **autumn of 1933** MacBride to Joseph MacGarrity, 19 Oct. 1933, in McGarrity papers Ms 17,546 NLI. There were five meetings in all. Seán Russell accompanied MacBride to the last of these meetings. **Ireland, or two** Twomey to Neenan, 19 July 1932, in MTUCDA, P69/185 (269–71). **rouse up the people** C/S to Seamus Lennon, 23 July 1932, in MTUCDA, P69/52 (9). **summer of 1932** GHQ Order to local units, calling on them to organise rallies with speakers from 'national, revolutionary and Trade Union' bodies, 6 July 1932, in MTUCDA, P69/158 (287). **Limerick during July** Frank Ryan and Peader O'Donnell were the IRA speakers. In Cork they were joined by TDs TP Dowdall and Martin Corry, in Limerick by D. Bourke TD and in Sligo by Mayor Lynch. *Irish Press*, 16, 18 and 22 July 1932.

PAGE 129 on legal tactics Chairman AC to Acting Secretary Clan na Gael, 30 July 1932, in MTUCDA, P69/185 (253–5). **Britain was at hand** See reports of support from Clare, Kerry and Limerick County Councils and the Limerick Labour Party and ITGWU in *Limerick Leader*, 23 July 1932. For report on Army manoeuvres see *Irish Press*, 29 July 1932. **disposal of the government** Policy Document, 23 March 1932, in MTUCDA, P69/53 (377–80). The implicit acceptance of partition in this scenario will be returned to in a later chapter. **strengthen their position** AC to Secretary Clan na Gael, 7 May 1932, in MTUCDA, P69/185 (298–302). **to organize them** Twomey to Neenan, 19 July 1932, P69/185 (269–71). **weaken Fianna Fáil** Twomey to McGarrity, 25 Aug. 1932 in MTUCDA, P69/185 (216).

PAGE 130 decide to co-operate' Twomey to Quirke, 4 Jan., and Quirke to Twomey, 7 Jan. 1933 in MTUCDA, P69/53 (357–360). See Chapter One. **back Fianna Fáil** Twomey to Neenan, 15 September 1932, in MTUCDA, P69/185 (190–1).**British Empire'** *An Phoblacht*, 14 Jan. 1933. **majority government** Gallagher, *Irish elections*, pp 175–6. **harness this discontent** A/G to Commanders of Independent Units, 18 Feb. 1933, in MTUCDA, P69/187 (1–). **he probably realized** Gilmore to Chairman AC, 16 Sept. and Chairman AC to Gilmore, 6 Oct. 1932, in MTUCDA, P69/53 (367–9). Gilmore contrasted his views on the likelihood of revolution with those of Peadar O'Donnell, who Gilmore suggested believed that all that was lacking in Ireland was 'someone to assume leadership'.

PAGE 131 an independent force *Notes of General Army Convention*, (GAC) Mar. 1933, in MTUCDA, P69/187 (90–118). The fact that MacBride had briefly been on the staff of the *Evening Press* had also led to some suspicion of him within the IRA. A/G to O/C Dublin Brigade, 6 June 1932, in MTUCDA, P69/155 (73). **with his allegation** O'Donnell to Cumann na mBan Executive, 20 Apr. 1934, in Humphreys papers, UCDA, P106/1154 (4). At that meeting O'Donnell claimed that MacBride had stated that he would favour the IRA giving up its arms if Fianna Fáil abolished the oath, the governor generalship and withheld the annuities. Gilmore alleged that MacBride had made this statement to him during 1932 following a meeting between Gilmore, Twomey and de Valera. Gilmore Notes. **to change later** Barry complained that *An Phoblacht* spent too much time attacking the goverment and not enough attacking the British. C/S to Seán Buckley, 6 Dec. and reply, 11 Dec. 1932, in MTUCDA, P69/54 (46–7) & (50–1). **had been a failure** During

Nov. 1932 only three local FF Cumann had sought information about the boycott campaign. Report by Secretary National Committee Boycott British League, 22 Nov. 1932, in Humphreys papers, UCDA, P106/2101 (10–22). **military expertise** Notes of 1933 GAC, P69/187 (75–79). **wing of Fianna Fáil** Ryan's resignation was announced in *An Phoblacht*, 1 Apr. 1933. Sheehy Skeffington to Twomey, 2 Apr. 1933, in MTUCDA, P69/53 (167–69). **by their activities** McGarrity to Twomey, 3 Oct. 1933, in McGarrity papers, Ms 17,490 NLI.

PAGE 132 **1934 local election** Twomey to McGarrity, 26 Oct. 1933, in McGarrity papers, Ms 17,490 NLI. The issue of standing candidates in the local elections had been discussed at the 1933 GAC but voted down. Notes of 1933 GAC, in MTUCDA, P69/187 (90–118) **government's supporters** MacBride was convinced that 'great pressure' was being exerted from within Fianna Fáil on de Valera to make him enter into an agreement with the IRA. MacBride to McGarrity, 19 Oct. 1933, Ms 17,456 NLI. **task more difficult** Notes of 1933 GAC, P69/187 (75–6). **a 'new' IRA** Notes of March 1934 GAC, in MacEntee papers, UCDA, P67/525. **against confrontation** Ryan noted how at one time FF claimed to value the IRA but 'now they treat us with contempt'.

PAGE 133 **was failing them** Meeting of Cumann na mBan Executive and AC Representatives, 18 Apr. 1934, in Humphreys papers, UCDA, P106/1153 (1–4). **by the government's policies** Twomey to McGarrity, 7 October 1935, in McGarrity papers, Ms 17,490 NLI. **much commented on** See comments on de Valera's reply to a letter from McGarrity asking him to bring about an 'understanding' with the IRA in R. Fanning, '"The rule of order": Eamon de Valera and the IRA, 1923–40' in O'Carroll and Murphy (eds) *De Valera and his times*, pp 161–71 and English, *Radicals*, pp 173–4 and 240. **base of support** *Irish Independent*, 10 Dec. 1936. Whether or not Russell was acting on official IRA instructions is harder to judge. His visit to de Valera was revealed by him in a letter to the press and was one of the charges made against him at his IRA court martial. Russell to McGarrity, 29 Jan. 1937, in McGarrity papers, Ms 17,485 NLI. **would not leave it** O/C North Clare to A/G, 23 May 1932, in MTUCDA, P69/155 (195). **an IRA member** C/S to M. MacNamara, 23 Feb. 1933, in MTUCDA, P69/53 (290–2). **and his organization** Seán Lanigan at the 1933 GAC, Notes of GAC, P69/187 (103). **including Seán T. O'Kelly** A/G to O/C Dublin Brigade, 6 June and C/S to O/C Dublin Brigade, 10 June 1932, in MTUCDA, P69/155 (71–3). There seem to have been at least six IRA members or reservists who worked as drivers for ministers. I/O Dub. Bdge. to D/I, 28 July 1932, in MTUCDA, P69/199 (102).

PAGE 134 for his son W.J. Ryan to Twomey, 2 Aug. 1932, in MTUCDA, P69/54 (219–20). **ensure its success** D. Healy to Twomey, (nd) in MTUCDA, P69/55 (26–7). **of appointments there** A/G to O/C Cavan Batt, 28 January 1933, in MTUCDA, P69/55 (30). **ex-Free State officer** O/C, Carrickmacross Batt. to A/G, 14 March 1933 in Aiken papers, UCDA, P104/2848. **able to help her** Tom Derrig to Twomey, 4 February 1933, in MTUCDA, P69/55 (33). **secure him the post** MacEvilly, IRA chief, pp 176–81. **a secondary school teacher** Secretary, An Roinn Oideachais, to Ó Maoileóin, 4 Jan. 1933, copy forwarded to Twomey, in MTUCDA, P69/53 (356). **government at all** Unsigned letter to Joseph J. Maguire, 5 Jan. 1933, in MTUCDA, P69/55 (17–18). **local IRA members** I/O Kenmare to D/I, 9 Apr. 1934, in Jus 8/319 NAI. **members in the county** See statement in *Kerry Champion*, 26 Jan. 1935. **to get jobs** Tom Maguire at the 1933 GAC, Notes of GAC, P69/187 (116). **as IRA officers** A/G to Adjt. Dingle Batt. 25 Aug. 1932, in MTUCDA, P69/158 (201) **and IRA days** 10,000 in Dublin, *Irish Press*, 28 Mar. 1932, 8,000 in Galway, *Connaught Tribune*, 2 Apr. 1932, 5,000 in Drumshambo, *Sligo Champion*, 2 Apr. 1932, 4,000 in *Tipperary Town* and 10,000 in Stranorlar, Co. Donegal, 3,000 in Castleisland, 2,700 in Caherciveen and 500 in Listowel Co. Kerry. *Kerry Champion*, 2 Apr. 1932. **and that's everything** Seán McCool, to Frank Ryan, 28 Mar. 1932, in MTUCDA, P69/235 (5–6). McCool estimated 10,000 had marched at Drumboe, headed by 350 IRA members.

PAGE 135 that spring *Longford Leader*, 15 Oct. 1932, *Sligo Champion*, 8 Oct. 1932 and *Kerry*

Champion, 16 and 30 Apr. 1932. **Bodenstown in June** Richard Walsh (Mayo South), Stephen Jordan (Galway) and John Flynn (Kerry). *Irish Press*, 20 June 1932. **Wexford and Offaly** In Dublin the Noel Lemass Cumann marched with the IRA, in Sligo Alderman Lynch again chaired proceedings, and in Tullamore Councillor PF Adams chaired the commemoration. *Irish Press*, 17 Apr. 1933 and *Offaly Independent*, 22 Apr.1933. **the IRA's statement** Garda report, 4 Apr.1934, in Jus 8/314 NAI. **republican army'** *Clare Champion*, 12 May 1934. **Easter ceremony** *An Phoblacht*, 7 Apr. 1934 and Garda report, 1 Apr. 1934, in Jus 8/315 NAI. **local IRA units** Local reports to Secretary Wolfe Tone Commemoration, 19 June 1935, in Humphrey's papers, UCDA, P106/2107 (20) and (31). **rank and file** The 'Torch – symbol of a resurgent nation' was chosen 'so the men of 1916 could be honoured without contributing to another organization'. FF Ard Fheis, *Irish Independent*, 5 Dec. 1935. **the new badges** *Irish Independent*, 27 Mar. and *Kerry Champion*, 6 Apr. 1935. **the new emblem** *Irish Press*, 18 Apr. 1935. **Dublin Tram strike** Twomey, 29 Mar. 1935, in Humphreys papers, UCDA, P106/1688. **of the CID** *An Phoblacht*, 5 Nov. 1932 and *Irish Independent*, 7 Nov. 1932. **a local IRA member** Séamus de Búrca to Peadar O'Donnell, 7 Nov. 1932, in MTUCDA, P69/158 (34–5).

PAGE 136 a British war film *Irish Press*, 9 Nov. 1933 and *An Phoblacht*, 11 Nov. 1933. **condemned these arrests** General Secretary Fianna Fáil to Minister for Justice, 17 Oct. 1933, in D/J H306/31 NAI. **an opposition senator** *An Phoblacht*, 23 Sept. 1933. **of the prisoners** *Kerry Champion*, 25 Nov., 9 and 16 Dec. 1933. **military tribunal** Despite the advice of the attorney general who did not favour censorship of it, *An Phoblacht* was subject to repeated raids and seizures from late Dec. 1933 onwards. See Att. Gen. to Dept of Justice, 27 Nov. 1934 in Jus 8/68 NAI. **for the IRA electorally** Seán O'Farrell topped the poll in Carrick on Shannon. As well as another councillor in Leitrim, IRA supporters won seats in Longford (2), Westmeath (2), Ennis, Tralee, and Letterkenny. *Leitrim Observer, Longford Leader, Westmeath Independent, Clare Champion* and *Kerry Champion*, 30 June 1934. **Fianna Fáil candidates** See GHQ to Listowel, 16 July 1934, in Aiken papers, UCDA, P104/2854 (23). **1933 and 1935** Between 10 Oct. 1933 and 16 Feb. 1935 *An Phoblacht* carried reports of 24 FF Cumann passing anti-government motions. **about ill-treatment** *Kerry Champion*, 26 Jan. 1935. **'in subjection'** Report, 27 Feb. 1935 in Jus 8/398 NAI. **in the Curragh** Tralee Urban District Council to Secretary Department of Justice, 10 Jan. 1935, in Aiken papers, UCDA, P104/2801 (100). **Tipperary and Kerry** Gortagarry FF Cumann, 21 Jan., Ballymackey Cumann, 16 Jan., Toomevara Parish Council, 22 Jan., all Tipperary and Thomas Ashe FF Cumann, Tralee, 11 Jan. 1935. All in Aiken papers, UCDA, P104/2801 (85, 87, 93, 100, 103). **republican organizations** *Donegal Democrat*, 29 June 1935. **party' cumainn** *Notes on the Republican Congress Movement*, MacEntee papers, UCDA, P67/527, p. 18. **and Denis Daly** Kissane to Frank Aiken, 13 Feb., McEllistrim to Aiken, 4 Feb. and Daly to Aiken, 5 Feb. 1935, in Aiken papers, UCDA, P104/2801 (77–83). **coercion of Republicans** Twomey to Mary MacSwiney, 24 Jan. 1935, in MacSwiney papers, UCDA, P48A/199.

PAGE 137 helped our party' Duagh FF to Eamon Kissane TD, 8 Feb. 1935, in Aiken papers, UCDA, P104/2801 (77–8). **of his movements** D. Curran to Secretary Dept. of Defence, 31 Dec. 1934, in Aiken papers, UCDA, P104/2801 (108). **the Cosgrave government** P.A. Tierney to Frank Aiken, 18 January 1935, in Aiken papers, UCDA, P104/2801 (94–5). **from the IRA** Daly to Aiken, 5 Feb. and McEllistrim to Aiken, 4 Feb. 1935, in Aiken papers, UCDA, P104/2801 (80–3). McEllistrim believed that it was sometimes necessary to 'go out of ones way to please small boys'. **against the imperialist's** The IRA's Anti-Imperialist rally in Sligo saw crowds cheer O'Donnell and Ryan with shouts of 'up de Valera'. *Irish Press*, 18 July 1932. At a commemoration in Clara, Co. Offaly in Apr. 1932 the IRA's Seán McGuinness had told the 6,000 strong crowd that a least now an 'honest man – de Valera' was at the helm of government. *Offaly Independent*, 2 Apr. 1932. **Land and Fisheries** Speech in Longford quoted in Kerry Champion, 27 July 1932. **of our people** Senator Michael Comyn speaking on the 22 Aug. 1933, in *Seanad Debates*, 18. **of the party** McCool to C/S, 10 Jan. 1933, in MTUCDA, P69/53 (16–17). **Irish Republican Army** *An*

Phoblacht, 1 Jan. 1933. Twomey assessed the makeup of the UFA as 'largely Fianna Fáil, Republican and a few sort of neutral'. Twomey to McGarrity, 26 Oct. 1933, in McGarrity papers, Ms 17,490 NLI. **members of the ACA** O/C North Mayo Batt to A/G, 20 and 22 Jan. 1933, in MTUCDA, P69/53 (121–4).

PAGE 138 Fianna Fáil crowd Manning, *Blueshirts,* pp 41–2. and *Irish Independent,* 10 Nov.1932. **by Fianna Fáil supporters** Twomey to McGarrity, 26 Oct. 1933, in McGarrity papers, Ms 17,490 NLI. **for armed clashes'** C/S to O/C Cork No. 1 Bgde, 10 Sept. 1932, in MTUCDA, P69/155 (39). **they were dismissed** See O'Halpin, *Defending Ireland,* pp 112–13, and Findings of Kilrush Inquiry, Sept. 1932 in Jus 8/376 NAI. **not be attempted** C/S to O/C Cork No. 1, 10 Sept. 1932, in MTUCDA, P69/155 (39). **with baton charges** Brady, *Guardians,* pp 185–6 and *Cork Examiner,* 6 Nov. 1932. **beaten up yesterday** O/C Cork No. 1 Bdge to C/S, 7 Nov. 1932, in MTUCDA, P69/155 (34). **official sanction** Manning, *Blueshirts,* pp 33–4. **during 1932** Numerous examples are cited by Brady in *Guardians,* pp 163–4, Foley, *Legion,* pp 107–8, and Coogan, *De Valera,* p. 465. Brady believes all his sources for these events were oral, citing David Neligan, Bill O'Connell and James Moore, all of Garda 'S' Branch. To author, 29 May 2001. *Garda Review* during this period, while outspoken on issues like pay cuts and voting rights for gardaí does not mention any cases of intimidation by the IRA. See *Garda Review,* Dec. 1931 to Dec. 1933. **looking for years** A/G to Adjt Tralee Battn. 22 June 1932, in MTUCDA, P69/155 (113). **splendid just now!'** Secretary AC to Secretary Clan, 30 July 1932, in MTUCDA, P69/185 (253–5). **was the reality** This was mirrored in the reaction in Britain to Fianna Fáil's election victory. See D. McMahon, *Republicans and Imperialists.* (Yale, 1984) chapter 2 and E. O'Halpin, "Weird Prophecies": British Intelligence and Anglo-Irish Relations, 1932–3' in Kennedy and Morrison Skelly (eds), *Irish foreign policy 1919-1966* (Dublin, 2000) pp 61–3. Headlines in the British press such as 'Fear gripped Ireland dreads the coming of the morrow' were not uncommon. *Sunday Express,* 24 July 1932. Twomey collected cuttings of a number of these type of reports. See MTUCDA, P69/52 (266–7). **of the opposition** Secretary, FF Club, Achill to Secretary D/J, 30 Dec. 1933, in D/J H306/31 NAI.

PAGE 139 the IRA's rally The IRA saw the threat as evidence that FF 'intended to fight for revolutionary leadership'. Army Council to Clan, 7 May 1932, in MTUCDA, P69/185 (298–302).**'chance to govern'** Dublin Bdge. I/O to D/I, 28 July 1932, in MTUC-DA, P69/199 (102). **refused to do so** AC to Clan, 30 July 1932, in MTUCDA, P69/185 (253–5). **College Green** *Irish Press,* 29 July 1932. **run the government** Dublin Bdge I/O to D/I, 20 August 1932, and I/O to D/I (nd) in MTUCDA, P69/199 (90) and (94). **on the organization** C/S to O/C Dublin Bdge, 29 Apr. 1933, in MTUCDA, P69/53 (87–8). **'harebrained lot'** Tom Barry to C/S, 3 Apr. 1933, in MTUCDA, P69/53 (212). **to the gardaí** Garda report, 13 Oct. 1933 in Jus 8/715 NAI.

PAGE 140 Fianna Fáil event C/S, 11 May 1933, in MTUCDA, P69/53 (20). **in the matter** Twomey to Seán Lynch, 23 Mar. 1934, O'Mahony. **ordered to leave** *Offaly Independent,* 23 July 1932. **occupation of the lodge** McGuinness claimed the 'local IRA and Fianna Fáil' were instigators of the occupation. F. Ryan to Twomey, July 1932, in MTUCDA, P69/158 (259–60). **silent on the matter** Reports by McGuinness, 20 & 25 July 1932, in MTUCDA, P69/158 (246–56). **for this agitation** C/S to O/C Offaly, 27 June 1932 in MTUCDA, P69/158 (245). **in the conquest'** Report on affair by Frank Ryan, 24 June 1932, in MTUC-DA, P69/158 (259) and *An Phoblacht,* 30 July 1932. **an eviction'** Exchange between Councillor P. Adams and Offaly Chairman James O'Connor, reported in *Offaly Independent,* 30 July 1932. **land reform** Peadar O'Donnell had enthusiastically reported from Offaly in *An Phoblacht,* 6 August 1932. Chairman AC to Secretary Clan, 8 Nov 1932, in MTUCDA, P69/185 (154–6) The IRA issued a statement to Dublin Trades Council denying instigating the strike, 11 Nov. 1932, in MTUCDA, P69/71 For the background to the case see Luke Gibbons, 'Labour and Local History – The case of Jim Gralton' in *Saothar,* 14, (1989) pp 85–95 P. Feeley, *The Gralton Affair* (Dublin, 1983) p. 30. Erskine Childer's Cumann, Arklow, Patriotswell Cumann, Co. Limerick and Fr. John Murphy

Cumann. Gralton himself had been a member of the Drumsna FF club. Feeley, *Gralton*, p. 46. Confidential Notes, MacEntee papers, UCDA, P67/534 p. 38.
PAGE 141 divided on the issue The O'Flannagan Cumann, North City. A resolution from this cumann distributed at strike meetings also called for the release of IRA prisoners. Garda report, 13 March 1935 in Jus 8/405 NAI. **grassroots revolt** See report on the Fianna Fáil Ard Fheis in *Republican Congress*, 14 Dec. 1935. **section of the party** Patrick McGuinness of Kinnitty was to the fore in raising protests about republican prisoners at the 1933 Ard Fheis. That Ard Fheis also saw complaints that the Knights of Columbanous represented 'a new ascendancy'. See *Irish Press*, 9 Nov. 1933. **to economic chaos** Twomey at the 1933 GAC, Notes of GAC, P69/187 (100). **Chamber of Commerce element'** Twomey to McGarrity, 26 October 1933, McGarrity papers, Ms 17,490 NLI.
 to republicanism' Twomey to Mary MacSwiney, 24 Jan. 1935, in MacSwiney papers, UCDA, P48A/199. **'mainstream' as well** English has made this point about the republican left, but it applies to the entire IRA leadership in this period. English, *Radicals*, p. 194.
PAGE 142 was clearly political As Seán Lemass explained, there were in Ireland 'young men to whom military manoeuvres are an attraction and who if they do not get the military associations they desire in an official organization may be induced to seek it in illegal organizations'. See L. Joye, 'Aiken's Slugs': The reserve of the Irish Army under Fianna Fáil' in J. Augusteijn (ed.), *Ireland in the 1930s* (Dublin, 1999). pp 143–62. **untried republicans'** Twomey to McGarrity, 26 Oct. 1933, McGarrity papers, Ms 17, 490 NLI. **in their areas** Notes of 1934 GAC, MacEntee papers, UCDA, P67/525. **on Volunteer halls** See *Confidential Notes*, MacEntee papers, UCDA, P67/534 pp 28–31. **with Fianna Fáil** *Kerry Champion*, 4 August 1934. **local public works** In Kenmare the local FF secretary expected 3 IRA men he helped gain employment for to join the new force. Promises of work on their return from training was also made in a 'covert way'. I/O Kenmare Batt. to D/I, 9 and 18 Apr., 1934, in Jus 8/319 NAI. **preferential treatment** The Military Service Pensions Act was introduced to provide pensions for Anti–Treaty veterans. The IRA regarded this as a 'bribe.' However the organization did favour pensions for disabled veterans. *An Phoblacht*, 18 Sept. 1934. **'coercion' period** I/O Dub. Brigade to D/I, 28 July 1932, in MTUCDA, P69/199 (102). **1916 veterans** *Irish Press*, 6 Apr. 1935. **'to grumble about it'** *Kerry Champion*, 23 Dec. 1933. **the 'new IRA'** *Kerry Champion*, 9 Feb. 1935. **of the IRA** *Kerry Champion*, 26 Jan. 1935
PAGE 143 'racketering organization' De Valera to National Executive of Fianna Fáil, 28 Mar. 1935, in D/T S. 7495 NAI. **'the new IRA'** *Kerry Champion*, 9 Feb. 1935. **by their leaders** Miss Kay Breen of Kerry co. council and the FF national executive, one of the party's most dogged defenders in these debates. *Kerry News*, 7 Jan. 1935. **the title IRA** Speech at Galway, 11 Aug. 1936, in *National discipline and majority rule* (Dublin, 1936). p. 11. **to make peace'** *Irish Independent*, 4 June 1935. Barry replied to this accusation and the debate continued through the letters pages of the *Irish Press* for several weeks. Copies in Aiken papers, UCDA, P104/1283 (1–5). Among a number of Anti-Treaty veterans who defended Barry's record was FF TD Tom Hales. See *An Phoblacht*, 25 May 1935. **where you served** *Irish Press*, 22 June 1936. **than its enemies** *Irish Press*, 9 Nov. 1933. **of Fine Gael** *Irish Press* editorial, 5 April 1935. **from the 'left'** *Irish Press* editorial, 2 Apr. 1935. **or the other'** *Kerry Champion*, 23 Dec. 1933. **person and property'** Aiken to D. Curran, 10 Jan. 1935, in Aiken papers, UCDA, P104/2801 (113). **was possible** De Valera at Enniscorthy, 2 August 1936, in *National discipline*, p. 3. **inferiority complex'** Seán Moylan at the 1933 FF Ard Fheis, *Irish Press*, 9 Nov. 1933. **government was employing** Seán T. O'Kelly at the 1932 FF Ard Fheis, *Irish Independent*, 9 Nov. 1932. **by IRA propaganda** FF claimed that of 1,800 cumann only 12 had refused to distribute the emblem. *Irish Press*, 18 Apr. 1935. **during 1936** For Hale's resignation see *Irish Times*, 26 June 1936. In Galway on the 13 Aug. Count Plunkett polled just 2,696 votes to Fianna Fáil's 39,982 and in Wexford on the 17 of Aug. Stephen Hayes only 1,301 to Fianna Fáil's 23,263. Gallagher, *Irish elections* p. 206.
PAGE 144 organization had become Garda reports, 31 December 1934, in Jus 8/68 NAI.

certainly did so Fine Gael's attempts to link Fianna Fáil to the killing of More O'Ferrall meant that at local council level FF members often refused to condemn the IRA's action. See *Dáil Debates*, 55, 7 Mar. 1935, and FF reaction to motion calling for condemnation of the killing on Longford Co. Council, *Irish Press*, 11 Mar. 1935. **claims to patriotism** De Valera at Galway, 11 Aug. 1936, in *National discipline*, p. 8. **and running away'** Frank Gallagher to McGarrity, 25 June 1938, in McGarrity papers, Ms 17,544 (1) NLI.

Chapter Eight

PAGE 145 commemorations were banned See reports from 1928 in Prohibited Meetings File, HA/32/1/465 in PRONI. **in the six counties** See A/G to O/C Ulster No. 4 Bdge. 23 Jan. 1930, for report on arrest of Tyrone officer for posession of 21 *An Phoblachts*, in MTUCDA, P69/152 (114–7). **to the Free State** Patrick Thornbury from the Falls Road, a former O/C of IRA prisoners on board the *Argenta* was arrested in 1926 and deported on release in 1927. P. Thornbury File, HA/32/1/513, in PRONI. **into submission** É. Phoenix, *Northern nationalism, nationalist politics* (Belfast, 1994) p. 251. **very 'existence'** IRA GHQ Report, 15 Apr. 1924, in MTUCDA, P69/145 (310). **Irish nationalism** D. Kennedy, *The widening gulf* (Belfast, 1988) p. 202. **Northern Ireland at birth** B. A. Follis, *A state under siege.* (Oxford, 1995) p. 115. **Protestant majority** M. Laffan, 'Violence and terror in twentieth-century Ireland: IRB and IRA' in Mommsen and Hirschfeld (eds), *Social protest, violence and terror in nineteenth- and twentieth-century Europe* (London, 1982) pp 155–74 Ballymacarrett Research Group, *Lagan enclave – a history of conflict in the Short Strand 1886–1997* (Belfast, 1997) p. 41. See also Jim McDermott, *Northern divisions* (Belfast, 2001), pp 244–79. **the National Army** Staunton, *Nationalists of Northern Ireland*, p. 71. McDermott, *Northern Divisions*, pp 161–176.

PAGE 146 to their peace' D/I Report, 9 Aug. 1924, in MTUCDA, P69/179 (123). **was just 628** General Report for IRA Executive, 10 Aug. 1924, in MTUCDA, P69/180 (25).**in their passivity** Report of Inspection Officer, 20 May 1925, in MTUCDA, P69/47 (242–3). **is widespread** AC Report 11 Feb. 1926, in MTUCDA, P69/181 (60). **to 517 men** AC Estimates, 1 Nov. 1926, in MTUCDA, P69/181 (5). Other units numbers stood at Armagh (142), Antrim (23), Derry (40), Down (40) and Tyrone (30). **for the IRA** RUC report, 24 Apr. 1930, in HA/32/1/465 in PRONI. Only 20 had attended the banned commemoration in Derry, with around 450 turning out in Belfast. **opposition to develop** D/I Report, 9 Aug. 1924, MTUCDA, P69/179 (122). **to the Belfast IRA** I/O Ulster No. 1 to D/I, 25 November 1926, in MTUCDA, P69/193 (86–94). **and the Markets** O/C Ulster No.1 to A/G, April 1931 in MTUCDA P69/151 (70–71). **for example** Matthews, from Bombay Street, had been interned on the *Argenta*. Matthews File, HA/5/2361 in PRONI. **through Saor Éire** O/C Belfast to C/S, 8 May 1932, in MTUCDA P69/52 (190). **political organization** Clar 1933 GAC, in MTUCDA, P69/53 (276–7 & 286).

PAGE 147 on a train *Irish News*, 27 June 1932. **be very bad** O/C Tirconaill No. 2 Batt to C/S 4 July & C/S reply, 6 July 1932 in MTUCDA, P69/52 (112–3). **in sectarian conflict** A/G to O/C No. 3 Ulster, 9 July 1932, in MTUCDA, P69/155 (64). **religious antagonisms** *Irish Independent*, 11 July 1932. **mass of the people** O'Donnell to Cumann na mBan Executive, 20 Apr. 1934, in Humphreys papers, UCDA, P106/1154. **the United Irishmen** *An Phoblacht*, 16 July 1932 & Coogan, *IRA*, pp 170–2. **attractive to Protestants** Some months later an IRA unit in Cabra Co. Down was on the verge of collapse because the local parish priest read 'refused the boys absolution unless they gave up the army. He has warned them off the pulpit, stressing the Communistic danger'. Adjt No.1 Area Ulster to A/G, 20 November 1932, in MTUCDA, P69/158 (26–31).

PAGE 148 the dark ages *Belfast Weekly Telegraph*, 16 July 1932. **At Bartholomew** *Belfast Newsletter*, 13 July 1932. **to beat the IRA** *Belfast Newsletter*, 11 July 1932. **IRA 'humour'** *Northern Whig*, 11 July 1932. **those of the Pope** *Irish Independent*, 13 July 1932. **National Anthem'** *Northern Whig*, 13 July 1932. **as a sectarian action** Kennedy *Widening gulf*, pp

164–5. **northern Protestants** Kennedy, *Widening Gulf,* pp 196–9. **address by Orangemen** A/G to O/C No.3 Ulster, 9 July 1932, in MTUCDA, P69/155 (64). **intent on trouble** C/S to O/C No.1 Ulster, 7 July 1932, in MTUCDA, P69/52 (103). **in their districts** O/C Belfast to C/S, 10 July 1932, in MTUCDA P69/52 (85). **'warning notices'** I/O Belfast to D/I, 21 July 1932, in MTUCDA P69/199 (111–4).

PAGE 149 the least effect' O/C Ulster No.3 to A/G IRA 12 September 1932, in MTUC-DA, P69/158 (163–6). **'burnt them'** Minutes of 1933 GAC in MTUCDA P69/187 (90–118). Murray's Battalion stood at 240 Volunteers in July 1932. Report, Adjt. Ulster No.2 to A/G IRA 8th July 1932 in MTUCDA, P69/156 (175). **is glossed over** I/O Belfast to D/I, 21 July 1932, in MTUCDA, P69/199 (111–14). **condemnation of the IRA** *Dundalk Examiner,* 16 July 1932. **marchers well away** O/C Belfast to C/S, 10 July 1932, in MTUC-DA P69/52 (85). **pass off peacefully** Headline in *Belfast Weekly Telegraph,* 16 July 1932. **Scarva, Co. Down** *Irish Independent,* 15 July 1932. **the Falls Road** *Irish News,* 13 & 14 July 1932. **recalled to Belfast** Adjt No. 1 Ulster to A/G, July 1932, in MTUCDA P69/158 (228–33).

PAGE 150 the coming week I/O to D/I, 10 July 1932, in MTUCDA, P69/199 (126). **carried out successfully** Adjt. Ulster No.1 to A/G, July 1932, in MTUCDA, P69/156 (167). **at street corners** I/O Belfast to D/I, 21 July 1932, in MTUCDA, P69/199 (111–14). **Northern Ireland's history** T. Hennessey, *A history of Northern Ireland, 1920–1996* (London, 1997) p. 59. **were killed** Both men were killed in Nationalist areas. It has been asserted by both Chris Ryder and Paddy Devlin that the RUC were given permission to use guns in Nationalist areas but only their batons in Unionist districts. See C. Ryder, *The RUC* (London, 1989) pp 68–9. and P. Devlin, *Yes – We have no bananas* (Belfast, 1981) pp 130–1. **'Irish Revolution' had begun** *An Phoblacht,* 22 Oct. 1932 and 15 Oct. 1932. **trench and barricade** *Northern Whig,* 17 Oct. 1932. **largely as individuals** Those include Liam Mulholland, Bob Bradshaw, Eamon Ó Cianáin and Barney Boswell. For Mulholland and Boswell, see Munck and Rolston, *Belfast,* pp 169 & 176. For Bradshaw and O'Cianain, see MacEoin, *Twilight years,* pp 425 & 690. **in the city'** I/O Belfast to D/I IRA, 24 May 1932, in MTUC-DA, P69/199 (166). **help from either** I/O Belfast to D/I IRA, 21 July 1932, in MTUCDA, P69/199 (111–4). **amongst them** D/I IRA to I/O Belfast, 30 July 1932, in MTUCDA, P69/199 (111–4).

PAGE 151 better organized I/O Belfast to D/I IRA, 15 Sept. 1932, in MTUCDA, P69/199 (99). **access to arms** I/O Belfast to D/I IRA, 10 Oct. 1932, in MTUCDA, P69/199 (12). **for stone throwing** Acting Adjt. Belfast Batt to A/G, Oct. 1932, in MTUC-DA, P69/156 (25–38). **ODR strike** By 1934, of the IRA's 460 members in Belfast, only 150 were employed. See p. 21. **never been republicans** Mike Millote, *Communism in modern Ireland* (Dublin, 1984). p. 125. **co-operation unlikely** I/O Belfast to D/I, 10 October 1932, in MTUCDA, P69/199 (12). **leadership's analysis** See interview with Peter Carelton in UinSeánn MacEoin, *Survivors,* p. 308. **the ODR strike** Notes of 1933 GAC, MTUCDA, P69/187 (95).

PAGE 152 from Dublin killed The dead men were James McWilliams and James Patterson. *Irish News,* 2 Feb. 1933. **refusing them refreshments** *Irish News,* 10 Feb. 1933. **organization involved** It has been asserted in the past that only 'leftist' sections of the IRA were active during the strike. See M. Farrell, *Northern Ireland, the orange state* (London, 1980), p. 133 and Devlin, *Yes,* p. 141. **bridge at Dunmurray** *Irish News,* 13 Feb. 1933. **during the strike** See Coogan, *The IRA,* p. 172 for rumours. **for use there** 'Q' to C/S, 28 Feb. 1933, in MTUCDA, P69/53 (296–8). **on strike breakers** Constable John Ryan, a native of Tipperary. *Irish News,* 1 Mar. 1933. **at their hands** MacEoin, *Twilight years,* pp 425–6 and Ryder, *RUC,* p. 69. **be the pogromists** C/S to 'Thomais,' 23 Mar. 1933, in MTUCDA, P69/53 (268–70). **of mutual interest'** A/G IRA to Commander of every Independent Unit, statement to be read at all Battalion Staff Meetings in preparation for GAC, 18 February 1933 in MTUCDA, P69/187 (1–3). **no sackings of strikers** *An Phoblacht,* 15 Apr. 1933.

PAGE 153 deal fell through O/C Belfast to C/S 30 April 1933, in MTUCDA, P69/53

(83). **during this period** Quinn, *A rebel voice.* p. 21. **during the 1930s** 'There were Protestants in a fair amount of the companies, odd ones you know, but there were Protestants ... there was no such thing, to be honest about it, as sectarianism' Liam Mulholland in Munck and Rolston, *Belfast*, p. 189. A number of IRA members from Protestant backgrounds are mentioned in Uinseann MacEoin, *Harry: the story of Harry White of Belfast* (Dublin, 1985). They include John Graham, the editor of the 1940s *Republican News*, Gideon Close and Bill Smith. p. 147. **during the strike** Minutes of GAC 1933, MTUCDA, P69/187 (113). **and exploitation** A/G to Commander of every Independent Unit, MTUCDA, P69/187 (1–3). **kept up the fight** Minutes of GAC, MTUCDA, P69/187 (110). **retire in 1933** Joseph Devlin (1871–1934). Irish Parliamentary Party MP for North Kilkenny 1904–6, West Belfast 1906–1922, Grand Master AOH from 1904, defeated de Valera in West Belfast 1918, Stormont and Westminster MP until his death. Rumours that he had met the IRA are mentioned in Phoenix, *Northern nationalism* p. 372 & Munck & Rolston, *Belfast*, p. 188. **members in Belfast** Chairman Army Council to members of the IRA Executive, 18 November 1932, in MTUCDA P69/155 (30). **supported unanimously** Minutes of GAC 1933, MTUCDA, P69/187 (110). **for these deaths** *Irish News*, 9, 14, 16 and 18 Oct. 1933. The RUC Constable was Charles Glennon, a native of Westmeath. *An Phoblacht* claimed the dead Catholic, Dan O'Boyle, was a republican sympathizer, 21 Oct. 1933. **'pogrom' was likely** Twomey to McGarrity, 26 Oct. 1933, in McGarrity papers, Ms 17,490 NLI.
PAGE 154 in his place Thornbury File HA/32/1/513 in PRONI and *An Phoblacht*, 25 Nov. 1933. Thornbury's exclusion order was not lifted until November 1946, along with those of Moss Twomey and Maud Gonne. **and a butcher** McCool would remain active in the IRA until the late 1940s. He became the organization's chief of staff in 1942 and was also interned in the Curragh that year. He was prominent in the various factional disputes there. On release he stood as a Republican candidate in the 1943 general election contesting Donegal East and secured 1,961 votes. McCool was an unsuccesful Clann na Poblachta candidate at the 1948 general election. See *Notes on certain individuals* in MacEntee papers UCDA P67/550 pp 159–160 and 'Internee Groups' File PM 1498, MA. **No. 2 battalion** See p. 20. **in South Down** *An Phoblacht*, 25 Nov. 1933. **tired of courting'** *Derry Journal*, 20 Nov. 1933. **McCarroll himself** *Derry Journal*, 28 Nov. 1933 and E. McCann, *War and an Irish town* (London, 1993) p. 253. **the Church was'** *Irish News*, 27 Nov. 1933. **by the Unionists** *Irish News*, 28 and 30 Nov. 1933. Cahir Healy (1877–1970). Active in Sinn Féin 1916–22, interned on the *Argenta*, Westminister MP for Fermanagh and South Tyrone 1931–5, and Stormont MP for Fermanagh 1925–65. **in Crumlin Road** *An Phoblacht*, 2 Dec. 1933. **Director of Elections** He was replaced by Mick Price of the Army Council.
PAGE 155 versus exploiter' *Derry Journal*, 27 Nov. 1933 and *An Phoblacht*, 2nd Dec.1933. **Table 14** *Irish News*, 2 Dec. 1933. **smaller constituency** *An Phoblacht*, 9 Dec. 1933. **the IRA and him** Devlin himself claimed that his illness meant he could not campaign effectively and that he would have otherwise claimed an extra 2,000 votes. He also suggested the IRA employed widespread personation during the voting. Joe Devlin to Hannah Keating, 13th December 1933, in Devlin papers T/2424 (3) in PRONI. **to the 'Hibernians'** *An Phoblacht*, 9 Dec. 1933. **voted against us** McCarroll to Healy 4 Dec. 1933. McCarroll could not resist a last dig at his opponents telling Healy that 'from what I saw of them on polling day, I am glad not to have their support for their chief agent in one centre is a jail-bird while another was a professional boxer of no character'. Cahir Healy papers D2991/A–B in PRONI. It was anything but a 'comfortable' victory for the Nationalists. McCann, *War*, p. 255. **bigotry** *An Phoblacht*, 20 Dec. 1933. **count in Belfast** MacEoin, *Harry*, p. 43.
PAGE 156 clear out of Ireland Patrick MacLogan File, HA/32/1/610 in PRONI. A civil servant has scribbled around the above quote from the *Armagh Guardian* of 25 May 1934 'isn't this enough to warrant exclusion?' **in January 1934** *An Phoblacht*, 3 Feb. 1934. **to do the same** *Northern Whig*, 23 Dec. 1933. One of the other prisoners who signed the undertaking was George Nash, who had been the prospective IRA candidate for Co. Down. **within the IRA** *Irish Worker' Voice*, 13 Jan. 1934. **the 1935 riots** Hennessey, *Northern Ireland*, pp

62–8. Paul Bew has argued that the fragmentation of Unionism during the early 1930s was reflected in both the ODR riots and the growth of the UPL. See P. Bew and C. Norton., 'The Unionist state and the outdoor relief riots of 1932' in the *Economic and Social Review* 10:3 (1979) 255–6. **in Marine Street** J. Bardon, *A history of Ulster* (Belfast, 1992) p. 539. **break such a ban** K. Jeffery, 'Parades, police and government in Northern Ireland, 1922–1969', in T.G. Fraser (ed.), *The Irish parading tradition* (Basingstoke, 2000) pp 78–94. **with bullet wounds** *Irish News*, 13 July 1935. **memories of 1922** *Irish News*, 15 July 1935.
PAGE 157 caused the blookshed *Belfast Newsletter*, 13 July 1935. **igniting the rioting** *Belfast Newsletter*, 17 July and *Irish News*, 1 Aug. 1935. **Orange bandsmens' conduct** Jeffery, 'Parades, police and government' p. 85. **access to arms** I/O Belfast to D/I, 10 July 1932, in MTUCDA P69/199 (126). **paid out to Catholics** Bardon, *History of Ulster*, pp 539–2. **left in Belfast** MacEoin, *Harry*, p. 44 and Munck & Rolston, *Belfast*, p. 182. The quote is from Jack Brady. **several from Belfast** *Notes on Events*, in MacEntee papers, UCDA, P67/534 p. 44. *Irish News*, 15 July 1935. **in Dundalk'** *Irish News*, 20 July 1935. **while Catholic were** Munck & Rolston, *Belfast*, p. 57. Unfortunately the RUC's reports on the riots are as yet unavailable to researchers.
PAGE 158 its fellow countrymen' *Irish News*, 4 Nov. 1935. **for Armagh** *Irish News*, 5 Nov. 1935. **an effective campaign** See Healy to R. O'Connor of Omagh, 5 Oct. 1935 & to de Valera 23 Oct.1935 in Cahir Healy papers D2991/A–B in PRONI. **an election pact** See D. Kennedy, 'Catholics in Northern Ireland, 1926–39' in F. MacManus (ed.), *The years of the great test, 1926–39* (Dublin, 1967). pp 138–49. **from the election** *Republican Congress*, 11 Nov. 1935. **with republicans** See Gilmore to Healy 25 Oct. 1935 suggesting Healy convene a conference of Republican and Labour opinion to fight the election on an anti-partition basis. Healy reply, 27 Oct. 1935. While there were major political differences between Healy and the Congress, he had spoken at a London rally organized by them the previous summer. Cahir Healy papers D2991/A–B in PRONI. **not support them** *Irish News*, 11 Nov. 1935. **in your hand'** *Irish News*, 7 and 11 Nov. 1935. **the republican campaign** Although there were hostile references to the IRA's percieved disdain for sectarian politicking. Staunton, *Nationalists of Northern Ireland*, pp 123–4. **during the election** *Republican Congress*, 23 Nov. 1935.
PAGE 159 injured in Co. Down *Irish News*, 14 and 15 Nov. 1935. **written on them** *Irish News*, 16 Nov. 1935. **has been challenged** *Irish News*, 18 Nov. 1935. **of armed Catholics?** Munck and Rolston, *Belfast*, p. 184, English, *Radicals*, p. 138, M. Elliot, *The Catholics of Ulster* (London, 2000). p. 403.
PAGE 160 service taking place The RUC would also prevent possible breaches of the ban elswhere. In 1931 the visiting speaker and the local IRA O/C were arrested at an attempted commemoration in Newry. Acting O/C Newry to A/G, 6 April 1931, in MTUCDA, P69/151 (65). **place of a commemoration** Prohibited Meetings File HA/32/1/465 in PRONI. The RUC claimed it was seditious speeches made by Frank Ryan in Belfast and Seán MacSweeney in Derry at Easter 1928 that prompted the ban. The reaction to Ryan's speech does point to contradictions within republican support in the north. While Ryan told the crowd that the 'fight was not one of religion ... but ... to drive the English out of the country' many in the audience sang 'Faith of our Fathers' as well as 'The Soldiers Song'. The RUC used the ceremonies to assess the ebbs and flows of republican support. From 1930 onwards they were noticing increasing numbers of young people in Belfast wearing Easter lilies. After some deliberation, the RUC decided that while sale of these 'Republican poppies' was prohibited, wearers would not be interfered with unless they were in an area where their presence could lead to a breach of the peace. **sectarian rationale'** English, *Radicals*, p. 201. **the Unionist Party** Twomey to McGarrity, 23 June 1931, in McGarrity papers, Ms 17,490, NLI. **is in question?** JB to Editor, *An Phoblacht*, 21 Nov. 1932, & O/C Belfast to C/S, 17 Apr.1933 in MTUCDA, P69/158 (28) and P69/53 (131–4). **leadership in 1938** There were accusations that the Belfast IRA, in alliance with Seán Russell and Joe McGarrity sabatoged planned IRA

operations in order to undermine the Dublin leadership. See Statement to GAC 1938, from the outgoing AC and Executive in Aiken papers, UCDA, P104/2833 (1–3). **the Stephen Hayes affair** Stephen Hayes, was kidnapped during 1941 by members in the belief that he was a government spy. He was due to be murdered but managed to escape. A fantastical confession was produced which claimed the Irish government was behind most of the IRA's activities from 1939 onwards. Copy in Humphreys papers, UCDA, P106/2097. A summary of the affair is contained in B. Bell, *Secret army*, pp 199–214.

Chapter Nine

AGE 161 on a regular basis Andy Cooney during 1926 and 1929, Frank Ryan in early 1930, Moss Twomey later that year, Mick Price during the 'coercion' period of late 1931, and Seán Russell in the autumn of 1932. **in July 1922** Fitzpatrick, *The two Irelands*, p. 214 and Cancellation of General Order No. 22, in MTUCDA, P69/206 (52). **'Ireland's foe'** *An t-Óglách*, May 1925, in Aiken papers, UCDA, P104/1281. **'the enemy's game'** O/C Western Division, 18 May 1925 in MTUCDA, P69/207 (86). **would be left** O/C Connemara, 28 Apr. 1925 in MTUCDA, P69/207 (97). **Foreign Reserve** Cancellation of GO. 22, (N/D) in MTUCDA, P69/206 (52).

PAGE 162 under its authority AC Report to GAC, Autumn 1925, in MTUCDA, P69/181 (91). **ordered by the IRA** Application Form for Transfer to Foreign Reserve List in MTUCDA, P69/167 (49). See Appendix 11. **for example** Memorandum to Members of Army Council on USA Organization, 11 Feb. 1926, in MTUCDA, P69/181 (62–4). **in republican politics** In 1932 for example the Clan was complaining about how few Tipperary IRA members in the US had contacted it. A/G to O/C Tipp Battn., 3 July 1932, in MTUCDA, P69/158 (284). **Clan na Gael** *An t-Óglách*, Apr. 1929, in FitzGerald papers, UCDA, P80/881 (7). **Table 15** Foreign Reserve Lists, 1924–6 in MTUCDA, P69/167 (94–99), P69/168 (1–5), P69/170 (1–50), P69/172, P69/183 (7) (91–2). The 'other' was Argentina. **the Great Depression** See K. Kenny, *The American Irish. A history* (Harlow, 2000) p. 182 and Chris McNickle, 'When New York was Irish, and after', in R.H. Bayor and T.J. Meagher (eds), *The New York Irish* (Baltimore, 1996) pp 337–56. **Table 16** Calculated from Foreign Reserve Lists, in MTUCDA, P69/167 (94–9), P69/168 (1–5), P69/170 (1–50), P69/172, P69/183 (7) & (91–2).

PAGE 163 to New York List for transfer to Foreign Reserve, (N/D) in MTUCDA, P69/183 (91–2). **attached to that unit** McLaughlin travelled to New York in Oct. 1925. Transfer form in MTUCDA, P69/169 (4). He was shot dead during a robbery at his workplace in Dec. 1930. The return of his remains to Ireland saw a major IRA mobilization and confrontation with the gardaí and army at his funeral. See *An Phoblacht*, 14 and 20 June 1931 and Calendar, in *Notes on Events*, in MacEntee papers, UCDA, P67/534 p. 6. **to dissuade him** Transfer Form, 20 August 1926 in MTUCDA, P69/167 (4) and Chairman AC to An Timthire, IRA, 3 June 1927 in MTUCDA, P69/183 (6). **who left Ireland** 37 out of 41 on lists for transfer, P69/183 (91–2). **escape from prison** McGuinness escaped from Mountjoy in November 1925 and returned to Ireland during 1930. O/C Offaly to A/G, 17 May 1932, in MTUCDA, P69/157 (34–6). Keogh escaped from Dundrum Asylum in May 1926. Report, 7 May 1929, FitzGerald papers, UCDA, P80/851 (11). **of Philadelphia** See Cronin, *McGarrity papers*, pp 16–17 and 28–36 for background to McGarrity's early career. **their consent obtained'** Text of Agreement, 15 Sept. 1926 in MTUCDA, P69/185 (257). **for the organization** AC to An Timthire (Neenan's title), Oglaigh na h-Éireann, USA and Canada, 9 Feb. 1927, in MTUCDA, P69/183 (113–14) See interview in MacEoin, *Survivors* pp 235–258 and O'Malley Notebooks, UCDA, P17b/112. Neenan's allowance from the IRA was $40 a week. See Dispatch, 10 Nov. 1926, in MTUCDA, P69/183 (175). **it would be** See pp 31–32 above. **to operate effectively** Memorandum for Clan na Gael Executive from IRA Representative, 25 Aug.1932, in MTUCDA, P69/185 (220). **'mainstay' of the clan** List of camps in records of Clan Convention, 12–14 July 1929, in McGarrity papers, Ms 17,534 (4) NLI. 'Mainstay' quote from An Timthire Dispatch, 18 May 1927 in MTUCDA, P69/183 (36). There were also a small number of branches in Canada. **social centre** From 1927 until 1931 the halls were situated at 66th St, Broadway, and from 1931 at 147 Columbus Avenue. An Timthire Dispatch, 18 May 1927 in MTUCDA, P69/183 (35) and Charles McGinnitty to *An Phoblacht*, 5 Mar. 1931 in MTUCDA, P69/233 (186). **yearly beauty contest** Leaflet advertising Labor Night dance, 7 Sept. 1931 and 'Message to all Lovers of Irish Freedom' from the Brooklyn and Queens Ladies IRA Auxiliaries, (N/D) in MTUCDA, P69/233 (117–18).

PAGE **164 in New York** Figure for boat trip from Clan Secretary to P. Castiglioni, 8 July 1930 and Neenan to Gannon, 15 men's clubs and 4 women's, 11 June 1930, in McGarritty papers, Ms 17,467 (5) NLI. **in Manhattan and Brooklyn** Leaflet in MTUCDA, P69/233 (118). **to just 1,722** Clan Convention Notes, July 1929, in McGarrity papers, Ms 17,534 (4) NLI. **sent to the US** List of areas to receive copies during June 1931 in MTUCDA, P69/52 (271). The New York area received 120 of these **copies of the week** New York were sent 100, Boston 40, Chicago 75, Cleveland 35 and Philadelphia 40. List in MTUC-DA, P69/222 (5). **the entire United States** List of subscribers, May 1932 in MTUCDA, P69/233 (69). They included James Gralton of New York, who would return home to Leitrim later that year. **through lily sales** See Cumann na mBan to An Timthire, 23 Dec. 1929, McGarrity papers, Ms 17,534 (3) NLI. **of three dances** Neenan to J. Stanton, 24 Mar. 1930 in McGarrity papers, Ms 17,467 (7) NLI. **in Chicago during 1930** J. Keating, Chicago to Neenan, 18 May 1930 and Neenan to Keating, 8 July 1930 in McGarrity papers, Ms 17,467 (1) NLI. **his fare during 1931** O/C West Limerick to A/G, 28 Mar. 1931 & A/G to O/C W. Limk, 31 Mar. 1931, in MTUCDA. P69/151 (106–3). **for their treatment** Pete Kearney to Chairman Army Council, 9 Sept. 1932 in MTUCDA, P69/185 (180). Of these men, one died, while the rest recovered, seven going back to Ireland and five remaining in the US. **a year in 1932** Secretary Clan na Gael to Chairman AC, 7 Sept. 1932, in MTUCDA, P69/185 (209–12). **during May 1930** Report by Jack Ashe of Springfield, Mass, 9 May 1930 in McGarrity papers, Ms 17,467 (3) NLI. **in 1921** Kenny, *American Irish*, p. 199. See also report that 1923 AOH Convention strongly supported the establishment of the Free State, in British Consulate General (NYC), report, 26 July 1923, in D/T S 1976 NAI. **supporters of the IRA** For the disillusioning effect of the split on Irish American activists see F.M. Carroll, *American opinion and the Irish question 1910–23* (Dublin, 1978) pp 177–87. **organization in the US** AC to An Timthire, 1 Aug. 1929 in McGarrity papers, Ms 17,534 (3) NLI. Comhairle na Poblachta was a short-lived political initiative launched by the IRA in late 1928.

PAGE **165 joined the clan** Secretary Army Council to Chairman Clan na Gael, 21 Nov. 1929, in McGarrity papers, Ms 17,534 (3) NLI. **organization to the Clan** Clan Executive Report, 28 Oct. 1929, in McGarrity papers, Ms 17,534 (3) NLI. For more on Cooney's mission see MacEvilly, *IRA chief,* pp 159–64. **across the US** The Clan Convention was held on 30 and 31 Aug. and 1 Sept. 1930; in McGarrity papers, Ms 17,535 (3). **we are not sincere'** C/S to Chairman and Executive, Clan na Gael, 11 Dec. 1930, in MTUCDA, P69/61 (5–10). Personally Twomey hugely enjoyed his travels in the US. He travelled from New York, through Cleveland, Chicago and Buffalo to San Francisco. See letters to Kathleen Twomey, 28 Sept., and 13 and 17 Oct. 1930. Fr. Maurice Twomey Jr. **of militant nationalism** Report of Chairman, Clan na Gael Executive, Clan Convention, 5–7 Sept. 1936, in McGarrity papers, Ms 17,542 (4) NLI. **spineless and afraid'?** Proposed circular to Clan, 15 June 1932. McGarrity also included a warning to the IRA to 'beware of spineless inaction'. The Clan executive convinced him not to send out the circular. In MTUC-DA, P69/185 (287). **the military side** 'Q' to C/S, 4 Oct. 1932 in MTUCDA, P69/185 (172–5). **to the new government** Clan na Gael to Chairman Army Council, 4 Aug. 1934 in McGarrity papers, Ms 17,539 NLI and Neenan to Twomey, 28 Aug. 1932 in MTUCDA, P69/185 (213). **members from Ireland** Russell report on Clan Convention of 3 Sept. 1932, report dated 20 Nov. 1932 in MTUCDA, P69/185 (148–52). **in late 1932** Secretary Clan na Gael to Chairman Army Council, 18 Dec. 1932 in MTUCDA, P69/185 (97–99).

PAGE **166 the highest authority** IRA Statement on 1933 Election, to all Clan Districts and Camps, 10 Jan. 1933 in MTUCDA, P69/185 (75). The new agreement was signed on behalf of the IRA by Twomey and Mick Price, 27 March 1933 in P69/185 (31). **us new members'** An Timthire Dispatch, 21 Dec. 1926, in MTUCDA, P69/183 (157). **are most convincing** McGarrity to Army Council, 7 Dec. 1929, quoted in Tarpey, op. cit. p. 257. **attack Northern Ireland** Clan to Chairman Army Council, 8 Oct. 1934 in McGarrity papers, Ms 17,539, NLI. **political direction** See Richard Dunphy, 'The soldiers set out: Reflections on the formation of Fianna Fáil.' in Hannon and Gallagher (eds), *Taking the long view*. **harboured this suspicion** Army Council to Chairman Clan na Gael, 27 Jan. 1930 in McGarrity papers, Ms 17,535 (1) NLI. **in the general election** Kearney to Chairman Army Council, 10 May 1932, in MTUCDA P69/185 (294–7). **objections** Telegram from 'Collins' to Clan: 'Must have remittance immediately, and protest your reason for withholding it.' (N/D) in MTUCDA P69/185 (290). **end of May** Kearney to Chairman Army Council, 31 May 1932, in MTUCDA, P69/185 (291–3) **political pronouncements** Kearney to Chairman AC, 10 May 1932, in MTUCDA, P69/185 (294–7). It should be noted that at the IRA's 1933 and 1934 conventions, Kearney, by then resident in Ireland would defend the need for radical social policies. See Notes of 1933 GAC, in MTUCDA, P69/187 (99–100) and Notes of 1934 GAC, MacEntee papers, UCDA, P67/525. **1932 Convention** Russell Report, 20 Nov. 1932, in MTUCDA P69/185 (148–52). **the IRA's position** Kearney to Chairman Army Council, 26 June 1932, in MTUCDA P69/185 (279–81). Kearney was in the US from 1924 until 1933, when he returned to Ireland and took up a position with IRA GHQ. **economic programme** Notes of 1933 GAC, in MTUCDA, P69/187 (100). **allowed to remain** An Timthire Dispatch, 18 May 1927 and 20 May 1927, in MTUCDA P69/183 (35–36) and (45). **the IRA would be** Dunphy, 'The Soldiers Set Out' & Coogan, *De Valera*, pp 389–98. **and IRA events** Founded in the 1870 as a populist radical newspaper by Patrick Ford. It strongly supported the Land League in Ireland and trade unionism in the US. The *Irish World* defended IRA activities in Ireland as well as supporting Fianna Fáil, and denounced Free State government as British puppets. The paper supported some labour organizations while also containing anti-Semitic and anti-communist articles. **divided on the issue** Report, 6 Nov. 1929, in McGarrity papers, Ms 17,534 (1) NLI.

PAGE **167 within its ranks** Kearney to Chairman AC, 10 May 1932, in MTUCDA, P69/185 (294–7). **among the clan** McGinnitty to Manager, *An Phoblacht*, 28 Apr. 1932, in MTUCDA, P69/233 (164). McGinnitty wrote that newsreel footage of the release of IRA prisoners during March 1932 had provided Clan members with a morale boost before their Easter commemorations. **'badly understood'** Chairman Army Council to Secretary Clan na Gael, 13 Feb. 1933, in MTUCDA P69/185 (91). **pro-de Valera** See *Irish World*, 3 and 10 Dec. 1932, and IRA criticism 14 Dec. 1932 in MTUCDA, P69/185 (138). Ryan's resignation letter to Connnie Neenan, 20 Dec. 1932 in MTUCDA P69/185 (132). Ryan had been a Clan member since 1892, see interview in *An Phoblacht*, 29 Oct. 1932. **held for the IRA!** Secretary Clan na Gael to Chairman AC, 3 October 1932, in MTUCDA, P69/185 (159–161). **many Irish emigrants** To Manager, *An Phoblacht*, 6 May 1931, in MTUCDA, P69/233 (173–4). **for revolutionary activity** See *Irish World*, 7 Nov. 1931 on the 'New Penal Laws.' The paper itself was banned in Ireland under the new legislation in Oct. 1931. *An Phoblacht* of 12 Mar. 1932 published a list of over 200 Irish American sporting and political bodies that had denounced the 'Coercion Bill.' **worked as miners** Report by Seán O'Deorain to McGarrity, 6 Nov. 1929, in McGarrity papers, Ms 17,534 (1). At one stage Butte had the highest Irish percentage population of any city in the US. It had a long Nationalist and Labour tradition. See D. M. Emmons, *The Butte Irish 1875–1925* (Chicago, 1990) **during the 1930s** J.B. Freeman, 'Irish workers in the twentieth-century United States: the case of the transport worker's Union.' in *Saothar* 8 (1982) 24–45. **the majority of them** McNickle argues that as the many of the Irish were part of an aspiring middle class at the time, the

Depression seemed to cut off their hopes of 'making it' and was relatively worse for them than other sectors of society. McNickle, 'When New York was Irish' in *New York Irish*, pp 352–3. **for support by 1933** The Clan helped McGarrity financially through his wife, with the IRA's knowledge, but without that of McGarritty himself. See Neenan to Twomey, 17 Dec. 1932 and 21 Mar. 1933 in MTUCDA P69/185 (137) and (50). **in that year** Army Council to An Timthire, 27 Jan. 1930 in McGarrity papers, Ms 17,535 NLI.

PAGE 168 in the country at large Clan Convention, 30 Aug. to 1 Sept. 1930 in McGarrity papers, Ms 17,535 (3) NLI. **were unemployed** P.J. Gannon and W. Kerrisk, 4 May and 4 June 1930 in McGarrity papers, Ms 17,467 (1) NLI. **who have jobs'** Moss Twomey to Kathleen Twomey, Detroit, 28 Sept. 1930. **feeling of dispair'** Moss Twomey to Kathleen Twomey, Butte, 13 Oct. 1930 and Klamath Falls, Oregon, 17 Oct. 1930. **from the US** Memorandum for Clan, 25 Aug. 1932 in MTUCDA P69/185 (220). **'treasury was depleted'** Kearney to Chairman Army Council, 31 May 1932 P69/185 (291–3).**for a rainy day** Kearney to Chairman Army Council, 26 June 1932, P69/185 (279–81). **'New York is broke'** Neenan to Twomey, 28 Aug. 1932 in MTUCDA, P69/185 (213). **about money** Memorandum, 25 Aug. 1932, P69/185 (220). **Butte gloomy 'Q'** to C/S, 7 Sept. 1932 in MTUCDA, P69/185 (209–12). **until next year** Army Finances Report, Dec. 1932 in MTUCDA, P69/54 (58–59). **forget them'** Neenan to Manager *An Phoblacht*, 30 Dec. 1932 in MTUCDA, P69/234 (4). For example, he reported that the only one Clan member in Buffalo had a job. **even that year** Edward Quinn, Chicago to *An Phoblacht*, 30 Nov. 1932, in MTUCDA, P69/227 (37). **the organization's treasury** Clan na Gael to Army Council, 30 Dec. 1932 in MTUCDA, P69/185 (103). **to collect money** McGarrity to Twomey, 3 Dec. 1933, in McGarrity papers, Ms 17,490 NLI. **'republican bonds'** Fitzpatrick, *Two Irelands*, p. 80.

PAGE 169 were to be repaid For the background to this issue see Coogan, *Long fellow*, pp 391, 416–18 and 439–41. **it can be secured** Army Council to Secretary Clan na Gael, 13 Feb. 1933, in MTUCDA, P69/185 (86). **the IRA later on** Clan na Gael to Chairman, Army Council, 7 Mar. 1933, in MTUCDA, P69/185 (60–62). **from Co. Kerry** James Connolly IRA Club Agenda, 31 Oct. 1932, in MTUCDA, P69/223 (4). **to cease doing so** McGinnitty to Manager *An Phoblacht*, 1 Aug. 1932, in MTUCDA, P69/233 (43). **in New York** Letter to Manager *An Phoblacht*, Oct. 1934 in MTUCDA, P69/227 (5) and *Republican Congress*, 13 July 1935. **to complain about it** Twomey to McGarrity, 7 Oct. 1935 in McGarrity papers, Ms 17,490 NLI.

PAGE 170 deaf ears in Ireland Gilmore Notes. **30,000 members** Freeman 'Irish Workers' in *Saothar* 8, p. 25. *Irish Democrat*, 26 June 1937. **Irish-Jewish conflict** See S. Cronin, *James Connolly and the Transport Workers Union of America* (Dublin, 1983) and R.H. Bayor, *Neighbors in conflict* (Baltimore, 1978). **criticism in Ireland** His attack on de Valera was contained in the TWU's *Transport Bulletin*, May 1945. While Ireland's neutrality was not popular with Irish Americans the attack on de Valera did cause much dissension. The *Irish Press*, 21 June 1945 quotes the *Gaelic American*, 19 May 1945, describing Quill a 'half-baked Red from the Bronx'. Quill's activities gained him a substantial Garda file, see Jus 8/931 NAI. **transit unionism** J.B. Freeman, *In Transit* (Oxford, 1989), p. 34. **in 1932** Sacco and Vanzetti faced execution on bombing charges. The Scottsboro boys were a group of young blacks on death row following accusations of rape. *An Phoblacht*, 17 Aug. 1927 and 5 Nov. 1932. **labour radical** *An Phoblacht*, 27 Sept. 1930 and 3 June 1933.

in Nicaragua See support for San Francisco General Strike, *An Phoblacht*, 21 May 1934 and US textile strike, 8 Sept. 1934. **see they were** Chairman Army Council to An Timthire, 9 Feb. 1927 in MTUCDA, P69/183 (111). **'winning his war'** *An Phoblacht*, 25 Feb. 1933 and 23 May 1933. **Fr Charles Coughlin** See p. 184 of New York Twomey to McGarrity, 7 Oct. 1935, in McGarrity papers, Ms 17,490 NLI. **by that time** See for example Paul O'Connor, Boston, to *An Phoblacht* 24 July 1934, asking that the paper no longer be sent because 'it has such a small circulation here' in MTUCDA, P69/232 (3). **for the IRA** See Cronin, *McGarrity papers*, pp 160–74 and also *Frank Ryan*, pp 175–9. Also J.B. Bell, *Secret army*, pp 145–67. **would revive again** Twomey to McGarrity, 27 Dec. 1937, in McGarrity papers, Ms 17,490, NLI. **enthusiasm with them** There were 500 present at a republican gathering in San Francisco and 50 in Butte, but only 24 in Chicago. Reports, 3 Aug. and 16 Aug. 1937 in McGarrity papers, Ms 17,485 NLI. **leadership after 1936** See Statement to the General Army Convention (1938) from the outgoing IRA leadership in Aiken papers, UCDA, P104/2833 (1–3). Also Russell to McGarrity 29 Jan., 7 May, and 5 Nov. 1937 in McGarrity papers, Ms 17,485 NLI.

PAGE 171 **the surrounding region** Foreign Reserve List, in MTUCDA, P69/172. **members in Britain** Army Council Report, 1 Nov. 1926, in MTUCDA, P69/181 (5). **Table 17** Foreign Reserve reports, in MTUCDA, P69/171 (2), & P69/172. **not acted on** Memorandum to members of the Army Council on future organization in Britain, 21 Feb. 1926, in MTUCDA, P69/181 (65–66). **still only 38** Report, Aug. 1930 in MTUCDA, P69/153 (203). **to just 20** O/C No. 2 Area Britain, to A/G 23 Apr. 1932, in MTUCDA, P69/121 (27). **Irish in Britain** There were 14 Sinn Féin Cumann in Britain in Dec. 1929, see report in Jus 8/675, NAI. **into Sinn Féin** See for example, Easter Week commemoration events, 17 Apr. 1933 in Joseph H. Fowler papers, Ms 27,097 (2/1) NLI. **in the North of England** See *Manchester Guardian*, 23 Nov. 1931 for estimate of 'over a thousand Irish men and women' attending ceremony in Bootle cemetery, Liverpool and 28 Nov. 1932 for a procession, 'some thousands strong' in Moston, north Manchester. **Seamus Barrett** See MTUCDA, P69/121 (1–28). Barrett owned a grocer's and wholesaler's shop in Deansgate. *An Phoblacht*, 4 Mar. 1927. **on the Labour party** A/G to O/C No.2, (n/d) in MTUCDA, P69/152 (214). All of the prisoners were being held in Maidstone prison, *An Phoblacht*, 8 Dec. 1928. **the prisoners issue** O/C No. 2 Area, Britain to A/G, 10 Feb. 1930 in MTUCDA, P69/152 (215).

PAGE 172 **Manchester, spoke** *An Phoblacht*, 10 May and 24 May 1930. **not be tolerated** Various reports, Oct. 1932, in MTUCDA, P69/121 (1–28). **feud during 1925** Pete Hughes to Frances Carty, 8 May 1925, in MTUCDA, P69/62 (17–18). **of this period** See O/C No. 1 Area Britain to A/G, 9 May 1932, for complaints of intimidation of republicans and surveillance of Irish clubs and dance halls, in Aiken papers, UCDA, P104/2836. **general army conventions** Notes of these Conventions in MTUCDA, P69/187 and MacEntee papers, P67/525. **often tenuous** Frank Corrigan, 'The bombing campaign' O'Mahoney. **Charles Donnelly** Joseph O'Connor, *Even the olives are bleeding* (Dublin, 1992). pp 78–9. **participation in them** B. McWilliams, Irish Anti-Imperialist League, to *An Phoblacht*, 25 Sept. 1932, in MTUCDA, P69/158 (52–3) and A/G to O/C No.1 Area Britain, 12 Oct. 1932, in MTUCDA, P69/158 (50). **in Britain itself** See Memorandum, MTUCDA, P69/181 (65–6). It is possible Seán Russell was the author of this document. **and ceilidhthe'** A/G to C/S, 6 May 1938 in McGarrity papers, Ms 17,544 (5) NLI.

PAGE 173. **over 200 republicans** See Bowyer Bell, op.cit. for deaths. 98 IRA members were jailed and 164 men and women deported. See *Notes on Events*, in MacEntee papers, UCDA, P67/534 (Appendix). **to New Zealand** List, 60 went to Melbourne and 24 to Sydney, 1 Apr. 1931, in MTUCDA, P69/233 (92). **economic struggle'** Seán O'Carroll, Sydney, to *An Phoblacht*, 15 May 1934, in MTUCDA, P69/224 (12–13). **dominance among immigrants** Manager, *The Tribune* to *An Phoblacht*, 'People here seem to prefer reading "The Irish Review" an Australian Irish monthly'. 6 June 1935, in MTUCDA, P69/224 (4–5). **rallies in Ireland** See Garda report on rally in Dublin's Mansion House, 24 Sept. 1930 with Indian speaker Krishno Deonarine, along with Seán MacBride and Peadar O'Donnell, in Jus 8/682 NAI. **a speaking tour** Political Prisoners Committee to Gandhi, 19 Sept. 1931, in Humphreys papers, UCDA, P106/1314. **during 1932** Chairman AC to Secretary Clan, 8 Nov. 1932, in MTUCDA, P69/185 (157–8). **if it were possible** An Timthire dispatch, 9 Feb. 1927, in MTUCDA, P69/183 (110). Also see *An Phoblacht*, 2 July 1926, 27 Aug. 1927. **in the city** An Timthire dispatch, 3 Feb. 1927, in MTUCDA, P69/183 (121). **(was) Imperialistic'** An Timthire dispatch, 20 Apr. 1927, in MTUCDA, P69/183 (45). The *Irish World* did feature pro-Chinese articles in Apr. 1927. See issue of 23 Apr. **were satisfactory** Army Council Report, 17 Feb. 1927, in MTUCDA, P69/48 (118–9). **in 1916** *An Phoblacht*, 6 Dec. 1930. **in the US** Army Council to An Timthire, 25

Feb. 1930, in McGarrity papers, Ms 17, 535 (2) NLI. **had visited Russia** See Michael McInerney, 'Gerry Boland's story' in the *Irish Times*, 11 Oct. 1968. Documents relating to their contacts were discovered by the gardaí in 1931. See p. 43.
PAGE 174 country in 1930 Dates from *Notes on Communism in Saorstat Eireann* in MacEntee papers, UCDA, P67/523. **during 1931** See Notes on Certain Individuals, Appendix IX, in MacEntee papers, UCDA, P67/550. **notifying his superiors** See Adjt North Kilkenny Batt, to A/G, 19 Sept. 1930, in MTUCDA, P69/153 (4–5). Boran was company O/C for the IRA in the Castlecomer district. **in Frankfurt** *Notes on Communism*, P67/523. **front organization** Garda report, 3 Sept. 1930, in FitzGerald papers, UCDA, P80/905. **the IRA in Ireland** Emmet O'Connor, 'Jim Larkin and the Communist Internationals, 1923–9', in *Irish Historical Studies* 123 (May 1999). pp 357–2. **'reactionary regime'** *An Phoblacht*, 27 May 1933. **under Italian invasion** *An Phoblacht*, 28 March 1936. **towards the IRA** See Hoven and Clissman's analysis of the IRA in *Der Vorkampfer*, Oct. 1932 in MTUCDA, P69/157 (12). Hoven had met MacBride at the 1929 Frankfurt Anti-imperialist conference. In 1937 he allegedly accompanied Tom Barry on a visit to Germany. Clissman returned to Dublin in 1936 where he again met members of the IRA and Republican Congress. 'The German agents' in *Notes on IRA Activities*, MacEntee papers, P67/550 p. 131. **the final chapter** For various views on this see R. English, 'Socialist Republicanism in independent Ireland, 1922–49' in Regan and Cronin (eds), *Ireland: The politics of Independence, 1922–49* (London, 2000) pp 84–97. Bell, *Secret army*, pp 215–35, MacEoin, *Twilight years*, pp 857–62 and Jim McVeigh, *Executed: Tom Williams and the IRA* (Belfast, 1999) pp 16–17.

Chapter Ten
PAGE 175 by that method *The Nation*, 10 Aug. 1929. **outside its ranks** As Twomey put it 'Everybody is agreed armed force must be the ultimate weapon'. Twomey to McGarrity, 26 Oct. 1933, in McGarrity papers, Ms 17,490 NLI. **new political departures** O/C Boyne Batt. at Officer's Meeting, 9 Apr. 1927 and Seán Lanigan, Limerick, at 1933 GAC, in MTUCDA, P69/48 (162) & P69/187 (94). **for a social policy** Barry to Twomey, 13 May 1932, in MTUCDA, P69/52 (63). **military force** Notes of 1933 GAC, MTUCDA, P69/187 (77). **'what they can get'** Seamus Mallin at the 1934 GAC, MacEntee papers, in UCDA, P67/525. **in Leinster House** MacBride at the 1934 Convention, P67/525, *An Phoblacht*, 21 Apr.1934, **a new Citizen's Army** O'Donnell in *Republican Congress*, 5 May 1934 and Ryan at the 1933 GAC, MTUCDA, P69/187 (94).
PAGE 176 to dash them again Report on 1933 GAC, MTUCDA, P69/187 (77) & Clan to AC, 8 Oct. 1934, in McGarrity papers, Ms 17,539 NLI. **and recruiting** Staff Officer 'J.J.' report on Kerry, 18 Jan. 1931, in MTUCDA, P69/153 (14–18). **to radical policies** McHugh, 'Voices of the Rearguard', p. 493. **for political parties'** Officer's meeting, 9 Apr. 1927, MTUCDA, P69/48 (162). **Protestant strikers** See Chapter 8. **exploited by employers** Notes of 1933 GAC, MTUCDA, P69/187 (97) and *An Phoblacht*, 7 Apr.1934. **and railway strikes** See Chapter 8. **the Republican Congress** Fitzpatrick was singled out along with MacBride by Mick Price as a principal opponent of the left by 1934. Meeting between Cumann na mBan Executive and resigned IRA officers, 20 Apr. 1934, in Humphreys papers, UCDA, P106/1154 (1–5). **were politicians'** Twomey to C/S, 10 November 1924, in MTUCDA, P69/46 (32–3).
PAGE 177 Treaty to be signed Interview with the Chief of Staff of the IRA, 1927, in MTUCDA, P69/73 (65–72). **than treachery** *An Phoblacht*, 2 May 1931. **national independence** *An Phoblacht*, 16 May 1931. **We are revolutionaries'** Notes of 1933 GAC, MTUCDA, P69/187 (100). **a civilian political party** Twomey to McGarrity, 26 Oct. 1933, in McGarrity papers Ms 17,490 NLI. **would emerge** Twomey to McGarrity, 9 Dec. 1931, in McGarrity papers, Ms 17,490 NLI. **and social conditions** Twomey to McGarrity, 23 June 1931, in McGarrity papers, Ms 17,490 NLI. **in early 1931** AC to Secretary, Clan na Gael, 7 May 1932, in MTUCDA, P69/185 (298–302). The AC discussed it at their meeting of 14 Jan. 1931, in MTUCDA, P69/69 (2). **the IRA leadership** After he left the IRA Michael

Price claimed 1930 was the year the leadership made a definite shift towards taking a radical social and economic position. Meeting with Cumann na mBan Executive, 20 April 1934, in Humphreys papers, UCDA, 1154 (1). **have been launched** W.K. Anderson, *James Connolly and the Irish Left* (Dublin, 1994), p. 134. Coogan, *IRA*, p. 59. **by elections results** Twomey writing in *The Nation*, 10 Aug. 1929. **over life and death'** Seán Ryan, Tralee IRA O/C at the 1933 GAC, MTUCDA, P69/187 (96). **to be armed** AC to President of the Executive Council, 25 Nov. 1932, in MTUCDA, P69/155 (18–19).
PAGE 178 good of sovereignty' AC Statement, Aug. 1932, in MTUCDA, P69/53 (375–6). **Treaty had proven** MacBride to McGarrity, 19 Oct. 1933, in McGarrity papers, Ms 17,456 NLI. **allow an election** MacBride at the 1933 GAC, MTUCDA, P69/187 (102). **an IRA regime** J.J. Sheehy and Tadgh Lynch for example at the 1933 GAC, MTUCDA, P69/187 (100–1). **unaware of the fact** Twomey to Tom Barry, 24 May 1932, MTUCDA, P69/52 (63–4). **revolutionary organization** Notes of AC meeting, 27 Jan. 1927, in MTUCDA, P69/181 (3). **mass of the people** Notes of 1934 GAC, MacEntee papers, UCDA, P67/525.**of no property** O'Donoghue to Humphreys, Apr. 1935, in Humphreys papers, UCDA, P106/1748. **requires discipline'** George Plunkett at the 1933 GAC, MTUCDA, P69/187 (104). **freedom to organize** C. MacGinnity to AP, 16 Jan. 1933, in MTUCDA, P69/233 (19–21).
PAGE 179 during the same period Mick Fitzpatrick in 1927 and 1932 and David FitzGerald in 1930. The Irish section of the League against Imperialism was led by Seán MacBride and Seán McSwiney from 1928. *Notes on Communism in Saorstat Eireann*, in MacEntee papers, UCDA, P67/523. See also AC and Executive Minutes, 18 June and 1 Aug. 1930, in MTUCDA, P69/69 (2). **for a period** O'Connor, 'Jim Larkin' in *Irish Historical Studies*, 123 and Fitzpatrick to 'Lecky'; Mar. 1928, in Russian State Archives for Social and Political History (RGASPI) 495/89/52–25, courtesy of Emmet O'Connor. **also IRA members** Garda report, 16 June 1930, in FitzGerald papers, UCDA, P80/911 (2). Garda informant Patrick Carroll reported that 30 out of 63 WRP members were IRA. The WRP was succeeded by the Revolutionary Workers' Group which then became the Communist Party of Ireland. **social inequality** *An Phoblacht*, 14 Feb. 1931. This was in reply to an attack on nationalization by Mick Price himself a proponent of the 'Worker's Republic' in 1934. See *An Phoblacht*, 7 Feb. 1931. **a Communist organization** *An Phoblacht*, 16 May 1931. **its 1933 convention** Notes of 1933 GAC, MTUCDA, P69/187 (78). **of the population** Mary M. Banta, 'The Red scare in the Irish Free State', 1929–37, MA thesis, UCD, 1982 p. 238. **Dublin city council** Dunphy, *Fianna Fáil Power*, p. 135. **anti-communists** O'Connor, 'Jim Larkin', *Irish Historical Studies*, 123 p. 371. **Saor Éire** English, *Radicals*, p. 126. **a stagnant IRA** McHugh, *Voices of the rearguard*, p. 494. Jonathan Hamill's point that Saor Éire was a 'response to class divisions' rather than their 'instigator' is correct but hardly surprising since most political organizations develop policies in response to social conditions. 'Saor Éire and the IRA: An Exercise in Deception?' in *Saothar* 20 (1995) 56–66. **have escaped censure** AC to Secretary Clan na Gael, 7 May 1932, in MTUCDA, P69/185 (298–302).
PAGE 180 of Saor Éire 'Jim' to Annie O'Farrelly (*An Phoblacht*), 2 Dec. 1931, in MTUCDA, P69/243 (142). AC Minutes, 29 Dec. 1931, in MTUCDA, P69/71. **organizing Saor Éire** AC to Clan, 7 May 1932, in MTUCDA, P69/185 (298–302). **the latter body** O/C Offaly to A/G, 19 May 1932, in MTUCDA, P69/157 (22). **from communism** The 12 units were Meath, North Cork, North Tipperary, Mayo South, Drogheda, Listowel, Limerick City, Clare West, Sligo, Dublin No. 2, Cork No. 1 and Caherciveen. Specifically anti-Communist motions came from Dublin No. 4, the Dublin College Coy, and West Cork. Clár, 1933 GAC, in MTUCDA, P69/53 (273–286). **out of the organization** C. Boyle, Donegal and Dick Batterbury, Dublin at 1933 GAC, in MTUCDA, P69/187 (96 & 106). **be a communist** Notes of 1933 in MTUCDA, P69/187 (107–8). **rejected his ideas** Notes of 1933 GAC, in MTUCDA, P69/187 (101). **association with communism** Twomey had no sympathy with the attackers, thinking them mobilized by Dublin's populist Lord Mayor

Alfie Byrne. Twomey to Neenan, 28 March 1933, MTUCDA, P69/185 (21–5). George Gilmore had tried without success to get permission to take men to defend Connolly House. Entry, Jacob Diaries, 8 Apr. 1933, Ms 32,582 (72) NLI. **system in Ireland** *Irish Times*, 19 June 1933. *An Phoblacht*, 17 June 1933. **the Free State** Jacob Diaries, 18 June 1933, Ms 32,582 (72). **associated with it** Achill's Brian Corrigan told listeners he was not a communist but a supporter of a 'worker's republic' during Sept. 1934. See Jus 8/342 NAI. See also Thomas Maguire at Westmeath County Council, where he answered the 'slur' that he was a communist. *Westmeath Independent*, 14 July 1934. **from defending it** Notes of 1933 GAC, MTUCDA, P69/187 (95). **recruit to the IRA** Notes of 1933 GAC, MTUCDA, P69/187 (77).

PAGE 181 to reform capitalism *An Phoblacht*, 10 & 17 Nov. 1934. **up another flag?** Sheehy, Tom Maguire (Westmeath) and Seán Mitchell (Cork), Notes of 1933 GAC, MTUCDA, P69/187 (98, 101–2). **commanding officer** Leitrim Batt. Convention report, 1933, MTUCDA, P69/187 (13). This also may have reflected lack of confidence in speaking in front of visiting senior officers. **these policies** Twomey himself made a similar point to Uinseann MacEoin, in *Twilight years*, p. 843. **defending Gralton** *An Phoblacht*, 4 & 11 Mar. 1933. The IRA's A/G statement to the Gralton Defence meeting in Dublin's Rotunda is often quoted as an example of the IRA's reluctance to defend Gralton. The Leitrim IRA condemned it as *too* sympathetic to him. Clár, 1933 GAC, in MTUCDA, P69/53 (278–9). **on the matter** The committee consisted of Andy Cooney, Tom Barry, J.J. Sheehy, Davy Matthews and George Plunkett. Possibly not the most sympathetic quintet the IRA could have chosen. Notes of 1933 GAC, MTUCDA, P69/187 (79–80). **his dance hall!!** Twomey to Neenan, 3 March 1933, see Chapter Three. Luke Gibbons, 'Labour and local history: the case of Jim Gralton', in *Saothar* 14 (1989) 85–95. A member of the Leitrim IRA at the time, Packy Earley, believes it was IRA members who fired on Gralton's hall. To author, 30 August 2001. **after 1936** F. McGarry, 'Catholics first and politicians afterwards': the Labour Party and the Workers' Republic, 1936–39' in *Saothar* 25 (2000). **'irreligious'** Notes of 1933 GAC, in MTUCDA, P69/187 (77) This was passed unanimously.

PAGE 182 benefit the community Oglaigh na h-Eireann, *Constitution and governmental programme for the republic of Ireland* (Dublin, January 1934). **struggle for instance** English, 'Socialism and republican schism in Ireland: the emergence of the Republican Congress in 1934' in *Irish Historical Studies* 105 (May 1990) 49–65 **Hilaire Belloc** Organized around a Distributist League in Britain. Barberis et al., *Encyclopaedia of British and Irish Political Organizations* (London, 2000) pp 209–10. **Clifford Douglas** In Britain represented by the Social Credit Party. In Alberta, Canada, the Social Credit Party actually formed a government in 1935 and existed until the 1980s. *Encyclopaedia of British and Irish*, pp 226–9. Twomey was critical of the Douglas variant of Social Credit, however. *An Phoblacht*, 9 Feb. 1935. **socialism or communism** See motion from Glasgow Sinn Féin at 1932 Ard Fheis, that as the banking system was the root of 'social evils' that the Douglas Social Credit scheme be proposed as an alternative. In MTUCDA, P69/54 (159–65). **Catholic, roots** Distributist ideas were still apparent within Provisional Sinn Féin's policies during the 1970s. Bob Purdie, 'Reconsideration's on Republicanism and Socialism' in Morgan and Purdie (eds), *Ireland, divided nation, divided class* (London, 1980) pp 74–95. **'pagan and unchristian'** *An Phoblacht*, 17 June 1932. **'knocking it down'** Twomey to Seamus Lennon, 6 Aug. 1932, in MTUCDA, P69/52 (2–3). **credit and the banks** Twomey to Neenan, 15 Sept. 1932, in MTUCDA, P69/185 (195–9). **any social strata** R. Dunphy, 'The enigma of Fianna Fáil: party strategy, social classes and the politics of hegemony' in Cronin and Regan, *The politics of Independence*, pp 67–83.

PAGE 183 in the area Adjt. Dingle Batt. to A/G, 12 Sept. 1932, in MTUCDA, P69/156 (88–90). **for them to feed** Adjt. North Mayo to A/G, 2 Aug. 1932, in MTUCDA, P69/158 (236–9). **and urban poor** A/G to Adjt Dingle Batt., 7 Oct. 1932, in MTUCDA, P69/156 (83–4). **demands heard instead** Twomey to Seamus Lennon, 6 Aug. 1932, in MTUCDA, P69/52 (2–3). Lennon had been a member of the Second Dáil for Carlow-Kilkenny. **the**

land situation Report on conference of 2 Oct. 1932, in MTUCDA, P69/54 (37–41). **stuff of fantasy** *An Phoblacht*, 1 Oct. 1932. **an inevitable collapse** A/G to Adjt Dingle Batt, P69/156 (83–4) and A/G to Commander of each Independent Unit, 18 Feb. 1933, in MTUCDA, P69/187 (1–3). **longer term anyway** Twomey to Neenan, 8 Nov. 1932, in MTUCDA, P69/185 (165–7) and A/G to Commander, P69/187 (1–3). **'co-operative redistribution'** MacBride and Donal O'Connor at the 1934 GAC, MacEntee papers, UCDA, P67/525. **in their formulation** Donal O'Connor at the 1934 GAC, MacEntee papers, UCDA, P67/525. **in the 'Constitution'** 'That the complete transport system of Dublin should be at the mercy of a private monopoly is a matter affecting the welfare of all Dublin citizens ... further the AC is interested as the governmental programme of the IRA on the question of transports provides:-Railways, canals, air and waterways ... shall be operated as a body set up by the National Economic Council'. AC Statement, *Irish Press*, 25 Mar. 1935. **during the 1940s** See *Explanations please – They say they are not Communists!* an anti-Clann na Poblachta pamphlet produced during the run up to the 1948 general election. The pasts of MacBride, O'Donoghue and Fitzpatrick are used to claim that they were still under communist influence. Copy in MacEntee papers, UCDA, P67/522 (1).

PAGE 184 'radio priest' *An Phoblacht*, 21 July & 27 Oct. 1934 and 19 Jan. 1935 Kenny, *American Irish*, pp 207–8. **virulent anti-Semite** Albert Fried, *FDR and his enemies*, (New York, 1999) pp 110–20, 145–58. While *An Phoblacht* was promoting Coughlin he was claiming he disavowed 'racial Hitlerism' and 'industrial Fascism' along with Communism. *An Phoblacht*, 18 May 1935. **too same route** Speakers at Dublin street meetings organized by the Financial Freedom Federation occasionally used anti-Semitic rhetoric. See Garda report, 17 Dec. 1934, in Jus 8/341 NAI. Seamus Lennon would write for the anti-Semitic publication *Penapa* . Copy of Dec. 1940 in MacEntee papers, UCDA, P67/544 (1). **there before them** To C/S, 9 Dec. 1926, in MTUCDA, P69/47 (200–32). **for fascist influence** As suggested by Garvin in *1922 – The birth of Irish democracy*, (Dublin, 1996), p. 22. **had happened in Germany** Twomey to McGarrity, 26 Oct. 1933, in McGarrity papers, Ms 17,490 NLI. **favourable to Hitler** *An Phoblacht*, 21 Aug. 1934. **our Celtic nature** Address to Cumann na mBan Convention, 1934, in Humphreys papers, UCDA, P106/1152 (1). **joining the party** National Convention report, 7&8 Nov. 1936, in Jus 8/68 NAI. **'Christian Justice'** 'An Open Letter to Young Irishmen' Dec. 1939, in Jus 8/752 NAI. **'King nor Dictator'** *War News*, 18 Nov. 1939, in PRONI HA4/2/32. **as 'Liberators'** 'Ireland's Answer' in D/T S 11564 A NAI. **the Nazi leadership** See *War News* of 17 Aug. and 14 Dec. 1940, in Jus 8/752 NAI. **driving from Europe** *War News*, Feb. 1941 and (nd) 1941, in Jus 8/752 NAI.

PAGE 185 Irish Nazi Supporters See reports on Coras na Poblachta in Jus 8/888 NAI and in *Notes on IRA Activities*, in MacEntee papers, UCDA, P67/550 p. 48. **marginality by 1940** Tom Garvin has argued that since 1922 the IRA can 'rightly be described as national socialist.' In *Irish Times*, 19 Feb. 1999. **general election!** Military Intelligence reports on IRA political attitudes, 5 March 1942 and 17 and 19 June 1943, in G2/X/0058 MA. Reports on splits in the Curragh Internment Camp, in P.M. 1498 MA. **is extremely difficult** Ó hUid was editor of *War News* for a period and may have introduced some of its anti-Semitism. Jim O'Donovan was described to me as 'Nazi to the core' by one IRA veteran but this is strenuously contested by Joe Briscoe, O'Donovan's dentist for many years and a prominent member of the Jewish community. Jim Savage to author, 9 Apr. 2000 and Briscoe to author, 7 Feb. 2002. **it would focus on** 'Lines on which paper is to be run' 1926, in MTUCDA, P69/181 (41). **about the border** *An Phoblacht*, 29 July 1933. **its northern policy** A/G to Commanders, Each Independent Unit, 18 Feb. 1933, in MTUCDA, P69/187 (1–3). **should be a prioity** Clár 1933 GAC, in MTUCDA, P69/53 (281–2). **developed in Dublin** See a complaint that leaflets from Dublin were 'a little too much inclined to the economic side of our freedom'. O/C No. 1 Ulster to C/S, 10 July 1932, in MTUCDA, P69/52 (84). **'nothing except religion'** Chair AC to Secretary Clan, 13 Feb. 1933, in

MTUCDA, P69/185 (89). Unsigned to McGarrity, 23 Apr. 1937?, in McGarrity papers, Ms 17,490 NLI. **was an enemy** McGarrity, 13 Sept. 1930, in MTUCDA, P69/61 (1–4). **PAGE 186 world view anyway** Patterson, *Politics of illusion*, pp 62–6 and English, *Radicals*, pp 132–8. **Clan na Gael** Clan na Gael to Chairman AC, 8 Oct. 1934, in McGarrity papers, Ms 17,539 NLI. **obstacle before them'** *Irish Independent*, 20 June 1938. **military operations** Unsigned pre-Convention document, 23 Mar. 1932, in MTUCDA, P69/53 (377–80). **republic was declared** The first Clann na Poblachta National Executive included MacBride, O'Donoghue, Killeen and Fitzpatrick from the 1933 AC, and former leading officers like McCool, Con Lehane, (who became a TD in 1948), Tomás Ó Maoileóin, Michael Ferguson, Mick Kelly, Dick Batterbury and James Hannigan were all involved at various stages. *Irish Times*, 8 July 1946 and 1 Dec. 1947. Clann candidates for Ard Chomhairle, Ard Fheis, 1953, in Humphreys papers, UCDA, P106/2152. In contrast Padraig MacLogan and J.J. Sheehy were the only senior figures to remain within the ranks of mainstream republicanism. **oppose it militarily** O'Donoghue to Humphreys, Apr. 1935, in Humphreys papers, UCDA, P106/1748. **the southern state** Notes of 1933 GAC, in MTUCDA P69/187 (92) and meeting wth Cumann na mBan Executive, 20 Apr. 1934, in Humphreys papers, UCDA, P106/1154 (4). **from Fianna Fáil** Buckley became a TD for Cork West in 1938. Gallagher, *Irish elections*, p. 221. Hilliard, who the gardaí had once considered a 'dangerous type', was elected for Meath-Westmeath in 1943. He later served as Minister for Post and Telegraphs and Minister for Defence between 1959 and 1969. Eoin O'Duffy to Ministers, 27 July 1931, in D/T S 5864 B NAI. Browne & Farrell, *Magill book of Irish elections*, p. 293.
PAGE 187 time to time' *Notes on the Republican Congress Movement*, MacEntee papers, UCDA, P67/527, p. 22. **get the Republic'** Meeting with Cumann na mBan Executive, 20 Apr. 1934, in Humphreys papers, UCDA, P106/1154 (4). **begin an insurrection** Twomey at Roscommon, Garda report, 22 May 1934, in Jus 8/313 NAI. **existent ones** English, *Radicals*, p. 240. **over a decade later** garda report, 2 Dec. 1929, in D/T S 5864 A NAI. O'Donoghue to Donnybrook Clann na Poblachta meeting, 4 Mar. 1948, in Humphreys papers, UCDA, P106/2142. That O'Donoghue was making this statement 12 years on is also evidence of how unpopular those murders were. **and civil war** D. Fitzpatrick, 'Militarism in Ireland, 1900–1922', in Bartlett and Jeffery (eds), *A military history of Ireland* (Cambridge, 1996) pp 379–406.
PAGE 188 revolutionary tradition In 1934 Ernest Blythe argued that the Blueshirts were the 'authentic successors' of the IRA of 1919–21. As the author of a article arguing for 'ruthless warfare' in *An t-Óglách* of 1918 he was in a position to do this. *Irish Press*, 19 Nov. 1934 and Fitzpatrick, *Two Irelands*, p. 73. **violence in Ireland** Figure from Hart, 'The geography of revolution in Ireland, 1917–1923' in *Past and Present*, 155, pp 142–76. **linked to politics** Estimated from fatalities caused by the IRA (16), IRA fatalities *directly* caused by external violence not accidents or suicide (2), and deaths of RUC (1), Blueshirt (1), Rail Strike (2), sectarian assassination (2). Victims of the Belfast riots of 1935 (13) responsibility for which cannot be assessed. **much of Europe** 155 died in political violence in the German state of Prussia alone between Jan. and Sept. 1932. Eve Rosenhaft, *Beating the Fascists?* (Cambridge, 1983) p. 7. **a republican backlash** Brady, *Guardians*, pp 167–8. **shrunk by 1935** Though it had not disappeared. See the *Irish Press*, 11 Dec. 1935, bemoaning the 'objection of giving information to the Gardai' which was a 'relic' of the past when conditions 'were very different' than in 1935. **Irish Freedom'** Letter seeking information on how to join the IRA from James O'Keeffe, Cashel, Co. Tipperary, 19 Apr. 1932, in MTUCDA, P69/155 (261).
PAGE 189 most of this period The clampdown of late 1931–32 and the rioting in Belfast during 1935 being two exceptions. **some young men** This especially seems to have been the case in Kerry. See comments by Frank Aiken to D. Curran, 10 Jan. 1935, in Aiken papers, UCDA, P104/2801 (113). **it would have failed** Seán Ryan of Tralee, Notes of 1933 GAC, In MTUCDA, P69/187 (105) and O/C Caherciveen, Notes of 1934 GAC,

MacEntee papers, UCDA, P67/525. **envy of the unsuccessful'** Liam T. Cosgrave to Cardinal McRory, 10 September 1931, 'Memorandum Regarding the Activities of Certain Organizations' in D/T S 5864 B NAI. James Hogan made a similar point that 'many a good Catholic has become a revolutionary socialist before he realised it at all'. Hogan, *Could Ireland become Communist?* (Dublin, 1935) p. xxvi. **post-1932** Real improvements in housing, and increased spending on unemployment insurance and issistance, old age pensions and on public works were achieved under Fianna Fáil. C. Ó Gráda, *Ireland: a new economic history, 1780–1939* (Oxford, 1994) pp 420 & 440–41.
PAGE 190 social vision Compare for example *An Phoblacht* from 1926–1936 with the 1950s *United Irishman*.

Appendices

PAGE 191 for a long period A/G to O/C Cork No. 1, 27 Sept. 1930 in MTUCDA, P69/153 (122). **left the organization** C/S report, 9 Aug. 1924, in MTUCDA, P69/179 (126–9). Minutes of IRA Executive, 11–12 July 1923, in MTUCDA, P69/179 (68–70). **IRA's social policies** Barry to Twomey, 13 May 1932, in MTUCDA, P69/52 (63–4). **Kilmichael and Crossbarry** Ryan, *Tom Barry Story*, pp 12, & 17–19. P. Hart, *The IRA and its Enemies, Violence and Community in Cork, 1916–1923* (Oxford, 1999) pp 30–2. **of Cumann na mBan** A sister of Michael Price she had participated in the 1916 Rising. As Leslie de Barra she was a founder of the Irish Red Cross and its chairwomen for over 20 years. McRedmond, *Irish Lives*, p. 73. Also 'Leslie Bean de Barra' in D. Ó Dulaing, *Voices of Ireland* (Dublin, 1984) pp 90–106. **post until 1965** Ryan, *Tom Barry story*, p. 153. **the IRA's enemies** He expressed disappointment that Cork Labour TD T.J. Murphy had a paralysed arm and therefore could not be 'dealt with in a fitting manner.' Barry to Twomey, 23 Dec. 1932, in MTUCDA, P69/155 (3). **to his nature** During 1925 he was paying the hospital expenses of a young women badly injured during fighting in Clonmel in the civil war. As he commanded the anti-Treaty forces in the town he felt responsible for her injuries. Barry to Aiken, 29 Jan. 1925, in MTUCDA, MTUCDA, P69/141 (4). **offensive in Northern Ireland** Oglaigh na h-Éireann Statement to General Army Convention, (1938), in Aiken papers, UCDA, P104/2833 (1–3). **with Nazi Germany** Barry to Humphreys, 12 June 1976, in Humphreys papers, UCDA, P106/839. Irish Military Intelligence, however, believed Barry had made contact with the Nazis before his resignation as C/S. Report, 16 Nov. 1942, in G2/X/0093 M.A. Ryan, *Barry story*, p. 146. **Cork Borough bye-election** Ryan, *Barry story*, pp 153–5 & *War News*, early 1941, in Jus 8/752 NAI. **published in 1949** It has remained in print ever since. Latest edition, Tralee, 1989. **died in 1980** Fionntan O'Laighin, 'Tom Barry' in *Spirit of freedom – The Bobby Sands commemoration school prize essay*, (Dublin, 1983) pp 60–7. Barry refused a request to sign an appeal for IRA prisoners during 1976. He argued that the IRA had 'only themselves to blame' for losing support after some recent activities. Barry to Humphreys, (N/D) in Humphreys papers, UCDA, P106/1566. Also *Sunday Independent*, 7 Mar. 1976. **of cancer in 1933** *Notes on Communism*, in MacEntee papers, UCDA, P67523. Donation of £55 towards Fitzgerald's medical bill in C/S to Irish National Aid, 12 Dec. 1932, in MTUCDA, P69/54 (64). *An Phoblacht*, 9 Sept. 1933, *Republican Congress*, 8 Sept. 1934.
PAGE 192 interned in 1923 *Notes on Individuals*, in MacEntee papers, UCDA, P67/550 p. 156. Report on revolutionary organizations, 4 Apr. 1930 in D/T S 5864 A NAI. Garda report, 14 Apr. 1930, in FitzGerald papers, UCDA, P80/916. **Irish Communist Party** Department of Defence mss, in Mulcahy papers, UCDA, P7a/87. I am grateful to Emmet O'Connor for bringing this to my attention. **in the same area** The union's full title was Irish National Union of Vintners Grocers and Allied Trades Assistants. *Notes on Individuals*, in MacEntee papers, UCDA, P67/550 p. 156. Garda report, 9 Jan. 1934, in Jus 8/68 NAI. **Workers Revolution Party** *Notes on Communism*, in MacEntee papers, UCDA, P67/523. **within the IRA** Notes of 1933 GAC, in MTUCDA, P69/187 (87) & Notes of 1934 GAC, in MacEntee papers, UCDA, P67/525. **Dublin Transport Strike** *Irish Times*, 22

Dec. 1934. Garda report, 27 Mar. 1935, in Jus 8/405 NAI. **his seat until 1951** *Notes on Individuals,* in MacEntee papers, UCDA, P67/550 p. 156. *Irish Times,* 8 July 1946. Browne and Farrell, *Magill book,* p. 126. **during the civil war** McRedmond, *Irish lives,* p. 116. O'Farrell, *Who's who,* p. 160. 'Who is George Gilmore?' in Humphreys papers, UCDA, P106/2436. O'Malley Notebooks, UCDA, P17b/106.

PAGE 193 the Dublin IRA Garda report, 7 May 1929, in FitzGerald papers, UCDA, P80/851 (11). MacEoin, *Survivors,* pp 393–5. **at least one murder** D/J report on Patrick Carroll murder, 24 June 1931, in FitzGerald papers, UCDA, P80/856 (19). **Soviet Union in 1930** Gilmore Notes. **for Fianna Fáil** Brady, *Guardians of the peace,* p. 173. Entry, Jacob Diaries, 13 Mar. 1933, in Ms 32,582 (69) NLI. Gilmore complained during 1932 that he was 'completely fed up ... past, present and future.' Gilmore to Chairman AC, 16 Sept. 1932, in MTUCDA, P69/53 (367–9). Notes of 1933 GAC, in MTUCDA, P69/187 (103). **a high regard** Notes of 1934 GAC, in MacEntee papers, UCDA, P67/525. Gilmore thought O'Donnell the only man he knew who had the 'power to be a political leader.' O'Donnell considered that Gilmore had the "best mind" since Liam Mellows and was actually 'rather better than Mellows.' Entries Jacob Diaries, 11 & 31 Oct. 1934, Ms 32,582 (76) NLI. **into the 1940s** notes. O'Donnell & Gilmore, 'Invasion! What if the British come back? If the Germans land? If both come – What then? A Republican answer.' (1941) in A. Mitchell and P. O'Snodaigh, (eds), *Irish political documents, 1916–1949,* (Dublin, 1985), pp 225–8. **died in 1985** B. Bell, *Secret army,* p. 345. R. English, *Socialist intellectuals and the 1916–23 Irish Revolution* paper delivered at Symposium – 'The Nature of the Irish Revolution, 1913–23' at Queens University Belfast, 1999. **to smuggle arms** *Notes on Certain Individuals,* in MacEntee papers, UCDA, P67/550 p. 157. **in Crumlin Road** RUC report, 22 May 1936, in HA/32/1/628 PRONI. **until the late 1950s** Republican re-organization minutes, 25 Feb. 1945, in Humphreys papers, UCDA, P106/2140. *Irish Times,* 8 July 1946. Clann Ard Chomairle, 1953, in Humphreys papers, UCDA, P106/2152. Killeen owned a grocer's shop in Dublin in that period. Advertisment in Gerard Tighe papers, Ms 28,894 (B) 1 NLI. **and early 1930s** See GHQ Staff IRA, Jan. 1933, in Aiken papers, UCDA, P104/2822 (1). O'Duffy to Blythe, 5 July 1929, in Blythe papers, P24/477. RUC report, 17 Jan. 1933, in HA/32/1/465 PRONI. **Bulfin in 1926** MacEoin, *Survivors,* pp 105–26. Anthony J. Jordan, *Seán MacBride – a biography,* (Dublin, 1993) pp 19–27. Political History of Seán MacBride, in MacEntee papers, UCDA, P67/539 (1–2). O'Farrell, *Who's who,* p. 189. O'Malley Notebooks, UCDA, P17b/87.

PAGE 194 meeting in Tullamore Garda reports, 20 Apr. and 24 June 1929, in D/T S 5864 A NAI. Jordan, MacBride, p. 46. **of that body** Notes on Communism, UCDA, P67/523. Garda reports, 24 Sept. 1930 & 30 July 1931, in D/T S 5864 A NAI. *An Phoblacht,* 14 Feb. 1931. *Notes on Republican Congress Movement,* in MacEntee papers, UCDA, P67/527 p. 25. **on behalf of the IRA** C/S to O/C Cork No. 1 Bdge, 19 July 1932, in MTUCDA, P69/52 (54–57). MacBride to McGarrity, 19 Oct. 1933, in McGarrity papers, Ms 17,456 NLI. **for a period** Twomey to Sheehy Skeffington, 31 Mar. 1933, in MTUCDA, P69/53 (170). A/G to O/C Dublin Bdge, 6 June 1932, in MTUCDA, P69/155 (73). **during March 1935** Notes of 1934 GAC, in MacEntee papers, UCDA, P67/525. Garda report, 27 Mar. 1935, in Jus 8/405 NAI. **do so in 1940** *Irish Times,* 4 May 1936. *Notes on Individuals,* in MacEntee papers, UCDA, P67/550 p. 158. **and 1977 respectively** McRedmond, *Irish lives,* pp 179–80. **the IRA's leader** MacEoin, *Survivors,* p. 123. For a critical examination of various MacBride claims see MacDermott, *Clann na Poblachta,* pp 172–3. For connection to Germany, undated Army Intelligence File file in G2/X/0093 MA and Gilmore Notes. **a public house** RUC report, 5 June 1934, in HA/32/1/610 PRONI. *Notes on individuals,* in MacEntee papers, UCDA, P67/550 p. 160. **during 1946** O/C Offaly Batt to A/G, 28 May 1932, in MTUCDA, P69/155 (171). Notes of 1934 GAC, in MacEntee papers, UCDA, P67/525. See Chapter Eight for Stormont election.

PAGE 195 his death in 1964 MacEoin, *Twilight years,* pp 875–77. **or about him** By O'Donnell himself, *There will be another day.* About O'Donnell, McInerney, *Peadar*

O'Donnell: Irish social rebel, Grattan Freyer, *Peadar O'Donnell* (Lewisburg, 1973), Hegarty, *O'Donnell* & Ó Drisceoil, *Peadar O'Donnell*. **ITGWU in 1918** Anton McCabe, 'The Stormy petrel of the transport workers': Peadar O'Donnell, Trade Unionist, 1917–1920, in *Saothar* 19 (1994) 41–51. **Donegal in 1923** MacEoin, *Survivors*, pp 21–34. O'Malley Notebooks, UCDA, P17b/87,98. IRA Executive, 20 Sept. 1924, in MTUCDA, P69/179 (130). Ó Drisceoil, *O'Donnell*, pp 34–6. **Saor Éire in 1931** *Notes on Communism*, in MacEntee papers, UCDA, P67/523. *Notes on Individuals*, in MacEntee papers, UCDA, P67/550 p. 160. *Notes on Republican Congress Movement*, in MacEntee papers, UCDA, P67/527 pp 1–2 & 25. **dismissed by the IRA** O'Donnell to Cumann na mBan Executive, 20 Apr. 1934, in Humphreys papers, UCDA, P106/1154 (1–5). Notes of 1933 GAC, in MTUCDA, P69/187 (104). Complaint over censorship in letter to Twomey (N/D) in Aiken papers, UCDA, P104/2855. **his death in 1986** Ó Drisceoil, *O'Donnell*, pp 110–15 & 118–24. McCabe, p. 41. **the Civil War** Introduction to Sighle Humphreys papers, UCDA. O'Malley Notebooks, UCDA, P17b/91. Twomey to Neenan, 28 Mar. 1933, in MTUCDA, P69/185 (24).
PAGE 196 in Brussels *Notes on Communism*, in MacEntee papers, UCDA, P67/523. **from 1938–39** 'Boycott British' National Executive Minute Book, 1 Nov. 1932, in Humphreys papers, UCDA, P106/2101. *Irish News*, 14 Nov. 1935. The Russell leadership informed O'Donoghue they could no longer rely on his 'loyalty.' A/G to Staff Comdt 'E', 11 May 1938, in Humphreys papers, UCDA, P106/2042. **died in 1957** Clann na Poblachta election leaflet, Feb. 1948, in Humphreys papers, UCDA, P106/2160. O'Donoghue's running mate, Noel Browne was elected. **during 1930** Gallagher, *Irish elections*, p. 36. O'Duffy to Ministers, 5 July 1929, in Blythe papers, UCDA, P24/477. *Notes on Communism*, in MacEntee papers, UCDA, P67/523. **during 1933** Report on Leitrim Battalion Convention, Mar. 1933, in MTUCDA, P69/187 (4–14). **Carrick-on-Shannon that year** O'Farrell claimed to have forced the expulsion of a Garda from a GAA club over the Guard's attendance at a Jazz dance. *Irish Press*, 26 June 1934 **IRA shortly afterwards** *Leitrim Observer*, 3 Nov. 1934. Foley, *Legion of the rearguard*, p. 149. **by the gardaí** IRA GHQ Staff, Jan. 1933, in Aiken papers, UCDA, P104/2822 (1). Garda report, 4 July 1929, in D/T S 5864 A NAI. *Notes on Individuals*, in MacEntee papers, UCDA, P67/550 p.161. **politics during this period** Officer's meeting, 9 Apr. 1927, in MTUCDA, P69/48 (152–62). Notes of 1933 GAC, in MTUCDA, P69/187 (104). **accident in 1944** *Notes on Individuals*, in MacEntee papers, UCDA, P67/550 p. 161. *Irish Press*, 22 Jan. 1944. **during that period** Copy of entry in Register of Births. MacEoin, *Survivors*, p. 369. *Irish Press*, 17 Jan. 1944. Brothers Jack, Eamon and Charles were in the IRA. Sister Leslie was in the Cumann na mBan. She married Tom Barry. See above.
PAGE 197 October 1923 O'Farrell, *Who's who*, p. 189. **Ireland during that period** A/Commandant Dan Bryan to C/S, 2 Dec. 1925, in FitzGerald papers, UCDA, P80/849 (11). Report on revolutionary organizations, 4 Apr. 1930, in D/T S 5864 A NAI. **than Price** Twomey to McGarrity, 9 Dec. 1931, in McGarrity papers, Ms 17,490 NLI. **Workers Republic was achieved** *An Phoblacht*, 7 Feb. 1931. *Notes on the Republican Congress Movement*, in MacEntee papers, UCDA, P67/527, p. 25. Notes of 1933 GAC, in MTUCDA, P69/187 (90–117). Notes of 1934 GAC, in MacEntee papers, UCDA, P67/525. **strike of 1935** A/G to Commanders, 17 Apr. 1934, in Jus 8/319 NAI. Price to Humphreys, 13 & 19 July 1934, in Humphreys papers, UCDA, P106/1489 & P016/1491 (1–2). **died in 1944** Dunphy, *Making of Fianna Fáil power*, p. 201. *Irish Press*, 17 & 20 Jan. 1944. **Director of Munitions in 1920** Copy of entry in Register of Births. Notes on Individuals, in MacEntee papers, UCDA, P67/550 p. 162. S. O'Mahony, *Frongoch* (Dublin, 1995), p. 218. O'Farrell, *Who's who*, pp 91 & 192. **during 1929–31** Michael McInerney, Gerry Boland's story, *Irish Times*, 11 Oct. 1968. Army Intelligence report, 4 Dec. 1925, in FitzGerald papers, UCDA, P80/849 (12). See for example, 'Q' to A/G, report on South Galway, 27 Apr. 1931, in MTUCDA, P69/151 (33–4). **intervention from Belfast** See Chapters Eight & Nine. **of Price and O'Donnell** A/G to Commanders, 17 Apr. 1934, in Jus 8/319 NAI. **was court mar-**

tialled *Irish Independent*, 10 Dec. 1936. Russell to McGarrity, 29 Jan. 1937, in McGarrity papers, Ms 17,485 NLI. **political naiveté** IRA statement to GAC, 1938, in Aiken papers, UCDA, P104/2833 (1–30). Russell to Dr. Hans Luther, German Ambassador to the US, 15 Oct. 1936, in Ms 17,485 NLI.

PAGE 198 died at sea *Notes on Individuals*, in MacEntee papers, UCDA, P67/550 p. 162. **during 1951** Garda report in Jus 8/802 NAI & *United Irishman*, Oct. 1951. **in popular culture** Mentioned in songs by The Pogues and Christy Moore. See V. Clarke, *A drink with Shane MacGowan* (London, 2001) pp 274–80 and F. McGarry, *Irish politics and the Spanish Civil War,* (Cork, 1999) pp 48–49. **War of Independence** Cronin, *Frank Ryan,* pp 17–19. According to Gilmore, Ryan was 'very sensitive' about his lack of involvement in the War of Independence. Gilmore Notes. **medal for oratory** Cronin, *Frank Ryan,* pp 22–31. **IRA inspector officer** *Notes on Individuals*, in MacEntee papers, UCDA, P67/550 p. 162. *Notes on Communism*, in MacEntee papers, UCDA, P67/523. 'Eilis Ryan in her own words' in *Saothar,* 21, (1996) pp 129–146. Andrews, *Man of no property,* pp 71–72. As Staff Captain 'O'Reilly' Ryan displayed a little black humour sending to Jim Killeen, "the names of men I have inspired to die for Ireland. Trusting you can facilitate.' 'OR' to A/G, 9 Nov. 1929, in MTUCDA, P69/152 (254). **in April 1933** Notes on Individuals, in MacEntee papers, UCDA, P67/550 p. 162. Notes of 1933 GAC, in MTUCDA, P69/187 (94). **being a communist** A/G to Staff Captain O'Reilly, 13 May 1933, in Humphreys papers, UCDA, P106/2038. Mary MacSwiney to Ryan, 1 July 1936, in MacSwiney papers, UCDA, P48a/248(1)/3. **May of that year** Twomey to Neenan, 28 Mar. 1933, in MTUCDA, P69/185 (21–25). **Dublin municipal elections** Cronin, *Frank Ryan,* pp 54–71.

PAGE 199 death sentence commuted McGarry, *Irish politics,* pp 49–60 & 101–8. Notes on Individuals, in MacEntee papers, UCDA, P67/550 p. 162. **remains controversial** English, *Radicals,* p. 273. E. Staunton, 'Frank Ryan & collaboration: a reassessment', in *History Ireland,* Autumn 1997. **the 1920s and 1930s** *Notes on Individuals*, in MacEntee papers, UCDA, P67/550 p. 162. **to the title** J.J. Barrett, *Name of the game,* pp 112–22. Dwyer, *Tans, terror & troubles,* pp 299 & 378. **for IRA members** See Seán McCool to C/S, 28 Apr., and C/S to McCool, 11 May 1932, in MTUCDA, P69/52 (117). **social policies** He opposed the Kerry IRA's disruption of garda sports in 1931. Garda report, 27 July 1931, in D/T S 5864 B NAI. See also Chapter Three. Notes of 1933 GAC, in MTUCDA, P69/187 (101). **a more militant activist** Defence Conference Notes, 22 Dec. 1942, in Mulcahy papers, UCDA, P7a/217. Notes on Individuals, in MacEntee papers, UCDA, P67/550 p. 162. MacEoin, *Survivors,* pp354–62. **died in 1980** Barrett, *Name of the game,* p. 122. *An Phoblacht,* 19 Jan. 1980. **in the early 1930s** Maurice Jr., born 11 June 1932 & Máire, born 8 Nov. 1933. Information from M. Twomey Jr. **the Clan na Gael** Twomey to McGarrity, 27 Dec. 1937, in McGarrity papers, Ms 17,544 NLI. **from IRA activity** A/G to C/S, 6 May 1938, in McGarrity papers, Ms 17,544 NLI. **during 1940** Internment File, No. 96 CP 627, 3–20 June 1940 MA.

PAGE 200 IRA factions Notes on Individuals, in MacEntee papers, UCDA, P67/550 p. 163. Republican re-organization minutes, 25 Feb. 1945, in Humphreys papers, UCDA, P106/2140. **Bodenstown in 1971** *Irish Times,* 26 Apr. 1971. His reiteration of Tone's non-sectarian message received praise in an *Irish Times* editorial, 29 Apr. 1971. **Bureau of Military History** Twomey File, S.2136, 30/3/53–31/3/53 MA. **no wish to add to** Twomey to J.A. Murphy, 30 Aug. 1976. **in April 1978** *Irish Times,* 9 Oct. 1978. **enduring popularity** *Irish Press,* 10 Oct. 1978. Among the mourners were Todd and Neil Andrews of Fianna Fáil, Garrett FitzGerald of Fine Gael, Tomás MacGiolla of Official SF, Ruairí Ó Brádaigh and Dáithí Ó Conaill of Provisional SF and Michael Mullin of the ITGWU.

Bibliography

MANUSCRIPTS

University College Dublin Archives
Frank Aiken Papers, AUCD.
Dan Bryan Papers, AUCD.
Ernest Blythe Papers, AUCD.
Cowan Family Papers, AUCD.
Desmond FitzGerald Papers, AUCD.
Sighle Humphreys Papers, AUCD.
Seán MacEntee Papers, AUCD.
Mary MacSwiney Papers, AUCD.
Richard Mulcahy Papers, AUCD.
Eithne Coyle-O'Donnell Papers, AUCD.
Ernie O' Malley Notebooks, AUCD.
Moss Twomey Papers, AUCD.

National Library of Ireland
Joseph H. Fowler Papers, NLI.
Rosamond Jacob Papers, NLI.
Joseph McGarrity Papers, NLI.
Gerard Tighe Papers, NLI.

Military Archives, Cathal Brugha Barracks, Dublin
Internment File on Moss Twomey, No.96, C.P. 627,
3rd of June 1940–20th June 1940.
Bureau of Military History File S.2136, 30/3/53-31/3/53.
G.2./X/0058, IRA Activities.
G.2./X/0626, IRA Activities.
G.2./X/0093, IRA Activities.
P.M. 1498 – Internee Groups in the Curragh.

National Archives, Dublin
Department of Justice 'Jus 8', 1993 Release; 'Jus 10'; H280/37; H306/31.
Department of the Taoiseach, S 5864 A, B, C, D (Anti-State Activities); S 1976.
S 5943; S 6328; S 6433; S 7494 & 5; S 8878; S 11564 A, B, C, D (IRA Activities 1939–1945).

Public Records Office, Northern Ireland
Home Affairs Series, HA/32/1.
Cahir Healy Papers, Random Extracts, D2991/AB.

Private Papers
George Gilmore Notes (held by Anthony Coughlan).
Seán O'Mahony Collection.

Maurice Twomey Jr. (family letters).

Government Publications
Dail Debates 1926–1937.
Seanad Debates 1933.

TAPE

Bob Bradshaw Interview (Courtesy of Eunan O'Halpin).

NEWSPAPERS AND JOURNALS
as cited

MEMOIRS AND ORAL HISTORIES

Anon., *Tom Harte and his comrades of the forties* (Dublin, 1990).
Andrews, C.S., *Dublin made me: an autobiography* (Dublin, 2001).
——, *Man of no property* (Dublin, 2001).
Barrett, J.J., *In the name of the game* (Bray, 1997).
Barry, T., *Guerrilla days in Ireland* (Dublin, 1981).
Behan, B., *Borstal boy* (London, 1990).
——, B., *Confessions of an Irish rebel* (London, 1985).
Briscoe, R., *For the life of me* (London, 1958).
Byrne, P., *The Irish Republican Congress revisited* (London, 1991).
Clarke, K., *Revolutionary woman: Kathleen Clarke 1878–1972* (Dublin,1991).
Connolly-O'Brien, N.,*We shall rise again* (London, 1981).
Deasy, L., *Brother against brother* (Dublin, 1999).
Donnelly, M, (ed), *The Last Post* (Dublin, 1932).
Fianna Fáil, *National discipline and majority rule* (Dublin, 1936).
Friends of Soviet Russia, *The USSR through Irish eyes* (Dublin, 1929).
Gilmore, G., *The Irish Republican Congress* (Cork, 1974).
Gralton, M, *My Cousin Jimmy* (Leitrim, 1991).
Hartnett, N, (ed.), *Prison escapes* (Dublin, 1945).
Hayes, S., 'My Strange Story' in *The Bell,* July and August 1951.
Hogan, J., *Could Ireland become communist?* (Dublin, 1935).
Kearney, P., *Tributes to his memory* (Cork, 1970).
Munck, R., and Rolston, B., *Belfast in the Thirties. An oral history* (Belfast, 1987).
Macardle, D., *Tragedies of Kerry* (Dublin, 1991).
MacEoin, U., *The IRA in the twilight years, 1923–1948* (Dublin, 1997).
——, *Harry. The story of Harry White* (Dublin, 1985).
——, *Survivors* (Dublin, 1980).
McNally, J., *Morally good – politically bad* (Belfast, 1989).
Murphy, J., *When youth was mine* (Dublin, 1998).
Ó'Brádaigh, R., *'Dílseacht' – The story of Tom Maguire and the Second Dáil* (Dublin, 1997).
O'Connor, P., *A soldier of liberty* (Dublin, 1996).
O'Donnell, P., *The gates flew open* (London, 1932).
'Óglac', *Óglaig na hÉireann* (Dublin, 1932).
Oglaigh na h-Éireann, *Constitution and governmental programme* (Dublin, 1934).

O'Kelly, J.J., *The Sinn Féin outlook* Dublin, 1930).
——, *Stepping stones* (Dublin, 1939).
O'Malley, E., *The singing flame* (Dublin, 1978).
O'Neill J., *Blood-dark track: a family history* (London, 2001).
O'Riordan, M., *Connolly Column* (Dublin, 1979).
O'Tuile, P., *The life and times of Brian O'Higgins* (Navan, nd).
Robbins, R., *Under the starry plough* (Dublin, 1977).
Ryan, E., 'In her own words' in *Saothar* 21 (1996) 129–6.
'Seachránaidhe' (Frank Ryan), *Emancipation* (Dublin, 1929).
Saor Éire, *Indictment of capitalism in Ireland* (Dublin, 1931).
——, *Constitution and rules* (Dublin, 1931).
Wilson, L., *Growing up in the hungry, violent thirties* (Belfast, 1997).

BOOKS, ARTICLES, AND ESSAYS

Allen, G., *The Garda Siochána – policing independent Ireland, 1922–82* (Dublin, 1999).
Allen, K., *Fianna Fáil and Irish labour* (London, 1997).
Anderson, W.K., *James Connolly and the Irish left* (Dublin, 1994).
Augusteijn, J. *From public defiance to guerrilla warfare. The experience of ordinary volunteers in the Irish War of independence, 1916–1921* (Dublin, 1996).
——, (ed.), *Ireland in the 1930s: new perspectives* (Dublin, 1999).
——, 'Political violence and democracy. An analysis of the tensions within Irish republican strategy, 1913–2000' (unpublished).
Ballymacarret Research Group, *Lagan enclave. A history of conflict in the short strand 1886–1997* (Belfast, 1997).
Barberis, P., McHugh, J., Tyldesley, M., & Pendry, H., *Encyclopedia of British and Irish political organisations* (London, 2000).
Bardon, J., *A history of Ulster* (Belfast, 1992).
Bartlett, T., and Jeffery K., *A military history of Ireland* (Cambridge, 1996).
Bayor, R.H., *Neighbors in conflict. The Irish, Germans, Jews, and Italians of New York City, 1929–1941* (Baltimore, 1978).
Bayor, R.H., and Meagher T.J. (eds), *The New York Irish* (Baltimore, 1997).
Bell, J.B., *The Secret Army. The IRA 1916–1979* (Dublin, 1979).
——, 'The Thompson Sub Machine gun in Ireland, 1921' in *Irish Sword*, vol. 8:31 (Winter, 1967).
——, *The gun in politics: an analysis of Irish political conflict, 1916–1986* (New Brunswick 1987).
Bew, P., Hazelkorn, E. and Patterson, H., *The dynamics of Irish politics* (London, 1989).
Bew, P., and Norton, C., 'The Unionist state and the outdoor relief riots of 1932' in *Economic and Social Review* 10:3 (1979) 255–65.
——,'Sinn Féin, agrarian radicalism and the War of Independence, 1919–1921' in D.G., Boyce (ed), *The revolution in Ireland, 1879–1923* (Dublin, 1988).
Brennan, A., and Nolan, W., 'Nixie Boran and the colliery community of North Kilkenny' in Nolan and Whelan (eds), *Kilkenny: history and society* (Dublin, 1990).
Bolster, E., *The Knights of Saint Columbanus* (Dublin, 1979).
Boland, K., *The rise and decline of Fianna Fáil* (Dublin, 1982).
Bowler S., 'Seán Murray, 1898–1961, and the pursuit of Stalinism in one country' in *Saothar* 18 (1993) 41–53.

Bowman, J., *De Valera and the Ulster question, 1917–1973* (Oxford, 1982).

Boyce, D.G. (ed.), *The revolution in Ireland, 1879–1923* (Dublin, 1988)

Browne, T., *Ireland, a social and cultural history* (London, 1985).

Browne, V., and Farrell M., (eds), *Magill book of Irish politics* (Dublin, 1981).

Browne, V., 'The Peter Berry story' in *Magill* 3:9, June 1980.

Brady C., *Guardians of the peace* (Dublin, 1974).

Carroll D., *They have fooled you again: Michael O'Flanagan (1876–1942)* (Dublin, 1993).

Carroll, D., *Unusual suspects* (Dublin 1998).

Carroll, F.M., *American opinion and the Irish question, 1910–23* (Dublin, 1978).

Clarke, V., *A drink with Shane MacGowan* (London, 2001).

Columb, F., *The shooting of More O Ferrall* (Monaghan, 1996).

Coogan, T.P., *De Valera, long fellow, long shadow* (Dublin,1993).

——, *The IRA* (London, 1995).

Communist Party of Ireland, *Outline history* (Dublin, n.d.).

Cronin, M., *The Blueshirts and Irish politics* (Dublin 1997).

——, *Sport and nationalism in Ireland* (Dublin, 1999).

——, 'The Blueshirts in the Irish Free State, 1932–1935: the nature of Socialist republican and governmental opposition.' in Kirk and McElligot (eds), *Opposing Fascism. Community, authority and resistance.* (Cambridge, 1999).

——, and Regan, J.M. (eds), *Ireland: the politics of independence, 1922–49.* (Macmillian, 2000).

Cronin, S., *Frank Ryan. The search for the republic* (Dublin, 1980).

——, *The McGarrity Papers: revelations of the Irish revolutionary movement in Ireland and America, 1900–1940* (Tralee, 1972).

——, *Irish nationalism: a history of its roots and ideology* (Dublin, 1980).

——, *Washington's Irish policy, 1916–1986* (Dublin, 1987).

——, *The Transport Workers Union of America* (Dublin, 1983).

Cullen, M., and Luddy, M. (eds), *Female activists: Irish women and change, 1900–1960* (Dublin, 2001).

de Burca, M., *The GAA: a history of the Gaelic Athletic Association* (Dublin, 1999).

Devlin, P., *Yes, we have no bananas. Outdoor relief in Belfast, 1920–39* (Belfast, 1981).

Doherty, G., 'A Star Chamber affair – the death of Timothy Coughlan' in *History Ireland*, Spring 1993.

Duggan, J.P., *A history of the Irish army* (Dublin, 1991).

Dunphy, R., *The making of Fianna Fáil power in Ireland, 1923–1948* (Oxford, 1995).

——, 'The soldiers set out: Reflections on the formation of Fianna Fáil' in Hannon and Gallagher (eds) *Taking the long view. 70 Years of Fianna Fáil* (Dublin, 1996).

Dwyer, R.T., *Tans, terror and troubles: Kerry's real fighting story, 1913–23* (Dublin, 2001).

Edmonds, S., *The gun, the law, and the Irish people* (Tralee, 1971).

Elliot, M., *The Catholics of Ulster* (London, 2000).

Ellis, J., *The social history of the machine gun* (London, 1993).

Emmons, D.M., *The Butte Irish, 1875–1925* (Chicago, 1990).

English, R., *Ernie O'Malley: IRA intellectual* (Oxford, 1998).

——, *Radicals and the Republic. Socialist republicanism in the Irish Free State, 1925–1937* (Oxford 1994).

——, 'Peadar O'Donnell, Socialism and the Republic' in *Saothar* 13 (1989) 47–58.

——, '"Paying no heed to public clamour": Irish republican solipsism in the 1930s' in *Irish Historical Studies* 112 (November, 1993).

——,'Socialism and republican schism in Ireland: the emergence of the Republican

Congress in 1934.' in *Irish Historical Studies* 105 (May 1990).

——, 'Socialist intellectuals and the 1916–23 Irish Revolution.' Paper delivered at the symposium, 'The nature of the Irish Revolution, 1913–23' (September 1999), Queen's University, Belfast).

Fallon, C.H., *Soul of fire. A life of Mary McSwiney* (Cork, 1986).

Farrell, M., *Northern Ireland. The Orange State* (London 1980).

——, 'The extraordinary life and times of Seán MacBride' in *Magill* 6:3 and 4, Christmas 1982 and January 1983.

Farrell, J.T., *On Irish themes* (Philidelphia, 1982).

Farry, M., *The aftermath of revolution, Sligo, 1921–23* (UCD, 2000).

Feehan, J.M., *The shooting of Michael Collins: murder or accident?* (Dublin, 1981)

Feeley, P., *The Gralton affair* (Dublin 1983).

——, 'The siege of Great Strand Street' in the *Old Limerick Journal*, Winter 1981 and Spring 1982.

——, & O'Riordan M., *The rise and fall of Irish anti-Semitism* (Dublin, 1984).

Fitzpatrick, D., *Politics and Irish life* (Cork, 1998).

——, *The two Irelands, 1912–1939* (Oxford, 1998).

Fisk, R., *In time of war: Ireland, Ulster and the price of neutrality 1939–1945* (London 1983).

Foley, C., *Legion of the rearguard. The IRA and the modern Irish state* (London, 1992).

Follis, B.A., *A state under siege* (Oxford, 1995).

Foster, R.F., *Modern Ireland, 1600–1972* (London, 1989).

Freeman, J.B., *In transit. The Transport Workers Union in New York City, 1933–1966* (Oxford, 1989).

——, 'Irish Workers in the twentieth century United States: The case of the Transport Workers' Union' in *Saothar*, 8 (1982) 24–45.

Fried, A., *FDR and his enemies* (New York, 1999).

Gallagher, M. (ed.), *Irish elections, 1922–44: results and analysis* (Limerick, 1993).

Garvin, T., *The evolution of Irish nationalist politics* (Dublin, 1981).

——, *Nationalist revolutionaries in Ireland, 1858–1921* (Oxford, 1987).

——, *1922. The birth of Irish democracy* (Dublin, 1996).

Gibbons, L., *Transformations in Irish culture* (Cork, 1996).

——, 'Labour and local history. The case of Jim Gralton' in *Saothar* 14 (1989).

Greaves, C.D., *Liam Mellows and the Irish revolution* (London, 1987).

Hanley, B., 'The Volunteer Reserve and the IRA' in *Irish Sword* 83 (Summer 1998).

——, 'Moss Twomey, radicalism, and the IRA, 1931–33: a reassessment' in *Saothar* 26 (2001).

——, '"Just a battalion of armed catholics"? The IRA in Northern Ireland in the 1930s' in *Irish history: a research yearbook* 1 (2002).

Hammill, J., 'Saor Éire and the IRA; an exercise in deception?' in *Saothar* 20 (1995) 56–66.

Hart, P., *The IRA and its enemies: violence and community in Co. Cork, 1916–1923* (Oxford, 1998).

——, 'The Thompson submachine gun in Ireland revisited' in *Irish Sword* 77 (Summer 1995) 160–70.

——, 'Defining and debating the Irish revolution', Paper delivered at the symposium, 'The nature of the Irish revolution, 1913–23' (September 1999, Queen's University, Belfast).

——, 'The geography of revolution in Ireland, 1917–1923' in *Past and Present*, 155 (May 1997).

——, 'The social structure of the Irish Republican Army, 1916–1923' in *Historical Journal* 42:1 (March, 1999).

Hegarty, M., *Peadar O'Donnell* (Dublin, 1999).

Hennessey, T., *A history of Northern Ireland, 1920–1996* (London, 1997).

Hepburn, A.C., *A past apart: studies in the history of Catholic Belfast, 1850–1950* (Belfast, 1996).

Hickey, D.J., & Doherty, J.E., *A dictionary of Irish history, 1800–1980* (Dublin, 1987).

Holland, J., *The American connection* (Dublin, 1989).

Hopkinson, M., *Green against green.*, (Dublin, 1988).

Horgan, J., *Seán Lemass. The enigmatic patriot* (Dublin 1997).

——, *Noel Browne, passionate outsider* (Dublin, 2000).

——, *Irish media. A critical history since 1922* (London, 2001).

Jordan, A., *Seán MacBride* (Dublin, 1993).

Jeffery, K., 'The Great War in Modern Irish Memory' in Fraser and Jeffery (eds) *Men, women and war* (Dublin, 1993).

——, 'Parades, police and government in Northern Ireland, 1922–69' in T. G. Fraser (eds) *The Irish parading tradition. Following the drum* (2000).

Joye L., '"Aiken's slugs"; the Reserve of the Irish Army under Fianna Fáil' in J. Augusteijn (ed.), *Ireland in the 1930s* (Dublin, 1999).

Jung, P., 'The Thompson submachine gun during and after the Anglo-Irish war – the new evidence' in *Irish Sword* 84 (Winter 1998).

Kearans, K.C., *Dublin tenement life. An oral history* (Dublin 1994).

Kenny, K., *The American Irish* (Harlow, 2000).

Kennedy, D., *The widening gulf; Northern attitudes to the independent Irish State, 1919–49* (Belfast, 1988).

Keogh, D., *Jews in twentieth century Ireland* (Cork, 1998).

——, *Twentieth century Ireland: nation and state* (Dublin, 1994).

——, *Ireland and Europe, 1919–1948* (Dublin, 1988).

——, 'De Valera, the Catholic Church and the "Red Scare", 1931–2,' in O'Carroll and Murphy (eds), *De Valera and his times* (Cork, 1986).

Kissane, B., 'The not so amazing case of Irish democracy' in *Irish Political Studies* 10, (1995) 43–68.

Kleinrichert, D., *Republican internment and the prison ship Argenta, 1922* (Dublin, 2001).

Laffan, M, 'Violence and terror in twentieth-century Ireland: IRB and IRA' in Mommson and Hirschfeld (eds), *Social protest, violence and terror in nineteenth- and Twentieth-century Europe* (London, 1982).

——, *The resurrection of Ireland, Sinn Féin, 1916–23* (Oxford, 1999).

Lee, J, *Ireland, 1912–1985: politics and society* (Cambridge, 1989).

Leonard, J., 'The twinge of memory; Armistice Day and Remembrance Sunday in Dublin since 1919' in G. Walker and R. English (eds), *Unionism in modern Ireland* (1996).

Loughlin, J., 'Northern Ireland and British Fascism in the inter-war years' in *Irish Historical Studies* 116 (1995).

Lyons, F.S.L., *Ireland since the Famine* (London, 1971).

Malone, S., *Alias Seán Forde* (Dublin, 2001).

Manning, M., *The Blueshirts* (Dublin, 1987).

Maume, P., *The long gestation. Irish nationalist life, 1891–1918* (Dublin, 1999).

Macardle, D., *The Irish Republic* (London, 1939).

MacEvilly, M., 'IRA chief – A Life of Dr Andy Cooney' (unpublished manuscript, Dublin 1999).

MacInerney, M., *Peadar O'Donnell. Irish social rebel* (Dublin, 1974).

MacManus, F. (ed.), *The years of the great test, 1926–39* (Cork, 1967).

McCabe, A., ' "The stormy petrel of the transport workers". Peadar O'Donnell, trade unionist 1917–1920' in *Saothar* 19 (1994).

McCamley, B., *The role of the rank and file in the 1935 Dublin Tram and Bus strike* (Dublin, 1981).

McCann, E., *War and an Irish town* (London, 1993).

McCoole, S., *Guns and chiffon. Women revolutionaries and Kilmainham gaol* (Dublin, 1997).

McDermott, J., *Northern divisions. The Old IRA and the Belfast pogroms 1920–22* (Belfast, 2001).

McGarry, F., *Irish Politics and the Spanish civil war* (Cork, 1999).

——, ' "Catholics first and politicians afterwards": the Labour Party and the Workers' Republic, 1936–39, in *Saothar* 25, (2000), 57–66.

McKay, E., 'Changing with the tide: the Irish Labour Party, 1927–33', in *Saothar* 11, (1986), 27–38.

McMahon, D., *Republicans and imperialists. Anglo-Irish relations in the 1930s* (Yale, 1984).

McNiffe, L., *A History of the Garda Síochána* (Dublin, 1997).

McDermott, E., *Clann na Poblachta* (Cork, 1998).

Mc Redmond, L., *Modern Irish Lives* (Dublin, 1998)

McVeigh, J., *Executed: Tom Williams and the IRA* (Belfast, 1999).

Milotte, M., *Communism in modern Ireland: the pursuit of the Workers' Republic since 1916* (Dublin, 1984).

Mitchell, A., & Ó Snodaigh, P., *Irish political documents, 1916–1949* (Dublin, 1985).

Moran, G., (ed.), *Radical Irish priests* (Dublin, 1998)

Morgan A. and Purdie B. (ed.), *Ireland. Divided nation, divided class* (London, 1980).

Moroney, M., *George Plant and the rule of law* (Tipperary, 1989).

Mulvihill, M., *Charlotte Despard. A biography* (London, 1989).

Murphy, B.P., *Patrick Pearse and the lost republican ideal* (Dublin, 1991).

Murphy, J.A., 'The new IRA, 1925–62', in Williams (ed.), *Secret societies in Ireland* (Dublin, 1973).

Murray, P., *Oracles of God. The Roman Catholic Church and Irish politics, 1922–1937* (Dublin, 2000).

National Graves Association, *The last post* (Dublin, 1976).

Nevin, D., 'Radical movements in the twenties and thirties' in Williams (ed.), *Secret societies in Ireland* (Dublin, 1973).

O'Brien, B., *A pocket history of the IRA* (Dublin, 1997).

O'Carroll, J.P., and Murphy, J.A. (eds), *De Valera and his times* (Cork, 1983).

O'Connor, E., *A labour history of Ireland, 1824–1960* (Dublin, 1992).

——, 'Jim Larkin and the Communist Internationals, 1923–9', *Irish Historical Studies*, May 1999.

O'Connor, J., *Even the olives are bleeding. The life and times of Charlie Donnelly* (Dublin, 1992).

Ó Corráin, D. (ed.), *James Hogan: revolutionary, historian & political scientist* (Dublin, 2001).

O'Donnell, P., *There will be another day* (Dublin, 1963)

O'Donoghue, D., *Hitler's Irish voices* (Belfast, 1998).

O'Donoghue, F., *No other law. The story of Liam Lynch* (Dublin, 1986).

Ó Drisceoil, D., *Peadar O'Donnell* (Cork, 2001).

Ó Dulaing, D., *Voices of Ireland* (Dublin, 1984).

Ó hEithir, B., *The begrudger's guide to Irish Politics* (Dublin, 1986).

O'Farrell, P., *Who's who in the Irish war of independence and civil war, 1916–1923* (Dublin, 1997).

O'Gadhra, N., *The civil war in Connaught, 1922–1923* (Dublin, 1999).

Ó Gráda, C., *Ireland: a new economic history, 1780–1939* (Oxford, 1994).

O'Halloran, C., *Partition and the limits of Irish nationalism* (Dublin, 1987).

O'Halpin, E., *Defending Ireland. The Irish state and its enemies since 1922* (Oxford, 1999).

——, '"Weird prophecies": British intelligence and anglo-Irish relations, 1932–33' in Kennedy, M., Skelly, J.M., (eds), *Irish foreign policy 1919–1966. From independence to internationalism* (Dublin, 2000).

O'Mahony, S., *Frongoch. University of revolution* (Dublin, 1995).

O'Reilly, D., (ed.) *Accepting the challenge. The memiors of Michael Flannery* (Dublin, 2001).

O'Riordan, M., *Portrait of an Irish anti-Fascist – Frank Edwards 1907-1983* (Dublin, 1984).

——, 'Communism in Dublin in the 1930s: the struggle against fascism' in H.G. Klaus (ed.) *Strong words, brave deeds. The poetry, life and times of Thomas O'Brien* (Dublin, 1994).

O'Sullivan, M., *Brendan Behan. A life* (Dublin, 1997).

Patterson, H., 'Fianna Fáil and the working class: the origins of the enigmatic relationship', *Saothar* 13 (1988).

Patterson, H., *The politics of illusion: republicanism and socialism in modern Ireland* (London, 1989).

Phoenix, E., *Northern nationalism: nationalist politics, Partition and the Catholic minority in Northern Ireland, 1890–1940* (Belfast, 1994).

Rosenhaft, E., *Beating the Fascists? The German Communists and political violence, 1929–1933* (Cambridge, 1983).

Regan, J.M., *The Irish counter–revolution, 1921–1936* (Dublin, 1999).

Rumpf, E. & Hepburn, A.C., *Nationalism and socialism in twentieth century Ireland* (Liverpool, 1977).

Ryan, M., *The Tom Barry story* (Cork, 1982).

Ryder, C., *The RUC. A force under fire* (London, 1989).

Stephan, E., *Spies in Ireland* (London, 1963).

Stradling, R., *The Irish and the Spanish civil war, 1936–39. Crusades in conflict* (Manchester 1999).

Staunton, E., 'Frank Ryan & collaboration – a reassessment' in *History Ireland*, Autumn 1997.

——, *The nationalists of Northern Ireland, 1918–1973* (Dublin, 2001).

Townshend, C., *Political violence in Ireland* (Oxford, 1983).

Ward, M., *Unmanageable revolutionaries: women and Irish nationalism* (London, 1995).

——, *Hannah Sheehy Skeffington: a life* (Cork, 1997).

——, *Maud Gonne: a life* (London, 1993).

Walsh, P., *Republicanism and socialism. The politics of the republican movement, 1905 to 1994* (Belfast, 1994).

THESES

Banta, M.M., 'The Red scare in the Irish Free State, 1925–37', MA thesis (UCD, 1982).

Doyle, M., 'The Republican Congress: a study in Irish radicalism', MA thesis (UCD, 1988).

McHugh, J.P., 'Voices of the rearguard: a study of *An Phoblacht*. Irish republican thought in the post-revolutionary era, 1923–37', MA thesis (UCD, 1983).

O'Sullivan, C.M., 'The IRA takes constitutional action: a history of Clann na Phoblachta,

1946–65.' MA thesis (UCD, 1995).

Rouse, P, 'Sport and the politics of culture. A history of the GAA ban, 1884– 1971.' MA thesis (UCD, 1991).

Tarpey, sister, M.V., 'The role of Joseph McGarrity in the struggle for Irish Independence', PhD thesis (St John's University, New York, 1970).

Index

Aiken, Frank, 14, 90, 113, 114, 120, 126,
127, 128, 143, 207, 209
Ancient Order of Hibernians, 69, 75, 76,
78, 154, 163, 167
Animal Gangs, 83–4
anti–Semitism, 75–6, 96, 170, 184
An t–Oglach, 13, 161, 164
arms, 28–36, 202–3
Armistice Day, 12, 71–4, 120
Army Comrades Association, ACA,
(Blueshirts), 16, 17, 25, 32, 43, 46, 62,
84–90, 108, 137–8, 185, 187, 189

Barry, Tom, 19, 20, 65, 87, 90, 111, 127,
131, 143, 158, 176, 178, 180, 190
Blaney, Neil, 114, 135, 136, 209
Bodenstown commemoration, 15, 50–2,
94, 95, 98, 107–8, 112, 124, 135, 139,
206–7
Boland, Gerald, 117, 118, 121, 122, 123,
139, 173
Bradshaw, Bob, 35
Bradshaw, R.G., 23, 70
Briscoe, Robert, 33, 75–6, 118–20
British Fascisti, 46, 73
Boycott British campaign, 25, 50, 59–61,
131
'B' Specials, 146, 152

Catholic Church, 14, 17, 64–70, 96, 122,
149, 166, 179, 182
China, 174
Clan na Gael, 14, 33–4, 44, 51, 62,
162–70, 173, 174, 186
communications, 45
Communists, 49, 89, 109, 110
in Belfast, 150–1
at Bodenstown, 51, 107

IRA association with, 13, 54, 71, 122,
123, 154, 157, 169, 172, 173–4, 192
IRA divided over, 65–9, 105, 173–4,
178–81
popular hostility to, 41, 66, 108, 140,
141, 156
Connolly, O'Brien, Nora, 66, 106, 109–10
Connolly, Roddy, 109, 110
Cooney, Andy, 18, 28, 134, 162, 166
Corrigan, Brian, 21–2, 39–40, 65, 67
Cosgrave, W.T., 44, 96, 99, 124, 129, 189
Coughlan, Fr Charles, 170, 184
Coughlan, Timothy, 48, 49, 119
Coyle, Eithne, 97, 98, 102–3, 184
Cumann na gCailini, 51, 101
Cumann na mBan, 51, 95, 97–104, 171
Cumann na nGaedheal, 9, 31–2, 39, 42,
62, 68, 85, 86, 87, 115, 123, 124, 125,
129, 134, 137, 138, 141

Devlin, Joseph, 153, 154, 155, 158, 160,
186
Derrig, Tom, 114, 118, 134, 207, 208
Derry Journal, 22, 154
de Valera, Eamon, 60, 68, 71, 89, 168–9,
177, 186, 194, 197
in opposition, 113–25
in government, 129–43
talks with IRA, 127–8, 133
Stormont election 1933, 154–5

Easter Lily campaign, 99
Economic War, 15, 59, 60, 127, 128–9, 188
Edwards, Frank, 67, 69, 109
Egan, John, 144, 188, 206

Fahy, Martin, 39, 115, 122
Fahy, Fr John, 67

Fianna Fáil, 9, 12, 14, 29, 44, 51, 55, 63, 71, 77, 84, 93, 97, 186, 187, 188, 190, 209
   and ACA, 85, 86, 89
   and church, 64, 68, 70
   and Gardaí, 81, 118–20
   in government, 126–44
   in opposition, 113–25
   and 'Old IRA', 111–12
   and United States, 166–8
   and Volunteer Reserve, 90
Fitzgerald, David, 192
Fitzpatrick, Mick, 18, 20, 55, 56, 132, 173, 176, 192
Freemasons, 69, 78, 96

Gaelic Athletic Association, 62–4
Gardaí, 13, 17, 30, 38–39, 42–3, 44, 45, 46–9, 51, 55, 62, 64, 65, 67, 77
   IRA attitude to 78, 138
   IRA violence against, 57, 58–9, 71,79–82, 113
General Elections,
   1927: 12, 114–17, 209
   1932: 14, 124–5, 126, 210–12
   1933: 15, 129–30, 137
Gilmore, Charles, 23, 41, 105
Gilmore, George, 20, 23, 43, 73, 82, 89, 105, 106, 107, 108, 109, 118, 127, 130, 131, 133, 158, 169, 174, 181, 190–2
Gilmore, Harry, 23, 41, 105
Glynn, James, 24, 208
Gralton, James, 65, 66, 140–1, 181

Hales, Tom, 139, 143
Hayes, Sean, 122, 136
Healy, Cahir, 154, 155, 158
Houlihan, Patrick, 114, 209
Hughes, Cora, 103
Humphreys, Sighle, 9, 98, 99, 100, 102, 103, 195

India, 173
informers, 47–9

intelligence, 46–7
internal discipline, 37–44
Irish Citizen Army, 51, 68, 93, 103, 106, 109–10
Irish language, 61
Irish News, 154, 157, 159
Irish Press, 41, 51, 60, 84, 86, 129, 140, 143
Irish Worker's Voice, 109, 156, 168
Irish World, 166–7, 173

Killeen, Jim, 19, 20, 33, 36, 52, 111, 179, 193
Killilea, Mark, 114, 209
Knights of Columbanus, 69–70, 75, 78, 141, 155
Kyne, Martin, (Martin O'Cadhain), 22, 69

land agitation, 56–9, 120–2, 140, 182–3
Labour Party, 14, 25, 26, 54, 59, 89, 110, 125, 181, 182, 197
Larkin, Jim, 54
Lehane, Con, 23, 24, 155
Lemass, Sean, 117, 123, 207
Lavery, May, 98
Lynch, Tadgh, 22, 25, 89

MacBride, Maud Gonne, 59, 104, 118, 193
MacBride, Seán, 18, 19, 20, 38, 40, 60, 90, 94, 102, 107, 127, 128, 133, 150, 158, 178, 179, 181, 186, 193–4
MacEntee, Sean, 9, 25, 119, 134, 143
MacSwiney, Mary, 93, 94, 95, 96, 97, 98, 102
McCarroll, J.J., 154, 155
McCool, Sean, 22, 35, 89, 107, 134, 137, 147, 154, 155, 174, 176, 180
McEllistrim, Tom, 135, 136, 137, 209
McGarrity, Joseph, 14, 18, 124, 131, 133, 163, 165, 166, 167, 168, 169, 170, 185
McGuinness, Sean, 22, 57, 66, 81, 140, 163, 180
McKeon, Patrick, 22, 65–7

McLogan, Patrick, 20, 23, 154–6, 194
Matthews, Davy, 22, 96, 146, 148, 151, 153, 154, 156, 160, 176
Maguire, Tom, (Mayo), 93, 95, 114, 209
Maguire, Tom, (Westmeath), 23, 132–3
Membership estimates,
  1924: 11
  1926: 12
  1930: 13,
  1932–3: 16
  1934: 17
Mná na Poblachta, 98
Molony, Helena, 71, 94, 104
moneylending raids, 75–6
Mullins, Tommy, 123

The Nation, 118, 119, 120, 122, 123
National Army, 32, 46, 83, 111, 121
Nazi Germany, 18, 174, 184–5, 192, 194
Neenan, Con, 164, 167

O'Donnell, Peadar, 16, 20, 24, 43, 52, 54, 56, 57, 76, 82, 89, 93, 103, 105–6, 109, 118, 120–2, 125, 131, 133, 147, 159, 178, 181, 195, 207
O'Donoghue, Donal, 19, 20, 38, 56, 60, 75, 107, 154–5, 159–60, 178, 181, 187, 195–7
O'Duffy, Eoin, 34, 38, 80, 85, 90, 119, 120, 122, 177
O'Farrell, Sean, 20, 23, 54, 77, 89, 90, 196
O'Ferrall, Gerald More, 58–9, 144, 206
O'Flanagan, Fr Michael, 96
O'Higgins, Brian, 94, 96, 97
O'Higgins, Kevin, 49, 93, 114, 206
O'Higgins, T.F., 46, 138
O'Kelly, J.J., 94, 96
O'Kelly, S.T., 49, 70, 119, 133
O'Maoileoin, Tomas, 22, 134
'Old IRA', 58, 110–12
Orange Order, 15, 75, 76–77, 146–9, 156–7
Outdoor Relief strike, 15, 150–1, 153, 188

partition, effects of, 145, 146,
  IRA and, 186–7
An Phoblacht, 16, 20, 44, 50, 55, 68, 70, 76, 79, 85, 97, 105, 121, 145, 151
  and Dublin print strike, 56, 83–4,
  and Fianna Fáil, 117–23,
  and international issues, 170, 173–4
  and IRA policies, 176, 179, 180, 181, 183, 184, 185
  and popular culture, 61–2
  and Sinn Féin, 93–4
  sales of, 52–3
  in United States, 163, 164, 167, 168, 169
Plant, George, 44
Plunkett, George, 20, 23, 115, 196
Price, Mick, 12, 20, 37, 49, 75, 104–7, 109–10, 118, 134, 176, 196–197

Quill, Michael, 169–170
Quirke, Bill, 19, 129, 140

Rail Strike (1933), 151–3
Republican Congress, 17, 43, 62, 67, 73, 84, 89, 102–3, 104, 105–9, 132, 136, 141, 158, 159, 169, 172, 175, 176, 180
Rice, J.J., 22, 63
Royal Ulster Constabulary, 35, 45, 49, 83, 146, 150, 152, 153, 154, 155, 156, 157, 158, 159, 206
Russell, Sean, 12, 13, 15, 18, 19, 20, 33, 34, 35, 47, 116, 118, 133, 152, 158, 165, 168, 170, 172, 173, 176, 197–9
Ruttledge, Paddy, 121, 137, 207
Ryan, Frank, 20, 24, 53, 61, 71, 72, 73, 85, 87, 89, 100, 103, 105, 106, 107, 125, 131, 132, 135, 176, 178, 198-9
Ryan, T.J., 22, 48, 80–2, 119, 138

Saor Éire, 14, 61, 64, 94, 122, 123, 124, 146, 166, 177, 179–80, 193, 195, 196, 198
sectarianism, 69–70, 72, 74, 76–8, 146–9, 156–7, 159–60

Sheehy, J.J., 20, 43, 63, 89, 96, 132, 181, 199

Sheehy Skeffington, Hannah, 71, 104, 131

Sinn Féin, 12, 93–7, 114, 115–17, 146, 171, 179, 194, 196, 199, 209

Smith, Patrick, 114, 209

Social Credit, 182, 184

Somerville, Henry Boyle, 83, 144, 187, 206

Soviet Union, 13, 33, 123, 173, 174, 179, 192

Stormont elections (1933), 23, 153–5

strikes, IRA involvement in, 18, 41, 50, 54–6, 83–4, 106, 108, 110, 140–1, 150–3, 182

Traynor, Oscar, 93, 120, 139

training, 35–37, 201–2

Turley, Dan, 48–9, 206

Twomey, Maurice, (Moss), 9, 14, 15, 17, 18–19, 20, 34, 47, 49, 57, 71, 77, 100, 104, 107, 108, 200–1
  on military strategy, 31–2
  on discipline, 38–9

communications to, 45

on 'Boycott' campaign, 60

and Church, 64–7

on Knights of Columbanus, 69

on ACA, 85–7, 89

on Volunteer Reserve, 90, 142

and Sinn Féin, 93–5

on 'Old IRA', 111

and Fianna Fáil, 115, 117, 124, 126–36, 139–40

and Northern Ireland, 146, 147–8, 152–3,

in US, 165, 168

on Clan na Gael, 169, 170

in Britain, 172

and ideology, 175, 176–82, 184, 186

Ulster Protestant League, 156

Vaugh, James, 81, 206Volunteer Reserve, 17, 44, 90–2, 142

Ward, Terry, 22, 148–9

Whyte, Martin, 32